AF596056

CHARLES LAMB'S ESSAYS

AS FIRST PUBLISHED

IN THE

LONDON MAGAZINE

1820-1825

THE

LONDON MAGAZINE.

JULY to DECEMBER,

1820.

Why should not divers studies, at divers hours, delight, when the variety is able alone to refresh and repair us?

Ben Jonson's *Discoveries*.

VOL. II.

London:

Printed for

BALDWIN, CRADOCK, AND JOY.

1820.

C. Baldwin, Printer,
New Bridge-street, London.

RECOLLECTIONS OF THE SOUTH SEA HOUSE.

Reader, in thy passage from the Bank—where thou hast been receiving thy half-yearly dividends (supposing thou art a lean annuitant like myself)—to the Flower Pot, to secure a place for Dalston, or Shacklewell, or some other thy suburban retreat northerly,--didst thou never observe a melancholy-looking, handsome, brick and stone edifice, to the left—where Threadneedle-street abuts upon Bishopsgate? I dare say thou hast often admired its magnificent portals ever gaping wide, and disclosing to view a grave court, with cloisters, and pillars, with few or no traces of goers-in or comers-out—a desolation something like Balclutha's.*

This was once a house of trade,—a centre of busy interests. The throng of merchants was here—the quick pulse of gain—and here some forms of business are still kept up, though the soul be long since fled. Here are still to be seen stately porticos; imposing staircaises; offices roomy as the state apartments in palaces—deserted, or thinly peopled with a few straggling clerks; the still more sacred interiors of court and committee rooms, with venerable faces of beadles, door-keepers — directors seated in form on solemn days (to proclaim a dead dividend,) at long worm-eaten tables, that have been mahogany, with tarnished gilt-leather coverings, supporting massy silver inkstands long since dry;—the oaken wainscots hung with pictures of deceased governors and sub-governors, of queen Anne, and the two first monarchs of the Brunswick dynasty;—huge charts, which subsequent discoveries have antiquated;—dusty maps of Mexico, dim as dreams,—and soundings of the Bay of Panama!—The long passages hung with buckets, appended, in idle row, to walls, whose substance might defy any, short of the last, conflagration:—with vast ranges of cellarage under all, where dollars and pieces of eight once lay, an "unsunned heap," for Mammon to have solaced his solitary heart withal,—long since dissipated, or scattered into air at the blast of the breaking of that famous Bubble.——

Such is the *South Sea-house*. At least, such it was forty years ago, when I knew it,—a magnificent relic! What alterations may have been made in it since, I have had no opportunities of verifying. Time, I take for granted, has not freshened it. No wind has resuscitated the face of the sleeping waters. A thicker crust by this time stagnates upon it. The moths, that were then battening upon its obsolete ledgers and day-books, have rested from their depredations, but other light generations have succeeded, making fine fretwork among their single and double entries. Layers of dust have accumulated (a superfœtation of dirt!) upon the old layers, that seldom used to be disturbed, save by some curious finger, now and then, that wished to explore the mode of book-keeping in Queen Anne's reign; or, with less hallowed curiosity, sought to unveil some of the mysteries of that tremendous HOAX, whose extent the petty peculators of our day look back upon with the same expression of incredulous admiration, and hopeless ambition of rivalry, as

* I passed by the walls of Balclutha, and they were desolate.—Ossian.

would become the puny face of modern conspiracy contemplating the Titan size of Vaux's superhuman plot.

Peace to the manes of the Bubble! Silence and destitution are upon thy walls, proud house, for a memorial!

Situated as thou art, in the very heart of stirring and living commerce, —amid the fret and fever of speculation—with the Bank, and the 'Change, and the India-house about thee, in the hey-day of present prosperity, with their important faces, as it were insulting thee, their *poor neighbour out of business*—to the idle, and merely contemplative,—to such as me, old house! there is a charm in thy quiet: —a cessation—a coolness from business—an indolence almost cloistral—which is delightful! With what reverence have I paced thy great bare rooms and courts at eventide! They spoke of the past:—the shade of some dead accountant, with visionary pen in ear, would flit by me, stiff as in life. Living accounts and accountants puzzle me. I have no skill in figuring. But thy great dead tomes, which scarce three degenerate clerks of the present day could lift from their enshrining shelves—with their old fantastic flourishes, and decorative rubric interlacings—their sums in triple columniations, set down with formal superfluity of cyphers—with pious sentences at the beginning, without which our religious ancestors never ventured to open a book of business, or bill of lading—the costly vellum covers of some of them almost persuading us that we are got into some *better library*,—are very agreeable and edifying spectacles. I can look upon these defunct dragons with complacency. Thy heavy odd-shaped ivory-handled penknives (our ancestors had every thing on a larger scale than we have hearts for) are as good as any thing from Herculaneum. The pounce-boxes of our days have gone retrograde.

The very clerks which I remember in the South Sea-house—I speak of forty years back—had an air very different from those in the public offices that I have had to do with since. They partook of the genius of the place!

They were mostly (for the establishment did not admit of superfluous salaries,) bachelors. Generally (for they had not much to do) persons of a curious and speculative turn of mind. Old-fashioned, for a reason mentioned before. Humourists, for they were of all descriptions; and, not having been brought together in early life (which has a tendency to assimilate the members of corporate bodies to each other), but, for the most part, placed in this house in ripe or middle age, they necessarily carried into it their separate habits and oddities, unqualified, if I may so speak, as into a common stock. Hence they formed a sort of Noah's ark. Odd fishes. A lay-monastry. Domestic retainers in a great house, kept more for show than use. Yet pleasant fellows, full of chat—and not a few among them had arrived at considerable proficiency on the German flute.

The cashier at that time was one Evans, a Cambro-Briton. He had something of the choleric complexion of his countrymen stamped on his visnomy, but was a worthy sensible man at bottom. He wore his hair, to the last, powdered and frizzed out, in the fashion which I remember to have seen in caricatures of what were termed, in my young days, *Maccaronies*. He was the last of that race of beaux. Melancholy as a gib-cat over his counter all the forenoon, I think I see him, making up his cash (as they call it) with tremulous fingers, as if he feared every one about him was a defaulter; in his hypochondry ready to imagine himself one; haunted, at least, with the idea of the possibility of his becoming one: his tristful visage clearing up a little over his roast neck of veal at Anderton's at two (where his picture still hangs, taken a little before his death by desire of the master of the coffee-house, which he had frequented for the last five-and-twenty years), but not attaining the meridian of its animation till evening brought on the hour of tea and visiting. The simultaneous sound of his well-known rap at the door with the stroke of the clock announcing six, was a topic of never failing mirth in the families which this dear old bachelor gladdened with his presence. Then was his forte, his glorified hour! How would he chirp, and expand, over a muffin! How would he dilate into secret history! His countryman, Pennant himself, in particular, could not be more eloquent than he in relation to old and new London—the site of old theatres, churches, streets gone to decay—where Rosomund's pond stood—the Mulberry-gardens—and the Conduit in Cheap—with many a pleasant anecdote, derived from paternal tradition, of those grotesque figures which Hogarth has immortalized in his picture of *Noon*,—the worthy descendants of those heroic confessors, who, flying to this country, from the wrath of Louis the Fourteenth and his dragoons, kept alive the flame of pure religion in the sheltering obscurities of Hog-lane, and the vicinity of the Seven Dials!

Deputy, under Evans, was Thomas Tame. He had the air and stoop of a nobleman. You would have taken him for one, had you met him in one of the passages leading to Westminster-hall. By stoop, I mean that gentle bending of the body forwards, which, in great men, must be supposed to be the effect of an habitual condescending attention to the applications of their inferiors. While he held you in converse, you felt "strained to the height" in the colloquy. The conference over, you were at leisure to smile at the comparative insignificance of the pretensions which had just awed you. His intellect was of the shallowest order. It did not reach to a saw or a proverb. His mind was in its original state of white paper. A sucking babe might have posed him. What was it then? Was he rich? Alas, no! Thomas Tame was very poor. Both he and his wife looked outwardly gentlefolks, when I fear all was not well at all times within. She had a neat meagre person, which it was evident she had not sinned in over-pampering; but in its veins was noble blood. She traced her descent, by some labyrinth of relationship, which I never thoroughly understood,—much less can explain with any heraldic certainty at this time of day,—to the illustrious, but unfortunate house of Derwentwater. This was the secret of Thomas's stoop. This was the thought—the sentiment—the bright solitary star of your lives,—ye mild and happy pair,—which cheered you in the night of intellect, and in the obscurity of your station! This was to you instead of riches, instead of rank, instead of glittering attainments: and it was worth them all together. You insulted none with it; but, while you wore it as a piece of defensive armour only, no insult likewise could reach you through it. *Decus et solamen.*

Of quite another stamp was the then accountant, John Tipp. He neither pretended to high blood, nor in good truth cared one fig about the matter. He "thought an accountant the greatest character in the world, and himself the greatest accountant in it." Yet John was not without his hobby. The fiddle relieved his vacant hours. He sang, certainly, "with other notes than to the Orphean lyre." He did, indeed, scream and scrape most abominably. His fine suite of official rooms in Threadneedle-street, which, without any thing very substantial appended to them, were enough to enlarge a man's notions of himself that lived in them, (I know not who is the occupier of them now*) resounded fortnightly to the notes of a concert of "sweet breasts," as our ancestors would have called them, culled from club-rooms and orchestras—chorus singers—first and second violincellos—double basses—and clarionets—who ate his cold mutton, and drank his punch, and praised his ear. He sate like Lord Midas among them. But at the desk Tipp was quite another sort of creature. Thence all ideas, that were purely ornamental, were banished. You could not speak of any thing romantic without rebuke. Politics were excluded. A newspaper was thought too refined and abstracted. The whole duty of man consisted in writing off dividend warrants. The striking of the annual balance in the company's books (which, perhaps, differed from the balance of last year in the sum of 25*l.* 1*s.* 6*d.*) occupied his days and nights for a month previous. Not that Tipp was blind to the deadness of *things* (as they call them in the city) in his beloved house,

* I have since been informed, that the present tenant of them is a Mr. Lamb, a gentleman who is happy in the possession of some choice pictures, and among them a rare portrait of Milton, which I mean to do myself the pleasure of going to see, and at the same time to refresh my memory with the sight of old scenes. Mr. Lamb has the character of a right courteous and communicative collector.

or did not sigh for a return of the old stirring days, when South Sea hopes were young—(he was indeed equal to the weilding of any the most intricate accounts of the most flourishing company in these or those days):—but to a genuine accountant the difference of proceeds is as nothing. The fractional farthing is as dear to his heart as the thousands which stand before it. He is the true actor, who, whether his part be a prince or a peasant, must act it with like intensity. With Tipp form was every thing. His life was formal. His actions seemed ruled with a ruler. His pen was not less erring than his heart. He made the best executor in the world: he was plagued with incessant executorships accordingly, which excited his spleen and soothed his vanity in equal ratios. He would swear (for Tipp swore) at the little orphans, whose rights he would guard with a tenacity like the grasp of the dying hand, that commended their interests to his protection. With all this there was about him a sort of timidity—(his few enemies used to give it a worse name)—a something which, in reverence to the dead, we will place, if you please, a little on this side of the heroic. Nature certainly had been pleased to endow John Tipp with a sufficient measure of the principle of self-preservation. There is a cowardice which we do not despise, because it has nothing base or treacherous in its elements; it betrays itself, not you: it is mere temperament; the absence of the romantic and the enterprising; it sees a lion in the way, and will not, with Fortinbras, "greatly find quarrel in a straw," when some supposed honour is at stake. Tipp never mounted the box of a stage-coach in his life; or leaned against the rails of a balcony; or walked upon the ridge of a parapet; or looked down a precipice; or let off a gun; or went upon a water-party; or would willingly let you go if he could have helped it: neither was it recorded of him, that for lucre, or for intimidation, he ever forsook friend or principle.

Whom next shall we summon from the dusty dead, in whom common qualities become uncommon?—Can I forget thee, Henry Man, the wit, the polished man of letters, the *author*, of the South Sea House? who never enteredst thy office in a morning, or quitted it in mid-day—(what didst *thou* in an office?)—without some quirk that left a sting! Thy gibes and thy jokes are now extinct, or survive but in two forgotten volumes, which I had the good fortune to rescue from a stall in Barbican, not three days ago, and found thee terse, fresh, epigrammatic, as alive. Thy wit is a little gone by in these fastidious days—thy topics are staled by the "new-born gauds" of the time:—but great thou used to be in Public Ledgers, and in Chronicles, upon Chatham, and Shelbourn, and Rockingham, and Howe, and Burgoyne, and Clinton, and the war which ended in the tearing from Great Britain her rebellious colonies,—and Keppel, and Wilkes, and Sawbridge, and Bull, and Dunning, and Pratt, and Richmond,—and such small politics.——

A little less facetious, and a great deal more obstreperous, was fine rattling rattleheaded Plumer. He was descended,—not in a right line, reader, (for his lineal pretensions, like his personal, favoured a little of the sinister bend) from the Plumers of Hertfordshire. So tradition gave him out; and certain family features not a little sanctioned the opinion. Certainly old Walter Plumer (his reputed author) had been a rake in his days, and visited much in Italy, and had seen the world. He was uncle, bachelor-uncle, to the fine old whig still living, who has represented the county in so many successive parliaments, and has a fine old mansion near Ware. Walter flourished in George the Second's days, and was the same who was summoned before the House of Commons about a business of franks, with the old Duchess of Marlborough. You may read of it in Johnson's Life of Cave. Cave came off cleverly in that business. It is certain our Plumer did nothing to discountenance the rumour. He rather seemed pleased whenever it was, with all gentleness, insinuated. But, besides his family pretensions, Plumer was an engaging fellow, and sang gloriously.——

Not so sweetly sang Plumer as thou sangest, mild, child-like, pastoral M——; a flute's breathing less divinely whispering than thy Arcadian melodies, when, in tones worthy of Arden, thou didst chant that song sung by Amiens to the banished Duke, which proclaims the winter wind more lenient than for a man to be ungrateful. Thy sire was old surly M——, the unapproachable church-warden of Bishopsgate. He knew not what he did, when he begat thee, like spring, gentle offspring of blustering winter:—only unfortunate in thy ending, which should have been mild, conciliatory, swan-like.——

Much remains to sing. Many fantastic shapes rise up, but they must be mine in private:—already I have fooled the reader to the top of his bent;—else could I omit that strange creature Woollett, who existed in trying the question, and *bought litigations?*—and still stranger, inimitable, solemn Hepworth, from whose gravity Newton might have deduced the law of gravitation. How profoundly would he nib a pen—with what deliberation would he wet a wafer!——

But it is time to close—night's wheels are rattling fast over me—it is proper to have done with this solemn mockery.

Reader, what if I have been playing with thee all this while—peradventure the very *names,* which I have summoned up before thee, are fantastic — insubstantial — like Henry Pimpernel, and old John Naps of Greece:——

Be satisfied that something answering to them has had a being. Their importance is from the past.

Elia.

SONNET

To the Author of Poems published under the name of Barry Cornwall.

LET hate, or grosser heats, their foulness mask
In riddling *Junius*, or in *L——e's* name:
Let things eschew the light, deserving blame:
No cause hast thou to blush for thy sweet task.
Marcian Colonna is a dainty book;
And thy *Sicilian Tale* may boldly pass;—
Thy *Dream* 'bove all, in which, as in a glass,
On the great world's antique glories we may look.
No longer then, as "lowly substitute,
Factor, or PROCTOR, for another's gains,"
Suffer the admiring world to be deceived;
Lest thou thyself, by self of fame bereaved,
Lament too late the lost prize of thy pains,
And heavenly tunes, piped through an alien flute.

* * * *

TO R. S. KNOWLES, ESQ.

ON HIS TRAGEDY OF VIRGINIUS.

TWELVE years ago I knew you, KNOWLES, and then
Esteemed you a perfect specimen
Of those fine spirits warm-soul'd Ireland sends,
To teach us colder English how a friend's
Quick pulse should beat. I knew you brave, and plain,
Strong-sensed, rough-witted, above fear or gain;
But nothing further had the gift to 'spy.
Sudden you re-appear. With wonder I
Hear my old friend (turn'd SHAKSPEARE!) read a scene,
Only to *his* inferior in the clean
Passes of pathos: with such fence-like art,—
Ere we can see the steel, 'tis in our heart.
Almost without the aid, language affords,
Your piece seems wrought. That huffing medium, *words*,
(Which in the modern *Tamburlaines* quite sway
Our shamed souls from their bias) in your play
We scarce attend to. Hastier passion draws
Our tears on credit; and we find the cause
Some two hours after, spelling o'er again
Those strange few words at ease, that wrought the pain.
Proceed, old friend; and, as the year returns,
Still snatch some new old story from the urns
Of long-dead virtue. We, that knew before
Your worth, may *admire*, we cannot *love* you, more.

June, 1820. C. LAMB.

To the Editor.

Mr. Editor,—The riddling lines which I send you, were written upon a young lady, who, from her diverting sportiveness in childhood, was named by her friends THE APE. When the verses were written, L. M. had outgrown the title—but not the memory of it—being in her teens, and consequently past child-tricks. They are an endeavour to express that perplexity, which one feels at any alteration, even supposed for the better, in a beloved object; with a little oblique grudging at TIME, who cannot bestow new graces without taking away some portion of the older ones, which we can ill miss. * * * *

THE APE.

AN Ape is but a trivial beast,
  Men count it light and vain;
But I would let them have their thoughts,
  To have my Ape again.

To love a beast in any sort,
  Is no great sign of grace;
But I have loved a flouting Ape's
  'Bove any lady's face.

I have known the power of two fair eyes,
  In smile, or else in glance,
And how (for I a lover was)
  They make the spirits dance;

But I would give two hundred smiles,
  Of them that fairest be,
For one look of my staring Ape,
  That used to stare on me.

This beast, this Ape, it had a face——
  If face it might be styl'd——
Sometimes it was a staring Ape,
  Sometimes a beauteous child—

A Negro flat—a Pagod squat,
  Cast in a Chinese mold—
And then it was a Cherub's face,
  Made of the beaten gold!
But TIME, that's meddling, meddling still
  And always altering things—
And, what's already at the best,
  To alteration brings—

That turns the sweetest buds to flowers,
  And chops and changes toys—
That breaks up dreams, and parts old friends,
  And still commutes our joys—

Has changed away my Ape at last,
  And in its place convey'd,
Thinking therewith to cheat my sight,
  A fresh and blooming maid!

And fair to sight is she—and still
  Each day doth sightlier grow,
Upon the ruins of the Ape,
  My ancient play-fellow!

The tale of Sphinx, and Theban jests,
  I true in me perceive;
I suffer riddles; death from dark
  Enigmas I receive:

Whilst a hid being I pursue,
  That lurks in a new shape,
My darling in herself I miss—
  And, in my Ape, THE APE.

1806.

THE

London Magazine.

N° X. OCTOBER, 1820. VOL. II.

MISCELLANEOUS ARTICLES.

OXFORD IN THE VACATION.

CASTING a preparatory glance at the bottom of this article—as the wary connoisseur in prints, with cursory eye (which, while it reads, seems as though it read not,) never fails to consult the *quis sculpsit* in the corner, before he pronounces some rare piece to be a Vivares, or a Woollet——methinks I hear you exclaim, Reader, *Who is Elia?*

Because in my last I tried to divert thee with some half-forgotten humours of some old clerks defunct, in an old house of business, long since gone to decay, doubtless you have already set me down in your mind as one of the self-same college——a votary of the desk—a notched and cropt scrivener—one that sucks his sustenance, as certain sick people are said to do, through a quill.

Well, I do agnize something of the sort. I confess that it is my humour, my fancy—in the forepart of the day, when the mind of your man of letters requires some relaxation—(and none better than such as at first sight seems most abhorrent from his beloved studies)—to while away some good hours of my time in the contemplation of indigos, cottons, raw silks, piece-goods, flowered or otherwise. In the first place * * * * * * * *

and then it sends you home with such increased appetite to your books * * * * not to say, that your outside sheets, and waste wrappers of foolscap, do receive into them, most kindly and naturally, the impression of sonnets, epigrams, *essays*—so that the very parings of a counting-house are, in some sort, the settings up of an author. The enfranchised quill, that has plodded all the morning among the cart-rucks of figures and cyphers, frisks and curvets so at its ease over the flowery carpet-ground of a midnight dissertation.—It feels its promotion. * * * *
So that you see, upon the whole, the literary dignity of *Elia* is very little, if at all, compromised in the condescension.

Not that, in my anxious detail of the many commodities incidental to the life of a public office, I would be thought blind to certain flaws, which a cunning carper might be able to pick in this Joseph's vest. And here I must have leave, in the fulness of my soul, to regret the abolition, and doing-away-with altogether, of those consolatory interstices, and sprinklings of freedom, through the four seasons,—the *red-letter days*, now become, to all intents and purposes, *dead-letter days*. There was Paul, and Stephen, and Barnabas—

Andrew and John, men famous in old times

—we were used to keep all their days holy, as long back as I was at school at Christ's. I remember their effigies, by the same token, in the old

Basket Prayer Book There hung Peter in his uneasy posture——holy Bartlemy in the troublesome act of flaying, after the famous Marsyas by Spagnoletti——I honoured them all, and could almost have wept the defalcation of Iscariot—so much did we love to keep holy memories sacred:—only methought I a little grudged at the coalition of the *better Jude* with Simon—clubbing (as it were) their sanctities together, to make up one poor gaudy-day between them—as an economy unworthy of the dispensation.

These were bright visitations in a scholar's and a clerk's life—"far off their coming shone."—I was as good as an almanac in those days. I could have told you such a saint's-day falls out next week, or the week after Peradventure the Epiphany, by some periodical infelicity, would, once in six years, merge in a Sabbath. Now am I little better than one of the profane. Let me not be thought to arraign the wisdom of my civil superiors, who have judged the further observation of these holy tides to be papistical, superstitious. Only in a custom of such long standing, methinks, if their Holinesses the Bishops had, in decency, been first sounded——but I am wading out of my depths I am not the man to decide the limits of civil and ecclesiastical authority——I am plain Elia—no Selden, nor Archbishop Usher—though at present in the thick of their books, here in the heart of learning, under the shadow of the mighty Bodley.

I can here play the gentleman, enact the student. To such a one as myself, who has been defrauded in his young years of the sweet food of academic institution, no where is so pleasant, to while away a few idle weeks at, as one or other of the Universities. Their vacation too, at this time of the year, falls in so pat with *ours*. Here I can take my walks unmolested, and fancy myself of what degree or standing I please. I seem admitted *ad eundem*. I fetch up past opportunities. I can rise at the chapel-bell, and dream that it rings for *me*. In moods of humility I can be a Sizar, or a Servitor. When the peacock vein rises, I strut a Gentleman Commoner. In graver moments I proceed Master of Arts. Indeed I do not think I am much unlike that respectable character. I have seen your dim-eyed vergers, and bed-makers in spectacles, drop a bow or curtsey, as I pass, wisely mistaking me for something of the sort. I go about in black, which favours the notion. Only in Christ Church reverend quadrangle, I can be content to pass for nothing short of a Seraphic Doctor.

The walks at these times are so much one's own,—the tall trees of Christ's, the groves of Magdalen! The halls deserted, and with open doors, inviting one to slip in unperceived, and pay a devoir to some Founder, or noble or royal Benefactress (that should have been ours) whose portrait seems to smile upon their over-looked beadsman, and to adopt me for their own. Then, to take a peep in by the way at the butteries, and sculleries, redolent of antique hospitality: the immense caves of kitchens, kitchen fire-places, cordial recesses, ovens whose first pies were baked four centuries ago; and spits which have cooked for Chaucer! Not the meanest minister among the dishes but is hallowed to me through his imagination, and the Cook goes forth a Manciple.

Antiquity! thou wondrous charm, what art thou? that, being nothing, art every thing! when thou *wert*, thou wert not antiquity—then thou wert nothing, but had'st a remoter *antiquity*, as thou called'st it, to look back to with blind veneration, thou thyself being to thyself flat, jejune, *modern*! What mystery lurks in this retroversion? or what half Januses are we, that cannot look forward with the same idolatry with which we for ever revert! The mighty future is as nothing, being every thing! the past is every thing, being nothing!

What were thy *dark ages*? Surely the sun rose as brightly then as now, and man got him to his work in the morning Why is it that we can never hear mention of them without an accompanying feeling, as though a palpable obscure had dimmed the face of things, and that our ancestors wandered to and fro groping!

Above all thy rarities, old Oxenford, what do most arride and solace me, are thy repositories of mouldering learning, thy shelves——

What a place to be in is an old library! It seems as though all the souls of all the writers, that have bequeathed their labours to these Bodleians, were reposing here, as in some dormitory, or middle state. I do not want to handle, to profane, the leaves, their winding-sheets. I could as soon dislodge a shade. I seem to inhale learning, walking amid their foliage; and the odour of their old moth-scented coverings, is fragrant as the first bloom of those sciential apples which grew amid the happy orchard.

Still less have I curiosity to disturb the elder repose of MSS. Those *variæ lectiones*, so tempting to the more erudite palates, do but disturb and unsettle my faith.* I am no Herculanean raker. The credit of the three witnesses might have slept unimpeached for me. I leave these curiosities to Porson, and to G. D.—whom, by the way, I found busy as a moth over some rotten archive, rummaged out of some seldom-explored press, in a nook at Oriel. With long poring, he is grown almost into a book. He stood as passive as one by the side of the old shelves. I longed to new-coat him in Russia, and assign him his place. He might have mustered for a tall Scapula.

D. is assiduous in his visits to these seats of learning. No inconsiderable portion of his moderate fortune, I apprehend, is consumed in journeys between them and Clifford's-inn —— where, like a dove on the asp's nest, he has long taken up his unconscious abode, amid an incongruous assembly of attorneys, attorneys' clerks, apparitors, promoters, vermin of the law, among whom he sits, "in calm and sinless peace." The fangs of the law pierce him not—the winds of litigation blow over his humble chambers—the hard sheriff's officer moves his hat as he passes—legal nor illegal discourtesy touches him—none thinks of offering violence or injustice to him†—you would as soon "strike an abstract idea."

D. has been engaged, he tells me, through a course of laborious years, in an investigation into all curious matter connected with the two Universities; and has lately lit upon a MS. collection of charters, relative to C——, by which he hopes to settle some disputed points—particularly that long controvery between them as to priority of foundation. The ardor with which he engages in these liberal pursuits, I am afraid, has not met with all the encouragement it deserved, either here, or at C———. Your caputs and heads of colleges, care less than any body else about these questions.—Contented to suck the milky fountains of their Alma Maters, without enquiring into the venerable gentlewomen's years, they rather hold such curiosities to be impertinent—unreverend. They have their good glebe lands *in manu*, and care not much to rake into the title-deeds. I gather at least so much from other sources, for D. is not a man to complain.

D. started like an unbroke heifer, when I interrupted him. *A priori* it was not very probable that we should have met in Oriel. But D. would have done the same, had I accosted him on the sudden in his own walks in Clifford's Inn, or in the Temple. In addition to a provoking short-

---

* There is something to me repugnant, at any time, in written hand. The text never seems determinate. Print settles it. I had thought of the Lycidas as of a full-grown beauty—as springing up with all its parts absolute—till, in evil hour, I was shown the original written copy of it, together with the other minor poems of its author, in the Library of Trinity, kept like some treasure to be proud of. I wish they had thrown them in the Cam, or sent them, after the latter cantos of Spenser, into the Irish Channel. How it staggered me to see the fine things in their ore! interlined, corrected! as if their words were mortal, alterable, displaceable at pleasure! as if they might have been otherwise, and just as good! as if inspiration were made up of parts, and those fluctuating, successive, indifferent! I will never go into the work-shop of any great artist again, nor desire a sight of his picture, till it is fairly off the easel; no, not if Raphael were to be alive again, and painting another Galatea.

† Violence or injustice certainly none, Mr. Elia. But you will acknowledge, that the charming unsuspectingness of our friend has sometimes laid him open to attacks, which, though savouring (we hope) more of waggery than malice—such is our unfeigned respect for G. D.—might, we think, much better have been omitted. Such was that silly joke of L———, who, at the time the question of the Scotch Novels was first agitated, gravely assured our friend—who as gravely went about repeating it in all companies—that Lord Castlereagh had acknowledged himself to be the author of Waverly!—*Note—not by Elia.*

sightedness (the effect of late studies and watchings at the midnight oil) D. is the most absent of men. He made a call the other morning at our friend *M.'s* in Bedford-square; and, finding nobody at home, was ushered into the hall, where, asking for pen and ink, with great exactitude of purpose he enters me his name in the book—which ordinarily lies about in such places, to record the failures of the untimely or unfortunate visitor —and takes his leave with many ceremonies, and professions of regret. Some two or three hours after, his walking destinies returned him into the same neighbourhood again, and again the quiet image of the fire-side circle at *M.'s*——Mrs. *M.* presiding at it like a Queen Lar, with pretty *A. S.* at her side——striking irresistibly on his fancy, he makes another call (forgetting that they were "certainly not to return from the country before that day week") and disappointed a second time, enquires for pen and paper as before: again the book is brought, and in the line just above that in which he is about to print his second name, (his re-script)—his first name (scarce dry) looks out upon him like another Sosia, or as if a man should suddenly encounter his own duplicate!—The effect may be conceived. D. made many a good resolution against any such lapses in future. I hope he will not keep them too rigorously.

For with G. D.—to be absent from the body, is sometimes (not to speak it profanely) to be present with the Lord. At the very time when, personally encountering thee, he passes on with no recognition——or, being stopped, starts like a thing surprized —at that moment, reader, he is on Mount Tabor—or Parnassus—or cosphered with Plato—or, with Harrington, framing "immortal commonwealths"—devising some plan of amelioration to thy country, or thy species——peradventure meditating some individual kindness or courtesy, to be done to *thee thyself*, the returning consciousness of which made him to start so guiltily at thy obtruded personal presence.

D. commenced life, after a course of hard study in the "House of pure Emanuel," as usher to a knavish fanatic schoolmaster at * * *, at a salary of eight pounds per annum, with board and lodging. Of this poor stipend, he never received above half in all the laborious years he served this man. He tells a pleasant anecdote, that when poverty, staring out at his ragged knees, has sometimes compelled him, against the modesty of his nature, to hint at arrears, Dr. * * * would take no immediate notice, but, after supper, when the school was called together to even-song, he would never fail to introduce some instructive homily against riches, and the corruption of the heart occasioned through the desire of them—ending with "Lord, keep thy servants, above all things, from the heinous sin of avarice. Having food and raiment, let us therewithal be content. Give me Agar's wish,"——and the like;—which, to the little auditory, sounded like a doctrine full of Christian prudence and simplicity,—but to poor D. was a receipt in full for that quarter's demands at least.

And D. has been under-working for himself ever since;—drudging at low rates for unappreciating booksellers, —wasting his fine erudition in silent corrections of the classics, and in those unostentatious but solid services to learning, which commonly fall to the lot of laborious scholars, who have not the art to sell themselves to the best advantage. He has published poems, which do not sell, because their character is inobtrusive like his own,—and because he has been too much absorbed in ancient literature, to know what the popular mark in poetry is, even if he could have hit it. And, therefore, his verses are properly, what he terms them, *crotchets*; voluntaries; odes to Liberty, and Spring; effusions; little tributes, and offerings, left behind him, upon tables and window-seats, at parting from friends' houses; and from all the inns of hospitality, where he has been courteously (or ,but tolerably) received in his pilgrimage. If his muse of kindness halt a little behind the strong lines, in fashion in this excitement-craving age, his prose is the best of the sort in the world, and exhibits a faithful transcript of his own healthy natural mind, and cheerful innocent tone of conversation.

D. is delightful any where, but he is at the best in such places as these. He cares not much for Bath. He is out of his element at Buxton, at Scarborow, or Harrowgate. The Cam, and the Isis, are to him "better than all the waters of Damascus." On the Muses' hill he is happy, and good, as one of the Shepherds on the Delectable Mountains; and when he goes about with you to show you the halls and colleges, you think you have with you the Interpreter at the House Beautiful.

Elia.

Aug. 5th, 1820.
From my rooms facing the Bodleian.

Elia requests the Editor to inform W. K. that in his article on Oxford, under the initials G. D. it was his ambition to make more familiar to the public, a character, which, for integrity and single-heartedness, he has long been accustomed to rank among the best patterns of his species. That, if he has failed in the end which he proposed, it was an error of judgment merely. That, if in pursuance of his purpose, he has drawn forth some personal peculiarities of his friend into notice, it was only from conviction that the public, in living subjects especially, do not endure pure panegyric. That the anecdotes, which he produced, were no more than he conceived necessary to awaken attention to character, and were meant solely to illustrate it. That it is an entire mistake to suppose, that he undertook the character to set off his own wit or ingenuity. That, he conceives, a candid interpreter might find something intended, beyond a heartless jest. That G. D., however, having thought it necessary to disclaim the ancedote respecting Dr. ——, it becomes him, who never for a moment can doubt the veracity of his friend, to account for it from an imperfect remembrance of some story he heard long ago, and which, happening to tally with his argument, he set down too hastily to the account of G. D. That, from G. D.'s strong affirmations and proofs to the contrary, he is bound to believe it belongs to no part of G. D.'s biography. That the transaction, supposing it true, must have taken place more than forty years ago. That, in consequence, it is not likely to "meet the eye of many, who might be justly offended."

Finally, that what he has said of the Booksellers, referred to a period of many years, in which he has had the happiness of G. D.'s acquaintance; and can have nothing to do with any present or prospective engagements of G. D. with those gentlemen, to the nature of which he professes himself an entire stranger.

CHRIST'S HOSPITAL FIVE AND THIRTY YEARS AGO.

In Mr. Lamb's "Works," published a year or two since, I find a magnificent eulogy on my old school,* such as it was, or now appears to him to have been, between the years 1782 and 1789. It happens, very oddly, that my own standing at Christ's was nearly corresponding with his; and, with all gratitude to him for his enthusiasm for the cloisters, I think he has contrived to bring together whatever can be said in praise of them, dropping all the other side of the argument most ingeniously.

I remember L. at school; and can well recollect that he had some peculiar advantages, which I and others of his school-fellows had not. His friends lived in town, and were near at hand; and he had the privilege of going to see them, almost as often as he wished, through some invidious distinction, which was denied to us. The present worthy sub-treasurer to the Inner Temple can explain how that happened. He had his tea and hot rolls in a morning, while we were battening upon our quarter of a penny loaf—our *crug*—moistened with attenuated small beer, in wooden pig-

* Recollections of Christ's Hospital.

gins, smacking of the pitched leathern jack it was poured from. Our Monday's milk porritch, blue and tasteless, and the peas soup of Saturday, coarse and choking, were enriched for him with a slice of "extraordinary bread and butter," from the hot-loaf of the Temple. The Wednesday's mess of millet, somewhat less repugnant—(we had three banyan to four meat-days in the week)—was endeared to his palate with a lump of double-refined, and a smack of ginger (to make it go down the more glibly) or the fragrant cinnamon. In lieu of our *half-pickled* Sundays, or *quite fresh* boiled beef on Thursdays, (strong as *caro equina,*) with detestable marigolds floating in the pail to poison the broth—our scanty mutton crags on Fridays—and rather more savoury, but grudging, portions of the same flesh, rotten-roasted or rear, on the Tuesdays (the only dish which excited our appetites, and disappointed our stomachs, in almost equal proportion)—he had his hot plate of roast veal, or the more tempting griskin (exotics unknown to our palates) cooked in the paternal kitchen (a great thing), and brought him daily by his maid or aunt! I remember the good old relative (in whom love forbade pride,) squatting down upon some odd stone in a by-nook of the cloisters, disclosing the viands (of higher regale than those cates which the ravens ministered to the Tishbite); and the contending passions of L. at the unfolding. There was love for the bringer; shame for the thing brought, and the manner of its bringing; sympathy for those who were too many to share in it; and, at top of all, hunger (eldest, strongest, of the passions!) predominant, breaking down the stony fences of shame, and aukwardness, and a troubling over-consciousness.

I was a poor friendless boy. My parents, and those who should care for me, were far away. Those few acquaintances of theirs, which they could reckon upon being kind to me in the great city, after a little forced notice, which they had the grace to take of me on my first arrival in town, soon grew tired of my holyday visits. They seemed to them to recur too often, though I thought them few enough; and, one after another, they all failed me, and I felt myself alone among six hundred playmates.

O the cruelty of separating a poor lad from his early home-stead! The yearnings which I used to have towards it in those unfledged years! How, in my dreams, would my native town (far in the west) come back, with its church, and trees, and faces! How I would wake weeping, and in the anguish of my heart exclaim upon sweet Calne in Wiltshire!

To this late hour of my life, I trace impressions left by the recollection of those friendless holydays. The long warm days of summer never return but they bring with them a gloom from the haunting memory of those *whole-day-leaves*, when, by some strange arrangement, we were turned out, for the live-long day, upon our own hands, whether we had friends to go to, or none. I remember those bathing-excursions to the New-River, which L. recalls with such relish, better, I think, than he can—for he was a home-seeking lad, and did not much care for such water-pastimes:—How merrily we would sally forth into the fields; and strip under the first warmth of the sun; and wanton like young dace in the streams; getting us appetites for noon, which those of us that were pennyless (our scanty morning crust long since exhausted) had not the means of allaying—while the cattle, and the birds, and the fishes, were at feed about us, and we had nothing to satisfy our cravings—the very beauty of the day, and the exercise of the pastime, and the sense of liberty, setting a keener edge upon them!—How faint and languid, finally, we would return, towards night-fall, to our desired morsel, half-rejoicing, half reluctant, that the hours of our uneasy liberty had expired!

It was worse in the days of winter, to go prowling about the streets *objectless*—shivering at cold windows of print-shops, to extract a little amusement; or haply, as a last resort, in the hope of a little novelty, to pay a fifty-times repeated visit (where our individual faces should be as well known to the warden as those of his own charges) to the Lions in the Tower—to whose levée, by courtesy immemorial, we had a prescriptive title to admission.

L.'s governor (so we called the patron who presented us to the foundation) lived in a manner under his paternal roof. Any complaint which he had to make was sure of being attended to. This was understood at Christ's, and was an effectual screen to him against the severity of masters, or worse tyranny of the monitors. The oppressions of these young brutes are heart-sickening to call to recollection. I have been called out of my bed, and *waked for the purpose,* in the coldest winter nights—and this not once, but night after night—in my shirt, to receive the discipline of a leathern thong, with eleven other sufferers, because it pleased my callous overseer, when there has been any talking heard after we were gone to bed, to make the six last beds in the dormitory, where the youngest children of us slept, answerable for an offence they neither dared to commit, nor had the power to hinder.—The same execrable tyranny drove the younger part of us from the fires, when our feet were perishing with snow; and, under the cruellest penalties, forbad the indulgence of a drink of water, when we lay in sleepless summer nights, fevered with the season, and the day's sports.

There was one H——, who, I learned, in after days, was seen expiating some maturer offence in the hulks. (Do I flatter myself in fancying that this might be the planter of that name, who suffered —— at Nevis, I think, or St. Kits, —— some few years since? My friend Tobin was the benevolent instrument of bringing him to the gallows.) This petty Nero actually branded a boy, who had offended him, with a red hot iron; and nearly starved forty of us, with exacting contributions, to the one half of our bread, to pamper a young ass, which, incredible as it may seem, with the connivance of the nurse's daughter (a young flame of his) he had contrived to smuggle in, and keep upon the leads of the *ward,* as they called our dormitories. This game went on for better than a week, till the foolish beast, not able to fare well but he must cry roast meat—happier than Caligula's minion, could he have kept his own counsel—but foolisher, alas! than any of his species in the fables—waxing fat, and kicking, in the fulness of bread, one unlucky minute would needs proclaim his good fortune to the world below; and, laying out his simple throat, blew such a ram's horn blast, as (toppling down the walls of his own Jericho) set concealment any longer at defiance. The client was dismissed, with certain attentions, to Smithfield; but I never understood that the patron underwent any censure on the occasion. This was in the stewardship of L.'s admired Perry.

Under the same *facile* administration, can L. have forgotten the cool impunity with which the nurses used to carry away openly, in open platters, for their own tables, one out of two of every hot joint, which the careful matron had been seeing scrupulously weighed out for our dinners? These things were daily practised in that magnificent apartment, which L. (grown connoisseur since, we presume) praises so highly for the grand paintings "by Verrio, and others," with which it is "hung round and adorned." But the sight of sleek well-fed blue-coat boys in pictures, was, at that time, I believe, little consolatory to him, or us, the living ones, who saw the better part of our provisions carried away before our faces by harpies; and ourselves reduced (with the Trojan in the hall of Dido)

TO FEED OUR MIND WITH IDLE PORTRAITURE.

L. has recorded the repugnance of the school to *gags,* or the fat of fresh beef boiled; and sets it down to some superstition. But these unctuous morsels are never grateful to young palates (children are universally fat-haters) and in strong, coarse, boiled meats, *unsalted,* are detestable. A *gag-eater* in our time was equivalent to a *goul,* and held in equal detestation. **** suffered under the imputation.

> ——'twas said,
> He ate strange flesh.

He was observed, after dinner, carefully to gather up the remnants left at his table (not many, nor very choice fragments, you may credit me)—and, in an especial manner, these *disreputable morsels,* which he would convey away, and secretly stow in the settle that stood at his bed side. None saw when he ate them. It was rumoured that he privately devoured them in the night. He was watched, but no traces of such midnight practices were discoverable. Some reported, that, on leave-days, he had been seen to carry out of the bounds a large blue check handkerchief, full of something This then must be the accursed thing. Conjecture next was at work to imagine how he could dispose of it. Some said he sold it to the beggars. This belief generally prevailed He went about moping None spake to him. No one would play with him. He was excommunicated, put out of the pale of the school He was too powerful a boy to be beaten, but he underwent every mode of that negative punishment, which is more grievous than many stripes. Still he persevered. At length he was observed by two of his school-fellows, who were determined to get at the secret, and had traced him one leave-day for that purpose, to enter a large worn-out building (such as there exist specimens of in Chancery-lane, which are let out to various scales of pauperism) with open door, and a common stair-case. After him they silently slunk in, and followed by stealth up four flights, and saw him tap at a poor wicket, which was opened by an aged woman, meanly clad. Suspicion was now ripened into certainty. The informers had secured their victim. They had him in their toils. Accusation was formally preferred, and retribution most signal was looked for Mr. Halhaway, the then steward (for this happened a little after my time,) with that patient sagacity which tempered all his conduct, determined to investigate the matter, before he proceeded to sentence. The result was, that the supposed mendicants, the receivers, or purchasers of the mysterious scraps, turned out to be the parents of ——, an honest couple come to decay, —whom this seasonable supply had, in all probability, saved from mendicancy, and that this young stork, at the expence of his own good name, had all this while been only feeding the old birds!—The governors on this occasion, much to their honour, voted a present relief to the family of ——, and presented him with a silver medal. The lesson which the steward read upon RASH JUDGMENT, on the occasion of publicly delivering the medal to ——, I believe, would not be lost upon his auditory.—I had left school then, but I well remember ——. He was a tall, shambling youth, with a cast in his eye, not at all calculated to conciliate hostile prejudices. I have since seen him carrying a baker's basket. I think I heard he did not do quite so well by himself, as he had done by the old folks.

I was a hypochondriac lad; and the sight of a boy in fetters, upon the day of my first putting on the blue clothes, was not exactly fitted to assuage the natural terrors of initiation. I was of tender years, barely turned of seven; and had only read of such things in books, or seen them but in dreams. I was told he had *run away.* This was the punishment for the first offence —As a novice I was soon after taken to see the dungeons These were little, square, Bedlam cells, where a boy could just lie at his length upon straw and a blanket—a mattress, I think, was afterwards substituted—with a peep of light, let in ascance, from a prison-orifice at top, barely enough to read by Here the poor boy was locked in by himself all day, without sight of any but the porter who brought him his bread and water—who *might not speak to him*;—or of the beadle, who came twice a week to call him out to receive his periodical chastisement, which was almost welcome, because it separated him for a brief interval from solitude:—and here he was shut up by himself *of nights*, out of the reach of any sound, to suffer whatever horrors the weakn erves, and superstition incident to his time of life, might subject him to* This was the penalty for the second offence —Wouldst thou like, reader, to see what became of him in the next degree?

The culprit, who had been a third time an offender, and whose expulsion was at this time deemed irreversible, was brought forth, as at some solemn *auto da fe*, arrayed in uncouth and most appalling attire—all trace of his late "watchet weeds" careful-

* One or two instances of lunacy, or attempted suicide, accordingly, at length convinced the Governors of the impolicy of this part of the sentence, and the midnight torture to the spirits was dispensed with.—This fancy of dungeons for children, was a sprout of Howard's brain; for which (saving the reverence due to Holy Paul) methinks, I could willingly "spit upon his stony gaberdine."

ly effaced, he was exposed in a jacket, resembling those which London lamplighters formerly delighted in, with a cap of the same. The effect of this divestiture was such as the ingenious devisers of it could have anticipated. With his pale and frighted features, it was as if some of those disfigurements in Dante had seized upon him. In this disguisement he was brought into the hall (*L 's favourite state-room*), where awaited him the whole number of his school-fellows, whose joint lessons and sports he was thenceforth to share no more; the awful presence of the steward, to be seen for the last time; of the executioner beadle, clad in his state robe for the occasion; and of two faces more, of direr import, because never but in these extremities visible These were governors; two of whom, by choice, or charter, were always accustomed to officiate at these *Ultima Supplicia;* not to mitigate (so at least we understood it), but to enforce the uttermost stripe. Old Bamber Gascoigne, and Peter Aubert, I remember, were colleagues on one occasion, when the beadle turning rather pale, a glass of brandy was ordered to prepare him for the mysteries. The scourging was, after the old Roman fashion, long and stately. The lictor accompanied the criminal quite round the hall. We were generally too faint with attending to the previous *disguising circumstances*, to make accurate report with our eyes of the degree of corporal suffering inflicted. Report, of course, gave out the back knotty and livid. After scourging, he was made over, in his *San Benito*, to his friends, if he had any (but commonly such poor runagates were friendless), or to his parish officer, who, to enhance the effect of the scene, had his station allotted to him on the outside of the hall gate

These solemn pageantries were not played off so often as to spoil the general mirth of the community. We had plenty of exercise and recreation *after* school hours, and, for myself, I must confess, that I was never happier, than *in* them. The Upper and the Lower Grammar Schools were held in the same room; and an imaginary line only divided their bounds. Their character was as different as that of the inhabitants on the two sides of the Pyrennees. The Rev. James Boyer was the Upper Master; but the Rev. Matthew Field presided over that portion of the apartment, of which I had the good fortune to be a member. We lived a life as careless as birds. We talked and did just what we pleased, and nobody molested us. We carried an accidence, or a grammar, for form; but, for any trouble it gave us, we might take two years in getting through the verbs deponent, and another two in forgetting all that we had learned about them. There was now and then the formality of saying a lesson, but if you had not learned it, a brush across the shoulders, (just enough to disturb a fly), was the sole remonstrance. Field never used the rod; and in truth he wielded the cane with no great good will—holding it " like a dancer." It looked in his hands rather like an emblem, than an instrument of authority; and an emblem, too, he was ashamed of. He was a good easy man, that did not care to ruffle his own peace, nor perhaps set any great consideration upon the value of juvenile time. He came among us now and then, but often staid away whole days from us, and when he came, it made no difference to us—he had his private room to retire to, the short time he staid, to be out of the sound of our noise Our mirth and uproar went on. We had classics of our own, without being beholden to " insolent Greece or haughty Rome," that passed current among us—Peter Wilkins—the adventures of the Hon Capt. Robert Boyle—the Fortunate Blue Coat Boy—and the like Or we cultivated a turn for mechanic or scientific operations; making little sundials of paper; or weaving those ingenious parentheses, called *cat-cradles*, or making dry peas to dance upon the end of a tin pipe; or studying the art military over that laudable game " French and English,"—and a hundred other such devices to pass away the time—mixing the useful with the agreeable—as would have made the souls of Rousseau and John Locke chuckle to have seen us.

Matthew Field belonged to that class of modest divines who affect to mix in equal proportion the *gentleman*, the *scholar*, and the *Christian*, but, I know not how, the first ingredient is generally found to be the predominating dose in the composition. He was engaged in gay parties, or with his courtly bow at some Episcopal levée, when he should have been attending upon us. He had for many years the classical charge of a hundred children, during the four or five first years of their education; and his very highest form seldom proceeded further than two or three of the introductory fables of Phædrus How things were suffered to go on thus, I cannot guess. Boyer, who was the proper person to have remedied these abuses, always affected, perhaps felt, a delicacy in interfering in a province not strictly his own I have not been without my suspicions, that he was not altogether displeased at the contrast we presented to his end of the school. We were a sort of Helots to his young Spartans. He would sometimes, with ironic deference, send to borrow a rod of the Under Master, and then, with Sardonic grin, observe to one of his upper boys, "how neat and fresh the twigs looked" While his pale students were battering their brains over Xenophon and Plato, with a silence as deep as that enjoined by the Samite, we were enjoying ourselves at our ease in our little Goshen. We saw a little into the secrets of his discipline, and the prospect did but the more reconcile us to our lot. His thunders rolled innocuous for us; his storms came near, but never touched us; contrary to Gideon's miracle, while all around were drenched, our fleece was dry.* His boys turned out the better scholars; we, I suspect, have the advantage in temper. His pupils cannot speak of him without something of terror, allaying their gratitude; the remembrance of Field comes back with all the soothing images of indolence, and summer slumbers, and work like play, and innocent idleness, and Elysian exemptions, and life itself a "playing holyday"

Though sufficiently removed from the jurisdiction of Boyer, we were near enough (as I have said) to understand a little of his system. We occasionally heard sounds of the *Ululantes*, and caught glances of Tartarus. B. was a rabid pedant. His English style was crampt to barbarism His Easter Anthems (for his duty obliged him to those periodical flights) were grating as scrannel pipes.†—He would laugh, aye, and heartily, but then it must be at Flaccus's quibble about *Rex*——or at the *tristis severitas in vultu*, or *inspicere in patinas*, of Terence—thin jests, which at their first broaching could hardly have had *vis* enough to move a Roman muscle. —He had two wigs, both pedantic, but of differing omen. The one serene, smiling, fresh powdered, betokening a mild day. The other, an old discoloured, unkempt, angry caxon, denoting frequent and bloody execution. Woe to the school, when he made his morning appearance in his *passy*, or *passionate wig*. No comet expounded surer.—I B had a heavy hand. I have known him double his knotty fist at a poor trembling child (the maternal milk hardly dry upon its lips) with a "Sirrah, do you presume to set your wits at me?" —Nothing was more common than to see him make a head-long entry into the school-room, from his inner recess, or library, and, with turbulent eye, singling out a lad, roar out, "Od's my life, Sirrah," (his favourite adjuration) "I have a great mind to whip you,"—then, with as sudden a retracting impulse, fling back into his lair—and, after a cooling lapse of some minutes (during which all but the culprit had totally forgotten the context) drive headlong out again, piecing out his imperfect sense, as if it had been some Devil's Litany, with the expletory yell—"*and I* WILL *too*" —In his gentler moods, when the *rabidus furor* was assuaged, he had resort to an ingenious method, peculiar, for what I have heard, to himself, of whipping the boy, and reading the Debates, at the same time; a paragraph, and a lash between; which in those times, when parliamentary oratory was most at a height and flourishing in these realms, was not

* Cowley.

† In this and every thing B. was the Antipodes of his co-adjutor While the former was digging his brains for crude anthems, worth a pig-nut, F. would be recreating his gentlemanly fancy in the more flowery walks of the Muses. A little dramatic effusion of his, under the name of Vertumnus and Pomona, is not yet forgotten by the Chroniclers of that sort of literature. It was accepted by Garrick, but the town did not give it their sanction.—B. used to say of it, in a way of half-compliment, half-irony, that it was *too classical for representation*.

calculated to impress the patient with a veneration for the diffuser graces of rhetoric.

Once, and but once, the uplifted rod was known to fall ineffectual from his hand—when droll squinting W— having been caught putting the inside of the master's desk to a use for which the architect had clearly not designed it, to justify himself, with great simplicity averred, that *he did not know that the thing had been forwarned.* This exquisite irrecognition of any law antecedent to the *oral,* or *declaratory,* struck so irresistibly upon the fancy of all who heard it (the pedagogue himself not excepted) that remission was unavoidable.

L. has given credit to B.'s great merits as an instructor. Coleridge, in his literary life, has pronounced a more intelligible and ample encomium on them. The author of the Country Spectator doubts not to compare him with the ablest teachers of antiquity. Perhaps we cannot dismiss him better than with the pious ejaculation of C.—when he heard that his old master was on his death bed—"Poor I. B.!—may all his faults be forgiven; and may he be wafted to bliss by little cherub boys, all head and wings, with no *bottoms* to reproach his sublunary infirmities."

Under him were many good and sound scholars bred.—First Grecian of my time was Lancelot Pepys Stevens, kindest of boys and men, since Co-grammar-master (and inseparable companion) with Dr. T——e. What an edifying spectacle did this brace of friends present to those who remembered the anti-socialities of their predecessors!—You never met the one by chance in the street without a wonder, which was quickly dissipated by the almost immediate subappearance of the other. Generally arm in arm, these kindly coadjutors lightened for each other the toilsome duties of their profession, and when, in advanced age, one found it convenient to retire, the other was not long in discovering that it suited him to lay down the fasces also. O it is pleasant, as it is rare, to find the same arm linked in yours at forty, which at thirteen helped it to turn over the *Cicero De Amicitia,* or some tale of *Antique Friendship,* which the young heart even then was burning to anticipate!—Co-Grecian with S. was Th——, who has since executed with ability various diplomatic functions at the Northern courts. Th—— was a tall dark saturnine youth, sparing of speech, with raven locks. —Thomas Fanshaw Middleton followed him (now Bishop of Calcutta) a scholar and a gentleman, in his teens. He has the reputation of an excellent critic; and is author (besides the Country Spectator,) of a Treatise on the Greek Article, against Sharpe.—M. is said to bear his mitre high in India, where the *regni novitas* (I dare say) sufficiently justifies the bearing. A humility quite as primitive as that of Jewel or Hooker, might not be exactly fitted to impress the minds of those Anglo-Asiatic diocesans with a reverend for home institutions, and the church which those fathers watered. The manners of M. at school, though firm, were mild, and unassuming.—Next to M. (if not senior to him,) was Richards, author of the Aboriginal Britons, the most spirited of the Oxford Prize Poems; a pale, studious Grecian.—Then followed poor S——, ill-fated M——! of these the Muse is silent.

Finding some of Edward's race
Unhappy, pass their annals by.

Come back into memory, like as thou wert in the day-spring of thy fancies, with hope like a fiery column before thee—the dark pillar not yet turned.—Samuel Taylor Coleridge—Logician, Metaphysician, Bard!—How have I seen the casual passer, through the Cloisters, stand still, intranced with admiration, (while he weighed the disproportion between the *speech* and the *garb* of the young Mirandula,) to hear thee unfold, in thy deep and sweet intonations, the mysteries of Jamblichus, or Plotinus (for even in those years thou waxedst not pale at such philosophic draughts) or reciting Homer in his Greek, or Pindar —— while the walls of the old Grey Friars re-echoed to the accents of the *inspired charity-boy!*—"Many were the wit-combats," (to dally awhile with the words of old Fuller,) between him and C. V. Le G——, "which two I behold like a Spanish great gallion, and an English man of war; Master Coleridge, like the former, was built far higher in learning, solid, but slow in his performances. C. V. L., with the English man of war, lesser in bulk, but lighter in sailing, could turn with all tides, tack about, and take advantage of all winds, by the quickness of his wit and invention."

Nor shalt thou, their compeer, be quickly forgotten, Allen, with the cordial smile, and still more cordial laugh, with which thou wert wont to make the old Cloisters shake, in thy cognition of some poignant jest of theirs; or the anticipation of some more material, and, peradventure, practical one, of thine own. Extinct are those smiles, with that beautiful countenance, with which (for thou wert the Nireus *formosus* of the school,) in the days of thy maturer waggery, thou didst disarm the wrath of infuriated town-damsel, who, incensed by provoking pinch, turning tigress-like round, suddenly converted by thy angel-look, exchanged the half-formed terrible "*bl——*," for a gentler greeting—"*bless thy handsome face!*"

Next follow two, who ought to be now alive, and the friends of Elia—the junior Le G—— and F——; who impelled, the former by a roving temper, the latter by too quick a sense of neglect—ill capable of enduring the slights poor Sizars are sometimes subject to in our seats of learning—exchanged their Alma Mater for the camp; perishing, one by climate, and one on the plains of Salamanca:—Le G——, sanguine, volatile, sweet-natured; F—— dogged, faithful, anticipative of insult, warm-hearted, with something of the old Roman height about him.

Fine frank-hearted, Fr——, the present master of Hertford, with Marmaduke T——, mildest of Missionaries—and both my good friends still—close the catalogue of Grecians in my time.

ELIA.

THE TWO RACES OF MEN.

The human species, according to the best theory I can form of it, is composed of two distinct races, *the men who borrow*, and *the men who lend*. To these two original diversities may be reduced all those impertinent classifications of Gothic and Celtic tribes, white men, black men, red men. All the dwellers upon earth, "Parthians and Medes and Elamites," flock hither, and do naturally fall in with one or other of these primary distinctions. The infinite superiority of the former, which I choose to designate as the *great race*, is discernible in their figure, port, and a certain instinctive sovereignty. The latter are born degraded. "He shall serve his brethren." There is something in the air of one of this cast, lean, and suspicious; contrasting with the open, trusting, generous manners of the other.

Observe who have been the greatest borrowers of all ages—Alcibiades—Falstaff—Sir Richard Steele—our late incomparable Brinsley—what a family likeness in all four!

What a careless even deportment hath your borrower! what rosy gills! what a beautiful reliance on Providence doth he manifest,—taking no more thought than lilies! What contempt for money,—accounting it (yours and mine especially) no better than dross! What a liberal confounding of those pedantic distinctions of *meum* and *tuum!* or rather, what a noble simplification of language (beyond Tooke), resolving these supposed opposites into one clear intelligible pronoun adjective!—What near approaches doth he make to the primitive *community*,—to the extent of one half of the principle at least!—

He is the true taxer who "calleth all the world up to be taxed;" and the distance is as vast between him and *one of us*, as subsisted betwixt the *Augustan Majesty*, and the poorest *obolary Jew* that paid it tribute-pittance at Jerusalem!—His exactions too have such a cheerful, voluntary air! So far removed from your sour parochial or state-gatherers,—those ink-horn varlets, who carry their want of welcome in their faces! He cometh to you with a smile, and troubleth you with no receipt; confining himself to no set season. Every day is his Candlemas, or his Feast of Holy Michael. He applieth the *lene tormentum* of a pleasant look to your purse,—which to that gentle warmth expands her silken leaves, as naturally as the cloak of the traveller, for which sun and wind contended! He is the true Propontic which never ebbeth! The sea which taketh handsomely at each man's hand. In vain the victim, whom he delighteth to honour, struggles with destiny; he is in the net. Lend therefore cheerfully, O man ordained to lend—that thou lose not in the end, with thy worldly penny, the reversion promised. Combine not preposterously in thine own person the penalties of Lazarus and of Dives!—but, when thou seest the proper authority coming, meet it smilingly, as it were half-way. Come, a handsome sacrifice! See how light *he* makes of it! Strain not courtesies with a noble enemy.

Reflections like the foregoing were forced upon my mind by the death of my old friend Ralph Bigod, Esq., who departed this life on Wednesday evening; dying, as he had lived, without much trouble. He boasted himself a descendant from mighty ancestors of that name, who heretofore held ducal dignities in this realm. In his actions and sentiments he belied not the stock to which he pretended. Early in life he found himself invested with ample revenues; which, with that noble disinterestedness which I have noticed as inherent in men of the *great race*, he took almost immediate measures entirely to dissipate and bring to nothing: for there is something revolting in the idea of a king holding a private purse; and the thoughts of Bigod were all regal. Thus furnished, by the very act of disfurnishment; getting rid of the cumbersome luggage of riches, more apt (as one sings)

TO SLACKEN VIRTUE, AND ABATE HER EDGE,
THAN PROMPT HER TO DO AUGHT MAY MERIT PRAISE,

he set forth, like some Alexander, upon his great enterprise, "borrowing, and to borrow!"

In his periegesis, or triumphant progress throughout this island, it has been calculated that he laid a tythe part of the inhabitants under contribution. I reject this estimate as greatly exaggerated:—but having had the honour of accompanying my friend, divers times, in his perambulations about this vast city, I own I was greatly struck at first with the prodigious number of faces we met, who claimed a sort of respectful acquaintance with us. He was one day so obliging as to explain the phenomenon. It seems, these were his tributaries, feeders of his exchequer; gentlemen, his good friends (as he was pleased to express himself), to whom he had occasionally been beholden for a loan. Their multitudes did no way disconcert him. He rather took a pride in numbering them, and, with Comus, seemed pleased to be "stocked with so fair a herd."

With such sources, it was a wonder how he contrived to keep his treasury always empty. He did it by force of an aphorism, which he had often in his mouth, that "money kept longer than three days stinks". So he made use of it while it was fresh. A good part he drank away (for he was an excellent toss-pot), some he gave away, the rest he threw away, literally tossing and hurling it violently from him,—as boys do burrs, or as if it had been infectious,—into ponds, or ditches, or deep holes,—inscrutable cavities of the earth;—or he would bury it, (where he would never seek it again) by a river's side under some bank, which (he would facetiously observe) paid no interest—but out away from him it must go peremptorily, as Hagar's offspring into the wilderness, while it was sweet. He never missed it. The streams were perennial which fed his fisc. When new supplies became necessary, the first person that had the felicity to fall in with him, friend or stranger, was sure to contribute to the deficiency. For Bigod had an *undeniable* way with him He had a cheerful, open exterior, a quick jovial eye, a bald forehead, just touched with grey (*cana fides*) He anticipated no excuse, and found none. And, waiving for a while my theory as to the *great race*, I would put it to the most untheorising reader, who may at times have disposeable coin in his pocket, whether it is not more répugnant to the kindliness of his nature, to refuse such a one as I am describing, than to say *no* to a poor petitionary rogue (your bastard borrower), who by his mumping visnomy tells you, that he expects nothing better, and, therefore, whose preconceived notions and expectations you do in reality so much less shock in the refusal.

When I think of this man, his fiery glow of heart; his swell of feeling; how magnificent, how *ideal* he was; how great at the midnight hour; and when I compare with him the companions, with whom I have associated since; I grudge the saving of a few idle ducats, and think that I am fallen into the society of *lenders*, and *little men*.

To one like Elia, whose treasures are rather cased in leather covers, than closed in iron coffers, there is a class of alienators more formidable than that which I have touched upon; I mean, your *borrowers of books*—those mutilators of collections, spoilers of the symmetry of shelves, and creators of odd volumes There is Comberbatch, matchless in his depredations!

That foul gap in the bottom shelf facing you, like a great eye-tooth knocked out—(you are now with me in my little back study in Bloomsbury, reader!)——with the huge Switzer-like tomes on each side (like the Guildhall giants, in their reformed posture, guarding of nothing (once held the tallest of my folios) *Opera Bonaventuræ*, choice and massy divinity), to which its two supporters (school divinity also, but of a lesser calibre,—Bellarmine, and Holy Thomas), showed but as dwarfs,—itself an Ascapart!—*that* Comberbatch abstracted upon the faith of a theory he holds, which is more easy, I confess, for me to suffer by than to refute, namely, that "the title to property in a book, (my Bonaventure, for instance), is in exact ratio to a person's powers of understanding and appreciating the same." Should he go on acting upon this theory, which of our shelves is safe?

That slight vacuum in the left hand

case—two shelves from the ceiling—scarcely distinguishable but by the quick eye of a loser——was whilom the commodious resting place of Browne on Urn Burial. C. will hardly allege that he knows more about that treatise than I do, who introduced it to him, and was indeed the first (of the moderns) to discover its beauties—but so have I known a foolish lover to praise his mistress in the presence of a rival more qualified to carry her off than himself.—Just below, Dodsley's dramas want their fourth volume, where Vittoria Corombona is! The remainder nine are as distasteful as Priam's refuse sons, when the Fates *borrowed* Hector. Here stood the Anatomy of Melancholy, in sober state.—There loitered the Complete Angler; quietly as in life, by some stream side.—In yonder nook, John Buncle, a widower-volume, with "eyes closed," mourns his ravished mate.

One justice I must do my friend, that if he sometimes, like the sea, sweeps away a treasure; at another time, sea-like, he throws up as rich an equivalent to match it. I have a small under-collection of this nature (my friend's gatherings in his various calls), picked up, he has forgotten at what odd places; and deposited, with as little memory at mine. I take in these orphans, the twice-deserted. These proselytes of the gate are welcome as the true Hebrews. There they stand in conjunction, natives, and naturalized. The latter seem as little disposed to inquire out their true lineage, as I am.—I charge no warehouse-room for these deodands, nor shall ever put myself to the ungentlemanly trouble of advertising a sale of them to pay expenses.

To lose a volume to C. carries some sense and meaning in it. You are sure that he will make one hearty meal on your viands, if he can give no account of the platter after it. But what moved thee, wayward, spiteful * * to be so importunate to carry off with thee, in spite of tears and adjurations to thee to forbear, the letters of that princely woman, the thrice noble Margaret Newcastle?—knowing at the time, and knowing that I knew also, thou most assuredly would'st never turn over one leaf of the illustrious folio.—what but the mere spirit of contradiction, and childish love of getting the better of thy friend?—Then, worst cut of all! to transport it with thee to the Gallican land—

Unworthy land to harbour such a sweetness,
A virtue in which all ennobling thoughts dwelt,
Pure thoughts, kind thoughts, high thoughts, her sex's wonder!

—— hadst thou not thy play-books, and books of jests and fancies, about thee, to keep thee merry, even as thou keepest all companies with thy quips, and mirthful tales?—Child of the Green Room, it was unkindly done of thee. Thy wife too, that part-French, better-part-Englishwoman!—that *she* could fix upon no other treatise to bear away, in kindly token of remembering us, than the works of Fulke Greville, Lord Brook—of which no Frenchman, nor woman of France, Italy, or England, was ever by nature constituted to comprehend a tittle!—*Was there not Zimmerman on Solitude?*

Reader, if haply thou art blessed with a moderate collection, be shy of showing it; or if thy heart overfloweth to lend them, lend thy books; but let it be to such a one as S. T. C. —he will return them (generally anticipating the time appointed) with usury; enriched with annotations, tripling their value. I have had experience. Many are these precious MSS. of his—(in *matter* oftentimes, and almost in *quantity*, not unfrequently, vying with the originals)—in no very clerkly hand—legible in my Daniel, in old Burton, in Sir Thomas Browne; and those abstruser cogitations of the Greville, now, alas! wandering in Pagan lands.——I counsel thee, shut not thy heart, nor thy library, from S. T. C.

ELIA.

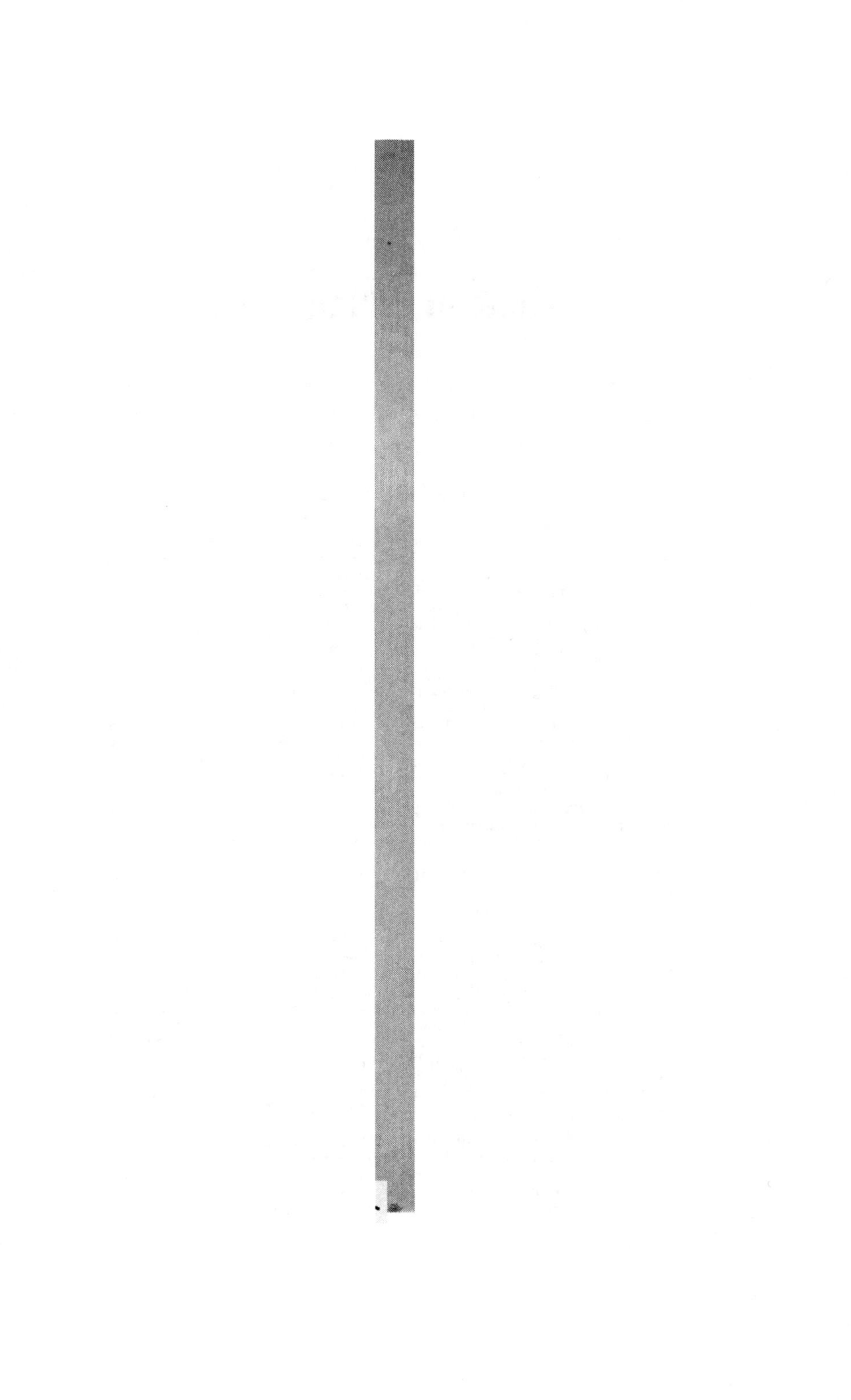

THE

London Magazine.

N° XIII. JANUARY, 1821. Vol. III.

NEW YEAR'S EVE.

Every man hath two birth-days: two days, at least, in every year, which set him upon revolving the lapse of time, as it affects his mortal duration. The one is that which in an especial manner he termeth *his*. In the gradual desuetude of old observances, this custom of solemnizing our proper birth-day hath nearly passed away; or is left to children, who reflect nothing at all about the matter, nor understand any thing in it beyond cake and orange. But the birth of a New Year is of an interest too wide to be pretermitted by king or cobbler. No one ever regarded the First of January with indifference. It is that from which all date their time, and count upon what is left. It is the nativity of our common Adam.

Of all sound of all bells—(bells, the music most bordering upon heaven)—most solemn and touching is the peal which rings out the Old Year. I never hear it without a gathering-up of my mind to a concentration of all the images that have been diffused over the past twelvemonth; all I have done, or suffered; performed, or neglected; in that regretted time. I begin to know its worth, as when a person dies. It takes a personal colour; nor was it a poetical flight in a contemporary, when he exclaimed

> I saw the skirts of the departing Year.

It is no more than what in sober sadness every one of us seems to be conscious of in that awful leave-taking. I am sure I felt it, and all felt it with me, last night; though some of my companions affected rather to manifest an exhilaration at the birth of the coming year, than any very tender regrets for the decease of its predecessor. But I am none of those who—

> Welcome the coming, speed the parting guest.

I am naturally, beforehand, shy of novelties; new books, new faces, new years,—from some mental twist which makes it difficult in me to face the prospective. I have almost ceased to hope; and am sanguine only in the prospects of other (former) years. I plunge into foregone visions and conclusions. I encounter pell-mell with past disappointments. I am armour-proof against old discouragements. I forgive, or overcome in fancy, old adversaries. I play over again *for love*, as the gamesters phrase it, games, for which I once paid so dear. I would scarce now have any of those untoward accidents and events of my life reversed. I would no more alter them than the incidents of some well-contrived novel. Methinks, it is better that I should have pined away seven of my goldenest years, when I was thrall to the fair hair, and fairer eyes, of Alice W——n, than that so passionate a love-adventure should be lost. It was better that our family should have missed that legacy, which old Dorrell cheated us of, than that I should have at this moment two thousand pounds *in banco*, and be without the idea of that specious old rogue.

In a degree beneath manhood, it is my infirmity to look back upon those early days. Do I advance a paradox, when I say, that, skipping over the intervention of forty years, a man may have leave to love *himself*, without the imputation of self-love?

If I know aught of myself, no one whose mind is introspective—and mine is painfully so—can have a less respect for his present identity, than I have for the man, Elia. I know him to be light, and vain, and humoursome, a notorious * * *; addicted to * * * *: averse from counsel, neither taking it, nor offering it,—* * * besides; a stammering buffoon; what you will; lay it on, and spare not; I subscribe to it all, and much more, than thou canst be willing to lay at his door — — — but for the child Elia—that "other me," there in the back-ground—I must take leave to cherish the remembrance of that young master—with as little reference, I protest, to this stupid changeling of five-and-forty, as if it had been a child of some other house, and not of my parents. I can cry over its patient small-pox at five, and rougher medicaments. I can lay its poor fevered head upon the sick pillow at Christ's, and wake with it in surprise at the gentle posture of maternal tenderness hanging over it, that unknown had watched its sleeps. I know how it shrank from any the least colour of falsehood.—God help thee, Elia, how art thou changed! Thou art sophisticated.—I know how honest, how courageous (for a weakling) it was—how religious, how imaginative, how hopeful! From what have I not fallen, if the child I remember was indeed myself,—and not some dissembling guardian, presenting a false identity, to give the rule to my unpractised steps, and regulate the tone of my moral being!

That I am fond of indulging, beyond a hope of sympathy, in such retrospection, may be the symptom of some sickly idiosyncrasy, or is it owing to another cause; simply, that being without wife or family, I have not learned to project myself enough out of myself; and having no offspring of my own to dally with, I turn back upon memory, and adopt my own early idea, as my heir and favorite? If these speculations seem fantastical to thee, reader—(a busy man perchance), if I tread out of the way of thy sympathy, and am singularly-conceited only; I retire, impenetrable to ridicule, under the phantom cloud of Elia.

The elders, with whom I was brought up, were of a character not likely to let slip the sacred observance of any old institution, and the ringing out of the Old Year was kept by them with circumstances of peculiar ceremony.—In those days the sound of those midnight chimes, though it seemed to raise hilarity in all around me, never failed to bring a train of pensive imagery into my fancy. Yet I then scarce conceived what it meant, or thought of it as a reckoning that concerned me. Not childhood alone, but the young man till thirty, never feels practically that he is mortal. He knows it indeed, and, if need were, he could preach a homily on the fragility of life; but he brings it not home to himself, any more than in a hot June we can appropriate to our imagination the freezing days of December. But now—shall I confess a truth?—I feel these audits but too powerfully. I begin to count the probabilities of my duration; and to grudge at the expenditure of moments and shortest periods, like miser's farthings. In proportion as the years both lessen and shorten, I set more count upon their periods, and would fain lay my ineffectual finger upon the spoke of the great wheel. I am not content to pass away "like a weaver's shuttle." Those metaphors solace me not, nor sweeten the unpalatable draught of mortality. I care not to be carried with the tide, that smoothly bears human life to eternity, and reluct at the inevitable course of destiny. I am in love with this green earth; the face of town and country, the unspeakable rural solitudes, and the sweet security of streets. I would set up my tabernacle here. I am content to stand still at the age to which I am arrived; I, and my friends. To be no younger, no richer, no handsomer. I do not want to be weaned by age, or drop, like mellow fruit, as they say, into the grave.—Any alteration, on this earth of mine, in diet, or in lodging, puzzles and discomposes me. My household-gods plant a terrible fixed foot, and are not rooted up without blood. They do not willingly seek Lavinian shores. A new state of being staggers me

Sun, and sky, and breeze, and solitary walks, and summer holydays, and the greenness of fields, and the delicious juices of meats and fishes, and society, and the chearful glass, and candle-light, and fireside conversations, and innocent vanities, and jests, and *irony itself*—do these things go out with life?

Can a ghost laugh, or shake his gaunt sides, when you are pleasant with him?

And you, my midnight darlings, my Folios! must I part with the intense delight of having you, (huge armfuls) in my embraces? Must knowledge come to me, if it come at all, by some awkward experiment of intuition, and no longer by this familiar process of reading?

Shall I enjoy friendships there, wanting the smiling indications which point me to them here,—the recognizable face—the "sweet assurance of a look"—?

In winter this intolerable disinclination to dying—to give it its mildest name—does more especially haunt and beset me In a genial August noon, beneath a sweltering sky, death is almost problematic. At those times do such poor snakes as myself enjoy an immortality. Then we expand, and burgeon Then are we as strong again, as valiant again, as wise again, and a great deal taller. The blast that nips and shrinks me, puts me in thoughts of death. All things allied to the insubstantial, wait upon that master feeling; cold, numbness, dreams, perplexity; moonlight itself, with its shadowy and spectral appearances, — that cold ghost of the sun, or Phœbus' sickly sister, like that innutritious one denounced in the Canticles:—I am none of her "minions"—I hold with the Persian.

Whatsoever thwarts, or puts me out of my way, brings death into my mind All partial evils, like humours, run into that capital plague-sore—I have heard some profess an indifference to life Such hail the end of their existence as a port of refuge, and speak of the grave as of some soft arms, in which they may slumber as on a pillow Some have wooed death — — — but out upon thee, I say, thou foul ugly phantom! I detest, abhor, execrate, and (with Friar John) give thee to six score thousand devils, as in no instance to be excused or tolerated, but shunned as a universal viper; to be branded, proscribed, and spoken evil of! In no way can I be brought to digest thee, thou thin, melancholy, *Privation*, or more frightful and confounding *Positive!*

Those antidotes, prescribed against the fear of thee, are altogether frigid and insulting, like thyself. For what satisfaction hath a man, that he shall "lie down with kings and emperors in death," who in his life-time never greatly coveted the society of such bed-fellows?—or, forsooth, that "so shall the fairest face appear"—Why, to comfort me, must Alice W——n be a goblin? More than all, I conceive disgust at those impertinent and misbecoming familiarities, inscribed upon your ordinary tomb-stones. Every dead man must take upon himself to be lecturing me with his odious truism, that "such as he now is, I must shortly be" Not so shortly, friend, perhaps, as thou imaginest. In the meantime I am alive. I move about. I am worth twenty of thee. Know thy betters! Thy New Years' Days are past. I survive, a jolly candidate for 1821. Another cup of wine—and while that turn-coat bell, that just now mournfully chanted the obsequies of 1820 departed, with changed notes lustily rings in a successor, let us attune to its peal the song made on a like occasion by hearty chearful Mr. Cotton.—

THE NEW YEAR.

Hark, the cock crows, and yon bright star
Tells us, the day himself's not far,
And see where, breaking from the night,
He gilds the western hills with light.
With him old Janus doth appear,
Peeping into the future year,
With such a look as seems to say,
The prospect is not good that way
Thus do we rise ill sights to see,
And 'gainst ourselves to prophecy;
When the prophetic fear of things
A more tormenting mischief brings,
More full of soul-tormenting gall,
Than direst mischiefs can befall.
But stay! but stay! methinks my sight,
Better inform'd by clearer light,
Discerns sereneness in that brow,
That all contracted seem'd but now.

His * revers'd face may show distaste,
And frown upon the ills are past;
But that which this way looks is clear,
And smiles upon the New-born year.
He looks too from a place so high,
The Year lies open to his eye;
And all the moments open are
To the exact discoverer.
Yet more and more he smiles upon
The happy revolution.
Why should we then suspect or fear
The influences of a year,
So smiles upon us the first morn,
And speaks us good so soon as born?
Plague on't! the last was ill enough,
This cannot but make better proof;
Or, at the worst, as we brush'd thro'
The last, why so we may this too;
And then the next in reason shou'd
Be superexcellently good:
For the worst ills (we daily see)
Have no more perpetuity,
Than the best fortunes that do fall;
Which also bring us wherewithal
Longer their being to support,
Than those do of the other sort;
And who has one good year in three,
And yet repines at destiny,
Appears ungrateful in the case,
And merits not the good he has.
Then let us welcome the New Guest
With lusty brimmers of the best;
Mirth always should Good Fortune meet,
And renders e'en Disaster sweet:
And though the Princess turn her back,
Let us but line ourselves with sack,
We better shall by far hold out,
Till the next Year she face about.

How say you, reader—do not these verses smack of the rough magnanimity of the old English vein? Do they not fortify like a cordial; enlarging the heart, and productive of sweet blood, and generous spirits, in the concoction? Where be those puling fears of death, just now expressed, or affected?—Passed like a cloud—absorbed in the purging sunlight of clear poetry—clean washed away by a wave of genuine Helicon, your only Spa for these hypochondries—And now another cup of the generous!—and a merry New Year, and many of them, to you all, my masters!

1st Jan. 1821. ELIA.

MRS. BATTLE'S OPINIONS ON WHIST.

"A CLEAR fire, a clean hearth,* and the rigour of the game." This was the celebrated *wish* of old Sarah Battle (now with God) who, next to her devotions, loved a good game at whist. She was none of your lukewarm gamesters, your half and half players, who have no objection to take a hand, if you want one to make up a rubber; who affirm that they have no pleasure in winning; that they like to win one game, and lose another;† that they can while away an hour very agreeably at a card-table, but are indifferent whether they play or no,—and will desire an adversary, who has slipt a wrong card, to take it up and play another. These insufferable triflers are the curse of a table. One of these flies will spoil a whole pot. Of such it may be said, that they do not play at cards, but only play at playing at them.

Sarah Battle was none of that breed. She detested them, as I do, from her heart and soul; and would not, save upon a striking emergency, willingly seat herself at the same table with them. She loved a thorough-paced partner, a determined enemy. She took, and gave no concessions. She hated favours. She never made a revoke, nor ever passed it over in her adversary without ex-

* This was before the introduction of rugs, reader. You must remember the intolerable crash of the unswept cinder, betwixt your foot and the marble.

† As if a sportsman should tell you, he liked to kill a fox one day, and lose him the next.

acting the utmost forfeiture. She fought a good fight: cut and thrust. She held not her good sword (her cards) "like a dancer." She sate bolt upright; and neither showed you her cards, nor desired to see yours. All people have their blind side—their superstitions; and I have heard her declare, under the rose, that Hearts was her favourite suit.

I never in my life—and I knew Sarah Battle many of the best years of it—saw her take out her snuff-box when it was her turn to play; or snuff a candle in the middle of a game, or ring for a servant, till it was fairly over. She never introduced, or connived at, miscellaneous conversation during its process. As she emphatically observed, cards were cards: and if I ever saw unmingled distaste in her fine last-century countenance, it was at the airs of a young gentleman of a literary turn, who had been with difficulty persuaded to take a hand, and who, in his excess of candour, declared, that he thought there was no harm in unbending the mind now and then, after serious studies, in recreations of that kind! She could not bear to have her noble occupation, to which she wound up her faculties, considered in that light. It was her business, her duty, the thing she came into the world to do,—and she did it. She unbent her mind afterwards—over a book.

Pope was her favourite author: his Rape of the Lock her favourite work. She once did me the favour to play over with me (with the cards) his celebrated game of Ombre in that poem; and to explain to me how far it agreed with, and in what points it would be found to differ from, traydrille. Her illustrations were apposite and poignant; and I had the pleasure of sending the substance of them to Mr. Bowles; but I suppose they came too late to be inserted among his ingenious notes upon that author.

Quadrille, she has often told me, was her first love; but whist had engaged her maturer esteem. The former, she said, was showy and specious, and likely to allure young persons. The uncertainty and quick shifting of partners—a thing which the constancy of whist abhors,—the dazzling supremacy and regal investiture, of Spadille—absurd, as she justly observed, in the pure aristocracy of whist, where his crown and garter give him no proper power above his brother-nobility of the Aces,—the giddy vanity, so taking to the inexperienced, of playing alone;—above all, the over-powering attractions of a *Sans Prendre Vole*,—to the triumph of which there is certainly nothing parallel, or approaching, in the contingencies of whist;—all these, she would say, make quadrille a game of captivation to the young and enthusiastic. But whist was the *solider* game. that was her word. It was a long meal; not, like quadrille, a feast of snatches. One or two rubbers might co-extend in duration with an evening. They gave time to form rooted friendships, to cultivate steady enmities. She despised the chance-started, capricious, and ever fluctuating alliances of the other. The skirmishes of quadrille, she would say, reminded her of the petty ephemeral embroilments of the little Italian states, depicted by Machiavel; perpetually changing postures and connexions; bitter foes to-day, sugared darlings to-morrow; kissing and scratching in a breath;—but the wars of whist were comparable to the long, steady, deep-rooted, rational, antipathies of the great French and English nations.

A grave simplicity was what she chiefly admired in her favourite game. There was nothing silly in it, like the nob in cribbage. Nothing superfluous. No *flushes*—that most irrational of all pleas, that a reasonable being can set up:—that any one should claim four by virtue of holding cards of the same shape and colour, without reference to the playing of the game, or the individual worth or pretensions of the cards themselves! She held this to be a solecism; as pitiful an ambition at cards as alliteration is in authorship. She despised superficiality, and looked deeper than the colours of things.—Suits were soldiers, she would say; and must have a uniformity of array to distinguish them: but what should we say to a foolish squire, who should claim a merit from dressing up his tenantry in red jackets, that never were to be marshalled—never to take the field?—She even wished that whist were more simple than it is; and, in my mind, would have stript it of some appendages, which, in the state of human frailty, may be venially, and even commendably, allowed of. She saw no reason for the deciding of the trump by the turn of the card. Why not one suit always trumps?—Why two colours, when the shape of the suits would have sufficiently distinguished them without it?—

"But the eye, my dear Madam, is agreeably refreshed with the variety. Man is not a creature of pure reason—he must have his senses delightfully appealed to. We see it in Roman Catholic countries, where the music and the paintings draw in many to worship, whom your quaker spirit of unsensualizing would have kept out.—You, yourself, have a pretty collection of paintings—but confess to me, whether, walking in your gallery at Sandham, among those clear Vandykes, or among the Paul Potters in the anti-room, you ever felt your bosom glow with an elegant delight, at all comparable to *that* you have it in your power to experience most evenings over a well-arranged assortment of the court cards?—the pretty antic habits, like heralds in a procession—the gay triumph-assuring scarlets—the contrasting deadly-killing sables—the "hoary majesty of spades"—Pam in all his glory!—

"All these might be dispensed with, and, with their naked names upon the drab pasteboard, the game might go on very well, picture-less. But the *beauty* of cards would be extinguished for ever. Stripped of all that is imaginative in them, they must degenerate into mere gambling.—Imagine a dull deal-board, or drum head, to spread them on, instead of that nice verdant carpet (next to nature's), fittest arena for those courtly combatants to play their gallant jousts and turneys in!—Exchange those delicately-turned ivory markers—(work of Chinese artist, unconscious of their symbol,—or as profanely slighting their true application as the arrantest Ephesian journeyman that turned out those little shrines for the goddess)—exchange them for little bits of leather (our ancestor's money) or chalk and a slate!"—

The old lady, with a smile, confessed the soundness of my logic; and to her approbation of my arguments on her favorite topic that evening, I have always fancied myself indebted for the legacy of a curious cribbage board, made of the finest sienna marble, which her maternal uncle (old Walter Plumer, whom I have elsewhere celebrated) brought with him from Florence:—this, and a trifle of five hundred pounds, came to me at her death.

The former bequest (which I do not least value) I have kept with religious care; though she herself, to confess a truth, was never greatly taken with cribbage. It was an essentially vulgar game, I have heard her say,—disputing with her uncle, who was very partial to it. She could never heartily bring her mouth to pronounce "*go*"—or "*that's a go.*" She called it an ungrammatical game. The pegging teazed her. I once knew her to forfeit a rubber (a five dollar stake), because she would not take advantage of the turn-up knave, which would have given it her, but which she must have claimed by the disgraceful tenure of declaring "*one for his heels.*" There is something extremely genteel in this sort of self-denial. Sarah Battle was a gentlewoman born.

Piquet, she held the best game at the cards for two persons, though she would ridicule the pedantry of the terms—such as pique—repique—the capot—they savoured (she thought) of affectation. But games for two, or even three, she never greatly cared for. She loved the quadrate, or square. She would argue thus:—Cards are warfare: the ends are gain, with glory. But cards are war, in disguise of a sport: when single adversaries encounter, the ends proposed are too palpable. By themselves, it is too close a fight; with spectators, it is not much bettered. No looker-on can be interested, except for a bet, and then it is a mere affair of money; he cares not for your luck *sympathetically*, or for your play.—Three are still worse, a mere naked war of every man against every man, as in cribbage, without league or alliance, or a rotation of petty and contradictory interests, a succession of heartless leagues, and not much more hearty infractions of them, as in traydrille.—But in square games (*she meant whist*) all that is possible to be attained in card-playing is accomplished. There are the incentives of profit with honour, common to every species—though the *latter* can be but very imperfectly enjoyed in those other games, where the spectator is only feebly a participator. But the parties in whist are spectators and principals too. They are a theatre to themselves, and a looker-on is not wanted He is rather worse than nothing, and an impertinence. Whist abhors neutrality, or interests beyond its sphere You glory in some surprising stroke of skill or fortune, not because a cold—or even an interested—by-stander witnesses it, but because your *partner* sympathises in the contingency. You win for two. You triumph for two. Two are exalted. Two again are mortified; which divides their disgrace, as the conjunction doubles (by taking off the invidiousness) your glories. Two losing to two are better reconciled, than one to one in that close butchery. The hostile feeling is weakened by multiplying the channels War becomes a civil game.—By such reasonings as these the old lady was accustomed to defend her favourite pastime.

No inducement could ever prevail upon her to play at any game, where chance entered into the composition, *for nothing*. Chance, she would argue—and here again, admire the subtlety of her conclusion!—chance is nothing, but where something else depends upon it It is obvious, that cannot be *glory*. What rational cause of exultation could it give to a man to turn up size ace a hundred times together by himself? or before spectators, where no stake was depending?—Make a lottery of a hundred thousand tickets with but one fortunate number—and what possible principle of our nature, except stupid wonderment, could it gratify to gain that number as many times successively, without a prize?—Therefore she disliked the mixture of chance in back-gammon, where it was not played for money She called it foolish, and those people idiots, who were taken with a lucky hit under such circumstances! Games of pure skill were as little to her fancy. Played for a stake, they were a mere system of over-reaching. Played for glory, they were a mere setting of one man's wit,—his memory, or combination-faculty rather—against another's; like a mock engagement at a review, bloodless and profitless.—She could not conceive a *game* wanting the sprightly infusion of chance,—the handsome excuses of good fortune. Two people playing at chess in a corner of a room, whilst whist was stirring in the centre, would inspire her with insufferable horror and ennui. Those well-cut similitudes of Castles, and Knights, the *imagery* of the board, she would argue, (and I think in this case justly) were entirely misplaced and senseless. Those hard head-contests can in no instance ally with the fancy. They reject form and colour. A pencil, and dry slate (she used to say) were the proper arena for such combatants.

To those puny objectors against cards, as nurturing the bad passions,—(dropping for awhile the speaking mask of old Sarah Battle) I would retort, that man is a gaming animal. He must be always trying to get the better in something or other.—that this passion can scarcely be more safely expended than upon a game at cards. that cards are a temporary illusion, in truth, a mere drama, for we do but *play* at being mightily concerned, where a few idle shillings are at stake, yet, during the illusion, we *are* as mightily concerned as those whose stake is crowns and kingdoms. They are a sort of dream-fighting; much ado; great battling, and little bloodshed; mighty means for disproportioned ends; quite as diverting, and a great deal more innoxious, than many of those more serious *games* of life, which men play, without esteeming them to be such.

P S.—With great deference to the old lady's judgment on these matters, I think I have experienced some moments in my life, when playing at cards *for nothing* has even been agreeable. When I am in sickness, or not in the best spirits, I sometimes call for the cards, and play a game at piquet *for love* with my cousin Bridget—*Bridget Elia*.

I grant there is someting sneaking in it: but with a tooth-ache, or a sprained ancle,—when you are subdued and humble,—you are glad to put up with an inferior spring of action.—

There is such a thing in nature, I am convinced, as *sick whist*.—

I grant it is not the highest style of man—I deprecate the manes of Sarah Battle—she lives not, alas! to whom I should apologize.—

At such times, those *terms* which my old friend objected to, come in as something admissible.—I love to get a tierce, or a quatorze, though they mean nothing. I am subdued to an inferior interest. Those shadows of winning amuse me.

That last game I had with my sweet cousin (I capotted her)—(dare I tell thee, how foolish I am?)—I wished it might have lasted for ever, though we gained nothing, and lost nothing, though it was a mere shade of play: I would be content to go on in that idle folly for ever. The pipkin should be ever boiling, that was to prepare the gentle lenitive to my foot, which Bridget was doomed to apply to it, after the game was over: and, as I do not much relish appliances, there it should ever bubble. Bridget and I should be ever playing.

Elia.

A CHAPTER ON EARS.

I HAVE no ear.—

Mistake me not, reader,—nor imagine that I am by nature destitute of those exterior twin appendages, hanging ornaments, and (architecturally speaking) handsome volutes to the human capital. Better my mother had never borne me.—I am, I think, rather delicately than copiously provided with those conduits; and I feel no disposition to envy the mule for his plenty, or the mole for her exactness, in those ingenious labyrinthine inlets—those indispensable side-intelligencers.

Neither have I incurred, or done any thing to incur, with Defoe, that hideous disfigurement, which constrained him to draw upon assurance —to feel quite unabashed,* and at ease upon that article. I was never, I thank my stars, in the pillory; nor,

* Earless on high stood, unabash'd, Defoe.—*Dunciad.*

You have claim to a seat here at my right hand, as patron of the stammerers. You left your work, if I remember Herodotus correctly, at eight hundred million toises, or thereabout, above the level of the sea. Bless us, what a long bell you must have pulled, to call your top workmen to their nuncheon on the low grounds of Sennaar. Or did you send up your garlick and onions by a rocket? I am a rogue if I am not ashamed to show you our Monument on Fish-street Hill, after your altitudes. Yet we think it somewhat.

What, the magnanimous Alexander in tears?—cry, baby, put its finger in its eye, it shall have another globe, round as an orange, pretty moppet!

Mister Adams——'odso, I honour your coat—pray do us the favour to read to us that sermon, which you lent to Mistress Slipslop—the twenty and second in your portmanteau there—on Female Incontinence—the same — it will come in most irrelevantly and impertinently seasonable to the time of the day.

Mr. ——, you look wise. Pray correct that error.——

Mr. Hazlitt, I cannot indulge you in your definition. I must fine you a bumper, or a paradox. We will have nothing said or done syllogistically this day. Remove those logical forms, waiter, that no gentleman break the tender shins of his apprehension stumbling across them.

Master Stephen, you are late.—Ha! Cokes, is it you?—Aguecheek, my dear knight, let me pay my devoir to you.—Master Shallow, your worship's poor servant to command.—Master Silence, I will use few words with you.—Slender, it shall go hard if I edge not you in somewhere.—You six will engross all the poor wit of the company to day.—I know it, I know it.

Ha! honest R——, my fine old Librarian of Ludgate, time out of mind, art thou here again? Bless thy doublet, it is not over-new, threadbare as thy stories:—what dost thou flitting about the world at this rate?—Thy customers are extinct, defunct, bed-rid, have ceased to read long ago.—Thou goest still among them, seeing if, peradventure, thou canst hawk a volume or two.—Good Grenville S——, thy last patron, is flown.

> King Pandion, he is dead,
> All thy friends are lapt in lead—

Nevertheless, noble R——, come in, and take your seat here, between Armado and Quisada, for in true courtesy, in gravity, in fantastic smiling to thyself, in courteous smiling upon others, in the goodly ornature of well-apparelled speech, and the commendation of wise sentences, thou art nothing inferior to those accomplished Dons of Spain. The spirit of chivalry forsake me for ever, when I forget thy singing the song of Macheath, which declares that he might be *happy with either*, situated between those two ancient spinsters—when I forget the inimitable formal love which thou didst make, turning now to the one, and now to the other, with that Malvolian smile—as if Cervantes, not Gay, had written it for his hero; and as if thousands of periods must revolve, before the mirror of courtesy could have given his invidious preference between a pair of so goodly-propertied and meritorious-equal damsels. * * *

* * * * * * *

To descend from these altitudes, and not to protract our Fools' Banquet beyond its appropriate day,—for I fear the second of April is not many hours distant—in sober verity I will confess a truth to thee, reader. I love a *Fool*—as naturally, as if I were of kith and kin to him. When a child, with child-like apprehensions, that dived not below the surface of the matter, I read those *Parables*, not guessing at their involved wisdom, I had more yearnings towards that simple architect, that built his house upon the sand, than I entertained for his more cautious neighbour; I grudged at the hard censure pronounced upon the quiet soul that kept his talent; and, prizing their simplicity beyond the more provident, and, to my apprehension, somewhat *unfeminine* wariness of their competitors, I felt a kindliness, that almost amounted to a *tendre*, for those five thoughtless virgins.—I have never made an acquaintance since, that lasted; or a friendship, that answered; with any that had not some tincture of the absurd in their characters. I venerate an honest obliquity of understanding. The more laughable blunders a man shall commit in your company, the more tests he giveth you, that he will not betray or overreach you. I love the safety, which a palpable hallucination warrants; the security, which a word out of season ratifies. And take my word for this, reader, and say, a fool told it you, if you please, that he who hath not a dram of folly in his mixture, hath pounds of much worse matter in his composition. It is observed, that "the foolisher the fowl or fish,—woodcocks,—dotterells,—cod's-heads, &c.—the finer the flesh thereof," and what are commonly the world's received fools, but such whereof the world is not worthy? and what have been some of the kindliest patterns of our species, but so many darlings of absurdity, minions of the goddess, and her white boys?—Reader, if you wrest my words beyond their fair construction, it is you, and not I, that are the *April Fool.*

ELIA.

1st April, 1821.

THE CONFESSIONS OF H. F. V. H. DELAMORE, ESQ.

Sackville-street, 25th March, 1821.

Mr. Editor,—A correspondent in your last Number,* blesses his stars, that he was never yet in the pillory; and, with a confidence which the uncertainty of mortal accidents but weakly justifies, goes on to predict that he never shall be. Twelve years ago, had a Sibyl prophesied, to me, that I should live to be set in a worse place, I should have struck her for a lying beldam. There are degradations below that which he speaks of.

I come of a good stock, Mr. Editor. The Delamores are a race singularly tenacious of their honour; men who, in the language of Edmund Burke, feel a stain like a wound. My grand uncle died of a fit of the sullens for the disgrace of a public whipping at Westminster. He had not then attained his fourteenth year. Would I had died young!

For more than five centuries, the current of our blood hath flowed unimpeachably. And must it stagnate now?

Can a family be tainted backwards?—can posterity purchase disgrace for their progenitors?—or doth it derogate from the great Walter of our name, who received the sword of knighthood in Cressy field, that one of his descendants once sate * * * * * * * * * * * ?

Can an honour, fairly achieved in *quinto Edwardi Tertii*, be reversed by a slip in *quinquagesimo Georgii Tertii?*—how stands the law?—what *dictum* doth the college deliver?—O Clarencieux! O Norroy!

Can a reputation, gained by hard watchings on the cold ground, in a suit of mail, be impeached by hard watchings on the cold ground in other circumstances—was the endurance equal?—why is the guerdon so disproportionate?

A priest mediated the ransom of

* Elia:—Chapter on Ears.

the too valorous Reginald, of our house, captived in Lord Talbot's battles. It was a clergyman, who by his intercession abridged the period of my durance.

Have you touched at my wrongs yet, Mr Editor?—or must I be explicit as to my grievance?

Hush, my heedless tongue

Something bids me—"Delamore, be ingenuous"

Once then, and only once———

Star of my nativity, hide beneath a cloud, while I reveal it!

Ancestors of Delamore, lie low in your wormy beds, that no posthumous hearing catch a sound!

Let no eye look over thee, while thou shalt peruse it, reader!

Once———these legs, with Kent in the play, though for far less ennobling considerations, did wear "cruel garters."

Yet I protest it was but for a thing of nought—a fault of youth, and warmer blood—a calendary inadvertence I may call it—or rather a temporary obliviousness of the day of the week—timing my Saturnàlia amiss.—

Streets of Barnet, infamous for civil broils, ye saw my shame!—did not your Red Rose rise again to dye my burning cheek?

It was but for a pair of minutes, or so—yet I feel, I feel, that the gentry of the Delamores is extinguished for ever —

Try to forget it, reader.—

(Signed)

HENRY FRANCIS VERE HARRINGTON DELAMORE.

A QUAKER'S MEETING

Still-born Silence! thou that art
Flood-gate of the deeper heart!
Offspring of a heavenly kind!
Frost o' the mouth, and thaw of the mind!
Secrecy's confident, and he
Who makes religion mystery!
Admiration's speaking'st tongue!
Leave, thy desert shades among,
Reverend hermits' hallowed cells,
Where retired devotion dwells!
With thy enthusiasms come,
Seize our tongues, and strike us dumb! *

Reader, would'st thou know what true peace and quiet mean; would'st thou find a refuge from the noises and clamours of the multitude; would'st thou enjoy at once solitude and society; would'st thou possess the depth of thy own spirit in stillness, without being shut out from the consolatory faces of thy species; would'st thou be alone, and yet accompanied; solitary, yet not desolate; singular, yet not without some to keep thee in countenance; a unit in aggregate; a simple in composite.—come with me into a Quaker's Meeting.

Dost thou love silence deep as that "before the winds were made?" go not out into the wilderness, descend not into the profundities of the earth; shut not up thy casements; nor pour wax into the little cells of thy ears, with little-faith'd self-mistrusting Ulysses—Retire with me into a Quaker's Meeting.

For a man to refrain even from good words, and to hold his peace, it is commendable; but for a multitude, it is great mastery.

What is the stillness of the desert, compared with this place? what the uncommunicating muteness of fishes?—here the goddess reigns and revels.—"Boreas, and Cesias, and Argestes loud," do not with their inter-confounding uproars more augment the brawl—nor the waves of the blown Baltic with their clubbed

* From "Poems of all sorts" by Richard Fleckno, 1653.

sounds—than their opposite (Silence her sacred self) is multiplied and rendered more intense by numbers, and by sympathy. She too hath her deeps, that call unto deeps. Negation itself hath a positive more and less; and closed eyes would seem to obscure the great obscurity of midnight.

There are wounds, which an imperfect solitude cannot heal. By imperfect I mean that which a man enjoyeth by himself. The perfect is that which he can sometimes attain in crowds, but no where so absolutely as in a Quaker's Meeting — Those first hermits did certainly understand this principle, when they retired into Egyptian solitudes, not singly, but in shoals, to enjoy one another's want of conversation. The Carthusian is bound to his brethren by this agreeing spirit of incommunicativeness. In secular occasions, what so pleasant as to be reading a book through a long winter evening, with a friend sitting by—say, a wife —he, or she, too, (if that be probable), reading another, without interruption, or oral communication?—can there be no sympathy without the gabble of words?—away with this inhuman, shy, single, shade-and-cavern-haunting solitariness. Give me, Master Zimmerman, a sympathetic solitude.

To pace alone in the cloisters, or side aisles of some Cathedral, time-stricken;

> Or under hanging mountains,
> Or by the fall of fountains;

is but a vulgar luxury, compared with that which those enjoy, who come together for the purposes of more complete, abstracted solitude. This is the loneliness "to be felt"—The Abbey Church of Westminster hath nothing so solemn, so spirit-soothing, as the naked walls and benches of a Quaker's Meeting. Here are no tombs, no inscriptions,

> ——— sands, ignoble things,
> Dropt from the ruined sides of kings—

but here is something, which throws Antiquity herself into the foreground—SILENCE—eldest of things —language of old Night—primitive Discourser—to which the insolent decays of mouldering grandeur have but arrived by a violent, and, as we may say, unnatural progression.

> How reverend is the view of these hushed heads,
> Looking tranquillity!

Nothing-plotting, nought-caballing, unmischievous synod! convocation without intrigue! parliament without debate! what a lesson dost thou read to council, and to consistory!—if my pen treat of you lightly—as haply it will wander—yet my spirit hath gravely felt the wisdom of your custom, when sitting among you in deepest peace, which some out-welling tears would rather confirm than disturb, I have reverted to the times of your beginnings, and the sowings of the seed by Fox and Dewesbury.—I have witnessed that, which brought before my eyes your heroic tranquillity, inflexible to the rude jests, and serious violences of the insolent soldiery, republican or royalist, sent to molest you—for ye sate betwixt the fires of two persecutions, the out-cast and off-scowring of church and presbytery—I have seen the reeling sea-ruffian, who had wandered into your receptacle, with the avowed intention of disturbing your quiet, from the very spirit of the place receive in a moment a new heart, and presently sit among ye as a lamb amidst lambs. And I remembered Penn before his accusers, and Fox in the bail-dock, where he was lifted up in spirit, as he tells us, and "the Judge and the Jury became as dead men under his feet."

Reader, if you are not acquainted with it, I would recommend to you, above all church-narratives, to read Sewel's History of the Quakers. It is in folio, and is the abstract of the journals of Fox, and the primitive Friends. It is far more edifying and affecting than any thing you will read of Wesley and his colleagues. Here is nothing to stagger you, nothing to make you mistrust, no suspicion of alloy, no drop or dreg of the worldly or ambitious spirit. You will here read the true story of that much-injured, ridiculed man (who perhaps hath been a by-word in your mouth,)—James Naylor: what dreadful sufferings, with what patience, he endured even to the boring through of his tongue with red-hot irons without a murmur; and with what strength of mind, when the delusion he had fallen into, which they stigmatized for blasphemy, had given way to clearer thoughts, he could renounce his error, in a strain of the beautifullest humility, yet keep his first grounds, and be a Quaker still!—so different from the practice of your common converts from enthusiasm, who when they apostatize, *apostatize all*, and think they can never get far enough from the society of their former errors, even to the renunciation of some saving truths, with which they had been mingled, not implicated.

Get the Writings of John Woolman by heart; and love the early Quakers.

How far the followers of these good men in our days have kept to the primitive spirit, or in what proportion they have substituted formality for it, the Judge of Spirits can alone determine. I have seen faces in their assemblies, upon which the dove sate visibly brooding. Others again I have watched, when my thoughts should have been better engaged, in which I could possibly detect nothing but a blank inanity. But quiet was in all, and the disposition to unanimity, and the absence of the fierce controversial workings.—If the spiritual pretensions of the Quakers have abated, at least they make few pretences. Hypocrites they certainly are not, in their preaching. It is seldom indeed that you shall see one get up amongst them to hold forth. Only now and then a trembling, female, generally *ancient*, voice is heard—you cannot guess from what part of the meeting it proceeds—with a low, buzzing, musical sound, laying out a few words which "she thought might suit the condition of some present," with a quaking diffidence, which leaves no possibility of supposing that any thing of female vanity was mixed up, where the tones were so full of tenderness, and a restraining modesty.—The men, for what I have observed, speak seldomer.*

Once only, and it was some years ago, I witnessed a sample of the old Foxian orgasm. It was a man of giant stature, who, as Wordsworth phrases it, might have danced "from head to foot equipt in iron mail." His frame was of iron too. But *he* was malleable. I saw him shake all over with the spirit—I dare not say, of delusion—the strivings of the outer man were unutterable—he seemed not to speak, but to be spoken from—I saw the strong man bowed down, and his knees to fail—his joints all seemed loosening—it was a figure to set off against Paul Preaching—the words he uttered were few, and sound—he was evidently resisting his will—keeping down his own word-wisdom with more mighty effort, than the world's orators strain for theirs. "He was a WIT in his youth," he told us, with expressions of a sober remorse. And it was not till long after the impression had begun to wear away, that I was enabled, with something like a smile, to recall the striking incongruity of the confession—understanding the term in its worldly acceptation—with the frame and physiognomy of the person before me. His brow would have scared away the Levities—the Joci Risus-que—faster than the Loves fled the face of Dis at Enna.—By *wit*, even in his youth, I will be sworn he understood something far within the limits of an allowable liberty.

More frequently the Meeting is broken up without a word having been spoken. But the mind has been fed. You go away with a sermon, not made with hands. You have been in the milder caverns of Trophonius; or as in some den, where that fiercest and savagest of all wild creatures, the TONGUE, that unruly member, has strangely lain tied up and captive. You have bathed with stillness.—O when the spirit is sore fretted, even tired to sickness of the janglings, and nonsense-noises of the world, what a balm and a solace it is, to go and seat yourself, for a quiet half hour, upon some undisputed corner of a bench, among the gentle Quakers!

Their garb and stillness conjoined, present a uniformity, tranquil, and

* Is this confined to *Quaker Meetings*?—ED.

herd-like—as in the pasture—"forty feeding like one."—

The very garments of a Quaker seem incapable of receiving a soil; and cleanliness in them to be something more than the absence of its contrary. Every Quakeress is a lily; and when they come up in bands to their Whitsun-conferences, whitening the easterly streets of the metropolis, from all parts of the United Kingdom, they show like troops of the Shining Ones.—

Elia.

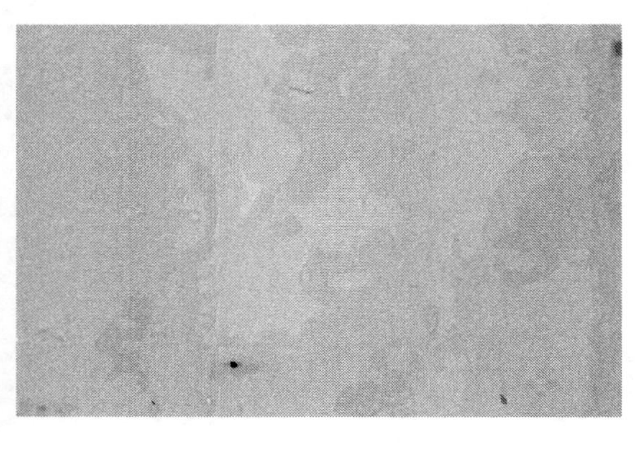

THE OLD AND THE NEW SCHOOLMASTER.

My reading has been lamentably desultory and immethodical. Odd, out of the way, old English plays, and treatises, have supplied me with most of my notions, and ways of feeling. In every thing that relates to *science*, I am a whole Encyclopædia behind the rest of the world. I should have scarcely cut a figure among the franklins, or country gentlemen, in king John's days. I know less geography than a school-boy of six weeks' standing. To me a map of old Ortelius is as authentic as Arrowsmith. I do not know whereabout Africa merges into Asia; whether Ethiopia lie in one or other of those great divisions; nor can form the remotest conjecture of the position of New South Wales, or Van Dieman's Land. Yet do I hold a correspondence with a very dear friend in the first-named of these two Terræ Incognitæ. I have no astronomy. I do not know where to look for the Bear, or Charles's Wain; the place of any star; or the name of any of them at sight. I guess at Venus only by her brightness—and if the sun on some portentous morn were to make his first appearance in the West, I verily believe, that, while all the world were gasping in apprehension about me, I alone should stand unterrified, from sheer incuriosity and want of observation. Of history and chronology I possess some vague points, such as one cannot help picking up in the course of miscellaneous study; but I never deliberately sat down to a chronicle, even of my own country. I have most dim apprehensions of the four great monarchies; and sometimes the Assyrian, sometimes the Persian, floats as *first* in my fancy. I make the widest conjectures concerning Egypt, and her shepherd kings. My friend *M.*, with great pains-taking, got me to think I understood the first proposition in Euclid, but gave me over in despair at the second. I am entirely unacquainted with the modern languages; and, like a better man than myself, have "small Latin and less Greek." I am a stranger to the shapes and texture of the commonest trees, herbs, flowers—not from the circumstance of my being town-born—for I should have brought the same inobservant spirit into the world with me, had I first seen it in "on Devon's leafy shores,"—and am no less at a loss among purely town-objects, tools, engines, mechanic processes.—Not that I affect ignorance—but my head has not many mansions, nor spacious; and I have been obliged to fill it with such cabinet curiosities, as it can hold without aching. I sometimes wonder, how I have passed my probation with so little discredit in the world, as I have done, upon so meagre a stock. But the fact is, a man may do very well with a very little knowledge, and scarce be found out, in mixed company; every body is so much more ready to produce his own, than to call for a display of your acquisitions. But in a *tête-à-tête* there is no shuffling. The truth will out. There is nothing which I dread so much, as the being left alone for a quarter of an hour with a sensible, well-informed man, that does not know me. I lately got into a dilemma of this sort.—

In one of my daily jaunts between Bishopsgate and Shacklewell, the coach stopped to take up a staid-looking gentleman, about the wrong side of thirty, who was giving his parting directions (while the steps were adjusting), in a tone of mild authority, to a tall youth, who seemed to be neither his clerk, his son, nor his servant, but something partaking of all three. The youth was dismissed, and we drove on. As we were the sole passengers, he naturally enough addressed his conversation to me; and we discussed the merits of the fare, the civility and punctuality of the driver; the circumstance of an opposition coach having been lately set up, with the probabilities of its success—to all which I was enabled to return pretty satisfactory answers, having been drilled into this kind of etiquette by some years' daily practice of riding to and fro in the stage aforesaid—when he suddenly alarmed me by a startling question, whether I had seen the show of prize cattle that morning in Smithfield: Now as I had not seen it, and do not greatly care for such sort of exhibitions, I was obliged to return a cold negative. He seemed a little mortified, as well as astonished, at my declaration, as (it appeared) he was just come fresh from the sight, and doubtless had hoped to compare notes on the subject. However he assured me that I had lost a fine treat, as it far exceeded the show of last year. We were now approaching Norton Falgate, when the sight of some shop-goods *ticketed* freshened him up into a dissertation upon the cheapness of cottons this spring. I was now a little in heart, as the nature of my morning avocations had brought me into some sort of familiarity with the raw material; and I was surprised to find how eloquent I was becoming on the state of the India market—when, presently, he dashed my incipient vanity to the earth at once, by inquiring whether I had ever made any calculation as to the value of the rental of all the retail shops in London. Had he asked of me, what song the Sirens sang, or what name Achilles assumed when he hid himself among women, I might, with Sir Thomas Browne, have hazarded a "wide solution."* My companion saw my embarrassment, and, the almshouses beyond Shoreditch just coming in view, with great good-nature and dexterity shifted his conversation to the subject of public charities; which led to the comparative merits of provision for the poor in past and present times, with observations on the old monastic institutions, and charitable orders;—but, finding me ra-

* Urn Burial.

ther dimly impressed with some glimmering notions from old poetic associations, than strongly fortified with any speculations reducible to calculation on the subject, he gave the matter up; and, the country beginning to open more and more upon us, as we approached the turnpike at Kingsland (the destined termination of his journey), he put a home thurst upon me, in the most unfortunate position he could have chosen, by advancing some queries relative to the North Pole expedition. While I was muttering out something about the panorama of those strange regions (which I had actually seen), by way of parrying the question, the coach stopping relieved me from any further apprehensions. My companion getting out, left me in the comfortable possession of my ignorance; and I heard him, as he went off, putting questions to an outside passenger, who had alighted with him, regarding an epidemic disorder, that had been rife about Dalston; and which, my friend assured him, had gone through five or six schools in that neighbourhood. The truth now flashed upon me, that my companion was a schoolmaster; and that the youth, whom he had parted from at our first acquaintance, must have been one of the bigger boys, or the usher.

He was evidently a kind-hearted man, who did not seem so much desirous of provoking discussion by the questions which he put, as of obtaining information at any rate. It did not appear that he took any interest, either, in such kind of inquiries, for their own sake; but that he was in some way bound to seek for knowledge. A greenish coloured coat, which he had on, forbade me to surmise that he was a clergyman. The adventure gave birth to some reflections on the difference between persons of his profession in past and present times.

Rest to the souls of those fine old Pedagogues; the breed, long since extinct, of the Lilys, and the Linacres: who believing that all learning was contained in the languages which they taught, and despising every other acquirement as superficial and useless, came to their task as to a sport. Passing from infancy to age, they dreamed away all their days as in a grammar school. Revolving in a perpetual cycle of declensions, conjugations, syntaxes, and prosodies; renewing constantly the occupations which had charmed their studious childhood; rehearsing continually the part of the past; life must have slipped from them at last like one day. They were always in their first garden, reaping harvests of their golden time, among their *Flori* and their *Spici-legia*; in Arcadia still, but kings; the ferule of their sway not much harsher, but of like dignity with that mild sceptre attributed to king Basileus; the Greek and Latin, their stately Pamela and their Philoclea; with the occasional duncery of some untoward Tyro, serving for a refreshing interlude of a Mopsa, or a clown Damætas!

With what a savour doth the Preface to Colet's, or (as it is sometimes called) Paul's Accidence, set forth! "To exhort every man to the learning of grammar, that intendeth to attain the understanding of the tongues, wherein is contained a great treasury of wisdom and knowledge, it would seem but vain and lost labour; for so much as it is known, that nothing can surely be ended, whose beginning is either feeble or faulty; and no building be perfect, whereas the foundation and groundwork is ready to fail, and unable to uphold the burden of the frame." How well doth this stately preamble (comparable to those which Milton commendeth as "having been the usage to prefix to some solemn law, then first promulgated by Solon, or Lycurgus") correspond with and illustrate that pious zeal for conformity, expressed in a succeeding clause, which would fence about grammar-rules with the severity of faith-articles!—"as for the diversity of grammars, it is well profitably taken away by the king majesties wisdom, who foreseeing the inconvenience, and favourably providing the remedie, caused one kind of grammar by sundry learned men to be diligently drawn, and so to be set out, only everywhere to be taught for the use of learners, and for the hurt in changing of schoolmaisters." What a *gusto* in that which follows: "wherein it is profitable that he [the pupil] can orderly decline his noun, and his verb." *His* noun!

The fine dream is fading away fast; and the least concern of a teacher in the present day is to inculcate grammar rules.

The modern schoolmaster is expected to know a little of every thing, because his pupil is required not to be entirely ignorant of any thing. He must be superficially, if I may so say, omniscient. He is to know something of pneumatics, of chemistry; of whatever is curious, or proper to excite the attention of the youthful mind; an insight into mechanics is desirable, with a touch of statistics; the quality of soils, &c. botany, the constitution of his country, *cum multis aliis.* You may get a notion of some part of his expected duties by consulting the famous Tractate on Education addressed to Mr Hartlib.

All these things—these, or the desire of them—he is expected to instil, not by set lessons from professors, which he may charge in the bill, but at school-intervals, as he walks the streets, or saunters through green fields (those natural instructors), with his pupils. The least part of what is expected from him, is to be done in school-hours. He must insinuate knowledge at the *mollia tempora fandi.* He must seize every occasion—the season of the year—the time of the day—a passing cloud—a rainbow—a waggon of hay—a regiment of soldiers going by—to inculcate something useful. He can receive no pleasure from a casual glimpse of Nature, but must catch at it as an object of instruction. He must interpret beauty into the picturesque. He cannot relish a beggar-man, or a gypsy, for thinking of the suitable improvement. Nothing comes to him, not spoiled by the sophisticating medium of moral uses. The Universe,—that Great Book, as it has been called—is to him indeed, to all intents and purposes, a book, out of which he is doomed to read tedious homilies to distasting school-boys.—Vacations themselves are none to him, he is only rather worse off than before; for commonly he has some intrusive upper-boy fastened upon him at such times; some cadet of a great family; some neglected lump of nobility, or gentry; that he must drag after him to the play, to the Panorama, to Mr. Bartley's orrery, to the Panopticon, or into the country, to a friend's house, or his favourite watering-place. Wherever he goes, this uneasy shadow attends him. A boy is at his board, and in his path, and in all his movements. He is boy-rid, sick of perpetual boy.

Boys are capital fellows in their own way, among their mates; but they are unwholesome companions for grown people. The restraint is felt no less on the one side, than on the other.—Even a child, that "plaything for an hour," tires *always.* The noises of children, playing their own fancies—as I now hearken to them by fits, sporting on the green before my window, while I am engaged in these grave speculations—at my neat suburban retreat at Shacklewell—by distance made more sweet—inexpressibly take from the labour of my task. It is like writing to music. They seem to modulate my periods. They ought at least to do so—for in the voice of that tender age there is a kind of poetry, far unlike the harsh prose-accents of man's conversation.—I should but spoil their sport, and diminish my own sympathy for them, by mingling in their pastime.

I would not be domesticated all my days with a person of very superior capacity to my own—not, if I know myself at all, from any considerations of jealousy or self-comparison, for the occasional communion with such minds has constituted the fortune and felicity of my life—but the habit of too constant intercourse with spirits above you, instead of raising you, keeps you down. Too frequent doses of original thinking from others, restrain what lesser portion of that faculty you may possess of your own. You get entangled in another man's mind, even as you lose yourself in another man's grounds. You are walking with a tall varlet, whose strides out-pace yours to lassitude. The constant operation of such potent agency would reduce me, I am convinced, to imbecility. You may derive thoughts from others; your way of thinking, the mould in which your thoughts are cast, must be your own. Intellect may be imparted, but not each man's intellectual frame.—

As little as I should wish to be always thus dragged upwards, as little (or rather still less) is it desirable to be stunted downwards by your associates. The trumpet does not more stun you by its loudness, than a whisper teazes you by its provoking inaudibility.

Why are we never quite at our ease in the presence of a schoolmaster?—because we are conscious that he is not quite at his ease in ours. He is awkward, and out of place, in the society of his equals. He comes like Gulliver from among his little people, and he cannot fit the stature of his understanding to yours. He cannot meet you on the square. He wants a point given him, like an indifferent whist-player. He is so used to teaching, that he wants to be teaching *you*. One of these professors, upon my complaining that these little sketches of mine were any thing but methodical, and that I was unable to make them otherwise, kindly offered to instruct me in the method, by which young gentlemen in *his* seminary were taught to compose English themes.—The jests of a schoolmaster are coarse, or thin. They do not *tell* out of school. He is under the restraint of a formal and didactive hypocrisy in company, as a clergyman is under a moral one. He can no more let his intellect loose in society, than the other can his inclinations.—He is forlorn among his co-evals; *his juniors cannot be his friends.*

"I take blame to myself," said a sensible man of this profession, writing to a friend respecting a youth who had quitted his school abruptly, "that your nephew was not more attached to me. But persons in my situation are more to be pitied, than can well be imagined. We are surrounded by young, and, consequently, ardently affectionate hearts, but *we* can never hope to share an atom of their affections. The relation of master and scholar forbids this. *How pleasing this must be to you, how I envy your feelings*, my friends will sometimes say to me, when they see young men, whom I have educated, return after some years absence from school, their eyes shining with pleasure, while they shake hands with their old master, bringing a present of game to me, or a toy to my wife, and thanking me in the warmest terms for my care of their education. A holyday is begged for the boys; the house is a scene of happiness; I, only, am sad at heart.—This fine-spirited and warm-hearted youth, who fancies he repays his master with gratitude for the care of his boyish years—this young man—in the eight long years I watched over him with a parent's anxiety, never could repay me with one look of genuine feeling. He was proud, when I praised; he was submissive, when I reproved him; but he did never *love* me—and what he now mistakes for gratitude and kindness for me, is but the pleasant sensation, which all persons feel at revisiting the scene of their boyish hopes and fears; and the seeing on equal terms the man they were accustomed to look up to with reverence."

"My wife too," this interesting correspondent goes on to say, "my once darling Anna, is the wife of a schoolmaster.—When I courted her, when I married her—knowing that the wife of a schoolmaster ought to be a busy notable creature, and fearing that my gentle Anna would ill supply the loss of my dear bustling mother, just then dead, who never sat still, was in every part of the house in a moment, and whom I was obliged sometimes to threaten to fasten down in a chair, to save her from fatiguing herself to death—when I expressed my fears, that I was bringing her into a way of life unsuitable to her, she, who loved me tenderly, promised for my sake to exert herself to perform the duties of her new situation. She promised, and she has kept her word. What wonders will not a woman's love perform?—My house is managed with a propriety and decorum, unknown in other schools; my boys are well fed, look healthy, and have every proper accommodation; and all this performed with a careful economy, that never descends to meanness. But I have lost my gentle, *helpless* Anna!—When we sit down to enjoy an hour of repose after the fatigue of the day, I am compelled to listen to what have been her useful (and they are really useful) employments through the day, and what she proposes for her to-morrow's task. Her heart and her features are changed by the duties of her situation. To the boys, she never appears other than the *master's wife;* and she looks up to me, as to the *boys' master*, to whom all show of fond affection would be highly improper, and unbecoming the dignity of her situation and mine. Yet *this*—gratitude forbids me to hint to her. For my sake she submitted to be this altered creature, and can I reproach her for it?—These kind of complaints are not often drawn from me. I am aware that I am a fortunate, I mean, a prosperous man"—

My feelings prevent me from transcribing any farther.—For the communication of this letter I am indebted to my cousin Bridget.

ELIA.

MY RELATIONS.

I AM arrived at that point of life, at which a man may account it a blessing, as it is a singularity, if he have either of his parents surviving. I have not that felicity—and sometimes think feelingly of a passage in Browne's Christian Morals, where he speaks of a man that hath lived sixty or seventy years in the world. "In such a compass of time," he says, "a man may have a close apprehension what it is to be forgotten, when he hath lived to find none who could remember his father, or scarcely the friends of his youth, and may sensibly see with what a face in no long time OBLIVION will look upon himself."

I had an aunt, a dear and good one. She was one whom single blessedness had soured to the world. She often used to say, that I was the only thing in it which she loved; and, when she thought I was quitting it, she grieved over me with mother's tears. A partiality quite so exclusive, my reason cannot altogether approve. She was from morning till night poring over good books, and devotional exercises. Her favourite volumes were Thomas à Kempis, in Stanhope's translation; and a Roman Catholic Prayer Book, with the *matins* and *complines* regularly set down,—terms which I was at that time too young to understand. She persisted in reading them, although admonished daily concerning their Papistical tendency; and went to church every Sabbath, as a good Protestant should do. These were the only books she studied; though, I think, at one period of her life, she told me she had read with great satisfaction the Adventures of an Unfortunate Young Nobleman. Finding the door of the chapel in Essex-street open one day—it was in the infancy of that heresy—she went in, liked the sermon, and the manner of worship, and frequented it at intervals for some time after. She came not for doctrinal points, and never missed them. With some little asperities in her constitution, which I have above hinted at, she was a steadfast, friendly being, and a fine *old Christian*. She was a woman of strong sense, and a shrewd mind—extraordinary at a *repartee*, one of the few occasions of her breaking silence—else she did not much value wit. The only secular employment I remember to have seen her engaged in, was, the splitting of French beans, and dropping them into a China basin of fair water. The odour of those tender vegetables to this day comes back upon my sense, redolent of soothing recollections. Certainly it is the most delicate of culinary operations.

Male aunts, as somebody calls them, I had none—to remember. By the uncles' side I may be said to have been born an orphan. Brother, or sister, I never had any—to know them. A sister, I think, that should have been Elizabeth, died in both our infancies. What a comfort, or what a care, may I not have missed in her!—But I have cousins, sprinkled about in Hertfordshire—besides *two*, with whom I have been all my life in habits of the closest intimacy, and whom I may term cousins *par excellence*. These are James and Bridget Elia. They are older than myself by twelve, and ten, years; and neither of them seems disposed, in matters of advice and guidance, to waive any of the prerogatives, which primogeniture confers. May they continue still in the same mind; and when they shall be seventy-five, and seventy-three, years old (I cannot spare them sooner), persist in treating me in my grand climacteric precisely as a stripling, or younger brother!

James is an inexplicable cousin. Nature hath her unities, which not every critic can penetrate; or, if we feel, we cannot explain them. The pen of Yorick, and of none since his, could have drawn J. E. entire—those fine Shandian lights and shades, which make up his story. I must limp after in my poor antithetical manner, as the fates have given me grace and talent. J. E. then—to the eye of a common observer at least—seemeth made up of contradictory principles.—The genuine child of impulse, the frigid philosopher of prudence—the phlegm of my cousin's doctrine is invariably at war with his temperament, which is high sanguine. With always some fire-new project in his brain, J. E. is the systematic opponent of innovation, and crier down of every thing that has not stood the test of age and experiment. With a hundred fine notions chasing one another hourly in his fancy, he is startled at the least approach to the romantic in others; and, determined by his own sense in every thing, commends *you* to the guidance of common sense on all occasions.—With a touch of the eccentric in all which he does, or says, he is only anxious that *you* should not commit yourself by doing any thing absurd or singular. On my once letting slip at table, that I was not fond of a certain popular dish, he begged me at any rate not to *say* so—for the world would think me mad. He disguises a passionate fondness for works of high art (whereof he hath amassed a choice collection), under the pretext of buying only to sell again—that his enthusiasm may give no encouragement to yours. Yet, if it were so, why does that piece of tender, pastoral Dominichino hang still by his wall?—is the ball of his sight much more dear to him?—or what picture-dealer can talk like him?

Whereas mankind in general are observed to warp their speculative conclusions to the bent of their individual humours, *his* theories are sure to be in diametrical opposition to his constitution. He is courageous as Charles of Sweden, upon instinct; chary of his person, upon principle, as a travelling Quaker.—He has been preaching up to me, all my life, the doctrine of bowing to the great—the necessity of forms, and manner, to a man's getting on in the world. He himself never aims at either, that I can discover—and has a spirit, that would stand upright in the presence of the Cham of Tartary. It is pleasant to hear him discourse of patience—extolling it as the truest wisdom—and to see him during the last seven minutes that his dinner is getting ready. Nature never ran up in her haste a more restless piece of workmanship, than when she moulded this impetuous cousin—and Art never turned out a more elaborate orator than he can display himself to be, upon his favourite topic of the advantages of quiet, and contentedness in the state, whatever it be, that we are placed in. He is triumphant on this theme, when he has you safe in one of those short stages that ply for the western road, in a very obstructing manner, at the foot of John Murray's street—where you get in when it is empty, and are expected to wait till the vehicle hath completed her just freight—a trying three quarters of an hour to some people. He "wonders at your fidgetiness"—"where could we be better than we are, *thus sitting, thus consulting?*"—"prefers, for his part, a state of rest to locomotion,"—with an eye all the while upon the coachman—till at length, waxing out of all patience, at *your want of it*, he breaks out into a pathetic remonstrance at the fellow for detaining us so long over the time which he had professed, and declares peremptorily that "the gentleman in the coach is determined to get out, if he does not drive on that instant."

Very quick at inventing an argument, or detecting a sophistry, he is incapable of attending *you* in any chain of arguing. Indeed he makes wild work with logic; and seems to jump at most admirable conclusions by some process, not at all akin to it. Consonantly enough to this, he hath been heard to deny, upon certain occasions, that there exists such a faculty at all in man, as *reason*, and wondereth how man came first to have a conceit of it—enforcing his negation with all the might of *reasoning* he is master of. He has some speculative notions against laughter, and will maintain that laughing is not natural to *him*—when peradventure the next moment his lungs shall crow like Chanticleer. He says some of the best things in the world—and declareth, that wit is his aversion. It was he who said, upon seeing the Eton boys at play in their grounds—*What a pity to think, that these fine ingenuous lads in a few years will all be changed into frivolous Members of Parliament!*

His youth was fiery, glowing, tempestuous—and in age he discovereth no symptom of cooling. This is that which I admire in him. I hate people, who meet Time half-way. I am for no compromise with that inevitable spoiler. While he lives, J. E. will take his swing.—It does me good, as I walk towards the street of my daily avocation, on some fine May morning, to meet him marching in a quite opposite direction, with a jolly handsome presence, and shining sanguine face, that indicates some purchase in his eye—a Claude—or a Hobbima—for much of his enviable leisure is consumed at Christie's, and Phillips's—or where not—to pick up pictures, and such gauds. On these occasions he mostly stoppeth me, to read a short lecture on the advantage a person like me possesses above himself, in having his time occupied with business which he *must do*—assureth me that he often feels it hang heavy on his hands—wishes he had fewer holidays—and goes off—Westward Ho!—chanting a tune, to Pall Mall—perfectly convinced, that he has convinced me—while I proceed in my opposite direction tuneless.

It is pleasant again to see this Professor of Indifference doing the honours of his new purchase, when he has fairly housed it. You must view it in every light, till *he* has found the best—placing it at this distance, and at that, but always suiting the focus of your sight to his own. You must spy at it through your fingers, to catch the aerial perspective—though you assure him that to you the landscape shows much more agreeable without that artifice. Woe be to the luckless wight, who does not only not respond to his rapture, but who should drop an unseasonable intimation of preferring one of his anterior bargains to the present!—The last is always his best hit—his "Cynthia of the minute."—Alas! how many a mild Madonna have I known to *come in*—a Raphael!—keep its ascendancy for a few brief moons—then, after certain intermedial degradations, from the front drawing room to the back gallery, thence to the dark parlour,—adopted in turn by each of the Carracci, under successive lowering ascriptions of filiation, mildly breaking its fall—consigned to the oblivious lumber-room, *go out* at last a Lucca Giordano, or plain Carlo Maratti!—which things when I beheld—musing upon the chances and mutabilities of fate below, hath made me to reflect upon the altered condition of great personages, or that woeful Queen of Richard the Second—

> —— set forth in pomp,
> She came adorned hither like sweet May,
> Sent back like Hollowmass or shortest day.

With great love for *you*, J. E. hath but a limited sympathy with what you feel, or do. He lives in a world of his own, and makes slender guesses at what passes in your mind. He never pierces the marrow of your habits. He will tell an old established playgoer, that Mr. Such-a-one, of So-and-so (naming one of the theatres), is a very lively comedian—as a piece of news! He advertised me but the other day of some pleasant green lanes which he had found out for me, *knowing me to be a great walker*, in my own immediate vicinity—who have haunted the identical spot any time these twenty years!—He has not much respect for that class of feelings, which goes by the name of sentimental. He applies the definition of real evil to bodily sufferings exclusively—and rejecteth all others, as imaginary. He is affected by the sight, or the bare supposition, of a creature in pain, to a degree which I have never witnessed out of womankind. A constitutional acuteness to this class of sufferings may in part account for this. The animal tribe in particular he taketh under his especial protection. A broken-winded or spur-galled horse is sure to find an advocate in him. An over-loaded ass is his client for ever. He is the apostle to the brute kind—the never-failing friend of those who have none to care for them. The contemplation of a lobster boiled, or eels skinned *alive*, will wring him so, that "all for pity he could die." It will take the savour from his palate, and the rest from his pillow, for days and nights. With the intense feeling of Thomas Clarkson, he wanted only the steadiness of pursuit, and unity of purpose, of that "true yoke-fellow with Time," to have effected as much for the *Animal*, as *he* hath done for the *Negro Creation*. But my uncontrollable cousin is but imperfectly formed for purposes which demand co-operation. He cannot wait. His amelioration-plans must be ripened in a day. For this reason he has cut but an equivocal figure in benevolent societies, and combinations for the alleviation of human sufferings. His zeal constantly makes him to outrun, and put out, his co-adjutors. He thinks of relieving, — while they think of debating. He was black-balled out of a society for the Relief of **********, because the fervor of his humanity toiled beyond the formal apprehension, and creeping processes, of his associates. I shall always consider this distinction as a patent of nobility in the Elia family!

Do I mention these seeming inconsistencies to smile at, or upbraid, my unique cousin? Marry! heaven, and all good manners, and the understanding that should be between kinsfolk, forbid! — With all the strangenesses of this *strangest of the Elias*—I would not have him in one jot or tittle other than he is; neither would I barter or exchange my wild kinsman for the most exact, regular, and every-way-consistent kinsman breathing.

In my next, reader, I may perhaps give you some account of my cousin Bridget—if you are not already surfeited with cousins — and take you by the hand, if you are willing to go with us, on an excursion which we made a summer or two since, in search of *more cousins*—

Through the green plains of pleasant
Hertfordshire.

Till when, Farewell.

ELIA.

MACKERY END, IN HERTFORDSHIRE.

Bridget Elia has been my housekeeper for many a long year. I have obligations to Bridget, extending beyond the period of memory. We house together, old bachelor and maid, in a sort of double singleness; with such tolerable comfort, upon the whole, that I, for one, find in myself no sort of disposition to go out upon the mountains, with the rash king's offspring, to bewail my celibacy. We agree pretty well in our tastes and habits—yet so, as "with a difference." We are generally in harmony, with occasional bickerings—as *it should be among near relations*. Our sympathies are rather understood, than expressed; and once, upon my dissembling a tone in my voice more *kind* than ordinary, my cousin burst into tears, and complained that I was altered. We are both great readers in different directions. While I am hanging over (for the thousandth time) some passage in old Burton, or one of his strange contemporaries, she is abstracted in some modern tale, or adventure, whereof our common reading-table is daily fed with assiduously fresh supplies. Narrative teazes me. I have little concern in the progress of events. She must have *a story*—well, ill, or indifferently told—so there be life stirring in it, and plenty of good or evil accidents. The fluctuations of fortune in fiction—and almost in real life—have ceased to interest, or operate but dully upon me. Out-of-the-way humours and opinions—heads with some diverting twist in them—the oddities of authorship please me most. My cousin has a native disrelish of any thing that sounds odd or bizarre. Nothing goes down with her, that is quaint, irregular, or out of the road of common sympathy. She "holds Nature more clever." I can pardon her blindness to the beautiful obliquities of the Religio Medici; but she must apologize to me for certain disrespectful insinuations, which she has been pleased to throw out latterly, touching the intellectuals of a dear favourite of mine, of the last century but one—the thrice noble, chaste, and virtuous,—but again somewhat fantastical, and original-brain'd, generous Margaret Newcastle.

It has been the lot of my cousin, oftener perhaps than I could have wished, to have had for her associates and mine, free-thinkers—leaders, and disciples, of novel philosophies and systems; but she neither wrangles with, nor accepts, their opinions. That which was good and venerable to her, when she was a child, retains its authority over her mind still. She never juggles or plays tricks with her understanding.

We are both of us inclined to be a little too positive; and I have observed the result of our disputes to be almost uniformly this — that in matters of fact, dates, and circumstances, it turns out, that I was in the right, and my cousin in the wrong. But where we have differed upon moral points; upon something proper to be done, or let alone; whatever heat of opposition, or steadiness of conviction, I set out with, I am sure always, in the long run, to be brought over to her way of thinking.

I must touch upon the foibles of my kinswoman with a gentle hand, for Bridget does not like to be told of her faults. She hath an aukward trick (to say no worse of it) of reading in company: at which times she will answer *yes* or *no* to a question, without fully understanding its purport—which is provoking, and derogatory in the highest degree to the dignity of the putter of the said question. Her presence of mind is equal to the most pressing trials of life, but will sometimes desert her upon trifling occasions. When the purpose requires it, and is a thing of moment, she can speak to it greatly; but in matters, which are not *stuff of the conscience*, she hath been known sometimes to let slip a word less seasonably.

Her education in youth was not much attended to; and she happily missed all that train of female garniture, which passeth by the name of accomplishments. She was tumbled early, by accident or design, into a spacious closet of good old English reading, without much selection or prohibition, and browsed at will upon that fair and wholesome pasturage. Had I twenty girls, they should be brought up exactly in this fashion. I know not whether their chance in wedlock might not be diminished by it; but I can answer for it, that it makes (if the worst come to the worst) most incomparable old maids.

In a season of distress, she is the truest comforter; but in the teazing accidents, and minor perplexities, which do not call out the *will* to meet them, she sometimes maketh matters worse by an excess of participation. If she does not always divide your trouble, upon the pleasanter occasions of life she is sure always to treble your satisfaction. She is excellent to be at a play with, or upon a visit; but best, when she goes a journey with you.

We made an excursion together a few summers since, into Hertfordshire, to beat up the quarters of some of our less-known relations in that fine corn country.

The oldest thing I remember is Mackery End; or Mackarel End, as it is spelt, perhaps more properly, in some old maps of Hertfordshire; a farm-house, — delightfully situated within a gentle walk from Wheathampstead. I can just remember having been there, on a visit to a great-aunt, when I was a child, under the care of Bridget; who, as I have said, is older than myself by some ten years. *I wish that I could throw into a heap the remainder of our joint existences, that we might share them in equal division. But that is impossible.* The house was at that time in the occupation of a substantial yeoman, who had married my grandmother's sister. His name was Gladman. My grandmother was a Bruton, married to a Field. The Gladmans and the Brutons are still flourishing in that part of the county, but the Fields are almost extinct. More than forty years had elapsed since the visit I speak of; and, for the greater portion of that period, we had lost sight of the other two branches also. Who, or what sort of persons, inherited Mackery End—kindred or strange folk—we were afraid almost to conjecture, but determined some day to explore.

By somewhat a circuitous route, taking the noble park at Luton in our way from Saint Alban's, we arrived at the spot of our anxious curiosity about noon. The sight of the old farm-house, though every trace of it was effaced from my recollection, affected me with a pleasure which I had not experienced for many a year. For though *I* had forgotten it, *we* had never forgotten being there together, and we had been talking about Mackery End all our lives, till memory on my part became mocked with a phantom of itself, and I thought I knew the aspect of a place, which, when present, O how unlike it was to *that*, which I had conjured up so many times instead of it!

Still the air breathed balmily about it; the season was in the "heart of June," and I could say with the poet,

> But thou, that did'st appear so fair
> To fond imagination,
> Dost rival in the light of day
> Her delicate creation! *

Bridget's was more a *waking bliss* than mine, for she easily remembered her old acquaintance again—some altered features, of course, a little grudged at. At first, indeed, she was ready to disbelieve for joy; but the scene soon re-confirmed itself in her affections—and she traversed every out-post of the old mansion, to the wood-house, the orchard, the place where the pigeon-house had stood (house and birds were alike flown)—with a breathless impatience of recognition, which was more pardonable perhaps than decorous, at the age of fifty odd. But Bridget in some things is behind her years.

The only thing left was to get into the house—and that was a difficulty, which to me singly would have been insurmountable; for I am terribly shy in making myself known to strangers, and out-of-date kinsfolk. Love, stronger than scruple, winged my cousin in without me; but she soon returned with a creature, that might have sat to a sculptor for the image of Welcome. It was the youngest of the Gladmans; who, by marriage with a Bruton, had become mistress of the old mansion. A comely brood are the Brutons. Six of them, females, were noted as the handsomest young women in the county. But this *adopted Bruton*, in my mind, was better than they all—more comely. She was born too late to have remembered me. She just recollected in early life to have had her cousin Bridget once pointed out to her, climbing a style. But the name of kindred, and of cousinship, was enough. Those slender ties, that prove slight as gossamer in the rending atmosphere of a metropolis, bind faster, as we found it, in hearty, homely, *loving* Hertfordshire. In five minutes we were as thoroughly acquainted, as if we had been born and bred up together; were familiar, even to the calling each other by our Christian names. *So Christians should call one another.* To have seen Bridget, and her—it was like the meeting of the two Scriptural cousins! There was a grace and dignity, an amplitude of form and stature, answering to her mind, in this farmer's wife, which would have shined in a palace—or so we thought it. We were made welcome by husband and wife equally—we, and our friend that was with us.—I had almost forgotten him—but B. F. will not so soon forget that meeting, if peradventure he shall read this on the far distant shores where the Kangaroo haunts. The fatted calf was made ready, or rather was already so, as if in anticipation of our coming; and, after an appropriate glass of native wine, never let me forget, with what honest pride this hospitable cousin made us proceed to Wheathampstead, to introduce us (as some new-found rarity) to her mother and sister Gladmans, who did indeed know something more of us, at a time when she almost knew nothing.—With what corresponding kindness we were received by them also—how Bridget's memory, exalted by the occasion, warmed into a thousand half obliterated recollections of things and persons, to my utter astonishment, and her own—and to the astoundment of B. F. who sat by, *almost the only thing that was not a cousin there,*—old effaced images of more than half-forgotten names and circumstances still crowding back upon her, as wc ds written in lemon come out upon exposure to a *friendly warmth,*—when I forget all this, then may my country cousins forget me; and Bridget no more remember, that in the days of weakling infancy I was her tender charge—as I have been her care in foolish manhood since—in those pretty pastoral walks, long ago, about Mackery End, in Hertfordshire.

ELIA.

* Wordsworth, on Yarrow Visited.

JEWS, QUAKERS, SCOTCHMEN,

AND OTHER IMPERFECT SYMPATHIES.

I am of a constitution so general, that it consorts and sympathizeth with all things, I have no antipathy, or rather idiosyncracy in any thing. Those national repugnancies do not touch me, nor do I behold with prejudice the French, Italian, Spaniard, and Dutch.—*Religio Medici.*

THAT the author of the Religio Medici, mounted upon the airy stilts of abstraction, conversant about notional and conjectural essences, in whose categories of Being the possible took the upper hand of the actual, should have overlooked the impertinent individualities of such poor concretions as mankind, is not much to be admired. It is rather to be wondered at, that in the genus of animals he should have condescended to distinguish that species at all. For myself—earth-bound and fettered to the scene of my activities,—

Standing on earth, not rapt above the sky,

I confess that I do feel the differences of mankind, national or individual, to an unhealthy excess. I can look with no indifferent eye upon things or persons. Whatever is, is to me a matter of taste or distaste; or when once it becomes indifferent, it begins to be disrelishing. I am, in plainer words, a bundle of prejudices—made up of likings and dislikings—the veriest thrall to sympathies, dispathies, antipathies. In a certain sense, I hope it may be said of me, that I am a lover of my species. I can feel for all indifferently, but I cannot feel towards them all equally. The more purely-English word that expresses sympathy will better explain my meaning. I can be a friend to a worthy man, who upon another account cannot be my mate or *fellow*. I cannot *like* all people alike.*

I have been trying all my life to like Scotchmen, and am obliged to desist from the experiment in despair. They cannot like me—and in truth, I never knew one of that nation who attempted to do it. There is something more plain and ingenuous in their mode of proceeding. We know one another at first sight. There is an order of imperfect intellects (under which mine must be content to rank) which in its constitution is essentially anti-Caledonian. The owners of the sort of faculties I allude to have minds rather suggestive than comprehensive. They have no pretences to much clearness or precision in their ideas, or in their manner of expressing them. Their intellectual wardrobe (to confess fairly) has few whole pieces in it. They are content with fragments and scattered pieces of Truth. She presents no full

* I would be understood as confining myself to the subject of *imperfect sympathies.* To nations or classes of men there can be no direct *antipathy.* There may be individuals born and constellated so opposite to another individual nature, that the same sphere cannot hold them. I have met with my moral antipodes, and can believe the story of two persons meeting (who never saw one another before in their lives) and instantly fighting.

———We by proof find there should be
'Twixt man and man such an antipathy,
That though he can show no just reason why
For any former wrong or injury,
Can neither find a blemish in his fame,
Nor aught in face or feature justly blame,
Can challenge or accuse him of no evil,
Yet notwithstanding hates him as a devil.

The lines are from old Heywood's "Hierarchie of Angels," and he subjoins a curious story in confirmation, of a Spaniard who attempted to assassinate a King Ferdinand of Spain, and being put to the rack could give no other reason for the deed but an inveterate antipathy which he had taken to the first sight of the King.

——— The cause which to that act compell'd him
Was, he ne'er loved him since he first beheld him.

front to them—a feature or side-face at the most. Hints and glimpses, germs and crude essays at a system, is the utmost they pretend to. They beat up a little game peradventure—and leave it to knottier heads, more robust constitutions, to run it down. The light that lights them, is not steady and polar, but mutable and shifting, waxing, and again waning. Their conversation is accordingly. They will throw out a random word in or out of season, and be content to let it pass for what it is worth They cannot speak always as if they were upon their oath—but must be understood, speaking or writing, with some abatement. They seldom wait to mature a proposition, but e'en bring it to market in the green ear. They delight to impart their defective discoveries as they arise, without waiting for their full developement. They are no systematizers, and would but err more by attempting it. Their minds, as I said before, are suggestive merely. The brain of a true Caledonian (if I am not mistaken) is constituted upon quite a different plan. Its Minerva is born in panoply You are never admitted to see his ideas in their growth—if indeed, they do grow, and are not rather put together upon principles of clock-work. You never catch his mind in an undress He never hints or suggests any thing, but unlades his stock of ideas in perfect order and completeness. He has no falterings of self-suspicion Surmises, guesses, suppositions, half-intuitions, demi-consciousnesses, misgivings, partial illuminations, "dim instincts," embryo conceptions, and every stage that stops short of absolute certainty and conviction—his intellectual faculty seems a stranger to He brings his total wealth into company, and gravely unpacks it. His riches are always about him. He never stoops to catch a glittering something in your presence, to share it with you before he quite knows whether it be true touch or not. You cannot cry *halves* to any thing that he finds. He does not find, but bring You never witness his first apprehension of a thing. His understanding is always at its meridian—you never see the first dawn, the early streaks. The twilight of dubiety never falls upon him. Is he orthodox—he has no doubts. Is he an infidel—he has none either Between the affirmative and the negative there is no border-land with him You cannot hover with him upon the confines of truth, or wander in the maze of a probable argument. He always keeps the path You cannot make excursions with him—for he sets you right. His taste never fluctuates. His morality never abates. He cannot compromise, or understand middle actions. There can be but a right and a wrong. His conversation is as a book. His affirmations have the sanctity of an oath You must speak upon the square with him. He stops a metaphor like a suspected person in an enemy's country. "A healthy book!"—said one of his countrymen to me, who had ventured to give that appellation to John Buncle,—"did I catch rightly what you said? I have heard of a man in health, and of a healthy state of body, but I do not see how that epithet can be properly applied to a book" Above all, you must beware of indirect expressions before a Caledonian. Clap an extinguisher upon your irony, if you are unhappily blest with a vein of it. Remember you are upon your oath.—I have a print of a graceful female after Leonardo da Vinci, which I was showing off to Mr. ****. After he had examined it minutely, I ventured to ask him how he liked MY BEAUTY (a foolish name it goes by among my friends)—when he very gravely assured me, that "he had considerable respect for my character and talents" (so he was pleased to say), "but had not given himself much thought about the degree of my personal pretensions." The misconception staggered me, but did not seem much to disconcert him —Persons of this nation are particularly fond of affirming a truth—which nobody doubts. They do not so properly affirm, as annunciate it. They do indeed appear to have such a love of truth—as if, like virtue, it were valuable for itself—that all truth becomes equally valuable, whether the proposition that contains it be new or old, disputed, or such as is impossible to become a subject of disputation. I was present not long since at a party of North Britons where a son of Burns was expected; and happened to drop a silly expression (in my south British way), that I wished it were the father instead of the son—when four of them started up at once to inform me, that "that was impossible, because he was dead." An impracticable wish, it seems, was more than they could conceive. Swift has hit off this part of their character, namely their love of truth, in his biting way, but with an illiberality that necessarily confines the passage to the margin.* The tediousness of the Scotch is certainly proverbial. I wonder if they ever tire one another! —In my early life I had a passionate fondness for the poetry of Burns. I have sometimes foolishly hoped to ingratiate myself with his countrymen by expressing it. But I have always found that a true Scot resents your admiration of his compatriot, even more than he would your contempt of him. The latter he imputes to your "imperfect acquaintance with many of the words which he uses;" and the same objection makes it a presumption in you to suppose that you can admire him. I have a great mind to give up Burns. There is certainly a bragging spirit of generosity, a swaggering assertion of independence, and *all that*, in his writings. Thomson they seem to have forgotten. Smollett they have neither forgotten nor forgiven for his delineation of Rory and his companion, upon their first introduction to our metropolis.—Speak of Smollett as a great genius, and they will retort upon you Hume's History compared with *his* Continuation of it. What if the historian had continued Humphrey Clinker?

I have, in the abstract, no disrespect for Jews. They are a piece of stubborn antiquity, compared with which, Stonehenge is in its nonage. They date beyond the pyramids. But I should not care to be in habits of familiar intercourse with any of that nation. I confess that I have not the nerves to enter their synagogues. Old prejudices cling about me. I cannot shake off the story of Hugh of Lincoln. Centuries of injury, contempt, and hate, on the one side,—of cloaked revenge, dissimulation, and hate, on the other, between our and their fathers, must, and ought, to affect the blood of the children. I cannot believe it can run clear and kindly yet, or that a few fine words, such as candour, liberality, the light of a nineteenth century, can close up the breaches of such a mighty antipathy. A Hebrew is no where congenial to me. He is least distasteful on 'Change—for the mercantile spirit levels all distinctions, as all are beauties in the dark. I boldly confess that I do not relish the approximation of Jew and Christian, which has become so fashionable. The reciprocal endearments have, to me, something hypocritical and unnatural in them. I do not like to see the Church and Synagogue kissing and congeeing in awkward postures of an affected civility. If *they* are converted, why do they not come over to us altogether? Why keep up a form of separation, when the life of it is fled? If they can sit with us at table, why do they keck at our cookery? I do not understand these half-convertites. Jews christianizing—Christians judaizing—puzzle me. I like fish or flesh. A moderate Jew is a more confounding piece of anomaly than a wet Quaker. The spirit of the synagogue is essentially *separative*. B—— would have been more in keeping if he had abided by the faith of his forefathers. There is a fine scorn in his face, which nature meant to be ——of Christians. The Hebrew spirit is strong in him in spite of his proselytism. He cannot conquer the Shibboleth. How it breaks out, when he sings, "The Children of

* There are some people who think they sufficiently acquit themselves, and entertain their company with relating of facts of no consequence, not at all out of the road of such common incidents as happen every day; and this I have observed more frequently among the Scots than any other nation, who are very careful not to omit the minutest circumstances of time or place; which kind of discourse, if it were not a little relieved by the uncouth terms and phrases, as well as accent and gesture peculiar to that country, would be hardly tolerable.—*Hints towards an Essay on Conversation.*

Israel passed through the Red Sea!" The auditors, for the moment, are as Egyptians to him, and he rides over our necks in triumph There is no mistaking him.—B—— has a strong expression of sense in his countenance, and it is confirmed by his singing. The foundation of his vocal excellence is sense He sings with understanding, as Kemble delivered dialogue. He would sing the Commandments, and give an appropriate character to each prohibition. His nation, in general, have not oversensible countenances. How should they?—but you seldom see a silly expression among them. Gain, and the pursuit of gain, sharpen a man's visage. I never heard of an idiot being born among them.—Some admire the Jewish female physiognomy. I admire it—but with trembling. Jael had those full dark inscrutable eyes.

In the negro countenance, you will often meet with strong traits of benignity. I have felt yearnings of tenderness towards some of these faces—or rather masks—that have looked out kindly upon one in casual encounters in the streets and highways I love what Fuller beautifully calls—these "images of God cut in ebony." But I should not like to associate with them, to share my meals and my good-nights with them—because they are black.

I love Quaker ways, and Quaker worship. I venerate the Quaker principles. It does me good for the rest of the day, when I meet any of their people in my path. When I am ruffled or disturbed by any occurrence, the sight, or quiet voice of a Quaker, acts upon me as a ventilator, lightening the air, and taking off a load from the bosom But I cannot like the Quakers (as Desdemona would say) "to live with them." I am all over sophisticated—with humours, fancies, craving hourly sympathy. I must have books, pictures, theatres, chit-chat, scandal, jokes, ambiguities, and a thousand whim-whams, which their simpler taste can do without. I should starve at their primitive banquet. My appetites are too high for the sallads which (according to Evelyn) Eve dressed for the angel, my gusto too excited

To sit a guest with Daniel at his pulse.

The indirect answers which Quakers are often found to return to a question put to them, may be explained, I think, without the vulgar assumption, that they are more given to evasion and equivocating than other people. They naturally look to their words more carefully, and are more cautious of committing themselves. They have a peculiar character to keep up on this head. They stand in a manner upon their veracity. A Quaker is by law exempted from taking an oath. The custom of resorting to an oath in extreme cases, sanctified as it is by all religious antiquity, is apt (it must be confessed) to introduce into the laxer sort of minds the notion of two kinds of truth—the one applicable to the solemn affairs of justice, and the other to the common proceedings of daily intercourse. As truth bound upon the conscience by an oath can be but truth, so in the common affirmations of the shop and the market-place, a latitude is expected, and conceded upon questions wanting this solemn covenant. Something less than truth satisfies It is common to hear a person say, "You do not expect me to speak as if I were upon my oath." Hence a great deal of incorrectness and inadvertency, short of falsehood, creeps into ordinary conversation; and a kind of secondary or laic-truth is tolerated, where clergy-truth—oath-truth, by the nature of the circumstances, is not required. A Quaker knows none of this distinction. His simple affirmation being received, upon the most sacred occasions, without any further test, stamps a value upon the words which he is to use upon the most indifferent topics of life. He looks to them, naturally, with more severity. You can have of him no more than his word He knows, if he is caught tripping in a casual expression, he forfeits, for himself at least, his claim to the invidious exemption. He knows, that his syllables are weighed—and how far a consciousness of this particular watchfulness, exerted against a person, has a tendency to produce indirect answers, and a diverting of the question by honest means, might be illustrated, and the practice justified, by a more sacred example than is proper perhaps to be more than hinted at upon this occasion. The admirable presence of mind, which is notorious in Quakers upon all contingencies, might be traced to this imposed self-watchfulness—if it did not seem rather an humble and secular scion of that old stock of religious constancy, which never bent or faltered, in the Primitive Friends, or gave way to the winds of persecution, to the violence of judge or accuser, under trials and racking examinations. "You will never be the wiser, if I sit here answering your questions till midnight," said one of those upright Justicers to Penn, who had been putting law-cases with a puzzling subtlety. "Thereafter as the answers may be," retorted the Quaker. The astonishing composure of this people is sometimes ludicrously displayed in lighter instances. I was travelling in a stage coach with three male Quakers, buttoned up in the straitest non-conformity of their sect. We stopped to bait at Andover, where a meal, partly tea apparatus, partly supper, was set before us. My friends confined themselves to the tea table. I in my way took supper. When the landlady brought in the bill, the eldest of my companions discovered that she had charged for both meals. This was resisted. Mine hostess was very clamorous and positive. Some mild arguments were used on the part of the Quakers, for which the heated mind of the good lady seemed by no means a fit recipient. The guard came in with his usual peremptory notice. The Quakers pulled out their money, and formally tendered it—so much for tea—I, in humble imitation, tendering mine—for the supper which I had taken. She would not relax in her demand. So they all three quietly put up their silver, as did myself, and marched out of the room, the eldest and gravest going first, with myself closing up the rear, who thought I could not do better than follow the example of such grave and warrantable personages. We got in. The steps went up. The coach drove off. The murmurs of mine hostess, not very indistinctly or ambiguously pronounced, became after a time inaudible—and now my conscience, which the whimsical scene had for a while suspended, beginning to give some twitches, I waited, in the hope that some justification would be offered by these serious persons for the seeming injustice of their conduct. To my great surprise, not a syllable was dropped on the subject. They sate as mute as at a meeting. At length the eldest of them broke silence, by enquiring of his next neighbour, "Hast thee heard how indigos go at the India House?" and the question operated as a soporific on my moral feeling as far as Exeter. ELIA.

THE OLD BENCHERS OF THE INNER TEMPLE.

I was born, and passed the first seven years of my life, in the Temple. Its church, its halls, its gardens, its fountain, its river, I had almost said; for in those young years, what was this king of rivers to me, but a stream that watered our pleasant places?—these are of my oldest recollections. I repeat, to this day, no verses to myself more frequently, or with kindlier emotion, than those of Spenser, where he speaks of this spot.

There when they came, whereas those bricky towers,
The which on Themmes brode aged back doth ride,
Where now the studious lawyers have their bowers,
There whylome wont the Templer knights to bide,
Till they decayd through pride.

Indeed, it is the most elegant spot in the metropolis. What a transition for a countryman visiting London for the first time—the passing from the crowded Strand or Fleet-street, by unexpected avenues, into its magnificent ample squares, its classic green recesses! What a cheerful, liberal look hath that portion of it, which, from three sides, overlooks the greater garden: that goodly pile

Of building strong, albeit of Paper hight,

confronting, with massy contrast, the lighter, older, more fantastically shrouded one, named of Harcourt, with the cheerful Crown-office Row (place of my kindly engendure), right opposite the stately stream, which washes the garden-foot with her yet scarcely trade-polluted waters, and seems but just weaned from her Twickenham Naiades! a man would give something to have been born in such places. What a collegiate aspect has that fine Elizabethan hall, where the fountain plays, which I have made to rise and fall, how many times! to the astoundment of the young urchins, my contemporaries, who, not being able to guess at its recondite machinery, were almost tempted to hail the wondrous work as magic! What an antique air had the now almost effaced sun-dials, with their moral inscriptions, seeming coevals with that Time which they measured, and to take their revelations of its flight immediately from heaven, holding correspondence with the fountain of light! How would the dark line steal imperceptibly on, watched by the eye of childhood, eager to detect its movement, never catched, nice as an evanescent cloud, or the first arrests of sleep!

Ah! yet doth beauty like a dial-hand
Steal from his figure, and no pace perceived!

What a dead thing is a clock, with its ponderous embowelments of lead and brass, its pert or solemn dulness of communication, compared with the simple altar-like structure, and silent heart-language of the old dial! It stood as the garden god of Christian gardens. Why is it almost everywhere vanished? If its business-use be superseded by more elaborate inventions, its moral uses, its beauty, might have pleaded for its continuance. It spoke of moderate labours, of pleasures not protracted after sun-set, of temperance, and good hours. It was the primitive clock, the horologe of the first world. Adam could scarce have missed it in Paradise. It was the measure appropriate for sweet plants and flowers to spring by, for the birds to apportion their silver warblings by, for flocks to pasture and be led to fold by. The shepherd "carved it out quaintly in the sun;" and, turning philosopher by the very occupation, provided it with mottos more touching than tombstones. It was a pretty device of the gardener, recorded by Marvell, who, in the days of artificial gardening, made a dial out of herbs and flowers. I must quote his verses a little higher up, for they are full, as all his serious poetry was, of a witty delicacy. They will not come in awkwardly, I hope, in a talk of fountains and sun-dials. He is speaking of sweet garden scenes.

What wondrous life in this I lead!
Ripe apples drop about my head.

artificial or not. I remember the astonishment it raised in me. He was a blustering, loud-talking person; and I reconciled the phenomenon to my ideas as an emblem of power—somewhat like the horns in the forehead of Michael Angelo's Moses. Baron Maseres, who walks (or did till very lately) in the costume of the reign of George the Second, closes my imperfect recollections of the old benchers of the Inner Temple.

Fantastic forms, whither are ye fled? Or, if the like of you exist, why exist they no more for me? Ye inexplicable, half-understood appearances, why comes in reason to tear away the preternatural mist, bright or gloomy, that enshrouded you? Why make ye so sorry a figure in my relation, who made up to me—to my childish eyes—the mythology of the Temple? In those days I saw Gods, as "old men covered with a mantle," walking upon the earth.—Let the dreams of classic idolatry perish,—extinct be the fairies and fairy trumpery of legendary fabling,—in the heart of childhood, there will, for ever, spring up a well of innocent or wholesome superstition—the seeds of exaggeration will be busy there, and vital—from every-day forms educing the unknown and the uncommon. In that little Goshen there will be light, when the grown world flounders about in the darkness of sense and materiality. While childhood, and while dreams, reducing childhood, shall be left, imagination shall not have spread her holy wings totally to fly the earth.

Elia.

P. S. I have done injustice to the soft shade of Samuel Salt. See what it is to trust to imperfect memory, and the erring notices of childhood! Yet I protest I always thought that he had been a bachelor! This gentleman, R. N. informs me, married young, and losing his lady in childbed within the first year of their union, fell into a deep melancholy, from the effects of which, probably, he never thoroughly recovered. In what a new light does this place his rejection (O call it by a gentler name!) of mild Susan P——, unravelling into beauty certain peculiarities of this very shy and retiring character!—Henceforth let no one receive the narratives of Elia for true records! They are, in truth, but shadows of fact—verisimilitudes, not verities—or sitting but upon the remote edges and outskirts of history. He is no such honest chronicler as R. N., and would have done better perhaps to have consulted that gentleman, before he sent these incondite reminiscences to press. But the worthy sub-treasurer—who respects his old and his new masters—would but have been puzzled at the indecorous liberties of Elia. The good man wots not, peradventure, of the license which *Magazines* have arrived at in this personal age, or hardly dreams of their existence beyond the *Gentleman's*—his furthest monthly excursions in this nature having been long confined to the holy ground of honest *Urban's* obituary. May it be long before his own name shall help to swell those columns of unenvied flattery!—Meantime, O ye new Benchers of the Inner Temple, cherish him kindly, for he is himself the kindliest of human creatures. Should infirmities over-take him—he is yet in green and vigorous senility—make allowances for them, remembering that "ye yourselves are old." So may the winged horse, your ancient badge and cognisance, still flourish! so may future Hookers and Seldens illustrate your church and chambers! so may the sparrows, in default of more melodious quiristers, unpoisoned hop about your walks! so may the fresh-coloured and cleanly nursery maid, who, by leave, airs her playful charge in your stately gardens, drop her prettiest blushing curtsey as ye pass, reductive of juvenescent emotion! so may the younkers of this generation eye you, pacing your stately terrace, with the same superstitious veneration, with which the child Elia gazed on the old worthies that solemnized the parade before ye!

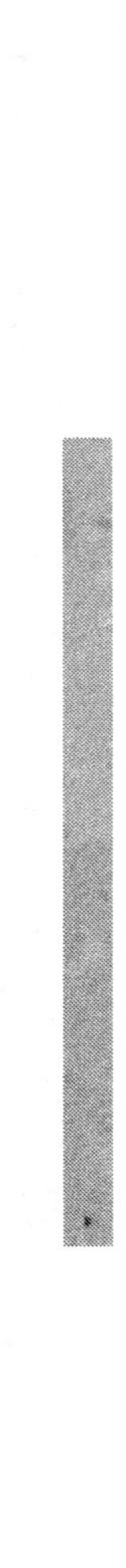

WITCHES, AND OTHER NIGHT-FEARS.

We are too hasty when we set down our ancestors in the gross for fools, for the monstrous inconsistencies (as they seem to us) involved in their creed of witchcraft. In the relations of this visible world we find them to have been as rational, and shrewd to detect an historic anomaly, as ourselves. But when once the invisible world was supposed to be opened, and the lawless agency of bad spirits assumed, what measures of probability, of decency, of fitness, or proportion—of that which distinguishes the likely from the palpable absurd—could they have to guide them in the rejection or admission of any particular testimony?—That maidens pined away, wasting inwardly as their waxen images consumed before a fire—that corn was lodged, and cattle lamed—that whirlwinds uptore in diabolic revelry the oaks of the forest—or that spits and kettles only danced a fearful-innocent vagary about some rustic's kitchen when no wind was stirring—were all equally probable where no law of agency was understood. That the prince of the powers of darkness, passing by the flower and pomp of the earth, should lay preposterous siege to the weak fantasy of indigent eld—has neither likelihood nor unlikelihood *a priori* to us, who have no measure to guess at his policy, or standard to estimate what rate those anile souls may fetch in the devil's market. Nor, when the wicked are expressly symbolized by a goat, was it to be wondered at so much, that *he* should come sometimes in that body, and assert

* She whom I seek, and find not, on the earth;

† ——More lovely, and less proud.

his metaphor.—That the intercourse was opened at all between both worlds was perhaps the mistake—but that once assumed, I see no reason for disbelieving one attested story of this nature more than another on the score of absurdity. There is no law to judge of the lawless, or canon by which a dream may be criticised.

I have sometimes thought that I could not have existed in the days of received witchcraft; that I could not have slept in a village where one of those reputed hags dwelt. Our ancestors were bolder or more obtuse. Amidst the universal belief that these wretches were in league with the author of all evil, holding hell tributary to their muttering, no simple Justice of the Peace seems to have scrupled issuing, or silly Headborough serving, a warrant upon them—as if they should subpœna Satan!—Prospero in his boat, with his books and wand about him, suffers himself to be conveyed away at the mercy of his enemies to an unknown island. He might have raised a storm or two, we think, on the passage. His acquiescence is in exact analogy to the non-resistance of witches to the constituted powers.—What stops the Fiend in Spenser from tearing Guyon to pieces—or who had made it a condition of his prey, that Guyon must take assay of the glorious bait—we have no guess. We do not know the laws of that country.

From my childhood I was extremely inquisitive about witches and witch-stories. My maid, and more legendary aunt, supplied me with good store. But I shall mention the accident which directed my curiosity originally into this channel. In my father's book-closet, the History of the Bible, by Stackhouse, occupied a distinguished station. The pictures with which it abounds—one of the ark, in particular, and another of Solomon's temple, delineated with all the fidelity of ocular admeasurement, as if the artist had been upon the spot—attracted my childish attention. There was a picture too, of the Witch raising up Samuel, which I wish that I had never seen. We shall come to that hereafter. Stackhouse is in two huge tomes—and there was a pleasure in removing folios of that magnitude, which, with infinite straining, was as much as I could manage, from the situation which they occupied upon an upper shelf. I have not met with the work from that time to this, but I remember it consisted of Old Testament stories, orderly set down, with the *objection* appended to each story, and the *solution* of the objection regularly tacked to that. The *objection* was a summary of whatever difficulties had been opposed to the credibility of the history, by the shrewdness of ancient or modern infidelity, drawn up with an almost complimentary excess of candour. The *solution* was brief, modest, and satisfactory. The bane and antidote were both before you. To doubts so put, and so quashed, there seemed to be an end for ever. The dragon lay dead, for the foot of the veriest babe to trample on. But—like as was rather feared than realized from that slain monster in Spenser—from the womb of those crushed errors, young dragonets would creep, exceeding the prowess of so tender a Saint George as myself to vanquish. The habit of expecting objections to every passage, set me upon starting more objections, for the glory of finding a solution of my own for them. I became staggered and perplexed, a sceptic in long coats. The pretty Bible stories which I had read, or heard read in church, lost their purity and sincerity of impression, and were turned into so many historic or chronologic theses to be defended against whatever impugners. I was not to disbelieve them, but—the next thing to that—I was to be quite sure that some one or other would, or had disbelieved them. Next to making a child an infidel, is the letting him know that there are infidels at all. Credulity is the man's weakness, but the child's strength. O, how ugly sound Scriptural doubts from the mouth of a babe and a suckling!—I should have lost myself in these mazes, and have pined away, I think, with such unfit sustenance as these husks afforded, but for a fortunate piece of ill-fortune, which about this time befel me. Turning over the picture of the ark with too much haste, I unhappily made a breach in its ingenious fabric—driving my inconsiderate fingers right through the two larger quadrupeds—the elephant, and the camel—that stare (as well they might) out of the two last windows next the steerage in that unique piece of naval architecture. Stackhouse was henceforth locked up, and became an interdicted treasure. With the book, the *objections* and *solutions* gradually cleared out of my head, and have seldom returned since in any force to trouble me.—But there was one impression which I had imbibed from Stackhouse, which no lock or bar could shut out, and which was destined to try my childish nerves rather more seriously.—That detestable picture!

I was dreadfully alive to nervous terrors. The night-time solitude, and the dark, were my hell. The sufferings I endured in this nature would justify the expression. I never laid my head on my pillow, I suppose, from the fourth to the seventh or eighth year of my life—so far as memory serves in things so long ago—without an assurance, which realized its own prophecy, of seeing some frightful spectre. Be old Stackhouse then acquitted in part, if I say that to his picture of the Witch raising up Samuel—(O that old man covered with a mantle!) I owe—not my midnight terrors, the hell of my infancy—but the shape and manner of their visitation. It was he who dressed up for me a hag that nightly sate upon my pillow—a sure bedfellow, when my aunt or my maid was far from me. All day long, while the book was permitted me, I dreamed waking over his delineation, and at night (if I may use so bold an expression) awoke into sleep, and found the vision true. I durst not, even in the day-light, once enter the chamber where I slept, without my face turned to the window, aversely from the bed where my witch-ridden pillow was.—Parents do not know what they do when they leave tender babes alone to go to sleep in the dark. The feeling about for a friendly arm—the hoping for a familiar voice—when they wake screaming—and find none to soothe them—what a terrible shaking it is to their poor nerves! The keeping them up till midnight, through candle-light and the unwholesome hours, as they are called,—would, I am satisfied, in a medical point of view, prove the better caution.—That detestable picture, as I have said, gave the fashion to my dreams—if dreams they were—for the scene of them was invariably the room in which I lay. Had I never met with the picture, the fears would have come self-pictured in some shape or other—

> Headless bear, black-man, or ape—

but, as it was, my imaginations took that form.—It is not book, or picture, or the stories of foolish servants, which create these terrors in children. They can at most but give them a direction. Dear little T. H. who of all children has been brought up with the most scrupulous exclusion of every taint of superstition—who was never allowed to hear of goblin or apparition, or scarcely to be told of bad men, or to read or hear of any distressing story—finds all this world of fear, from which he has been so rigidly excluded *ab extra*, in his own "thick-coming fancies;" and from his little midnight pillow, this nurse-child of optimism will start at shapes, unborrowed of tradition, in sweats to which the reveries of the cell-damned murderer are tranquillity.

Gorgons, and Hydras, and Chimæras dire—stories of Celæno and the Harpies—may reproduce themselves in the brain of superstition—but they were there before. They are transcripts, types—the archetypes are in us, and eternal. How else should the recital of that, which we know in a waking sense to be false, come to affect us at all?—or

> —— Names, whose sense we see not,
> Fray us with things that be not?

Is it that we naturally conceive terror from such objects, considered in their capacity of being able to inflict upon us bodily injury?—O, least of all! These terrors are of older standing. They date beyond body—or, without the body, they would have been the same. All the cruel, tormenting, defined devils in Dante—tearing, mangling, choking, stifling, scorching demons—are they one half so fearful to the spirit of a man, as the simple idea of a spirit unembodied following him—

> Like one that on a lonesome road
> Doth walk in fear and dread,
> And having once turn'd round, walks on,
> And turns no more his head;
> Because he knows a frightful fiend
> Doth close behind him tread.*

* Mr. Coleridge's Ancient Mariner.

That the kind of fear here treated of is purely spiritual—that it is strong in proportion as it is objectless upon earth—that it predominates in the period of sinless infancy—are difficulties, the solution of which might afford some probable insight into our ante-mundane condition, and a peep at least into the shadow-land of pre-existence.

My night-fancies have long ceased to be afflictive. I confess an occasional night-mare; but I do not, as in early youth, keep a stud of them. Fiendish faces, with the extinguished taper, will come and look at me; but I know them for mockeries, even while I cannot elude their presence, and I fight and grapple with them. For the credit of my imagination, I am almost ashamed to say how tame and prosaic my dreams are grown. They are never romantic,—seldom even rural. They are of architecture and of buildings—cities abroad, which I have never seen, and hardly have hope to see. I have traversed, for the seeming length of a natural day, Rome, Amsterdam, Paris, Lisbon—their churches, palaces, squares, market-places, shops, suburbs, ruins, with an inexpressible sense of delight—a map-like distinctness of trace—and a day-light vividness of vision, that was all but being awake. I have travelled among the Westmoreland fells—my highest Alps,—but they were objects too mighty for the grasp of my dreaming recognition; and I have again and again awoke with ineffectual struggles of the "inner eye," to make out a shape in any way whatever, of Helvellyn. Methought I was in that country, but the mountains were gone. The poverty of my dreams mortifies me. There is C——, at his will can conjure up icy domes, and pleasure-houses for Kubla Khan, and Abyssinian maids, and songs of Abara, and caverns,

Where Alph, the sacred river, runs,

to solace his night solitudes—when I cannot muster a fiddle. Barry Cornwall has his tritons and his nereids gamboling before him in nocturnal visions, and proclaiming sons born to Neptune—when my stretch of imaginative activity can hardly, in the night season, raise up the ghost of a fish-wife. To set my failures in somewhat a mortifying light—it was after reading the noble Dream of this poet, that my fancy ran strong upon these marine spectra; and the poor plastic power, such as it is, within me set to work, to humour my folly in a sort of dream that very night. Methought I was upon the ocean billows at some sea nuptials, riding and mounted high, with the customary train sounding their conchs before me, (I myself, you may be sure, the *leading god*,) and jollily we went careering over the main, till just where Ino Leucothea should have greeted me (I think it was Ino) with a white embrace, the billows gradually subsiding, fell from a sea-roughness to a sea-calm, and thence to a river-motion, and that river (as happens in the familiarization of dreams) was no other than the gentle Thames, which landed me, in the wafture of a placid wave or two, safe and inglorious somewhere at the foot of Lambeth palace.

The degree of the soul's creativeness in sleep might furnish no whimsical criterion of the quantum of poetical faculty resident in the same soul waking. An old gentleman, a friend of mine, and a humourist, used to carry this notion so far, that when he saw any stripling of his acquaintance ambitious of becoming a poet, his first question would be,—"Young man, what sort of dreams have you?" I have so much faith in my old friend's theory, that when I feel that idle vein returning upon me, I presently subside into my proper element of prose, remembering those eluding nereids, and that inauspicious inland landing.

ELIA.

THE

London Magazine.

Nº XXIII. NOVEMBER, 1821. Vol. IV.

GRACE BEFORE MEAT.

The custom of saying grace at meals had, probably, its origin in the early times of the world, and the hunter-state of man, when dinners were precarious things, and a full meal was something more than a common blessing; when a belly-full was a windfall, and looked like a special providence. In the shouts and triumphal songs, with which, after a season of sharp abstinence, a lucky booty of deer's or goat's flesh would naturally be ushered home, existed, perhaps, the germ of the modern grace. It is not otherwise easy to be understood, why the blessing of food—the act of eating—should have had a particular expression of thanksgiving annexed to it, distinct from that implied and silent gratitude with which we are expected to enter upon the enjoyment of the many other various gifts and good things of existence.

I own that I am disposed to say grace upon twenty other occasions in the course of the day besides my dinner. I want a form for setting out upon a pleasant walk, for a moonlight ramble, for a friendly meeting, or a solved problem. Why have we none for books, those spiritual repasts—a grace before Milton—a grace before Shakspeare—a devotional exercise proper to be said before reading the Fairy Queen?—but, the received ritual having prescribed these forms to the solitary ceremony of manducation, I shall confine my observations to the experience which I have had of the grace, properly so called; commending my new scheme for extension to a niche in the grand philosophical, poetical, and perchance in part heretical, liturgy, now compiling by my friend Homo Humanus, for the use of a certain snug congregation of Utopian Rabelæsian Christians, no matter where assembled.

The form then of the benediction before eating has its beauty at a poor man's table, or at the simple and unprovocative repasts of children. It is here that the grace becomes exceedingly graceful. The indigent man, who hardly knows whether he shall have a meal the next day or not, sits down to his fare with a present sense of the blessing, which can be but feebly acted by the rich, into whose minds the conception of ever wanting a dinner could never, but by some extreme theory, have entered. The proper end of food—the animal sustenance—is barely contemplated by them. The poor man's bread is his daily bread, literally his bread for the day. Their courses are perennial.

Again, the plainest diet seems the fittest to be preceded by the grace. That which is least stimulative to appetite, leaves the mind most free for foreign considerations. A man may feel thankful, heartily thankful, over a dish of plain mutton with turnips, and have leisure to reflect upon the ordinance and institution of eating, when he shall confess a perturbation of mind, inconsistent with the purposes of the grace, at the presence of venison or turtle. When I have sate (a *rarus hospes*) at rich men's tables, with the savoury soup and messes steaming up the nostrils, and moistening the lips of the guests with desire and a distracted choice, I have felt the introduction of that ceremony to be unseasonable. With the ravenous orgasm upon you, it seems impertinent to interpose a religious sentiment. It is a confusion of purpose to mutter out praises from a mouth that waters. The heats of epicurism put out the gentle flame of devotion. The incense which rises round is pagan, and the belly-god intercepts it for his own. The very excess of the provision beyond the needs, takes away all sense of proportion between the end and means. The giver is veiled by his gifts. You are startled at the injustice of returning thanks—for what? —for having too much, while so many starve. It is to praiset he Gods amiss.

I have observed this awkwardness felt, scarce consciously perhaps, by the good man who says the grace. I have seen it in clergymen and others—a sort of shame—a sense of the co-presence of circumstances which unhallow the blessing. After a devotional tone put on for a few seconds, how rapidly the speaker will fall into his common voice, helping himself or his neighbour, as if to get rid of some uneasy sensation of hypocrisy. Not that the good man was a hypocrite, or was not most conscientious in the discharge of the duty; but he felt in his inmost mind the incompatibility of the scene and the viands before him with the exercise of a calm and rational gratitude.

I hear somebody exclaim,—Would you have Christians sit down at table, like hogs to their troughs, without remembering the Giver?—no—I would have them sit down as Christians, remembering the Giver, and less like hogs. Or if their appetites must run riot, and they must pamper themselves with delicates for which east and west are ransacked, I would have them postpone their benediction to a fitter season, when appetite is laid; when the still small voice can be heard, and the reason of the grace returns—with temperate diet and restricted dishes. Gluttony and surfeiting are no proper occasions for thanksgiving. When Jeshurun waxed fat, we read that he kicked. Virgil knew the harpy-nature better, when he put into the mouth of Celæno any thing but a blessing. We may be gratefully sensible of the deliciousness of some kinds of food beyond others, though that is a meaner and inferior gratitude: but the proper object of the grace is sustenance, not relishes; daily bread, not delicacies; the means of life, and not the means of pampering the carcase. With what frame or composure, I wonder, can a city chaplain pronounce his benediction at some great Hall feast, when he knows that his last concluding pious word—and that, in all probability, the sacred name which he preaches—is but the signal for so many impatient harpies to commence their foul orgies, with as little sense of true thankfulness (which is temperance) as those Virgilian fowl! It is well if the good man himself does not feel his devotions a little clouded, those foggy sensuous steams mingling with, and polluting the pure altar sacrifice.

The severest satire upon full tables and surfeits is the banquet which Satan, in the Paradise Regained, provides for a temptation in the wilderness:—

A table richly spread in regal mode,
With dishes piled, and meats of noblest sort
And savour; beasts of chase, or fowl of game,
In pastry built, or from the spit, or boiled,
Gris-amber-steamed; all fish from sea or shore,
Freshet or purling brook, for which was drained
Pontus, and Lucrine bay, and Afric coast.

The Tempter, I warrant you, thought these cates would go down without the recommendatory preface of a benediction. They are like to be short graces where the devil plays the host.—I am afraid, the poet wants his usual decorum in this place. Was he thinking of the old Roman luxury, or of a gaudy day at Cambridge? This was a temptation fitter for a Heliogabalus. The whole banquet is too civic and culinary, and the accompaniments altogether a profanation of that deep, abstracted, holy scene. The mighty artillery of sauces, which the cook-fiend conjures up, is out of proportion to the simple wants and plain hunger of the guest. He that disturbed him in his dreams, from his dreams might have been taught better. To the temperate fantasies of the famished Son of God, what sort of feasts presented themselves?—He dreamed indeed,

——— As appetite is wont to dream,
Of meats and drinks, nature's refreshment sweet.

But what meats?—

Him thought, he by the brook of Cherith stood,
And saw the ravens with their horny beaks
Food to Elijah bringing, even and morn;
Though ravenous, taught to abstain from what they brought:
He saw the prophet also how he fled
Into the desart, and how there he slept
Under a juniper; then how awaked
He found his supper on the coals prepared,
And by the angel was bid rise and eat,
And ate the second time after repose,
The strength whereof sufficed him forty days:
Sometimes, that with Elijah he partook,
Or as a guest with Daniel at his pulse.

Nothing in Milton is finelier fancied than these temperate dreams of the divine Hungerer. To which of these two visionary banquets, think you, would the introduction of what is called the grace have been most fitting and pertinent?

Theoretically I am no enemy to graces; but practically I own that (before meat especially) they seem to involve something awkward and unseasonable. Our appetites, of one or another kind, are excellent spurs to our reason, which might otherwise but feebly set about the great ends of preserving and continuing the species. They are fit blessings to be contemplated at a distance with a becoming gratitude; but the moment of appetite (the judicious reader will apprehend me) is, perhaps, the least fit season for that exercise. The Quakers who go about their business, of every description, with more calmness than we, have more title to the use of these benedictory prefaces. I have always admired their silent grace, and the more because I have observed their applications to the meat and drink following to be less passionate and sensual than ours. They are neither gluttons nor wine-bibbers as a people. They eat, as a horse bolts his chopt hay, with indifference, calmness, and cleanly circumstances. They neither grease nor slop themselves. When I see a citizen in his bib and tucker, I cannot imagine it a surplice.

I am no Quaker at my food. I confess I am not indifferent to the kinds of it. Those unctuous morsels of deer's flesh were not made to be received with dispassionate services. I hate a man who swallows it, affecting not to know what he is eating. I suspect his taste in higher matters. I shrink instinctively from one who professes to like minced veal. There is a physiognomical character in the tastes for food. C—— holds that a man cannot have a pure mind who refuses apple-dumplings. I am not certain but he is right. With the decay of my first innocence, I confess a less and less relish daily for those innocuous cates. The whole vegetable tribe have lost their gust with me. Only I stick to asparagus, which still seems to inspire gentle thoughts. I am impatient and querulous under culinary disappointments, as to come home at the dinner hour, for instance, expecting some savoury mess, and to find one quite tasteless and sapidless. Butter ill melted—that commonest of kitchen failures—puts me beside my tenour. The author of the Rambler used to make inarticulate animal noises over a favourite food. Was this the music quite proper to be preceded by the grace? or would the pious man have done better to postpone his devotions to a season when the blessing might be contemplated with less perturbation? I quarrel with no man's tastes, nor would set my thin face against those excellent things in their way, jollity and feasting. But as these exercises, however laudable, have little in them of grace or gracefulness, a man should be sure, before he ventures so to grace them, that while he is pretending his devotions otherwhere, he is not secretly kissing his hand to some great fish—his Dagon—with a special consecration of no ark but the fat tureen before him. Graces are the sweet preluding strains to the banquets of angels and children; to the roots and severer repasts of the Chartreuse; to the slender, but not slenderly acknowledged, refection of the poor and humble man: but at the heaped-up boards of the pampered and the luxurious they become of dissonant mood, less timed and tuned to the occasion, methinks, than the noise of those better befitting organs would be, which children hear tales of, at Hog's Norton. We sit too long at our meals, or are too curious in the study of them, or too disordered in our application to them, or engross too great a portion of those good things (which should be common) to our share, to be able with any grace to say grace. To be thankful for what we grasp exceeding our proportion is to add hypocrisy to injustice. A lurking sense of this truth is what makes the performance of this duty so cold and spiritless a service at most tables. In houses where the grace is as indispensable as the napkin, who has not seen that never settled question arise, as to *who shall say it;* while the good man of the house and the visitor clergyman, or some other guest belike of next authority from years or gravity, shall be bandying about the office between them as a matter of compliment, each of them not unwilling to shift the awkward burthen of an equivocal duty from his own shoulders? I once drank tea in company with two Methodist divines of different persuasions, whom it was my fortune to introduce to each other for the first time that evening. Before the first cup was handed round, one of these reverend gentlemen put it to the other, with all due solemnity, whether he chose to *say any thing.* It seems it is the custom with some sectaries to put up a short prayer before this meal also. His reverend brother did not at first quite apprehend him, but upon an explanation, with little less importance he made answer, that it was not a custom known in his church; in which courteous evasion the other acquiescing for good manner's sake, or in compliance with a weak brother, the supplementary or tea-grace was waived altogether. With what spirit might not Lucian have painted two priests, of *his* religion, playing into each other's hands the compliment of performing or omitting a sacrifice,—the hungry God meantime, doubtful of his incense, with expectant nostrils hovering over the two flamens, and (as between two stools) going away in the end without his supper.

A short form upon these occasions is felt to be unreverend; a long one, I am afraid, cannot escape the charge of impertinence. I do not quite approve of the epigrammatic conciseness with which that equivocal wag (but my pleasant school-fellow) C. V. L., when importuned for a grace, used to enquire, first slyly leering down the table, "Is there no clergyman here?"—significantly adding, "thank G—." Nor do I think our old form at school quite pertinent, when we were used to preface our bald bread and cheese suppers with a preamble, connecting with that humble blessing a recognition of benefits the most awful and overwhelming to the imagination which religion has to offer. *Non tunc illis erat locus.* I remember we were put to it to reconcile the phrase "good creatures," upon which the blessing rested, with the fare set before us, wilfully understanding that expression in a low and animal sense, till some one recalled a legend, which told how in the golden days of Christ's, the young Hospitallers were wont to have smoking joints of roast meat upon their nightly boards, till some pious benefactor, commiserating the decencies, rather than the palates, of the children, commuted our flesh for garments, and gave us—*horresco referens*—trowsers instead of mutton.

ELIA.

THE LION'S HEAD.

Some of our Correspondents having expressed a wish to put their heads in the Lion's Mouth this month, he hath courteously consented, and promises not to "*wag his Tail*," till they have done.

Elia to his Correspondents.—A Correspondent, who writes himself Peter Ball, *or* Bell,—for his hand-writing is as ragged as his manners—admonishes me of the old saying, that some people (under a courteous periphrasis I slur his less ceremonious epithet) had need have good memories. In my "Old Benchers of the Inner Temple," I have delivered myself, and truly, a Templar born. Bell clamours upon this, and thinketh that he hath caught a fox. It seems that in a former paper, retorting upon a weekly scribbler who had called my good identity in question, (see P. S. to my "Chapter on Ears,") I profess myself a native of some spot near Cavendish Square, deducing my remoter origin from Italy. But who does not see, except this tinkling cymbal, that in that idle fiction of Genoese ancestry I was answering a fool according to his folly—that Elia there expresseth himself ironically, as to an approved slanderer, who hath no right to the truth, and can be no fit recipient of it? Such a one it is usual to leave to his delusions; or, leading him from error still to contradictory error, to plunge him (as we say) deeper in the mire, and give him line till he suspend himself. No understanding reader could be imposed upon by such obvious rhodomontade to suspect me for an alien, or believe me other than English.—To a second Correspondent, who signs himself "a Wiltshire man," and claims me for a countryman upon the strength of an equivocal phrase in my "Christ's Hospital," a more mannerly reply is due. Passing over the Genoese fable, which Bell makes such a ring about, he nicely detects a more subtle discrepancy, which Bell was too obtuse to strike upon. Referring to the passage (in page 484 of our second volume), I must confess, that the term "native town," applied to Calne, *primâ facie* seems to bear out the construction which my friendly Correspondent is willing to put upon it. The context too, I am afraid, a little favours it. But where the words of an author, taken literally, compared with some other passage in his writings, admitted to be authentic, involve a palpable contradiction, it hath been the custom of the ingenuous commentator to smooth the difficulty by the supposition, that in the one case an allegorical or tropical sense was chiefly intended. So by the word "native," I may be supposed to mean a town where I might have been born; or where it might be desirable that I should have been born, as being situate in wholesome air, upon a dry chalky soil, in which I delight; or a town, with the inhabitants of which I passed some weeks, a summer or two ago, so agreeably, that they and it became in a manner native to me. Without some such latitude of interpretation in the present case, I see not how we can avoid falling into a gross error in physics, as to conceive that a gentleman may be born in two places, from which all modern and ancient testimony is alike abhorrent. Bacchus cometh the nearest to it, whom I remember Ovid to have honoured with the epithet "Twice born."* But not to mention that he is so called (we conceive) in reference to the places *whence* rather than the places *where* he was delivered,—for by either birth he may probably be challenged for a Theban—in a strict way of speaking, he was a *filius femoris* by no means in the same sense as he had been before a *filius alvi*, for that latter was but a secondary and tralatitious way of being born, and he but a denizen of the second house of his geniture. Thus much by way of explanation was thought due to the courteous "Wiltshire man."—To "Indagator," "Investigator," "Incertus," and the rest of the pack, that are so importunate about the true localities of his birth—as if, forsooth, Elia were presently about to be passed to his parish—to all such churchwarden critics he answereth, that, any explanation here given notwithstanding, he hath not so fixed his nativity (like a rusty vane) to one dull spot, but that, if he seeth occasion, or the argument shall demand it, he will be born again, in future papers, in whatever place, and at whatever period, shall seem good unto him.

Modò me Thebis—modò Athenis. ELIA.

* Imperfectus adhuc infans genetricis ab alvo
Eripitur, patrioque tener (si credere dignum)
Insuitur femori.———
Tutaque bis geniti sunt incunabula Bacchi. *Metamorph.* lib. 3.

MY FIRST PLAY.

At the north end of Russell-court there yet stands a portal, of some architectural pretensions, though reduced to humble use, serving at present for an entrance to a wine vault. This old door-way, if you are young, reader, you may not know was the identical pit entrance to Old Drury—Garrick's Drury—all of it that is left. I never pass it without shaking some forty years from off my shoulders, recurring to the evening when I passed through it to see my *first play*. The afternoon had been wet, and the condition of our going (the elder folks and myself) was, that the rain should cease. With what a beating heart did I watch from the window the puddles, from the stillness of which I was taught to prognosticate the desired cessation! I seem to remember the last spurt, and the glee with which I ran to announce it.

We went with orders, which my godfather F. had sent us. He kept the oil shop (now Davies's) at the corner of Featherstone-buildings, in Holborn. F. was a tall grave person, lofty in speech, and had pretensions above his rank. He associated in those days with John Palmer, the comedian, whose gait and bearing he seemed to copy; if John (which is quite as likely) did not rather borrow somewhat of his manner from my godfather. He was also known to, and visited by, Sheridan. It was to his house in Holborn that young Brinsley brought his first wife on her elopement with him from a boarding-school at Bath—the beautiful Maria Linley. My parents were present (over a quadrille table) when he arrived in the evening with his harmonious charge.—From either of these connexions it may be inferred that my godfather could command an order for the then Drury-lane theatre at pleasure—and, indeed, a pretty liberal issue of those cheap billets, in Brinsley's easy autograph, I have heard him say was the sole remuneration which he had received for many years' nightly illumination of the orchestra and various avenues of that theatre—and he was content it should be so. The honour of Sheridan's familiarity—or supposed familiarity—was better to my godfather than money.

F. was the most gentlemanly of oilmen; grandiloquent, yet courteous. His delivery of the commonest matters of fact was Ciceronian. He had two Latin words almost constantly in his mouth (how odd sounds Latin from an oilman's lips!), which my better knowledge since has enabled me to correct. In strict pronunciation they should have been sounded *vice versâ*—but in those young years they impressed me with more awe than they would now do read aright from Seneca or Varro—in his own peculiar pronunciation, monosyllabically elaborated, or Anglicized, into something like *verse verse*. By an imposing manner, and the help of these distorted syllables, he climbed (but that was little) to the highest parochial honours which St. Andrew's has to bestow.

He is dead—and thus much I thought due to his memory, both for my first orders (little wondrous talismans!—slight keys, and insignificant to outward sight, but opening to me more than Arabian paradises!) and moreover, that by his testamentary beneficence I came into possession of the only landed property which I could ever call my own—situate near the road-way village of pleasant Puckeridge, in Hertfordshire. When I journeyed down to take possession, and planted foot on my own ground, the stately habits of the donor descended upon me, and I strode (shall I confess the vanity?) with larger paces over my allotment of three quarters of an acre, with its commodious mansion in the midst, with the feeling of an English freeholder that all betwixt sky and centre was my own. The estate has passed into more prudent hands, and nothing but an Agrarian can restore it.

In those days were pit orders. Beshrew the uncomfortable manager who abolished them!—with one of these we went. I remember the waiting at the door—not that which is left—but between that and an inner door in shelter—O when shall I be such an expectant again!—with the cry of nonpareils, an indispensible play-house accompaniment in those days. As near as I can recollect, the fashionable pronunciation of the theatrical fruiteresses then was, "Chase some oranges, chase some numparels, chase a bill of the play;"—chase *pro* chuse. But when we got in, and I beheld the green curtain that veiled a heaven to my imagination, which was soon to be disclosed——the breathless anticipations I endured! I had seen something like it in the plate prefixed to Troilus and Cressida, in Rowe's Shakspeare—the tent scene with Diomede—and a sight of that plate can always bring back in a measure the feeling of that evening.—The boxes at that time, full of well-dressed women of quality, projected over the pit; and the pilasters reaching down were adorned with a glistering substance (I know not what) under glass (as it seemed), resembling—a homely fancy—but I judged it to be sugar-candy—yet, to my raised imagination, divested of its homelier qualities, it appeared a glorified candy!—The orchestra lights at length arose, those "fair Auroras!" Once the bell sounded. It was to ring out yet once again—and, incapable of the anticipation, I reposed my shut eyes in a sort of resignation upon the maternal lap. It rang the second time. The curtain drew up—I was not past six years old—and the play was Artaxerxes!

I had dabbled a little in the Universal History—the ancient part of it—and here was the court of Persia. It was being admitted to a sight of the past. I took no proper interest in the action going on, for I understood not its import—but I heard the word Darius, and I was in the midst of Daniel. All feeling was absorbed in vision. Gorgeous vests, gardens, palaces, princesses, passed before me. I knew not players. I was in Persepolis for the time; and the burning idol of their devotions was as if the sun itself should have been brought down to minister at the sacrificial altar. I took those significations to be something more than elemental fires. Harlequin's Invasion followed; where, I remember, the transformation of the magistrates into reverend beldams seemed to me a piece of grave historic justice, and the taylor carrying his own head, to be as sober a verity as the legend of St. Denys.

The next play to which I was taken was the Lady of the Manor, of which, with the exception of some scenery, very faint traces are left in my memory. It was followed by a pantomime, called Lun's Ghost—a satiric touch, I apprehend, upon Rich, not long since dead—but to my apprehension (too sincere for satire), Lun was as remote a piece of antiquity as Lud—the father of a line of Harlequins—transmitting his dagger of lath (the wooden sceptre) through countless ages. I saw the primeval Motley come from his silent tomb in a ghastly vest of white patch-work, like the apparition of a dead rainbow. So Harlequins (thought I) look when they are dead.

My third play followed in quick succession. It was the Way of the World. I think I must have sat at it as grave as a judge; for, I remember, the hysteric affectations of good Lady Wishfort affected me like some solemn tragic passion. Robinson Crusoe followed; in which Crusoe, man Friday, and the parrot, were as good and authentic as in the story.—The clownery and pantaloonery of these pantomimes have clean passed out of my head. I believe, I no more laughed at them, than at the same age I should have been disposed to laugh at the grotesque Gothic heads (seeming to me then replete with devout meaning) that gape, and grin, in stone around the inside of the old Round Church (my church) of the Templars.

I saw these plays in the season 1781-2, when I was from six to seven years old. After the intervention of six or seven other years (for at school all play-going was inhibited) I again entered the doors of a theatre. That old Artaxerxes evening had never done ringing in my fancy. I expected the same feelings to come again with the same occasion. But we differ from ourselves less at sixty and sixteen, than the latter does from six. In that interval what had I not lost! At the first period I knew nothing, understood nothing, discriminated nothing. I felt all, loved all, wondered all—

Was nourished, I could not tell how—

I had left the temple a devotee, and was returned a rationalist. The same things were there materially; but the emblem, the reference, was gone!—The green curtain was no longer a veil, drawn between two worlds, the unfolding of which was to bring back past ages, to present "a royal ghost,"—but a certain quantity of green baize, which was to separate the audience for a given time from certain of their fellow-men who were to come forward and pretend those parts. The lights—the orchestra lights—came up a clumsy machinery. The first ring, and the second ring, was now but a trick of the prompter's bell—which had been, like the note of the cuckoo, a phantom of a voice, no hand seen or guessed at which ministered to its warning. The actors were men and women painted. I thought the fault was in them; but it was in myself, and the alteration which those many centuries—of six short twelvemonths—had wrought in me.—Perhaps it was fortunate for me that the play of the evening was but an indifferent comedy, as it gave me time to crop some unreasonable expectations, which might have interfered with the genuine emotions with which (with unmixed perception) I was soon after enabled to enter upon the first appearance to me of Mrs. Siddons in Isabella. Comparison and retrospection soon yielded to the present attraction of the scene; and the theatre became to me, upon a new stock, the most delightful of recreations.

ELIA.

DRAMATIC FRAGMENT.

Fie upon 't.
All men are false, I think. The date of love
Is out, expired, its stories all grown stale,
O'er-past, forgotten, like an antique tale
Of Hero and Leander. JOHN WOODVIL.

ALL are not false. I knew a youth who died
For grief, because his Love proved so,
And married with another.
I saw him on the wedding day,
For he was present in the church that day,
In festive bravery deck'd,
As one that came to grace the ceremony.
I mark'd him when the ring was given,
His countenance never changed;
And when the priest pronounced the marriage blessing,
He put a silent prayer up for the bride,
For so his moving lip interpreted.
He came invited to the marriage feast
With the bride's friends,
And was the merriest of them all that day:
But they, who knew him best, call'd it feign'd mirth;
And others said,
He wore a smile like death upon his face.
His presence dash'd all the beholders' mirth,
And he went away in tears.

What followed then?

Oh! then
He did not, as neglected suitors use,
Affect a life of solitude in shades,
But lived,
In free discourse and sweet society,
Among his friends who knew his gentle nature best.
Yet ever when he smiled,
There was a mystery legible in his face,
That whoso saw him said he was a man
Not long for this world.——
And true it was, for even then
The silent love was feeding at his heart
Of which he died:
Nor ever spake word of reproach,
Only he wish'd in death that his remains
Might find a poor grave in some spot, not far
From his mistress' family vault, "being the place
Where one day Anna should herself be laid." * * *

DREAM-CHILDREN; A REVERIE.

CHILDREN love to listen to stories about their elders, when *they* were children; to stretch their imagination to the conception of a traditionary great-uncle, or grandame, whom they never saw. It was in this spirit that my little ones crept about me the other evening to hear about their great-grandmother Field, who lived in a great house in Norfolk (a hundred times bigger than that in which they and Papa lived) which had been the scene—so at least it was generally believed in that part of the country—of the tragic incidents which they had lately become familiar with from the ballad of the Children in the Wood. Certain it is that the whole story of the children and their cruel uncle was to be seen fairly carved out in wood upon the chimney-piece of the great hall, the whole story down to the Robin Redbreasts, till a foolish rich person pulled it down to set up a marble one of modern invention in its stead, with no story upon it. Here Alice put out one of her dear mother's looks, too tender to be called upbraiding. Then I went on to say, how religious and how good their great-grandmother Field was, how beloved and respected by every body, though she was not indeed the mistress of this great house, but had only the charge of it (and yet in some respects she might be said to be the mistress of it too) committed to her by the owner, who preferred living in a newer and more fashionable mansion which he had purchased somewhere in the adjoining county; but still she lived in it in a manner as if it had been her own, and kept up the dignity of the great house in a sort while she lived, which afterwards came to decay, and was nearly pulled down, and all its old ornaments stripped and carried away to the owner's other house, where they were set up, and looked as awkward as if some one were to carry away the old tombs they had seen lately at the Abbey, and stick them up in Lady C.'s tawdry gilt drawing-room. Here John smiled, as much as to say "that would be foolish indeed." And then I told how, when she came to die, her funeral was attended by a concourse of all the poor, and some of the gentry too, of the neighbourhood for many miles round, to show their respect for her memory, because she had been such a good and religious woman; so good indeed that she knew all the Psaltery by heart, aye, and a great part of the Testament besides. Here little Alice spread her hands. Then I told what a tall, upright, graceful person their great-grandmother Field once was; and how in her youth she was esteemed the best dancer—here Alice's little right foot played an involuntary movement, till, upon my looking grave, it desisted—the best dancer, I was saying, in the county, till a cruel disease, called a cancer, came, and bowed her down with pain; but it could never bend her good spirits, or make them stoop, but they were still upright, because she was so good and religious. Then I told how she was used to sleep by herself in a lone chamber of the great lone house; and how she believed that an apparition of two infants was to be seen at midnight gliding up and down the great staircase near where she slept, but she said "those innocents would do her no harm;" and how frightened I used to be, though in those days I had my maid to sleep with me, because I was never half so good or religious as she—and yet I never saw the infants. Here John expanded all his eyebrows, and tried to look courageous. Then I told how good she was to all her grand-children, having us to the great house in the holydays, where I in particular used to spend many hours by myself, in gazing upon the old busts of the Twelve Cæsars, that had been Emperors of Rome, till the old marble heads would seem to live again, or I to be turned into marble with them; how I never could be tired with roaming about that huge mansion, with its vast empty rooms, with their worn-out hangings, fluttering tapestry, and carved oaken pannels, with the gilding almost rubbed out—sometimes in the spacious old-fashioned gardens, which I had almost to myself, unless when now and then a solitary gardening man would cross me—and how the nectarines and peaches hung upon the walls, without my ever offering to pluck them, because they were forbidden fruit, unless now and then,—and because I had more pleasure in strolling about among the old melancholy-looking yew trees, or the firs, and picking up the red berries, and the fir apples, which were good for nothing but to look at—or in lying about upon the fresh grass, with all the fine garden smells around me—or basking in the orangery, till I could almost fancy myself ripening too along with the oranges and the limes in that grateful warmth—or in watching the dace that darted to and fro in the fish pond, at the bottom of the garden, with here and there a great sulky pike hanging midway down the water in silent state, as if it mocked at their impertinent friskings,—I had more pleasure in these busy-idle diversions, than in all the sweet flavours of peaches, nectarines, oranges, and such like common baits of children. Here John slyly deposited back upon the plate a bunch of grapes, which, not unobserved by Alice, he had meditated dividing with her, and both seemed willing to relinquish them for the present as irrelevant. Then in somewhat a more heightened tone, I told how, though their great-grandmother Field loved all her grand-children, yet in an especial manner she might be said to love their uncle, John L——, because he was so handsome and spirited a youth, and a king to the rest of us; and, instead of moping about in solitary corners, like some of us, he would mount the most mettlesome horse he could get, when but an imp no bigger than themselves, and make it carry him half over the county in a morning, and join the hunters when there were any out—and yet he loved the old great house and gardens too, but had too much spirit to be always pent up within their boundaries—and how their uncle grew up to man's estate as brave as he was handsome, to the admiration of every body, but of their great-grandmother Field most especially; and how he used to carry me upon his back when I was a lame-footed boy—for he was a good bit older than me—many a mile when I could not walk for pain;—and how in after life he became lame-footed too, and I did not always (I fear) make allowances enough for him when he was impatient, and in pain, nor remember sufficiently how considerate he had been to me when I was lame-footed; and how when he died, though he had not been dead an hour, it seemed as if he had died a great while ago, such a distance there is betwixt life and death; and how I bore his death as I thought pretty well at first, but afterwards it haunted and haunted me; and though I did not cry or take it to heart as some do, and as I think he would have done if I had died, yet I missed him all day long, and knew not till then how much I had loved him. I missed his kindness, and I missed his crossness, and wished him to be alive again, to be quarreling with him (for we quarreled sometimes), rather than not have him again, and was as uneasy without him, as he their poor uncle must have been when the doctor took off his limb. Here the children fell a crying, and asked if their little mourning which they had on was not for uncle John, and they looked up, and prayed me not to go on about their uncle, but to tell them some stories about their pretty dead mother. Then I told how for seven long years, in hope sometimes, sometimes in despair, yet persisting ever, I courted the fair Alice W—n; and, as much as children could understand, I explained to them what coyness, and difficulty, and denial meant in maidens—when suddenly, turning to Alice, the soul of the first Alice looked out at her eyes with such a reality of re-presentment, that I became in doubt which of them stood there before me, or whose that bright hair was,—and while I stood gazing, both the children gradually grew fainter to my view, receding, and still receding, till nothing at last but two mournful features were seen in the uttermost distance, which, without speech, strangely impressed upon me the effects of speech; "We are not of Alice, nor of thee, nor are we children at all. The children of Alice call Bartrum father. We are nothing; less than nothing, and dreams. We are only what might have been, and must wait upon the tedious shores of Lethe millions of ages before we have existence, and a name"——and immediately awaking, I found myself quietly seated in my bachelor armchair, where I had fallen asleep, with the faithful Bridget unchanged by my side—but John L. (or James Elia) was gone for ever. ELIA.

ON SOME OF THE OLD ACTORS.

Of all the actors who flourished in my time—a melancholy phrase if taken aright, reader—Bensley had most of the swell of soul, was greatest in the delivery of heroic conceptions, the emotions consequent upon the presentment of a great idea to the fancy. He had the true poetical enthusiasm—the rarest faculty among players. None that I remember possessed even a portion of that fine madness which he threw out in Hotspur's famous rant about glory, or the transports of the Venetian incendiary at the vision of the fired city.* His voice had the dissonance, and at times the inspiriting effect of the trumpet. His gait was uncouth and stiff, but no way embarrassed by affectation; and the thorough-bred gentleman was uppermost in every movement. He seized the moment of passion with the greatest truth; like a faithful clock never striking before the time; never anticipating or leading you to anticipate. He was totally destitute of trick and artifice. He seemed come upon the stage to do the poet's message simply, and he did it with as genuine fidelity as the nuncios in Homer deliver the errands of the gods. He let the passion or the sentiment do its own work without prop or bolstering. He would have scorned to mountebank it; and betrayed none of that *cleverness* which is the bane of serious acting. For this reason, his Iago was the only endurable one which I remember to have seen. No spectator from his action could divine more of his artifice than Othello was supposed to

* How lovelily the Adriatic whore
Dress'd in her flames will shine—devouring flames—
Such as will burn her to her wat'ry bottom,
And hiss in her foundation. *Pierre, in Venice Preserved.*

do. His confessions in soliloquy alone put you in possession of the mystery. There were no bye-intimations to make the audience fancy their own discernment so much greater than that of the Moor—who commonly stands like a great helpless mark set up for mine Ancient, and a quantity of barren spectators, to shoot their bolts at. The Iago of Bensley did not go to work so grossly. There was a triumphant tone about the character, natural to a general consciousness of power; but none of that petty vanity which chuckles and cannot contain itself upon any little successful stroke of its knavery—which is common with your small villains, and green probationers in mischief. It did not clap or crow before its time. It was not a man setting his wits at a child, and winking all the while at other children who are mightily pleased at being let into the secret; but a consummate villain entrapping a noble nature into toils, against which no discernment was available, where the manner was as fathomless as the purpose seemed dark, and without motive. The part of Malvolio, in the Twelfth Night, was performed by Bensley, with a richness and a dignity of which (to judge from some recent castings of that character) the very tradition must be worn out from the stage. No manager in those days would have dreamed of giving it to Mr. Baddeley, or Mr. Parsons: when Bensley was occasionally absent from the theatre, John Kemble thought it no derogation to succeed to the part. Malvolio is not essentially ludicrous. He becomes comic but by accident. He is cold, austere, repelling; but dignified, consistent, and, for what appears, rather of an over-stretched morality. Maria describes him as a sort of Puritan; and he might have worn his gold chain with honour in one of our old round-head families, in the service of a Lambert, or a Lady Fairfax. But his morality and his manners are misplaced in Illyria. He is opposed to the proper *levities* of the piece, and falls in the unequal contest. Still his pride, or his gravity, (call it which you will) is inherent, and native to the man, not mock or affected, which latter only are the fit objects to excite laughter. His quality is at the best unlovely, but neither buffoon nor contemptible. His bearing is lofty, a little above his station, but probably not much above his deserts. We see no reason why he should not have been brave, honourable, accomplished. His careless committal of the ring to the ground (which he was commissioned to restore to Cesario), bespeaks a generosity of birth and feeling.* His dialect on all occasions is that of a gentleman, and a man of education. We must not confound him with the eternal low steward of comedy. He is master of the household to a great Princess, a dignity probably conferred upon him for other respects than age or length of service.† Olivia, at the first indication of his supposed madness, declares that she "would not have him miscarry for half of her dowry." Does this look as if the character was meant to appear little or insignificant? Once, indeed, she accuses him to his face—of what?—of being "sick of self-love,"—but with a gentleness and considerateness which could not have been, if she had not thought that this particular infirmity shaded some virtues. His rebuke to the knight, and his sottish revellers, is sensible and spirited; and when we take into consideration the unprotected condition of his mistress, and the strict regard with

---

* *Viola.* She took the ring from me; I'll none of it.

Mal. Come, Sir, you peevishly threw it to her; and her will is, it should be so returned. If it be worth stooping for, there it lies in your eye; if not, be it his that finds it.

† Mrs. Inchbald seems to have fallen into the common mistake of the character in some sensible observations, otherwise, upon this Comedy. "It might be asked," she says, "whether this credulous steward was much deceived in imputing a degraded taste, in the sentiments of love, to his fair lady Olivia, as she actually did fall in love with a domestic; and one, who from his extreme youth, was perhaps a greater reproach to her discretion, than had she cast a tender regard upon her old and faithful servant." But where does she gather the fact of his age? Neither Maria nor Fabian ever cast that reproach upon him.

to clear my cloudy face for two or three hours at least of its furrows? Was this the face—manly, sober, intelligent,—which I had so often despised, made mocks at, made merry with? The remembrance of the freedoms which I had taken with it came upon me with a reproach of insult. I could have asked it pardon. I thought it looked upon me with a sense of injury. There is something strange as well as sad in seeing actors—your pleasant fellows particularly—subjected to and suffering the common lot—their fortunes, their casualties, their deaths, seem to belong to the scene, their actions to be amenable to poetic justice only. We can hardly connect them with more awful responsibilities. The death of this fine actor took place shortly after this meeting. He had quitted the stage some months; and, as I learned afterwards, had been in the habit of resorting daily to these gardens almost to the day of his decease. In these serious walks probably he was divesting himself of many scenic and some real vanities—weaning himself from the frivolities of the lesser and the greater theatre—doing gentle penance for a life of no very reprehensible fooleries,—taking off by degrees the buffoon mask which he might feel he had worn too long—and rehearsing for a more solemn cast of part. Dying he "put on the weeds of Dominic."*

The elder Palmer (of stage-treading celebrity) commonly played Sir Toby in those days; but there is a solidity of wit in the jests of that half-Falstaff which he did not quite fill out. He was as much too showy as Moody (who sometimes took the part) was dry and sottish. In sock or buskin there was an air of swaggering gentility about Jack Palmer. He was a *gentleman* with a slight infusion of *the footman*. His brother Bob (of recenter memory) who was his shadow in every thing while he lived, and dwindled into less than a shadow afterwards—was a *gentleman* with a little stronger infusion of the *latter ingredient*; that was all. It is amazing how a little of the more or less makes a difference in these things. When you saw Bobby in the Duke's Servant,† you said, what a pity such a pretty fellow was only a servant. When you saw Jack figuring in Captain Absolute, you thought you could trace his promotion to some lady of quality who fancied the handsome fellow in his topknot, and had bought him a commission. Therefore Jack in Dick Amlet was insuperable.

Jack had two voices,—both plausible, hypocritical, and insinuating; but his secondary or supplemental voice still more decisively histrionic than his common one. It was reserved for the spectator; and the dramatis personæ were supposed to know nothing at all about it. The *lies* of young Wilding, and the *sentiments* in Joseph Surface, were thus marked out in a sort of italics to the audience. This secret correspondence with the company before the curtain (which is the bane and death of tragedy) has an extremely happy effect in some kinds of comedy, in the more highly artificial comedy of Congreve or of Sheridan especially, where the absolute sense of reality (so indispensable to scenes of interest) is not required, or would rather interfere to diminish your pleasure. The fact is, you do not believe in such characters as Surface—the villain of artificial comedy—even while you read or see them. If you did, they would shock and not divert you. When Ben, in Love for Love, returns from sea, the following exquisite dialogue occurs at his first meeting with his father—

Sir Sampson. Thou hast been many a weary league, Ben, since I saw thee.

Ben. Ey, ey, been! Been far enough,

* Dodd was a man of reading, and left at his death a choice collection of old English literature. I should judge him to have been a man of wit. I know one instance of an impromptu which no length of study could have bettered. My merry friend, Jem White, had seen him one evening in Aguecheek, and recognising Dodd the next day in Fleet Street, was irresistibly impelled to take off his hat and salute him as the identical Knight of the preceding evening with a "Save you, *Sir Andrew*." Dodd, not at all disconcerted at this unusual address from a stranger, with a courteous half-rebuking wave of the hand, put him off with an "Away, *Fool*."

† High Life Below Stairs.

an that be all—Well, father, and how do all at home? how does brother Dick, and brother Val?

Sir Sampson. Dick! body o' me, Dick has been dead these two years. I writ you word when you were at Leghorn.

Ben. Mess, that's true; Marry, I had forgot. Dick's dead, as you say—Well, and how?—I have a many questions to ask you—

Here is an instance of insensibility which in real life would be revolting, or rather in real life could not have co-existed with the warm-hearted temperament of the character. But when you read it in the spirit with which such playful selections and specious combinations rather than strict *metaphrases* of nature should be taken, or when you saw Bannister play it, it neither did, nor does wound the moral sense at all. For what is Ben—the pleasant sailor which Bannister gave us—but a piece of a satire—a creation of Congreve's fancy—a dreamy combination of all the accidents of a sailor's character—his contempt of money—his credulity to women—with that necessary estrangement from home which it is just within the verge of credibility to suppose *might* produce such an hallucination as is here described. We never think the worse of Ben for it, or feel it as a stain upon his character. But when an actor comes, and instead of the delightful phantom—the creature dear to half-belief—which Bannister exhibited—displays before our eyes a downright concretion of a Wapping sailor—a jolly warm-hearted Jack Tar—and nothing else—when instead of investing it with a delicious confusedness of the head, and a veering undirected goodness of purpose—he gives to it a downright daylight understanding, and a full consciousness of its actions; thrusting forward the sensibilities of the character with a pretence as if it stood upon nothing else, and was to be judged by them alone—we feel the discord of the thing; the scene is disturbed; a real man has got in among the dramatis personæ, and puts them out. We want the sailor turned out. We feel that his true place is not behind the curtain, but in the first or second gallery.

(*To be resumed occasionally.*)

ELIA.

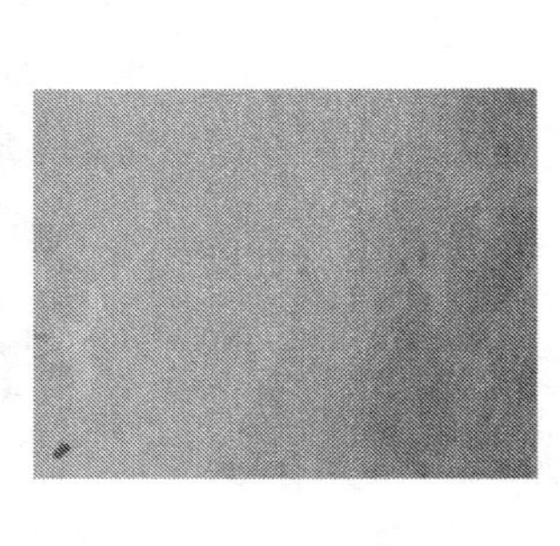

DISTANT CORRESPONDENTS.

In a Letter to B. F. Esq. at Sydney, New South Wales.

My dear F.—When I think how welcome the sight of a letter from the world where you were born must be to you in that strange one to which you have been transplanted, I feel some compunctious visitings at my long silence. But, indeed, it is no easy effort to set about a correspondence at our distance. The weary world of waters between us oppresses the imagination. It is difficult to conceive how a scrawl of mine should ever stretch across it. It is a sort of presumption to expect that one's thoughts should live so far. It is like writing for posterity; and reminds me of one of Mrs. Rowe's superscriptions, "Alcander to Strephon, in the shades." Cowley's Post-Angel is no more than would be expedient in such an intercourse. One drops a pacquet at Lombard-street, and in twenty-four hours a friend in Cumberland gets it as fresh as if it came in ice. It is only like whispering through a long trumpet. But suppose a tube let down from the moon, with yourself at one end, and *the man* at the other; it would be some baulk to the spirit of conversation, if you knew that the dialogue exchanged with that interesting theosophist would take two or three revolutions of a higher luminary in its passage. Yet for aught I know, you may be some parasangs nigher that primitive idea—Plato's man—than we in England here have the honour to reckon ourselves.

Epistolary matter usually compriseth three topics; news, sentiment, and puns. In the latter, I include all non-serious subjects; or subjects serious in themselves, but treated after my fashion, non-seriously.—And first, for news. In them the most desirable circumstance, I suppose, is that they shall be true. But what security can I have that what I now send you for truth shall not before you get it unaccountably turn into a lie? For instance, our mutual friend P. is at this present writing—*my Now*—in good health, and enjoys a fair share of worldly reputation. You are glad to hear it. This is natural and friendly. But at this present reading—*your Now*—he may possibly be in the Bench, or going to be hanged, which in reason ought to abate something of your transport (*i. e.* at hearing he was well, &c.), or at least considerably to modify it. I am going to the play this evening, to have a laugh with Joey Munden. You have no theatre, I think you told me, in your land of d——d realities. You naturally lick your lips, and envy me my felicity. Think but a moment, and you will correct the hateful emotion. Why, it is Sunday morning with you, and 1823. This confusion of tenses, this grand solecism of *two presents*, is in a degree common to all postage. But if I sent you word to Bath or the Devises, that I was expecting the aforesaid treat this evening, though at the moment you received the intelligence my full feast of fun would be over, yet there would be for a day or two after, as you would well know, a smack, a relish left upon my mental palate, which would give rational encouragement to you to foster a portion at least of the disagreeable passion, which it was in part my intention to produce. But ten months hence your envy or your sympathy would be as useless as a passion spent upon the dead. Not only does truth, in these long intervals, un-essence herself, but (what is harder) one cannot venture a crude fiction for the fear that it may ripen into a truth upon the voyage. What a wild improbable banter I put upon you some three years since—of Will Weatherall having married a servant-maid! I remember gravely consulting you how we were to receive her—for Will's wife was in no case to be rejected; and your no less serious replication in the matter; how tenderly you advised an abstemious introduction of literary topics before the lady, with a caution not to be too forward in bringing on the carpet matters more within the sphere of her intelligence; your deliberate judgment, or rather wise suspension of sentence, how far jacks, and spits, and mops, could with propriety be introduced as subjects; whether the conscious avoiding of all such matters in discourse would not have a worse look than the taking of them casually in our way; in what manner we should carry ourselves to our maid Becky, Mrs. William Weatherall being by; whether we should show more delicacy, and a truer sense of respect for Will's wife, by treating Becky with our customary chiding before her, or by an unusual deferential civility paid to Becky as to a person of great worth, but thrown by the caprice of fate into a humble station. There were difficulties, I remember, on both sides, which you did me the favour to state with the precision of a lawyer, united to the tenderness of a friend. I laughed in my sleeve at your solemn pleadings, when lo! while I was valuing myself upon this flam put upon you in New South Wales, the devil in England, jealous possibly of any lie-children not his own, or working after my copy, has actually instigated our friend (not three days since) to the commission of a matrimony, which I had only conjured up for your diversion. William Weatherall has married Mrs. Cotterel's maid. But to take it in its truest sense, you will see, my dear F., that news from me must become history to you; which I neither profess to write, nor indeed care much for reading. No person, under a diviner, can with any prospect of veracity conduct a correspondence at such an arm's length. Two prophets, indeed, might thus interchange intelligence with effect; the epoch of the writer (Habbakuk) falling in with the true present time of the receiver (Daniel); but then we are no prophets.

Then as to sentiment. It fares little better with that. This kind of dish, above all, requires to be served up hot; or sent off in water-plates, that your friend may have it almost as warm as yourself. If it have time to cool, it is the most tasteless of all cold meats. I have often smiled at a conceit of the late Lord C. It seems that travelling somewhere about Geneva, he came to some pretty green spot, or nook, where a willow, or something, hung so fantastically and invitingly over a stream—was it?—or a rock?—no matter—but the stillness and the repose, after a weary journey 'tis likely, in a languid moment of his Lordship's hot restless life, so took his fancy, that he could imagine no place so proper, in the event of his death, to lay his bones in. This was all very natural and excusable as a sentiment, and shows his character in a very pleasing light. But when from a passing sentiment it came to be an act; and when, by a positive testamentary disposal, his remains were actually carried all that way from England; who was there, some desperate sentimentalists excepted, that did not ask the question, Why could not his Lordship have found a spot as solitary, a nook as romantic, a tree as green and pendent, with a stream as emblematic to his purpose, in Surry, in Dorset, or in Devon? Conceive the sentiment hoarded up, freighted, entered at the Custom House (startling the tide-waiters with the novelty), hoisted into a ship. Conceive it pawed about and handled between the rude jests of tarpaulin ruffians—a thing of its delicate texture—the salt bilge wetting it till it became as vapid as a damaged lustring. Suppose it in material danger (mariners have some superstition about sentiments) of being tossed over in a fresh gale to some propitiatory shark (spirit of Saint Gothard, save us from a quietus so foreign to the deviser's purpose!) but it has happily evaded a fishy consummation. Trace it then to its lucky landing—at Lyons shall we say?—I have not the map before me—jostled upon four men's shoulders—baiting at this town—stopping to refresh at t'other village—waiting a passport here, a licence there; the sanction of the magistracy in this district, the concurrence of the ecclesiastics in that canton; till at length it arrives at its destination, tired out and jaded, from a brisk sentiment, into a feature of silly pride or tawdry senseless affectation. How few sentiments, my dear F., I am afraid we can set down, in the sailor's phrase, as quite sea-worthy.

Lastly, as to the agreeable levities, which, though contemptible in bulk, are the twinkling corpuscula which should irradiate a right friendly epistle—your puns and small jests are, I apprehend, extremely circumscribed in their sphere of action. They are so far from a capacity of being packed up and sent beyond sea, they will scarce endure to be transported by hand from this room to the next. Their vigour is as the instant of their birth. Their nutriment for their brief existence is the intellectual atmosphere of the by-standers: or this last is the fine slime of Nilus—the *melior lutus*,—whose maternal recipiency is as necessary as the *sol pater* to their equivocal generation. A pun hath a hearty kind of present ear-kissing smack with it; you can no more transmit it in its pristine flavour, than you can send a kiss.—Have you not tried in some instances to palm off a yesterday's pun upon a gentleman, and has it answered? Not but it was new to his hearing, but it did not seem to come new from you. It did not hitch in. It was like picking up at a village ale-house a two days old newspaper. You have not seen it before, but you resent the stale thing as an affront. This sort of merchandise above all requires a quick return. A pun, and its recognitory laugh, must be co-instantaneous. The one is the brisk lightning, the other the fierce thunder. A moment's interval, and the link is snapped. A pun is reflected from a friend's face as from a mirror. Who would consult his sweet visnomy, if the polished surface were two or three minutes (not to speak of twelve-months, my dear F.) in giving back its copy?

I cannot image to myself whereabout you are. When I try to fix it, Peter Wilkins's island comes across me. Sometimes you seem to be in the *Hades of Thieves*. I see Diogenes prying among you with his perpetual fruitless lantern. What must you be willing by this time to give for the sight of an honest man! You must almost have forgotten how *we* look. And tell me, what your Sydneyites do? are they th**v*ng all day long? Merciful heaven, what property can stand against such a depredation! The kangaroos—your Aborigines—do they keep their primitive simplicity un-Europe-tainted, with those little short fore-puds, looking like a lesson framed by nature to the pickpocket! Marry, for diving into fobs they are rather lamely provided *a priori*; but if the hue and cry were once up, they would show as fair a pair of hind-shifters as the expertest loco-motor in the colony.—We hear the most improbable tales at this distance. Pray, is it true that the young Spartans among you are born with six fingers, which spoils their scanning?—It must look very odd; but use reconciles. For their scansion, it is less to be regretted, for if they take it into their heads to be poets, it is odds but they turn out, the greater part of them, vile plagiarists.—Is there much difference to see to between the son of a th**f, and the grandson? or where does the taint stop? Do you bleach in three or in four generations?—I have many questions to put, but ten Delphic voyages can be made in a shorter time than it will take to satisfy my scruples.—Do you grow your own hemp?—What is your staple trade, exclusive of the national profession, I mean? Your lock-smiths, I take it, are some of your great capitalists.

I am insensibly chatting to you as familiarly as when we used to exchange good-morrows out of our old contiguous windows, in pump-famed Hare-court in the Temple. Why did you ever leave that quiet corner?—Why did I?—with its complement of four poor elms, from whose smoke-dyed barks, the theme of jesting ruralists, I picked my first lady-birds! My heart is as dry as that spring sometimes proves in a thirsty August, when I revert to the space that is between us, a length of passage enough to render obsolete the phrases of our English letters before they can reach you. But while I talk, I think you hear me,—thoughts dallying with vain surmise—

> Aye me! while thee the seas and sounding shores
> Hold far away.

Come back, before I am grown into a very old man, so as you shall hardly know me. Come, before Bridget walks on crutches. Girls whom you left children have become sage matrons, while you are tarrying there. The blooming Miss W—r (you remember Sally W—r) called upon us yesterday, an aged crone. Folks, whom you knew, die off every year. Formerly, I thought that death was wearing out,—I stood ramparted about with so many healthy friends. The departure of J. W. two springs back corrected my delusion. Since then the old divorcer has been busy. If you do not make haste to return, there will be little left to greet you, of me, or mine.

Something of home matters I could add; but *that,* with certain remembrances, never to be omitted, I reserve for the grave postscript to this light epistle; which postscript, for weighty reasons, justificatory in any court of feeling, I think better omitted in this first edition.

ELIA.

London, March 1, 1822.

THE

London Magazine.

N° XXVIII. APRIL, 1822. Vol. V.

THE OLD ACTORS.*

The artificial Comedy, or Comedy of manners, is quite extinct on our stage. Congreve and Farquhar show their heads once in seven years only to be exploded and put down instantly. The times cannot bear them. Is it for a few wild speeches, an occasional licence of dialogue? I think not altogether. The business of their dramatic characters will not stand the moral test. We screw every thing up to that. Idle gallantry in a fiction, a dream, the passing pageant of an evening, startles us in the same way as the alarming indications of profligacy in a son or ward in real life should startle a parent or guardian. We have no such middle emotions as dramatic interests left. We see a stage libertine playing his loose pranks of two hours' duration, and of no after consequence, with the severe eyes which inspect real vices with their bearings upon two worlds. We are spectators to a plot or intrigue (not reducible in life to the point of strict morality) and take it all for truth. We substitute a real for a dramatic person, and judge him accordingly. We try him in our courts, from which there is no appeal to the *dramatis personæ*, his peers. We have been spoiled with—not sentimental comedy—but a tyrant far more pernicious to our pleasures which has succeeded to it,—the exclusive and all-devouring drama of common life; where the moral point is every thing; where, instead of the fictitious half-believed personages of the stage (the phantoms of old comedy) we recognise ourselves, our brothers, aunts, kinsfolk, allies, patrons, enemies,—the same as in life,—with an interest in what is going on so hearty and substantial, that we cannot afford our moral judgment, in its deepest and most vital results, to compromise or slumber for a moment. What is *there* transacting, by no modification is made to affect us in any other manner than the same events or characters would do in our relationships of life. We carry our fire-side concerns to the theatre with us. We do not go thither, like our ancestors, to escape from the pressure of reality, so much as to confirm our experience of it; to make assurance double, and take a bond of fate. We must live our toilsome lives twice over, as it was the mournful privilege of Ulysses to descend twice to the shades. All that neutral ground of character which stood between vice and virtue; or which, in fact, was indifferent to neither, where neither properly was called in question—that happy breathing-place from the burden of a perpetual moral questioning—the sanctuary and quiet Alsatia of hunted casuistry—is broken up and disfranchised as injurious to the interests of society. The privileges of the place are taken away by law. We dare not dally with images or names of wrong. We bark like foolish dogs at shadows. We dread

* Vide No. XXVI. p. 174.

infection from the scenic representation of disorder; and fear a painted pustule. In our anxiety that our morality should not take cold, we wrap it up in a great blanket surtout of precaution against the breeze and sunshine.

I confess for myself that (with no great delinquencies to answer for) I am glad for a season to take an airing beyond the diocese of the strict conscience,—not to live always in the precincts of the law courts,—but now and then, for a dream-while or so, to imagine a world with no meddling restrictions—to get into recesses, whither the hunter cannot follow me—

> ——— Secret shades
> Of woody Ida's inmost grove,
> While yet there was no fear of Jove—

I come back to my cage and my restraint the fresher and more healthy for it. I wear my shackles more contentedly for having respired the breath of an imaginary freedom. I do not know how it is with others, but I feel the better always for the perusal of one of Congreve's—nay, why should I not add even of Wycherley's—comedies. I am the gayer at least for it; and I could never connect those sports of a witty fancy in any shape with any result to be drawn from them to imitation in real life. They are a world of themselves almost as much as fairy-land. Take one of their characters, male or female (with few exceptions they are alike), and place it in a modern play, and my virtuous indignation shall rise against the profligate wretch as warmly as the Catos of the pit could desire; because in a modern play I am to judge of right and wrong, and the standard of *police* is the measure of *poetical justice*. The atmosphere will blight it. It cannot thrive here. It is got into a moral world where it has no business; from which it must needs fall head-long; as dizzy and incapable of keeping its stand, as a Swedenborgian bad spirit that has wandered unawares within the sphere of one of his good men or angels. But in its own world do we feel that the creature is so very bad?

The Fainalls and the Mirabels, the Dorimants, and Lady Touchwoods, in their own sphere do not offend my moral sense—or, in fact, appeal to it at all. They seem engaged in their proper element. They break through no laws, or conscientious restraints. They know of none. They have got out of Christendom into the land—what shall I call it?—of cuckoldry—the Utopia of gallantry, where pleasure is duty, and the manners perfect freedom. It is altogether a speculative scene of things, which has no reference whatever to the world that is. No good person can be justly offended as a spectator, because no good person suffers on the stage. Judged morally, every character in these plays—the few exceptions only are *mistakes*—is alike essentially vain and worthless. The great art of Congreve is especially shown in this, that he has entirely excluded from his scenes,—some little generosities in the part of Angelica perhaps excepted,—not only any thing like a faultless character, but any pretensions to goodness or good feelings whatsoever. Whether he did this designedly, or instinctively, the effect is as happy, as the design (if design) was bold. I used to wonder at the strange power which his Way of the World in particular possesses of interesting you all along in the pursuits of characters, for whom you absolutely care nothing—for you neither hate nor love his personages—and I think it is owing to this very indifference for any, that you endure the whole. He has spread a privation of moral light, I will call it, rather than by the ugly name of palpable darkness, over his creations; and his shadows flit before you without distinction or preference. Had he introduced a good character, a single gush of moral feeling, a revulsion of the judgment to actual life and actual duties, the impertinent Goshen would have only lighted to the discovery of deformities, which now are none, because we think them none.

Translated into real life, the characters of his, and his friend Wycherley's dramas, are profligates and strumpets,—the business of their brief existence, the undivided pursuit of lawless gallantry. No other spring of action, or possible motive of conduct, is recognised; principles which universally acted upon must reduce this frame of things to a chaos. But we do them wrong in so translating them. No such effects are produced in *their* world. When we are among them, we are amongst a chaotic people. We are not to judge them by our usages. No reverend institutions are insulted by their proceedings,—for they have none among them. No peace of families is violated,—for no family ties exist among them. No purity of the marriage bed is stained,—for none is supposed to have a being. No deep affections are disquieted,—no holy wedlock bands are snapped asunder,—for affection's depth and wedded faith are not of the growth of that soil. There is neither right nor wrong,—gratitude or its opposite,—claim or duty,—paternity or sonship. Of what consequence is it to virtue, or how is she at all concerned about it, whether Sir Simon, or Dapperwit, steal away Miss Martha; or who is the father of Lord Froth's, or Sir Paul Pliant's children?

The whole is a passing pageant, where we should sit as unconcerned at the issues, for life or death, as at a battle of the frogs and mice. But, like Don Quixote, we take part against the puppets, and quite as impertinently. We dare not contemplate an Atlantis, a scheme, out of which our coxcombical moral sense is for a little transitory ease excluded. We have not the courage to imagine a state of things for which there is neither reward nor punishment. We cling to the painful necessities of shame and blame. We would indict our very dreams.

Amidst the mortifying circumstances attendant upon growing old, it is something to have seen the School for Scandal in its glory. This comedy grew out of Congreve and Wycherley, but gathered some allays of the sentimental comedy which followed theirs. It is impossible that it should be now acted, though it continues, at long intervals, to be announced in the bills. Its hero, when Palmer played it at least, was Joseph Surface. When I remember the gay boldness, the graceful solemn plausibility, the measured step, the insinuating voice—to express it in a word—the downright *acted* villany of the part, so different from the pressure of conscious actual wickedness,—the hypocritical assumption of hypocrisy,—which made Jack so deservedly a favourite in that character, I must needs conclude the present generation of play-goers more virtuous than myself, or more dense. I freely confess that he divided the palm with me with his better brother; that, in fact, I liked him quite as well. Not but there are passages,—like that, for instance, where Joseph is made to refuse a pittance to a poor relation,—incongruities which Sheridan was forced upon by the attempt to join the artificial with the sentimental comedy, either of which must destroy the other—but over these obstructions Jack's manner floated him so lightly, that a refusal from him no more shocked you, than the easy compliance of Charles gave you in reality any pleasure; you got over the paltry question as quickly as you could, to get back into the regions of pure comedy, where no cold moral reigns. The highly artificial manner of Palmer in this character counteracted every disagreeable impression which you might have received from the contrast, supposing them real, between the two brothers. You did not believe in Joseph with the same faith with which you believed in Charles. The latter was a pleasant reality, the former a no less pleasant poetical foil to it. The comedy, I have said, is incongruous; a mixture of Congreve with sentimental incompatibilities; the gaiety upon the whole is buoyant; but it required the consummate art of Palmer to reconcile the discordant elements.

A player with Jack's talents, if we had one now, would not dare to do the part in the same manner. He would instinctively avoid every turn which might tend to unrealize, and so to make the character fascinating. He must take his cue from his spectators, who would expect a bad man and a good man as rigidly opposed to each other, as the death-beds of those geniuses are contrasted in the prints, which I am sorry to see have disappeared from the windows of my old friend Carrington Bowles, of St. Paul's Church-yard memory—(an exhibition as venerable as the adjacent cathedral, and almost coeval) of the bad and good man at the hour of death; where the ghastly apprehensions of the former,—and truly the grim phantom with his reality of a toasting fork is not to be despised,—so finely contrast with the meek complacent kissing of the rod,—taking it in like honey and butter,—with which the latter submits to the scythe of the gentle bleeder, Time, who wields his lancet with the apprehensive finger of a popular young ladies' surgeon. What flesh, like loving grass, would not covet to meet half-way the stroke of such a delicate mower?—John Palmer was twice an actor in this exquisite part. He was playing to you all the while that he was playing upon Sir Peter and his lady. You had the first intimation of a sentiment before it was on his lips. His altered voice was meant to you, and you were to suppose that his fictitious co-flutterers on the stage perceived nothing at all of it. What was it to you if that half-reality, the husband, was overreached by the puppetry—or the thin thing (Lady Teazle's reputation) was persuaded it was dying of a plethory? The fortunes of Othello and Desdemona were not concerned in it. Poor Jack has past from the stage—in good time, that he did not live to this our age of seriousness. The fidgety pleasant old Teazle *King* too is gone in good time. His manner would scarce have past current in our day. We must love or hate—acquit or condemn—censure or pity—exert our detestable coxcombry of moral judgment upon every thing. Joseph Surface, to go down now, must be a downright revolting villain—no compromise—his first appearance must shock and give horror—his specious plausibilities, which the pleasurable faculties of our fathers welcomed with such hearty greetings, knowing that no harm (dramatic harm even) could come, or was meant to come of them, must inspire a cold and killing aversion. Charles (the real canting person of the scene—for the hypocrisy of Joseph has its ulterior legitimate ends, but his brother's professions of a good heart centre in down-right self-satisfaction) must be *loved*, and Joseph *hated*. To balance one disagreeable reality with another, Sir Peter Teazle must be no longer the comic idea of a fretful old bachelor bridegroom, whose teazings (while King acted it) were evidently as much played off at you, as they were meant to concern any body on the stage,—he must be a real person, capable in law of sustaining an injury—a person towards whom duties are to be acknowledged—the genuine crim-con antagonist of the villanous seducer, Joseph. To realize him more, his sufferings under his unfortunate match must have the downright pungency of life—must (or should) make you not mirthful but uncomfortable, just as the same predicament would move you in a neighbour or old friend. The delicious scenes which give the play its name and zest, must affect you in the same serious manner as if you heard the reputation of a dear female friend attacked in your real presence. Crabtree, and Sir Benjamin—those poor snakes that lived but in the sunshine of your mirth—must be ripened by this hot-bed process of realization into asps or amphisbænas; and Mrs. Candour—O! frightful! become a hooded serpent. Oh who that remembers Parsons and Dodd—the wasp and butterfly of the School for Scandal—in those two characters; and charming natural Miss Pope, the perfect gentlewoman as distinguished from the fine lady of comedy, in this latter part—would forego the true scenic delight—the escape from life—the oblivion of consequences—the holiday barring out of the pedant Reflection—those Saturnalia of two or three brief hours, well won from the world—to sit instead at one of our modern plays—to have his coward conscience (that forsooth must not be left for a moment) stimulated with perpetual appeals—dulled rather, and blunted, as a faculty without repose must be—and his moral vanity pampered with images of notional justice, notional beneficence, lives saved without the spectators' risk, and fortunes given away that cost the author nothing?

No piece was, perhaps, ever so completely cast in all its parts as this *manager's comedy*. Miss Farren had succeeded to Mrs. Abingdon in Lady Teazle; and Smith, the original Charles, had retired, when I first saw it. The rest of the characters, with very slight exceptions, remained. I remember it was then the fashion to cry down John Kemble, who took the part of Charles after Smith; but, I thought, very unjustly. Smith, I fancy, was more airy, and took the eye with a certain gaiety of person. He brought with him no sombre recollections of tragedy. He had not to expiate the fault of having pleased before hand in lofty declamation. He had no sins of Hamlet or of Richard to atone for. His failure in these parts was a passport to success in one of so opposite a tendency. But as far as I could judge, the weighty sense of Kemble made up for more personal incapacity than he had to answer for. His harshest tones in this part came steeped and dulcified in good humour. He made his defects a grace. His exact declamatory manner, as he managed it, only served to convey the points of his dialogue with more precision. It seemed to head the shafts to carry them deeper. Not one of his sparkling sentences was lost. I remember minutely how he delivered each in succession, and cannot by any effort imagine how any of them could be altered for the better. No man could deliver brilliant dialogue—the dialogue of Congreve or of Wycherley—because none understood it—half so well as John Kemble. His Valentine, in Love for Love, was, to my recollection, faultless. He flagged sometimes in the intervals of tragic passion. He would slumber over the level parts of an heroic character. His Macbeth has been known to nod. But he always seemed to me to be particularly alive to pointed and witty dialogue. The relaxing levities of tragedy have not been touched by any since him—the playful court-bred spirit in which he condescended to the players in Hamlet—the sportive relief which he threw into the darker shades of Richard—disappeared with him. Tragedy is become a uniform dead weight. They have fastened lead to her buskins. She never pulls them off for the ease of a moment. To invert a commonplace from Niobe, she never forgets herself to liquefaction. John had his sluggish moods, his torpors—but they were the halting stones and resting places of his tragedy—politic savings, and fetches of the breath—husbandry of the lungs, where nature pointed him to be an economist—rather, I think, than errors of the judgment. They were, at worst, less painful than the eternal tormenting unappeasable vigilance, the "lidless dragon eyes," of present fashionable tragedy. The story of his swallowing opium pills to keep him lively upon the first night of a certain tragedy, we may presume to be a piece of retaliatory pleasantry on the part of the suffering author. But, indeed, John had the art of diffusing a complacent equable dulness (which you knew not where to quarrel with) over a piece which he did not like, beyond any of his contemporaries. John Kemble had made up his mind early, that all the good tragedies, which could be written, had been written; and he resented any new attempt. His shelves were full. The old standards were scope enough for his ambition. He ranged in them absolute—and "fair in Otway, full in Shakspeare shone." He succeeded to the old lawful thrones, and did not care to adventure bottomry with a Sir Edward Mortimer, or any casual speculator that offered. I remember, too acutely for my peace, the deadly extinguisher which he put upon my friend G.'s "Antonio." G., satiate with visions of political justice (possibly not to be realized in our time), or willing to let the sceptical worldlings see, that his anticipations of the future did not preclude a warm sympathy for men as they are and have been—wrote a tragedy. He chose a story, affecting, romantic, Spanish—the plot simple, without being naked—the incidents uncommon, without being overstrained. Antonio, who gives the name to the piece, is a sensitive young Castilian, who, in a fit of his country honour, immolates his sister———

But I must not anticipate the catastrophe—the play, reader, is extant in choice English—and you will employ a spare half crown not injudiciously in the quest of it.

The conception was bold, and the dénouement—the time and place in which the hero of it existed, considered—not much out of keeping; yet it must be confessed, that it required a delicacy of handling both from the author and the performer, so as not much to shock the prejudices of a modern English audience. G., in my opinion, had done his part.

John, who was in familiar habits with the philosopher, had undertaken to play Antonio. Great expectations were formed. A philosopher's first play was a new æra. The night arrived. I was favoured with a seat in an advantageous box, between the author and his friend M—. G. sate cheerful and confident. In his friend M.'s looks, who had perused the manuscript, I read some terror. Antonio in the person of John Philip Kemble at length appeared, starched out in a ruff which no one could dispute, and in most irreproachable mustachios. John always dressed most provokingly correct on these occasions. The first act swept by, solemn and silent. It went off, as G. assured M., exactly as the opening act of a piece—the protasis—should do. The cue of the spectators was to be mute. The characters were but in their introduction. The passions and the incidents would be developed hereafter. Applause hitherto would be impertinent. Silent attention was the effect all-desirable. Poor M. acquiesced—but in his honest friendly face I could discern a working which told how much more acceptable the plaudit of a single hand (however misplaced) would have been than all this reasoning. The second act (as in duty bound) rose a little in interest; but still John kept his forces under—in policy, as G. would have it—and the audience were most complacently attentive. The protasis, in fact, was scarcely unfolded. The interest would warm in the next act, against which a special incident was provided. M. wiped his cheek, flushed with a friendly perspiration—'tis M's way of showing his zeal—"from every pore of him a perfume falls—" I honour it above Alexander's. He had once or twice during this act joined his palms in a feeble endeavour to elicit a sound—they emitted a solitary noise without an echo—there was no deep to answer to his deep. G. repeatedly begged him to be quiet. The third act at length brought on the scene which was to warm the piece progressively to the final flaming forth of the catastrophe. A philosophic calm settled upon the clear brow of G. as it approached. The lips of M. quivered. A challenge was held forth upon the stage, and there was promise of a fight. The pit roused themselves on this extraordinary occasion, and, as their manner is, seemed disposed to make a ring,—when suddenly Antonio, who was the challenged, turning the tables upon the hot challenger Don Gusman (who by the way should have had his sister) baulks his humour, and the pit's reasonable expectation at the same time, with some speeches out of the new philosophy against duelling. The audience were here fairly caught—their courage was up, and on the alert—a few blows, *ding dong*, as R——s the dramatist afterwards expressed it to me, might have done the business—when their most exquisite moral sense was suddenly called in to assist in the mortifying negation of their own pleasure. They could not applaud, for disappointment; they would not condemn, for morality's sake. The interest stood stone still; and John's manner was not at all calculated to unpetrify it. It was Christmas time, and the atmosphere furnished some pretext for asthmatic affections. One began to cough—his neighbour sympathised with him—till a cough became epidemical. But when, from being half-artificial in the pit, the cough got frightfully naturalised among the fictitious persons of the drama; and Antonio himself (albeit it was not set down in the stage directions) seemed more intent upon relieving his own lungs than the distresses of the author and his friends,—then G. "first knew fear;" and mildly turning to M., intimated that he had not been aware that Mr. K. laboured under a cold; and that the performance might possibly have been postponed with advantage for some nights further—still keeping the same serene countenance, while M. sweat like a bull. It would be invidious to pursue the fates of this ill-starred evening. In vain did the plot thicken in the scenes that followed, in vain the dialogue wax more passionate and stirring, and the progress of the sentiment point more and more clearly to the arduous developement which impended. In vain the action was accelerated, while the acting stood still. From the beginning, John had taken his stand; had wound himself up to an even tenor of stately declamation, from which no exigence of dialogue or person could make him swerve for an instant. To dream of his rising with the scene (the common trick of tragedians) was preposterous; for from the onset he had planted himself, as upon a terrace, on an eminence vastly above the audience, and he kept that sublime level to the end. He looked from his throne of elevated sentiment upon the under-world of spectators with a most sovran and becoming contempt. There was excellent pathos delivered out to them: an they would receive it, so; an they would not receive it, so. There was no offence against decorum in all this; nothing to condemn, to damn. Not an irreverent symptom of a sound was to be heard. The procession of verbiage stalked on through four and five acts, no one venturing to predict what would come of it, when towards the winding up of the latter, Antonio, with an irrelevancy that seemed to stagger Elvira herself—for she had been coolly arguing the point of honour with him—suddenly whips out a poniard, and stabs his sister to the heart. The effect was, as if a murder had been committed in cold blood. The whole house rose up in clamorous indignation demanding justice. The feeling rose far above hisses. I believe at that instant, if they could have got him, they would have torn the unfortunate author to pieces. Not that the act itself was so exorbitant, or of a complexion different from what they themselves would have applauded upon another occasion in a Brutus, or an Appius—but for want of attending to Antonio's *words*, which palpably led to the expectation of no less dire an event, instead of being seduced by his *manner*, which seemed to promise a sleep of a less alarming nature than it was his cue to inflict upon Elvira, they found themselves betrayed into an accompliceship of murder, a perfect misprision of parricide, while they dreamed of nothing less. M., I believe, was the only person who suffered acutely from the failure; for G. thenceforward, with a serenity unattainable but by the true philosophy, abandoning a precarious popularity, retired into his fast hold of speculation,—the drama in which the world was to be his tiring room, and remote posterity his applauding spectators at once, and actors.

ELIA.

THE

London Magazine.

Nº XXIX. MAY, 1822. Vol. V.

THE PRAISE OF CHIMNEY-SWEEPERS:

A MAY-DAY EFFUSION.

I like to meet a sweep—understand me—not a grown sweeper—old chimney-sweepers are by no means attractive—but one of those tender novices, blooming through their first nigritude, the maternal washings not quite effaced from the cheek—such as come forth with the dawn, or somewhat earlier, with their little professional notes sounding like the *peep peep* of a young sparrow; or liker to the matin lark should I pronounce them, in their aerial ascents not seldom anticipating the sun-rise?

I have a kindly yearning toward these dim specks—poor blots—innocent blacknesses—

I reverence these young Africans of our own growth—these almost clergy imps, who sport their cloth without assumption; and from their little pulpits (the tops of chimneys), in the nipping air of a December morning, preach a lesson of patience to mankind.

When a child, what a mysterious pleasure it was to witness their operation! to see a chit no bigger than one's-self enter, one knew not by what process, into what seemed the *fauces Averni*—to pursue him in imagination, as he went sounding on through so many dark stifling caverns, horrid shades!—to shudder with the idea that "now, surely, he must be lost for ever!"—to revive at hearing his feeble shout of discovered day-light—and then (O fulness of delight) running out of doors, to come just in time to see the sable phenomenon emerge in safety, the brandished weapon of his art victorious like some flag waved over a conquered citadel! I seem to remember having been told, that a bad sweep was once left in a stack with his brush to indicate which way the wind blew. It was an awful spectacle certainly; not much unlike the old stage direction in Macbeth, where the "Apparition of a child crowned, with a tree in his hand, rises."

Reader, if thou meetest one of these small gentry in thy early rambles, it is good to give him a penny. It is better to give him two-pence. If it be starving weather, and to the proper troubles of his hard occupation, a pair of kibed heels (no unusual accompaniment) be superadded, the demand on thy humanity will surely rise to a tester.

There is a composition, the ground-work of which I have understood to be the sweet wood 'yclept sassafras. This wood boiled down to a kind of tea, and tempered with an infusion of milk and sugar, hath to some tastes a delicacy beyond the China luxury. I know not how thy palate may relish it; for myself, with every deference to the judicious Mr. Read, who hath time out of mind kept open a shop (the only one he avers in London) for the vending of this "wholesome and pleasant beverage," on the south side of Fleet-street, as thou approachest Bridge-street—*the only Salopian house,*—I have never yet adventured to dip my own particular lip in a basin of his commended ingredients—a cautious premonition to the olfactories constantly whispering to me, that my stomach must infallibly, with all due courtesy, decline it. Yet I have seen palates, otherwise not uninstructed in dietetical elegances, sup it up with avidity.

I know not by what particular conformation of the organ it happens, but I have always found that this composition is surprisingly gratifying to the palate of a young chimney-sweeper—whether the oily particles (sassafras is slightly oleaginous) do attenuate and soften the fuliginous concretions, which are sometimes found (in dissections) to adhere to the roof of the mouth in these unfledged practitioners; or whether Nature, sensible that she had mingled too much of bitter wood in the lot of these raw victims, caused to grow out of the earth her sassafras for a sweet lenitive—but so it is, that no possible taste or odour to the senses of a young chimney-sweeper can convey a delicate excitement comparable to this mixture. Being penniless, they will yet hang their black heads over the ascending steam, to gratify one sense if possible, seemingly no less pleased than those domestic animals—cats—when they purr over a new found sprig of valerian. There is something more in these sympathies than philosophy can explicate.

Now albeit Mr. Read boasteth, not without reason, that his is the *only Salopian house;* yet be it known to thee, reader—if thou art one who keepest what are called good hours, thou art haply ignorant of the fact—he hath a race of industrious imitators, who from stalls, and under open sky, dispense the same savoury mess to humbler customers, at that dead time of the dawn, when (as extremes meet) the rake, reeling home from his midnight cups, and the hard-handed artisan leaving his bed to resume the premature labours of the day, jostle, not unfrequently to the manifest disconcerting of the former, for the honours of the pavement. It is the time when, in summer, between the expired and the not yet relumined kitchen-fires, the kennels of our fair metropolis give forth their least satisfactory odours. The rake, who wisheth to dissipate his o'er-night vapours in more grateful coffee, curses the ungenial fume, as he passeth; but the artisan stops to taste, and blesses the fragrant breakfast.

This is *Saloop*—the precocious herb-woman's darling—the delight of the early gardener, who transports his smoking cabbages by break of day from Hammersmith to Covent-garden's famed piazzas—the delight, and, oh I fear, too often the envy, of the unpennied sweep. Him shouldest thou haply encounter, with his dim visage pendant over the grateful steam, regale him with a sumptuous basin (it will cost thee but three half-pennies) and a slice of delicate bread and butter (an added halfpenny)—so may thy culinary fires, eased of the o'er-charged secretions from thy worse-placed hospitalities, curl up a lighter volume to the welkin—so may the descending soot never taint thy costly well-ingredienced soups—nor the odious cry, quick-reaching from street to street, of the *fired chimney,* invite the rattling engines from ten adjacent parishes, to disturb for a casual scintillation thy peace and pocket!

I am by nature extremely susceptible of street affronts; the jeers and taunts of the populace; the low-bred triumph they display over the casual trip, or splashed stocking, of a gentleman. Yet I can endure the jocularity of a young sweep with something more than forgiveness.—In the last winter but one, pacing along Cheapside with my accustomed precipitation when I walk westward, a treacherous slide brought me upon my back in an instant. I scrambled up with pain and shame enough—yet outwardly trying to face it down, as if nothing had happened—when the roguish grin of one of these young wits encountered me. There he stood, pointing me out with his dusky finger to the mob, and to a poor woman (I suppose his mother) in particular, till the tears for the exquisiteness of the fun (so he thought it) worked themselves out at the corners of his poor red eyes, red from many a previous weeping, and soot-inflamed, yet twinkling through all with such a joy, snatched out of desolation, that Hogarth —— but Hogarth has got him already (how could he miss him?) in the March to Finchley, grinning at the pye-man——there he stood, as he stands in the picture, irremovable, as if the jest was to last for ever—with such a maximum of glee, and minimum of mischief, in his mirth—for the grin of a genuine sweep hath absolutely no malice in it—that I could have been content, if the honour of a gentleman might endure it, to have remained his butt and his mockery till midnight.

I am by theory obdurate to the seductiveness of what are called a fine set of teeth. Every pair of rosy lips (the ladies must pardon me) is a casket, presumably holding such jewels; but, methinks, they should take leave to "air" them as frugally as possible. The fine lady, or fine gentleman, who show me their teeth, show me bones. Yet must I confess, that from the mouth of a true sweep a display (even to ostentation) of those white and shining ossifications, strikes me as an agreeable anomaly in manners, and an allowable piece of foppery. It is, as when

A sable cloud
Turns forth her silver lining on the night.

It is like some remnant of gentry not quite extinct; a badge of better days; a hint of nobility:—and, doubtless, under the obscuring darkness and double night of their forlorn disguisement, oftentimes lurketh good blood, and gentle conditions, derived from lost ancestry, and a lapsed pedigree. The premature apprenticements of these tender victims give but too much encouragement, I fear, to clandestine, and almost infantile abductions; the seeds of civility and true courtesy, so often discernible in these young grafts (not otherwise to be accounted for) plainly hint at some forced adoptions; many noble Rachels mourning for their children, even in our days, countenance the fact; the tales of fairy-spiriting may shadow a lamentable verity, and the recovery of the young Montagu be but a solitary instance of good fortune, out of many irreparable and hopeless *defiliations*.

In one of the state-beds at Arundel Castle, a few years since—under a ducal canopy—(that seat of the Howards is an object of curiosity to visitors, chiefly for its beds, in which the late Duke was especially a connoisseur)—encircled with curtains of delicatest crimson, with starry coronets inwoven—folded between a pair of sheets whiter and softer than the lap where Venus lulled Ascanius—was discovered by chance, after all methods of search had failed, at noon-day, fast asleep, a lost chimney-sweeper. The little creature, having somehow confounded his passage among the intricacies of those lordly chimneys, by some unknown aperture had alighted upon this magnificent chamber; and, tired with his tedious explorations, was unable to resist the delicious invitement to repose, which he there saw exhibited; so, creeping between the sheets very quietly, laid his black head upon the pillow, and slept like a young Howard.

Such is the account given to the visitors at the Castle.—But I cannot help seeming to perceive a confirmation of what I have just hinted at in this story. A high instinct was at work in the case, or I am mistaken. Is it probable that a poor child of that description, with whatever weariness he might be visited, would have ventured, under such a penalty as he would be taught to expect, to uncover the sheets of a Duke's bed, and deliberately to lay himself down between them, when the rug, or the carpet, presented an obvious couch, still far above his pretensions—is this probable, I would ask, if the great power of nature, which I contend for, had not been manifested within him, prompting to the adventure? Doubtless this young nobleman (for such my mind misgives me that he must be) was allured by some memory, not amounting to full consciousness, of his condition in infancy, when he was used to be lapt by his mother, or his nurse, in just such sheets as he there found, into which he was now but creeping back as into his proper *incunabula*, and resting place.—By no other theory, than by this sentiment of a pre-existent state (as I may call it), can I explain a deed so venturous, and, indeed, upon any other system, so indecorous, in this tender, but unseasonable, sleeper.

My pleasant friend Jem White

was so impressed with a belief of metamorphoses like this frequently taking place, that in some sort to reverse the wrongs of fortune in these poor changelings, he instituted an annual feast of chimney-sweepers, at which it was his pleasure to officiate as host and waiter. It was a solemn supper held in Smithfield, upon the yearly return of the fair of St. Bartholomew. Cards were issued a week before to the master-sweeps in and about the metropolis, confining the invitation to their younger fry. Now and then an elderly stripling would get in among us, and be good-naturedly winked at; but our main body were infantry. One unfortunate wight, indeed, who, relying upon his dusky suit, had intruded himself into our party, but by tokens was providentially discovered in time to be no chimney-sweeper (all is not soot which looks so), was quoited out of the presence with universal indignation, as not having on the wedding garment; but in general the greatest harmony prevailed. The place chosen was a convenient spot among the pens, at the north side of the fair, not so far distant as to be impervious to the agreeable hubbub of that vanity; but remote enough not to be obvious to the interruption of every gaping spectator in it. The guests assembled about seven. In those little temporary parlours three tables were spread with napery, not so fine as substantial, and at every board a comely hostess presided with her pan of hissing sausages. The nostrils of the young rogues dilated at the savour. James White, as head waiter, had charge of the first table; and myself, with our trusty companion Bigod, ordinarily ministered to the other two. There was clambering and jostling, you may be sure, who should get at the first table—for Rochester in his maddest days could not have done the humours of the scene with more spirit than my friend. After some general expression of thanks for the honour the company had done him, his inaugural ceremony was to clasp the greasy waist of old dame Ursula (the fattest of the three), that stood frying and fretting, half-blessing, half-cursing "the gentleman," and imprint upon her chaste lips a tender salute, whereat the universal host would set up a shout that tore the concave, while hundreds of grinning teeth startled the night with their brightness. O it was a pleasure to see the sable younkers lick in the unctuous meat, with *his* more unctuous sayings—how he would fit the tit bits to the puny mouths, reserving the lengthier links for the seniors—how he would intercept a morsel even in the jaws of some young desperado, declaring it "must to the pan again to be browned, for it was not fit for a gentleman's eating"—how he would recommend this slice of white bread, or that piece of kissing-crust, to a tender juvenile, advising them all to have a care of cracking their teeth, which "were their best patrimony"—how genteelly he would deal about the small ale, as if it were wine, naming the brewer, and protesting, if it were not good, he should lose their custom; with a special recommendation to "wipe the lip before drinking." Then we had our toasts—"The King,"—the "Cloth,"—which, whether they understood or not, was equally diverting and flattering;—and for a crowning sentiment, which never failed, "May the Brush supersede the Laurel." All these, and fifty other fancies, which were rather felt than comprehended by his guests, would he utter, standing upon tables, and prefacing every sentiment with a "Gentlemen, give me leave to propose so and so," which was a prodigious comfort to those young orphans; every now and then stuffing into his mouth (for it did not do to be squeamish on these occasions) indiscriminate pieces of those reeking sausages, which pleased them mightily, and was the savouriest part, you may believe, of the entertainment.

Golden lads and lasses must,
As chimney sweepers, come to dust—

James White is extinct, and with him these suppers have long ceased. He carried away with him half the fun of the world when he died—of my world at least. His old clients look for him among the pens; and, missing him, reproach the altered feast of St. Bartholomew, and the glory of Smithfield departed for ever.

Elia.

A COMPLAINT OF THE DECAY OF BEGGARS IN THE METROPOLIS.

The all-sweeping besom of societarian reformation—your only modern Alcides' club to rid the time of its abuses—is uplift with many-handed sway to extirpate the last fluttering tatters of the bugbear MENDICITY from the metropolis. Scrips, wallets, bags—staves, dogs, and crutches—the whole mendicant fraternity with all their baggage are fast posting out of the purlieus of this eleventh persecution. From the crowded crossing, from corners of streets and turnings of allies, the parting Genius of Beggary is "with sighing sent."

I do not approve of this wholesale going to work, this impertinent crusado, or *bellum ad exterminationem*, proclaimed against a species. Much good might be sucked from these Beggars.

They were the oldest and the honourablest form of pauperism. Their appeals were to our common nature; less revolting to an ingenuous mind than to be a supplicant to the particular humours or caprice of any fellow-creature, or set of fellow-creatures, parochial or societarian. Theirs were the only rates uninvidious in the levy, ungrudged in the assessment.

There was a dignity springing from the very depth of their desolation; as to be naked is to be so much nearer to the being a man, than to go in livery.

The greatest spirits have felt this in their reverses; and when Dionysius from king turned schoolmaster, do we feel any thing towards him but contempt? Could Vandyke have made a picture of him, swaying a ferula for a sceptre, which would have affected our minds with the same heroic pity, the same compassionate admiration, with which we regard his Belisarius begging for an *obolum*? Would the moral have been more graceful, more pathetic?

The Blind Beggar in the legend—the father of pretty Bessy—whose story doggrel rhymes and ale-house signs cannot so degrade or attenuate, but that some sparks of a lustrous spirit will shine through the disguisements—this noble Earl of Flanders (as indeed he was) and memorable sport of fortune, fleeing from the unjust sentence of his liege lord, stript of all, and seated on the flowering green of Bethnal, with his more fresh and springing daughter by his side, illumining his rags and his beggary—would the child and parent have cut a better figure, doing the honours of a counter, or expiating their fallen condition upon the three-foot eminence of some sempstering shop-board?

In tale or history your Beggar is ever the just antipode to your King. The poets and romancical writers (as dear Margaret Newcastle would call them) when they would most sharply and feelingly paint a reverse of fortune, never stop till they have brought down their hero in good earnest to rags and the wallet. The depth of the descent illustrates the height he falls from. There is no medium which can be presented to the imagination without offence. There is no breaking the fall. Lear, thrown from his palace, must divest him of his garments, till he answer "mere nature;" and Cresseid, fallen from a prince's love, must extend her pale arms, pale with other whiteness than of beauty, supplicating lazar alms with bell and clap-dish.

The Lucian wits knew this very well; and, with an opposite policy, when they would express scorn of greatness without the pity, they show us an Alexander in the shades cobbling shoes, or a Semiramis getting up foul linen.

How would it sound in song, that a great monarch had declined his affections upon the daughter of a baker! yet do we feel the imagination at all violated, when we read the "true ballad," where King Cophetua wooes the beggar maid?

Pauperism, pauper, poor man, are expressions of pity, but pity alloyed with contempt. No one properly contemns a beggar. Poverty is a comparative thing, and each degree of it is mocked by its "neighbour grice."* Its poor rents and comings-in are soon summed up and told. Its pretences to property are almost ludicrous. Its pitiful attempts to save

* Timon of Athens.

excite a smile. Every scornful companion can weigh his trifle-bigger purse against it. Poor man reproaches poor man in the streets with impolitic mention of his condition, his own being a shade better, while the rich pass by and jeer at both. No rascally comparative insults a Beggar, or thinks of weighing purses with him. He is not in the scale of comparison. He is not under the measure of property. He confessedly hath none, any more than a dog or a sheep. No one twitteth him with ostentation above his means. No one accuses him of pride, or upbraideth him with mock humility. None jostle with him for the wall, or pick quarrels for precedency. No wealthy neighbour seeketh to eject him from his tenement. No man sues him. No man goes to law with him. If I were not the independent gentleman that I am, rather than I would be a retainer to the great, a led captain, or a poor relation, I would chuse, out of the delicacy and true greatness of my mind, to be a Beggar.

Rags, which are the reproach of poverty, are the Beggar's robes, and graceful *insignia* of his profession, his tenure, his full dress, the suit in which he is expected to show himself in public. He is never out of the fashion, or limpeth awkwardly behind it. He is not required to put on court mourning. He weareth all colours, fearing none. His costume hath undergone less change than the Quaker's. His coat is coeval with Adam's. He is the only man in the universe who is not obliged to study appearances. The ups and downs of the world concern him no longer. He alone continueth in one stay. The price of stock or land affecteth him not. The fluctuations of agricultural or commercial prosperity touch him not, or at worst but change his customers. He is not expected to become bail or surety for any one. No man troubleth him with questioning his religion or politics. He is the only free man in the universe.

The Mendicants of this great city were so many of her sights, her lions. I can no more spare them than I could the Cries of London. No corner of a street is complete without them. They are as indispensable as the Ballad Singer; and in their picturesque attire as ornamental as the Signs of old London. They were the standing morals, emblems, mementos, dial-mottos, the spital sermons, the books for children, the salutary checks and pauses to the high and rushing tide of greasy citizenry—

——— Look
Upon that poor and broken bankrupt there.

Above all, those old blind Tobits that used to line the wall of Lincoln's Inn Garden, before modern fastidiousness had expelled them, casting up their ruined orbs to catch a ray of pity, and (if possible) of light, with their faithful Dog Guide at their feet, —whither are they fled? or into what corners, blind as themselves, have they been driven, out of the wholesome air and sun-warmth? immersed between four walls, in what withering poor-house do they endure the penalty of double darkness, where the chink of the dropt half-penny no more consoles their forlorn bereavement, far from the sound of the cheerful and hope-stirring tread of the passenger? Where hang their useless crutches? and who will farm their dogs?—Have the overseers of St. L—— caused them to be shot? or were they tied up in sacks, and dropt into the Thames, at the suggestion of B——, the mild Rector of P——?

Well fare the soul of unfastidious Vincent Bourne, most classical, and at the same time, most English, of the Latinists!—who has treated of this human and quadrupedal alliance, this dog and man friendship, in the sweetest of his poems, the *Epitaphium in Canem*, or, *Dog's Epitaph*. Reader, peruse it; and say, if customary sights, which could call up such gentle poetry as this, were of a nature to do more harm or good to the moral sense of the passengers through the daily thoroughfares of a vast and busy metropolis.

Pauperis hic Iri requiesco Lyciscus, herilis,
Dum vixi, tutela vigil columenque senectæ,
Dux cæco fidus: nec, me ducente, solebat,
Prætenso hinc atque hinc baculo, per iniqua locorum
Incertam explorare viam; sed fila secutus,
Quæ dubios regerent passûs, vestigia tuta

Fixit inoffenso gressu; gelidumque sedile
In nudo nactus saxo, quà prætereuntium
Unda frequens confluxit, ibi miserisque tenebras
Lamentis, noctemque oculis ploravit obortam.
Ploravit nec frustra; obolum dedit alter et alter,
Queis corda et mentem indiderat natura benignam.
Ad latus interea jacui sopitus herile,
Vel mediis vigil in somnis; ad herilia jussa
Auresque atque animum arrectus, seu frustula amicè
Porrexit sociasque dapes, seu longa diei
Tædia perpessus, reditum sub nocte parabat.
  Hi mores, hæc vita fuit, dum fata sinebant,
Dum neque languebam morbis, nec inerte senectâ;
Quæ tandem obrepsit, veterique satellite cæcum
Orbavit dominum: prisci sed gratia facti
Ne tota intereat, longos deleta per annos,
Exiguum hunc Irus tumulum de cespite fecit,
Etsi inopis, non ingratæ, munuscula dextræ;
Carmine signavitque brevi, dominumque canemque,
Quod memoret, fidumque canem dominumque benignum.

Poor Irus' faithful wolf-dog here I lie,
That wont to tend my old blind master's steps,
His guide and guard: nor, while my service lasted,
Had he occasion for that staff, with which
He now goes picking out his path in fear
Over the highways and crossings; but would plant,
Safe in the conduct of my friendly string,
A firm foot forward still, till he had reach'd
His poor seat on some stone, nigh where the tide
Of passers by in thickest confluence flow'd:
To whom with loud and passionate laments
From morn to eve his dark estate he wail'd.
Nor wail'd to all in vain: some here and there,
The well-disposed and good, their pennies gave.
I meantime at his feet obsequious slept;
Not all-asleep in sleep, but heart and ear
Prick'd up at his least motion; to receive
At his kind hand my customary crumbs,
And common portion in his feast of scraps;
Or when night warn'd us homeward, tired and spent
With our long day and tedious beggary.
  These were my manners, this my way of life,
Till age and slow disease me overtook,
And sever'd from my sightless master's side.
But lest the grace of so good deeds should die,
Through tract of years in mute oblivion lost,
This slender tomb of turf hath Irus reared,
Cheap monument of no ungrudging hand,
And with short verse inscribed it, to attest,
In long and lasting union to attest,
The virtues of the Beggar and his Dog.

These dim eyes have in vain explored for some months past a well-known figure, or part of the figure, of a man, who used to glide his comely upper half over the pavements of London, wheeling along with most ingenious celerity upon a machine of wood; a spectacle to natives, to foreigners, and to children. He was of a robust make, with a florid sailor-like complexion, and his head was bare to the storm and sunshine. He was a natural curiosity, a speculation to the scientific, a prodigy to the simple. The infant would stare at the mighty man brought down to his own level. The common cripple would despise his own pusillanimity, viewing the hale stoutness, and hearty heart, of this half-limbed giant. Few but must have noticed him; for the accident, which brought him low, took place during the riots of 1780, and he has been a groundling so long. He seemed earth-born, an Antæus, and to suck in fresh vigour from the soil which he neighboured. He was a grand fragment; as good as an Elgin marble. The nature, which should have recruited his reft legs and thighs, was not lost, but only retired into his upper parts, and he was half a Hercules. I heard a tremendous voice thundering and growling, as before an earthquake, and casting down my eyes, it was this mandrake reviling a steed that had started at his portentous appearance. He seemed to want but his just stature to have rent the offending quadruped in shivers. He was as the man-part of a Centaur, from which the horse-half had been cloven in some dire Lapithan controversy. He moved on, as if he could have made shift with yet half of the body-portion which was left him. The *os sublime* was not wanting; and he threw out yet a jolly countenance upon the heavens. Forty-and-two years had he driven this out of door trade, and now that his hair is grizzled in the service, but his good spirits no way impaired, because he is not content to exchange his free air and exercise for the restraints of a poor house, he is expiating his contumacy in one of those houses (ironically christened) of Correction.

Was a daily spectacle like this to be deemed a nuisance, which called for legal interference to remove? or not rather a salutary, and a touching object, to the passers-by in a great city? Among her shows, her museums, and supplies for ever-gaping curiosity (and what else but an accumulation of sights—endless sights—*is* a great city; or for what else is it desirable?) was there not room for one *Lusus* (not *Naturæ* indeed, but) *Accidentium*? What if in forty-and-two years' going about, the man had scraped together enough to give a portion to his child (as the rumour ran) of a few hundreds—whom had he injured? whom had he imposed upon? The contributors had enjoyed their *sight* for their pennies. What if after being exposed all day to the heats, the rains, and the frosts of heaven—shuffling his ungainly trunk along in an elaborate and painful motion—he was enabled to retire at night to enjoy himself at a club of his fellow cripples over a dish of hot meat and vegetables, as the charge was gravely brought against him by a clergyman deposing before a House of Commons' Committee—was *this*, or was his truly paternal consideration, which (if a fact) deserved a statue rather than a whipping post, and is inconsistent at least with the exaggeration of nocturnal orgies which he has been slandered with—a reason that he should be deprived of his chosen, harmless, nay edifying, way of life, and be committed in hoary age for a sturdy vagabond?—

There was a Yorick once, that would not have shamed him to have sate down at the cripples' feast, and would have thrown in his benediction, aye, and his mite too, for a companionable symbol. "Age, thou hast lost thy breed."—

Half of these stories about the prodigious fortunes made by begging are (I verily believe) misers' calumnies. One was much talked of in the public papers some time since, and the usual charitable inferences deduced. A clerk in the Bank was surprised with the announcement of a five hundred pound legacy left him by a person whose name he was a stranger to. It seems that in his daily morning walks from Peckham (or some village thereabouts) where he lived, to his office, it had been his practice for the last twenty years to drop his halfpenny duly into the hat of some blind Bartimeus, that sate begging alms by the way-side in the Borough. The good old beggar recognised his daily benefactor by the voice only; and, when he died, left all the amassings of his alms (that had been half a century perhaps in the accumulating) to his old Bank friend. Was this a story to purse up people's hearts, and pennies, against giving an alms to the blind?—or not rather a beautiful moral of well-directed charity on the one part, and noble gratitude upon the other?

I sometimes wish I had been that Bank clerk.

I seem to remember a poor old grateful kind of creature, blinking, and looking up with his no eyes in the sun—

Is it possible I could have steeled my purse against him?

Perhaps I had no small change.

Reader, do not be frightened at the hard words, imposition, imposture—*give, and ask no questions.* Cast thy bread upon the waters. Some have unawares (like this Bank clerk) entertained angels.

Shut not thy purse-strings always against painted distress. Act a charity sometimes. When a poor creature (outwardly and visibly such) comes before thee, do not stay to enquire whether the "seven small children," in whose name he implores thy assistance, have a veritable existence. Rake not into the bowels of unwelcome truth, to save a halfpenny. It is good to believe him. If he be not all that he pretendeth, *give*, and under a personate father of a family, think (if thou pleasest) that thou hast relieved an indigent bachelor. When they come with their counterfeit looks, and mumping tones, think them players. You pay your money to see a comedian feign these things, which, concerning these poor people, thou canst not certainly tell whether they are feigned or not.

"Pray God your honour relieve me," said a poor beadswoman to my friend L—— one day; "I have seen better days." "So have I, my good woman," retorted he, looking up at the welkin which was just then threatening a storm—and the jest (he will have it) was as good to the beggar as a tester.

It was at all events kinder than consigning her to the stocks, or the parish beadle—

But L. has a way of viewing things in rather a paradoxical light on some occasions. ELIA.

P. S. My friend Hume (not MP.) has a curious manuscript in his possession, the original draught of the celebrated "Beggar's Petition," (who cannot say by heart the "Beggar's Petition?") as it was written by some school usher (as I remember) with corrections interlined from the pen of Oliver Goldsmith. As a specimen of the doctor's improvement, I recollect one most judicious alteration—

A pamper'd menial drove me from the door.

It stood originally,

A livery servant drove me, &c.

Here is an instance of poetical or artificial language properly substituted for the phrase of common conversation; against Wordsworth.

I think I must get H. to send it to the LONDON, as a corollary to the foregoing.

N. B. I am glad to see JANUS veering about to the old quarter. I feared he had been rust-bound.

C. being asked why he did not like Gold's "London" as well as ours—it was in poor S.'s time—replied—

——Because there is no WEATHERCOCK,
And that's the reason why.

DETACHED THOUGHTS ON BOOKS AND READING.

To mind the inside of a book is to entertain one's self with the forced product of another man's brain. Now I think a man of quality and breeding may be much amused with the natural sprouts of his own.

Lord Foppington in the Relapse.

An ingenious acquaintance of my own was so much struck with this bright sally of his Lordship, that he has left off reading altogether, to the great improvement of his originality. At the hazard of losing some credit on this head, I must confess that I dedicate no inconsiderable portion of my time to other people's thoughts. I dream away my life in others' speculations. I love to lose myself in other men's minds. When I am not walking, I am reading; I cannot sit and think. Books think for me.

I have no repugnances. Shaftsbury is not too genteel for me, nor Jonathan Wild too low. I can read any thing which I call a *book*. There are things in that shape which I cannot allow for such.

In this catalogue of *books which are no books—biblia a-biblia*—I reckon Court Calendars, Directories, Pocket Books (the Literary excepted), Draught Boards bound and lettered at the back, Scientific Treatises, Almanacks, Statutes at Large; the works of Hume, Gibbon, Robertson, Beattie, Soame Jenyns, and, generally, all those volumes which "no gentleman's library should be without;" the Histories of Flavius Josephus (that learned Jew), and Paley's Moral Philosophy. With these exceptions, I can read almost any thing. I bless my stars for a taste so catholic, so unexcluding.

I confess that it moves my spleen to see these *things in books' clothing* perched upon shelves, like false saints, usurpers of true shrines, intruders into the sanctuary, thrusting out the legitimate occupants. To reach down a well-bound semblance of a volume, and hope it some kind-hearted play-book, then, opening what "seem its leaves," to come bolt upon a withering Population Essay. To expect a Steele, or a Farquhar, and find—Adam Smith. To view a well-arranged assortment of blockheaded Encyclopædias (Anglicanas or Metropolitanas) set out in an array of Russia, or Morocco, when a tythe of that good leather would comfortably re-clothe my shivering folios; would renovate Paracelsus himself, and enable old Raymund Lully—I have them both, reader—to look like himself again in the world. I never see these impostors, but I long to strip them, to warm my ragged veterans in their spoils.

To be strong-backed and neat-bound is the desideratum of a volume. Magnificence comes after. This, when it can be afforded, is not to be lavished upon all kinds of books indiscriminately. I would not dress a set of Magazines, for instance, in full suit. The dishabille, or half-binding (with Russia backs ever), is *our* costume. A Shakspeare, or a Milton (unless the first editions), it were mere foppery to trick out in gay apparel. The possession of them confers no distinction. The exterior of them (the things themselves being so common), strange to say, raises no sweet emotions, no tickling sense of property in the owner. Thomson's Seasons, again, looks best (I maintain it) a little torn, and dog's-eared. How beautiful to a genuine lover of reading are the sullied leaves, and worn out appearance, nay, the very odour (beyond Russia), if we would not forget kind feelings in fastidiousness, of an old "Circulating Library" Tom Jones, or Vicar of Wakefield! How they speak of the thousand thumbs, which have turned over their pages with delight!—of the lone sempstress, whom they may have cheered (milliner, or harder-working mantua-maker) after her long day's needle-toil, running far into midnight, when she has snatched an hour, ill spared from sleep, to steep her cares, as in some Lethean cup, in spelling out their enchanting contents! Who would have them a whit less soiled? What better condition could we desire to see them in?

In some respects the better a book is, the less it demands from binding. Fielding, Smollet, Sterne, and all that class of perpetually self-reproductive volumes——Great Nature's Stereotypes——we see them individually perish with less regret, because we know the copies of them to be "eterne." But where a book is at once both good and rare—where the individual is almost the species, and when *that* perishes,

We know not where is that Promethean torch
That can its light relumine—

such a book, for instance, as the Life of the Duke of Newcastle, by his Duchess—no casket is rich enough, no casing sufficiently durable, to honour and keep safe such a jewel.

Not only rare volumes of this description, which seem hopeless ever to be reprinted; but old editions of writers, such as Sir Philip Sidney, Bishop Taylor, Milton in his prose-works, Fuller—of whom we *have* reprints; yet the books themselves, though they go about, and are talked of here and there, we know, have not endenizened themselves (nor possibly ever will) in the national heart, so as to become stock books—it is good to possess these in durable and costly covers.—I do not care for a First Folio of Shakspeare. You cannot make a *pet* book of an author whom every body reads. I rather prefer the common editions of Rowe and Tonson, without notes, and with *plates*, which, being so execrably bad, serve as maps, or modest remembrancers, to the text; and without pretending to any supposeable emulation with it, are so much better than the Shakspeare gallery *engravings*, which *did*. I have a community of feeling with my countrymen about his Plays; and I like those editions of him best, which have been oftenest tumbled about and handled.—On the contrary, I cannot read Beaumont and Fletcher but in Folio. The Octavo editions are painful to look at. I have no sympathy with them, nor with Mr. Gifford's Ben Jonson. If they were as much read as the current editions of the other poet, I should prefer them in that shape to the older one.—I do not know a more heartless sight than the reprint of the Anatomy of Melancholy. What need was there of unearthing the bones of that fantastic old great man, to expose them in a winding-sheet of the latest edition to modern censure? what hapless stationer could dream of Burton ever becoming popular?—The wretched Malone could not do worse, when he bribed the sexton of Stratford church to let him white-wash the painted effigy of old Shakspeare, which stood there, in rude but lively fashion depicted, to the very colour of the cheek, the eye, the eye-brow, hair, the very dress he used to wear—the only authentic testimony we had, however imperfect, of these curious parts and parcels of him. They covered him over with a coat of white paint. By ——, if I had been a justice of peace for Warwickshire, I would have clapt both commentator and sexton fast in the stocks for a pair of meddling sacrilegious varlets.

I think I see them at their work—these sapient trouble-tombs.

Shall I be thought fantastical, if I confess, that the names of some of our poets sound sweeter, and have a finer relish to the ear—to mine, at least—than that of Milton or of Shakspeare? It may be, that the latter are more staled and rung upon in common discourse. The sweetest names, and which carry a perfume in the mention, are, Kit Marlowe, Drayton, Drummond of Hawthornden, and Cowley.

Much depends upon *when* and *where* you read a book. In the five or six impatient minutes, before the dinner is quite ready, who would think of taking up the Fairy Queen for a stop-gap, or a volume of Bishop Andrewes' sermons?

Milton almost requires a solemn service of music to be played, before you enter upon him. But he brings his music—to which, who listens, had need bring docile thoughts and purged ears.

Winter evenings—the world shut out—with less of ceremony the gentle Shakspeare enters. At such a season, the Tempest—or his own Winter's Tale—

These two poets you cannot avoid reading aloud—to yourself, or (as it chances) to some single person listening. More than one—and it degenerates into an audience.

Books of quick interest, that hurry on for incidents, are for the eye to glide over solely. It will not do to read them out. I could never listen to even the better kind of modern novels without extreme irksomeness.

A newspaper, read out, is intolerable. In some of the Bank offices it is the custom (to save so much individual time) for one of the clerks—who is the best scholar—to commence upon the Times, or the Chronicle, and recite its entire contents aloud *pro bono publico*. With every advantage of lungs and elocution—the effect is singularly vapid.—In barbers' shops, and public-houses, a fellow will get up, and spell out a paragraph, which he communicates as some discovery. Another follows with *his* selection. So the entire journal transpires at length by piece-meal. Seldom-readers are slow readers, and, without this expedient no one in the company would probably ever travel through the contents of a whole paper.

Newspapers always excite curiosity. No one ever lays one down without a feeling of disappointment.

What an eternal time that gentleman in black, at Nando's, keeps the paper! I am sick of hearing the waiter bawling out incessantly, "the Chronicle is in hand, Sir."

As in these little Diurnals I generally skip the Foreign News—the Debates—and the Politics—I find the Morning Herald by far the most entertaining of them. It is an agreeable miscellany, rather than a newspaper.

Coming in to an inn at night—having ordered your supper—what can be more delightful than to find lying in the window-seat, left there time out of mind by the carelessness of some former guest—two or three numbers of the old Town and Country Magazine, with its amusing *tête-a-tête* pictures.—"The Royal Lover and Lady G——;" "the Melting Platonic and the old Beau,"—and such like antiquated scandal? Would you exchange it—at that time, and in that place—for a better book?

Poor Tobin, who latterly fell blind, did not regret it so much for the weightier kinds of reading—the Paradise Lost, or Comus, he could have *read* to him—but he missed the pleasure of skimming over with his own eye—a magazine, or a light pamphlet.

I should not care to be caught in the serious avenues of some cathedral alone, and reading—*Candide!*

I do not remember a more whimsical surprise than having been once detected—by a familiar damsel—reclined at my ease upon the grass, on Primrose Hill (her Cythera), reading—*Pamela*. There was nothing in the book to make a man seriously ashamed at the exposure; but, as she seated herself down by me, and seemed determined to read in company, I could have wished it had been—any other book.—We read on very sociably for a few pages; and, not finding the author much to her taste, she got up, and—went away. Gentle casuist, I leave it to thee to conjecture, whether the blush (for there was one between us) was the property of the nymph, or the swain, in this dilemma. From me you shall never get the secret.

I am not much a friend to out-of-doors reading. I cannot settle my spirits to it. I knew a Unitarian minister, who was generally to be seen upon Snow-hill (as yet Skinner's-street *was not*), between the hours of ten and eleven in the morning, studying a volume of Lardner. I own this to have been a strain of abstraction beyond my reach. I used to admire how he sidled along, keeping clear of secular contacts. An illiterate encounter with a porter's knot, or a bread-basket, would have quickly put to flight all the theology I am master of, and have left me worse than indifferent to the five points.

I was once amused—there is a pleasure in *affecting* affectation—at the indignation of a crowd that was justling in with me at the pit door of Covent Garden theatre, to have a sight of Master Betty—then at once in his dawn and his meridian—in Hamlet. I had been invited quite unexpectedly to join a party, whom I met near the door of the play-house, and I happened to have in my hand a large octavo of Johnson and Steevens's Shakspeare, which, the time not admitting of my carrying it home, of course went with me to the theatre. Just in the very heat and pressure of the doors opening—the *rush*, as they term it—I deliberately held the volume over my head, open at the scene in which the young Roscious had been most cried up, and quietly read by the lamp-light. The clamour became universal. "The affectation of the fellow," cried one. "Look at that gentleman *reading*, papa," squeaked a young lady, who in her admiration of the novelty almost forgot her fears. I read on. "He ought to have his book knocked out of his hand," exclaimed a pursy cit, whose arms were too fast pinioned to his side to suffer him to execute his kind intention. Still I read on—and, till the time came to pay my money, kept as unmoved, as Saint Antony at his Holy Offices, with the satyrs, apes, and hobgoblins, mopping, and making mouths at him, in the picture, while the good man sits as undisturbed at the sight, as if he were sole tenant of the desart.—The individual rabble (I recognized more than one of their ugly faces) had damned a slight piece of mine but a few nights before, and I was determined the culprits should not a second time put me out of countenance.

There is a class of street-readers, whom I can never contemplate without affection—the poor gentry, who, not having wherewithal to buy, or hire, a book, filch a little learning at the open stalls—the owner, with his hard eye, casting envious looks at them all the while, and thinking when they will have done. Venturing tenderly, page after page, expecting every moment when he shall interpose his interdict, and yet unable to deny themselves the gratification, they "snatch a fearful joy." Martin B—, in this way, by daily fragments, got through two volumes of Clarissa, when the stall-keeper damped his laudable ambition, by asking him (it was in his younger days) whether he meant to purchase the work. M. declares, that under no circumstances of his life did he ever peruse a book with half the satisfaction which he took in those uneasy snatches. A quaint poetess of our day has moralized upon this subject in two very touching but homely stanzas.

THE TWO BOYS.

I saw a boy with eager eye
Open a book upon a stall,
And read, as he'd devour it all;
Which when the stall-man did espy,
Soon to the boy I heard him call,
"You, Sir, you never buy a book,
Therefore in one you shall not look."
The boy pass'd slowly on, and with a sigh
He wish'd he never had been taught to read,
Then of the old churl's books he should have had no need.

Of sufferings the poor have many,
Which never can the rich annoy:
I soon perceiv'd another boy,
Who look'd as if he'd not had any
Food, for that day at least—enjoy
The sight of cold meat in a tavern larder.
This boy's case, then thought I, is surely harder,
Thus hungry, longing, thus without a penny,
Beholding choice of dainty-dressed meat:
No wonder if he wish he ne'er had learn'd to eat.

ELIA.

(*To be continued.*)

CONFESSIONS OF A DRUNKARD.

Dehortations from the use of strong liquors have been the favourite topic of sober declaimers in all ages, and have been received with abundance of applause by water-drinking critics. But with the patient himself, the man that is to be cured, unfortunately their sound has seldom prevailed. Yet the evil is acknowledged, the remedy simple. Abstain. No force can oblige a man to raise the glass to his head against his will. 'Tis as easy as not to steal, not to tell lies.

Alas! the hand to pilfer, and the tongue to bear false witness, have no constitutional tendency. These are actions indifferent to them. At the first instance of the reformed will, they can be brought off without a murmur. The itching finger is but a figure in speech, and the tongue of the liar can with the same natural delight give forth useful truths, with which it has been accustomed to scatter their pernicious contraries. But when a man has commenced sot——

O pause, thou sturdy moralist, thou person of stout nerves and a strong head, whose liver is happily untouched, and ere thy gorge riseth at the *name* which I have written, first learn what the *thing* is; how much of compassion, how much of human allowance, thou may'st virtuously mingle with thy disapprobation. Trample not on the ruins of a man. Exact not, under so terrible a penalty as infamy, a resuscitation from a state of death almost as real as that from which Lazarus rose not but by a miracle.

Begin a reformation, and custom will make it easy. But what if the beginning be dreadful, the first steps not like climbing a mountain but going through fire? what if the whole system must undergo a change violent as that which we conceive of the mutation of form in some insects? what if a process comparable to flaying alive be to be gone through? is the weakness that sinks under such struggles to be confounded with the pertinacity which clings to other vices, which have induced no constitutional necessity, no engagement of the whole victim, body and soul?

I have known one in that state, when he has tried to abstain but for one evening,—though the poisonous potion had long ceased to bring back its first enchantments, though he was sure it would rather deepen his gloom than brighten it,—in the violence of the struggle, and the necessity he has felt of getting rid of the present sensation at any rate, I have known him to scream out, to cry aloud, for the anguish and pain of the strife within him.

Why should I hesitate to declare, that the man of whom I speak is myself? I have no puling apology to make to mankind. I see them all in one way or another deviating from the pure reason. It is to my own nature alone I am accountable for the woe that I have brought upon it.

I believe that there are constitutions, robust heads and iron insides, whom scarce any excesses can hurt; whom brandy (I have seen them drink it like wine), at all events whom wine, taken in ever so plentiful measure, can do no worse injury to than just to muddle their faculties, perhaps never very pellucid. On them this discourse is wasted. They would but laugh at a weak brother, who, trying his strength with them, and coming off foiled from the contest, would fain persuade them that such agonistic exercises are dangerous. It is to a very different description of persons I speak. It is to the weak, the nervous; to those who feel the want of some artificial aid to raise their spirits in society to what is no more than the ordinary pitch of all around them without it. This is the secret of our drinking. Such must fly the convivial board in the first instance, if they do not mean to sell themselves for term of life.

Twelve years ago I had completed my six and twentieth year. I had lived from the period of leaving school to that time pretty much in solitude. My companions were chiefly books, or at most one or two living ones of my own book-loving and sober stamp. I rose early, went to bed betimes, and the faculties which God had given me, I have reason to think, did not rust in me unused.

About that time I fell in with

some companions of a different order. They were men of boisterous spirits, sitters up a-nights, disputants, drunken; yet seemed to have something noble about them. We dealt about the wit, or what passes for it after midnight, jovially. Of the quality called fancy I certainly possessed a larger share than my companions. Encouraged by their applause, I set up for a profest joker! I, who of all men am least fitted for such an occupation, having, in addition to the greatest difficulty which I experience at all times of finding words to express my meaning, a natural nervous impediment in my speech!

Reader, if you are gifted with nerves like mine, aspire to any character but that of a wit. When you find a tickling relish upon your tongue disposing you to that sort of conversation, especially if you find a preternatural flow of ideas setting in upon you at the sight of a bottle and fresh glasses, avoid giving way to it as you would fly your greatest destruction. If you cannot crush the power of fancy, or that within you which you mistake for such, divert it, give it some other play. Write an essay, pen a character or description,—but not as I do now, with tears trickling down your cheeks.

To be an object of compassion to friends, of derision to foes; to be suspected by strangers, stared at by fools; to be esteemed dull when you cannot be witty, to be applauded for witty when you know that you have been dull; to be called upon for the extemporaneous exercise of that faculty which no premeditation can give; to be spurred on to efforts which end in contempt; to be set on to provoke mirth which procures the procurer hatred; to give pleasure and be paid with squinting malice; to swallow draughts of life-destroying wine which are to be distilled into airy breath to tickle vain auditors; to mortgage miserable morrows for nights of madness; to waste whole seas of time upon those who pay it back in little inconsiderable drops of grudging applause,—are the wages of buffoonery and death.

Time, which has a sure stroke at dissolving all connexions which have no solider fastening than this liquid cement, more kind to me than my own taste or penetration, at length opened my eyes to the supposed qualities of my first friends. No trace of them is left but in the vices which they introduced, and the habits they infixed. In them my friends survive still, and exercise ample retribution for any supposed infidelity that I may have been guilty of towards them.

My next more immediate companions were and are persons of such intrinsic and felt worth, that though accidentally their acquaintance has proved pernicious to me, I do not know that if the thing were to do over again, I should have the courage to eschew the mischief at the price of forfeiting the benefit. I came to them reeking from the steams of my late over-heated notions of companionship; and the slighest fuel which they unconsciously afforded, was sufficient to feed my old fires into a propensity.

They were no drinkers, but, one from professional habits, and another from a custom derived from his father, smoked tobacco. The devil could not have devised a more subtle trap to re-take a backsliding penitent. The transition, from gulping down draughts of liquid fire to puffing out innocuous blasts of dry smoke, was so like cheating him. But he is too hard for us when we hope to commute. He beats us at barter; and when we think to set off a new failing against an old infirmity, 'tis odds but he puts the trick upon us of two for one. That (comparatively) white devil of tobacco brought with him in the end seven worse than himself.

It were impertinent to carry the reader through all the processes by which, from smoking at first with malt liquor, I took my degrees through thin wines, through stronger wine and water, through small punch, to those juggling compositions, which, under the name of mixed liquors, slur a great deal of brandy or other poison under less and less water continually, until they come next to none, and so to none at all. But it is hateful to disclose the secrets of my Tartarus.

I should repel my readers, from a mere incapacity of believing me, were I to tell them what tobacco has been to me, the drudging service which I have paid, the slavery which I have vowed to it. How, when I have resolved to quit it, a feeling as of ingratitude has started up; how it has put on personal claims and made the demands of a friend upon me. How the reading of it casually in a book, as where Adams takes his whiff in the chimney-corner of some inn in Joseph Andrews, or Piscator in the Complete Angler breaks his fast upon a morning pipe in that delicate room *Piscatoribus Sacrum,* has in a moment broken down the resistance of weeks. How a pipe was ever in my midnight path before me, till the vision forced me to realize it,—how then its ascending vapours curled, its fragrance lulled, and the thousand delicious ministerings conversant about it, employing every faculty, extracted the sense of pain. How from illuminating it came to darken, from a quick solace it turned to a negative relief, thence to a restlessness and dissatisfaction, thence to a positive misery. How, even now, when the whole secret stands confessed in all its dreadful truth before me, I feel myself linked to it beyond the power of revocation. Bone of my bone——

Persons not accustomed to examine the motives of their actions, to reckon up the countless nails that rivet the chains of habit, or perhaps being bound by none so obdurate as those I have confessed to, may recoil from this as from an overcharged picture. But what short of such a bondage is it, which in spite of protesting friends, a weeping wife, and a reprobating world, chains down many a poor fellow, of no original indisposition to goodness, to his pipe and his pot?

I have seen a print after Corregio, in which three female figures are ministering to a man who sits fast bound at the root of a tree. Sensuality is soothing him, Evil Habit is nailing him to a branch, and Repugnance at the same instant of time is applying a snake to his side. In his face is feeble delight, the recollection of past rather than perception of present pleasures, languid enjoyment of evil with utter imbecility to good, a Sybaritic effeminacy, a submission to bondage, the springs of the will gone down like a broken clock, the sin and the suffering co-instantaneous, or the latter forerunning the former, remorse preceding action—all this represented in one point of time.—When I saw this, I admired the wonderful skill of the painter. But when I went away, I wept, because I thought of my own condition.

Of *that* there is no hope that it should ever change. The waters have gone over me. But out of the black depths, could I be heard, I would cry out to all those who have but set a foot in the perilous flood. Could the youth, to whom the flavor of his first wine is delicious as the opening scenes of life or the entering upon some newly discovered paradise, look into my desolation, and be made to understand what a dreary thing it is when a man shall feel himself going down a precipice with open eyes and a passive will,—to see his destruction, and have no power to stop it, and yet to feel it all the way emanating from himself; to perceive all goodness emptied out of him, and yet not to be able to forget a time when it was otherwise; to bear about the piteous spectacle of his own self-ruins:—could he see my fevered eye, feverish with last night's drinking, and feverishly looking for this night's repetition of the folly; could he feel the body of the death out of which I cry hourly with feebler and feebler outcry to be delivered,—it were enough to make him dash the sparkling beverage to the earth in all the pride of its mantling temptation; to make him clasp his teeth,

and not undo 'em
To suffer WET DAMNATION to run thro' 'em.

Yea, but (methinks I hear somebody object) if sobriety be that fine thing you would have us to understand, if the comforts of a cool brain are to be preferred to that state of heated excitement which you describe and deplore, what hinders in your own instance that you do not return to those habits from which you would induce others never to swerve? if the blessing be worth preserving, is it not worth recovering?

Recovering!—O if a wish could transport me back to those days of youth, when a draught from the next clear spring could slake any heats which summer suns and youthful exercise had power to stir up in the blood, how gladly would I return to thee, pure element, the drink of children, and of child-like holy hermit. In my dreams I can sometimes fancy thy cool refreshment purling over my burning tongue. But my waking stomach rejects it. That which refreshes innocence, only makes me sick and faint.

But is there no middle way betwixt total abstinence and the excess which kills you?—For your sake, reader, and that you may never attain to my experience, with pain I must utter the dreadful truth, that there is none, none that I can find. In my stage of habit (I speak not of habits less confirmed—for some of them I believe the advice to be most prudential) in the stage which I have reached, to stop short of that measure which is sufficient to draw on torpor and sleep, the benumbing apoplectic sleep of the drunkard, is to have taken none at all. The pain of the self-denial is all one. And what that is, I had rather the reader should believe on my credit, than know from his own trial. He will come to know it, whenever he shall arrive at that state, in which, paradoxical as it may appear, *reason shall only visit him through intoxication:* for it is a fearful truth, that the intellectual faculties by repeated acts of intemperance may be driven from their orderly sphere of action, their clear day-light ministeries, until they shall be brought at last to depend, for the faint manifestation of their departing energies, upon the returning periods of the fatal madness to which they owe their devastation. The drinking man is never less himself than during his sober intervals. Evil is so far his good.*

Behold me then, in the robust period of life, reduced to imbecility and decay. Hear me count my gains, and the profits which I have derived from the midnight cup.

Twelve years ago I was possessed of a healthy frame of mind and body. I was never strong, but I think my constitution (for a weak one) was as happily exempt from the tendency to any malady as it was possible to be. I scarce knew what it was to ail any thing. Now, except when I am losing myself in a sea of drink, I am never free from those uneasy sensations in head and stomach, which are so much worse to bear than any definite pains or aches.

At that time I was seldom in bed after six in the morning, summer and winter. I awoke refreshed, and seldom without some merry thoughts in my head, or some piece of a song to welcome the new-born day. Now, the first feeling which besets me, after stretching out the hours of recumbence to their last possible extent, is a forecast of the wearisome day that lies before me, with a secret wish that I could have lain on still, or never awaked.

Life itself, my waking life, has much of the confusion, the trouble, and obscure perplexity, of an ill dream. In the day time I stumble upon dark mountains.

Business, which, though never particularly adapted to my nature, yet as something of necessity to be gone through, and therefore best undertaken with cheerfulness, I used to enter upon with some degree of alacrity, now wearies, affrights, perplexes me. I fancy all sorts of discouragements, and am ready to give up an occupation which gives me bread, from a harassing conceit of incapacity. The slightest commission given me by a friend, or any small duty which I have to perform for myself, as giving orders to a tradesman, &c. haunts me as a labour impossible to be got through. So much the springs of action are broken.

The same cowardice attends me in all my intercourse with mankind. I dare not promise that a friend's honour, or his cause, would be safe in my keeping, if I were put to the expense of any manly resolution in defending it. So much the springs of moral action are deadened within me.

My favourite occupations in times past, now cease to entertain. I can do nothing readily. Application for

* When poor M——— painted his last picture, with a pencil in one trembling hand and a glass of brandy and water in the other, his fingers owed the comparative steadiness, with which they were enabled to go through their task in an imperfect manner, to a temporary firmness derived from a repetition of practices, the general effect of which had shaken both them and him so terribly.

ever so short a time kills me. This poor abstract of my condition was penned at long intervals, with scarcely any attempt at connexion of thought, which is now difficult to me.

The noble passages which formerly delighted me in history or poetic fiction, now only draw a few weak tears, allied to dotage. My broken and dispirited nature seems to sink before any thing great and admirable.

I perpetually catch myself in tears, for any cause, or none. It is inexpressible how much this infirmity adds to a sense of shame, and a general feeling of deterioration.

These are some of the instances, concerning which I can say with truth, that it was not always so with me.

Shall I lift up the veil of my weakness any further? or is this disclosure sufficient?

I am a poor nameless egotist, who have no vanity to consult by these Confessions. I know not whether I shall be laughed at, or heard seriously. Such as they are, I commend them to the reader's attention, if he finds his own case any way touched. I have told him what I am come to. Let him stop in time. ELIA.

THE LION'S HEAD.

Re-prints of ELIA.—Many are the sayings of *Elia*, painful and frequent his lucubrations, set forth for the most part (such his modesty!) without a name, scattered about in obscure periodicals and forgotten miscellanies. From the dust of some of these, it is our intention, occasionally, to revive a Tract or two, that shall seem worthy of a better fate; especially at a time like the present, when the pen of our industrious Contributor, engaged in a laborious digest of his recent Continental Tour, may haply want the leisure to expatiate in more miscellaneous speculations. We have been induced, in the first instance, to re-print a Thing, which he put forth in a friend's volume some years since, entitled the Confessions of a Drunkard, seeing that Messieurs the Quarterly Reviewers have chosen to embellish their last dry pages with fruitful quotations therefrom; adding, from their peculiar brains, the gratuitous affirmation, that they have reason to believe that the describer (in his delineations of a drunkard forsooth!) partly sate for his own picture. The truth is, that our friend had been reading among the Essays of a contemporary, who has perversely been confounded with him, a paper in which *Edax* (or the *Great Eater*) humorously complaineth of an inordinate appetite; and it struck him, that a better paper—of deeper interest, and wider usefulness—might be made out of the imagined experiences of a *Great Drinker*. Accordingly he set to work, and with that mock fervor, and counterfeit earnestness, with which he is too apt to over-realise his descriptions, has given us—a frightful picture indeed—but no more resembling the man *Elia*, than the fictitious *Edax* may be supposed to identify itself with Mr. L., its author. It is indeed a compound extracted out of his long observations of the effects of drinking upon all the world about him; and this accumulated mass of misery he hath centered (as the custom is with judicious essayists) in a single figure. We deny not that a portion of his own experiences may have passed into the picture, (as who, that is not a washy fellow, but must at some times have felt the after-operation of a too generous cup?)—but then how heightened! how exaggerated!—how little within the sense of the Review, where a part, in their slanderous usage, must be understood to stand for the whole!—but it is useless to expostulate with this Quarterly slime, brood of Nilus, watery heads with hearts of jelly, spawned under the sign of Aquarius, incapable of Bacchus, and therefore cold, washy, spiteful, bloodless.———Elia shall string them up one day, and show their colours—or rather how colourless and vapid the whole fry—when he putteth forth his long promised, but unaccountably hitherto delayed, Confessions of a Water-drinker.

A DISSERTATION UPON ROAST PIG.

MANKIND, says a Chinese manuscript, which my friend M. was obliging enough to read and explain to me, for the first seventy thousand ages ate their meat raw, clawing or biting it from the living animal, just as they do in Abyssinia to this day. This period is not obscurely hinted at by their great Confucius in the second chapter of his Mundane Mutations, where he designates a kind of golden age by the term Cho-fang, literally the Cooks' holyday. The manuscript goes on to say, that the art of roasting, or rather broiling (which I take to be the elder brother), was accidentally discovered in the manner following. The swine-herd, Ho-ti, having gone out into the woods one morning, as his manner was, to collect mast for his hogs, left his cottage in the care of his eldest son Bo-bo, a great lubberly boy, who being fond of playing with fire, as younkers of his age commonly are, let some sparks escape into a bundle of straw, which kindling quickly, spread the conflagration over every part of their poor mansion, till it was reduced to ashes. Together with the cottage (a sorry antediluvian makeshift of a building, you may think it), what was of much more importance, a fine litter of new-farrowed pigs, no less than nine in number, perished. China pigs have been esteemed a luxury all over the East from the remotest periods that we read of. Bobo was in the utmost consternation, as you may think, not so much for the sake of the tenement, which his father and he could easily build up again with a few dry branches, and the labour of an hour or two, at any time, as for the loss of the pigs. While he was thinking what he should say to his father, and wringing his hands over the smoking remnants of one of those untimely sufferers, an odour assailed his nostrils, unlike any scent which he had before experienced. What could it proceed from?—not from the burnt cottage—he had smelt that smell before—indeed this was by no means the first accident of the kind which had occurred through the negligence of this unlucky young fire-brand. Much less did it resemble that of any known herb, weed, or flower. A premonitory moistening at the same time overflowed his nether lip. He knew not what to think. He next stooped down to feel the pig, if there were any signs of life in it. He burnt his fingers, and to cool them he applied them in his booby fashion to his mouth. Some of the crumbs of the scorched skin had come away with his fingers, and for the first time in his life (in the world's life indeed, for before him no man had known it) he tasted—*crackling!* He stood in a posture of ideot wonder. Again he felt and fumbled at the pig. It did not burn him so much now, still he licked his fingers from a sort of habit. The truth at length broke into his slow understanding, that it was the pig that smelt so, and the pig that tasted so delicious; and, surrendering himself up to the new-born pleasure, he fell to tearing up whole handfuls of the scorched skin with the flesh next it, and was cramming it down his throat in his beastly fashion, when his sire entered amid the smoking rafters, armed with retributory cudgel, and finding how affairs stood, began to rain blows upon the young rogue's shoulders, as thick as hailstones, which Bo-bo heeded not any more than if they had been flies. The tickling pleasure, which he experienced in his lower regions, had rendered him quite callous to any inconveniences he might feel in those remote quarters. His father might lay on, but he could not beat him from his pig, till he had fairly made an end of it, when, becoming a little more sensible of his situation, something like the following dialogue ensued.

"You graceless whelp, what have you got there devouring? is it not enough that you have burnt me down three houses with your dog's tricks, and be hanged to you, but you must be eating fire, and I know not what—what have you got there, I say?"

"O father, the pig, the pig, do come and taste how nice the burnt pig eats."

The ears of Ho-ti tingled with horror. He cursed his son, and he cursed himself that ever he should beget a son that should eat burnt pig.

Bo-bo, whose scent was wonderfully sharpened since morning, soon raked out another pig, and fairly rending it asunder, thrust the lesser half by main force into the fists of Ho-ti, still shouting out "Eat, eat, eat the burnt pig, father, only taste —O Lord,"—with such-like barbarous ejaculations, cramming all the while as if he would choke.

Ho-ti trembled every joint while he grasped the abominable thing, wavering whether he should not put his son to death for an unnatural young monster, when the crackling scorching his fingers, as it had done his son's, and applying the same remedy to them, he in his turn tasted some of its flavour, which, make what sour mouths he would for a pretence, proved not altogether displeasing to him. In conclusion (for the manuscript here is a little tedious) both father and son fairly sate down to the mess, and never left off till they had dispatched all that remained of the litter.

Bo-bo was strictly enjoined not to let the secret escape, for the neighbours would certainly have stoned them for a couple of abominable wretches, who could think of improving upon the good meat which God had sent them. Nevertheless, strange stories got about. It was observed that Ho-ti's cottage was burnt down now more frequently than ever. Nothing but fires from this time forward. Some would break out in broad day, others in the night-time. As often as the sow farrowed, so sure was the house of Ho-ti to be in a blaze; and Ho-ti himself, which was the more remarkable, instead of chastising his son, seemed to grow more indulgent to him than ever. At length they were watched, the terrible mystery discovered, and father and son summoned to take their trial at Pekin, then an inconsiderable assize town. Evidence was given, the obnoxious food itself produced in court, and verdict about to be pronounced, when the foreman of the jury begged that some of the burnt pig, of which the culprits stood accused, might be handed into the box. He handled it, and they all handled it, and burning their fingers, as Bo-bo and his father had done before them, and nature prompting to each of them the same remedy, against the face of all the facts, and the clearest charge which judge had ever given,—to the surprise of the whole court, townsfolk, strangers, reporters, and all present, without leaving the box, or any manner of consultation whatever, they brought in a simultaneous verdict of Not Guilty.

The judge, who was a shrewd fellow, winked at the manifest iniquity of the decision; and, when the court was dismissed, went privily, and bought up all the pigs that could be had for love or money. In a few days his Lordship's town house was observed to be on fire. The thing took wing, and now there was nothing to be seen but fires in every direction. Fuel and pigs grew enormously dear all over the district. The insurance offices one and all shut up shop. People built slighter and slighter every day, until it was feared that the very science of architecture would in no long time be lost to the world. Thus this custom of firing houses continued, till in process of time, says my manuscript, a sage arose, like our Locke, who made a discovery, that the flesh of swine, or indeed of any other animal, might be cooked (*burnt*, as they called it) without the necessity of consuming a whole house to dress it. Then first began the rude form of a gridiron. Roasting by the string, or spit, came in a century or two later, I forget in whose dynasty. By such slow degrees, concludes the manuscript, do the most useful, and seemingly the most obvious arts, make their way among mankind.——

Without placing too implicit faith in the account above given, it must be agreed, that if a worthy pretext for so dangerous an experiment as setting houses on fire (especially in these days) could be assigned in favour of any culinary object, that pretext and excuse might be found in ROAST PIG.

Of all the delicacies in the whole *mundus edibilis*, I will maintain it to be the most delicate—*princeps obsoniorum*.

I speak not of your grown porkers —things between pig and pork—those hobbydehoys—but a young and tender suckling—under a moon old

—guiltless as yet of the stye—with no original speck of the *amor immunditiæ*, the hereditary failing of the first parent, yet manifest—his voice as yet not broken, but something between a childish treble, and a grumble—the mild forerunner, or *præludium*, of a grunt.

He must be roasted. I am not ignorant that our ancestors ate them seethed, or boiled—but what a sacrifice of the exterior tegument!

There is no flavour comparable, I will contend, to that of the crisp tawny, well-watched, not over-roasted, *crackling*, as it is well called—the very teeth are invited to their share of the pleasure at this banquet in overcoming the coy, brittle resistance—with the adhesive oleaginous—O call it not fat—but an indefinable sweetness growing up to it—the tender blossoming of fat—fat cropped in the bud—taken in the shoot—in the first innocence—the cream and quintessence of the child-pig's yet pure food——the lean, no lean, but a kind of animal manna—or, rather, fat and lean (if it must be so) so blended and running into each other, that both together make but one ambrosian result, or common substance.

Behold him, while he is doing—it seemeth rather a refreshing warmth, than a scorching heat, that he is so passive to. How equably he twirleth round the string!—Now he is just done. To see the extreme sensibility of that tender age, he hath wept out his pretty eyes—radiant jellies—shooting stars—

See him in the dish, his second cradle, how meek he lieth!—wouldst thou have had this innocent grow up to the grossness and indocility which too often accompany maturer swinehood? Ten to one he would have proved a glutton, a sloven, an obstinate, disagreeable animal—wallowing in all manner of filthy conversation—from these sins he is happily snatched away—

> *Ere sin could blight, or sorrow fade,*
> *Death came with timely care—*

his memory is odoriferous—no clown curseth, while his stomach half rejecteth, the rank bacon—no coalheaver bolteth him in reeking sausages—he hath a fair sepulchre in the grateful stomach of the judicious epicure—and for such a tomb might be content to die.

> He is the best of sapors——

Pine-apple is great. She is indeed almost too transcendant—a delight, if not sinful, yet so like to sinning, that really a tender-conscienced person would do well to pause—too ravishing for mortal taste, she woundeth and excoriateth the lips that approach her—like lovers' kisses, she biteth—she is a pleasure bordering on pain from the fierceness and insanity of her relish—but she stoppeth at the palate—she meddleth not with the appetite—and the coarsest hunger might barter her consistently for a mutton chop.

Pig—let me speak his praise—is no less provocative of the appetite, than he is satisfactory to the criticalness of the censorious palate. The strong man may batten on him, and the weakling refuseth not his mild juices.

Unlike to mankind's mixed characters, a bundle of virtues and vices, inexplicably intertwisted, and not to be unravelled without hazard, he is—good throughout. No part of him is better or worse than another. He helpeth, as far as his little means extend, all around. He is the least envious of banquets. He is all neighbours' fare.

I am one of those, who freely and ungrudgingly impart a share of the good things of this life which fall to their lot (few as mine are in this kind) to a friend. I protest I take as great an interest in my friend's pleasures, his relishes, and proper satisfactions, as in mine own. "Presents," I often say, "endear Absents." Hares, pheasants, partridges, snipes, barn-door chickens (those "tame villatic fowl"), capons, plovers, brawn, barrels of oysters, I dispense as freely as I receive them. I love to taste them, as it were, upon the tongue of my friend. But a stop must be put somewhere. One would not, like Lear, "give every thing." I make my stand upon pig. Methinks it is an ingratitude to the Giver of all good flavours, to extra-domiciliate, or send out of the house, slightingly, (under pretext of friendship, or I know not what) a blessing so particularly adapted, predestined, I may say, to my individual palate—it argues an insensibility.

I remember a touch of conscience in this kind at school. My good old aunt, who never parted from me at the end of a holiday without stuffing a sweet-meat, or some nice thing, into my pocket, had dismissed me one evening with a smoking plumb cake, fresh from the oven. In my way to school (it was over London bridge) a grey-headed old beggar saluted me (I have no doubt at this time of day that he was a counterfeit). I had no pence to console him with, and in the vanity of self-denial, and the very coxcombry of charity, school-boy-like, I made him a present of—the whole cake! I walked on a little, buoyed up, as one is on such occasions, with a sweet soothing of self-satisfaction; but before I had got to the end of the bridge, my better feelings returned, and I burst into tears, thinking how ungrateful I had been to my good aunt, to go and give her good gift away to a stranger, that I had never seen before, and who might be a bad man for aught I knew; and then I thought of the pleasure my aunt would be taking in thinking that I—I myself, and not another—would eat her nice cake—and what should I say to her the next time I saw her—how naughty I was to part with her pretty present—and the odour of that spicy cake came back upon my recollection, and the pleasure and the curiosity I had taken in seeing her make it, and her joy when she sent it to the oven, and how disappointed she would feel that I had never had a bit of it in my mouth at last—and I blamed my impertinent spirit of alms-giving, and out-of-place hypocrisy of goodness, and above all I wished never again to see the face of that insidious, good-for-nothing, old grey impostor.

Our ancestors were nice in their method of sacrificing these tender victims. We read of pigs whipt to death with something of a shock, as we hear of any other obselete custom. The age of discipline is gone by, or it would be curious to inquire (in a philosophical light merely) what effect this process might have towards intenerating and dulcifying a substance, naturally so mild and dulcet as the flesh of young pigs. It looks like refining a violet. Yet we should be cautious, while we condemn the inhumanity, how we censure the wisdom of the practice. It might impart a gusto—

I remember an hypothesis, argued upon by the young students, when I was at St. Omer s, and maintained with much learning and pleasantry on both sides, "Whether, supposing that the flavour of a pig who obtained his death by whipping (*per flagellationem extremam*) superadded a pleasure upon the palate of a man more intense, than any possible suffering we can conceive in the animal, is man justified in using that method of putting the animal to death?" I forget the decision.

His sauce should be considered. Decidedly, a few bread crumbs, done up with his liver and brains, and a dash of mild sage. But, banish, dear Mrs. Cook, I beseech you, the whole onion tribe. Barbecue your whole hogs to your palate, steep them in shalots, stuff them out with plantations of the rank and guilty garlick; you cannot poison them, or make them stronger than they are—but consider, he is a weakling—a flower.

ELIA.

A BACHELOR'S COMPLAINT OF THE BEHAVIOUR OF MARRIED PEOPLE.

As a single man, I have spent a good deal of my time in noting down the infirmities of Married People, to console myself for those superior pleasures, which they tell me I have lost by remaining as I am.

I cannot say that the quarrels of men and their wives ever made any great impression upon me, or had much tendency to strengthen in me those anti-social resolutions, which I took up long ago upon more substantial considerations. What oftenest offends me at the houses of married persons where I visit, is an error of quite a different description;—it is, that they are too loving.

Not too loving neither: that does not explain my meaning. Besides, why should that offend me? The very act of separating themselves from the rest of the world to have the fuller enjoyment of each other's society, implies that they prefer one another to all the world.

But what I complain of is, that they carry this preference so undisguisedly, they perk it up in the faces of us single people so shamelessly, you cannot be in their company a moment without being made to feel, by some indirect hint or open avowal, that *you* are not the object of this preference. Now there are some things which give no offence, while implied or taken for granted merely; but expressed, there is much offence in them. If a man were to accost the first homely-featured or plain-dressed young woman of his acquaintance, and tell her, bluntly, that she was not handsome or rich enough for him, and he could not marry her, he would deserve to be kicked for his ill manners; yet no less is implied in the fact, that having access and opportunity of putting the question to her, he has never yet thought fit to do it. The young woman understands this as clearly as if it were put into words; but no reasonable young woman would think of making this the ground of a quarrel. Just as little right have a married couple to tell me by speeches, and looks that are scarce less plain than speeches, that I am not the happy man,—the lady's choice. It is enough that I know I am not: I do not want this perpetual reminding.

The display of superior knowledge or riches may be made sufficiently mortifying; but these admit of a palliative. The knowledge which is brought out to insult me, may accidentally improve me; and in the rich man's houses and pictures,—his parks and gardens, I have a temporary usufruct at least. But the display of married happiness has none of these palliatives: it is throughout pure, unrecompensed, unqualified insult.

Marriage by its best title is a monopoly, and not of the least invidious sort. It is the cunning of most possessors of any exclusive privileges to keep their advantage as much out of sight as possible, that their less favoured neighbours, seeing little of the benefit, may the less be disposed to question the right. But these married monopolists thrust the most obnoxious part of their patent into our faces.

days, when he was "cherub Dicky."

What clipped his wings, or made it expedient that he should exchange the holy for the profane state; whether he had lost his good voice (his best recommendation to that office), like Sir John, "with hallooing and singing of anthems;" or whether he was adjudged to lack something, even in those early years, of the gravity indispensable to an occupation which professeth to "commerce with the skies"—I could never rightly learn; but we find him, after the probation of a twelvemonth or so, reverting to a secular condition, and become one of us.

I think he was not altogether of that timber, out of which cathedral seats and sounding boards are hewed. But if a glad heart—kind and therefore glad—be any part of sanctity, then might the robe of Motley, with which he invested himself with so much humility after his deprivation, and which he wore so long with so much blameless satisfaction to himself and to the public, be accepted for a surplice—his white stole, and *albe*.

The first fruits of his secularization was an engagement upon the boards of Old Drury, at which theatre he commenced, as I have been told, with adopting the manner of Parsons in old men's characters. At the period in which most of us knew him, he was no more an imitator than he was in any true sense himself imitable.

He was the Robin Good-Fellow of the stage. He came in to trouble all things with a welcome perplexity, himself no whit troubled for the matter. He was known, like Puck, by his note—*Ha! Ha! Ha!*—sometimes deepening to *Ho! Ho! Ho!* with an irresistible accession, derived perhaps remotely from his ecclesiastical education, foreign to his prototype, of—*O La!* Thousands of hearts yet respond to the chuckling *O La!* of Dicky Suett, brought back to their remembrance by the faithful transcript of his friend Mathews's mimicry. The "force of nature could no further go." He drolled upon the stock of these two syllables richer than the cuckoo.

Care, that troubles all the world, was forgotten in his composition. Had he had but two grains (nay, half a grain) of it, he could never have supported himself upon those two spider's strings, which served him (in the latter part of his unmixed existence) as legs. A doubt or a scruple must have made him totter, a sigh have puffed him down; the weight of a frown had staggered him, a wrinkle made him lose his balance. But on he went, scrambling upon those airy stilts of his, with Robin Good-Fellow, "thorough brake, thorough briar," reckless of a scratched face or a torn doublet.

Shakspeare foresaw him, when he framed his fools and jesters. They have all the true Suett stamp, a loose gait, a slippery tongue, this last the ready midwife to a without-pain-delivered jest; in words light as air, venting truths deep as the centre; with idlest rhymes tagging conceit when busiest, singing with Lear in the tempest, or Sir Toby at the buttery hatch.

Jack Bannister and he had the fortune to be more of personal favourites with the town than any actors before or after. The difference, I take it, was this:—Jack was more *beloved* for his sweet, good-natured, moral, pretensions. Dicky was more *liked* for his sweet, good-natured, no pretensions at all. Your whole conscience stirred with Bannister's performance of Walter in the Children in the Wood—how dearly beautiful it was!—but Dicky seemed like a thing, as Shakspeare says of Love, too young to know what conscience is. He put us into Vesta's days. Evil fled before him—not as from Jack, as from an antagonist,—but because it could not touch him, any more than a cannon-ball a fly. He was delivered from the burthen of that death; and, when Death came himself, not in metaphor, to fetch Dicky, it is recorded of him by Robert Palmer, who kindly watched his exit, that he received the last stroke, neither varying his accustomed tranquillity, nor tune, with the simple exclamation, worthy to have been recorded in his epitaph—*O La! —O La! Bobby!*

MR. MUNDEN.

Not many nights ago we had come home from seeing this extraordinary performer in Cockletop; and when we retired to our pillow, his whimsical image still stuck by us, in a manner as to threaten sleep. In vain we tried to divest ourselves of it by conjuring up the most opposite associations. We resolved to be serious. We raised up the gravest topics of life; private misery, public calamity. All would not do.

——— There the antic sate
Mocking our state—

his queer visnomy—his bewildering costume—all the strange things which he had raked together—his serpentine rod swagging about in his pocket—Cleopatra's tear, and the rest of his relics—O'Keefe's wild farce, and *his* wilder commentary—till the passion of laughter, like grief in excess, relieved itself by its own weight, inviting the sleep which in the first instance it had driven away.

But we were not to escape so easily. No sooner did we fall into slumbers, than the same image, only more perplexing, assailed us in the shape of dreams. Not one Munden, but five hundred, were dancing before us, like the faces which, whether you will or no, come when you have been taking opium—all the strange combinations, which this strangest of all strange mortals ever shot his proper countenance into, from the day he came commissioned to dry up the tears of the town for the loss of the now almost forgotten Edwin. O for the power of the pencil to have fixed them when we awoke! A season or two since there was exhibited a Hogarth gallery. We do not see why there should not be a Munden gallery. In richness and variety the latter would not fall far short of the former.

There is one face of Farley, one face of Knight, one face (but what a one it is!) of Liston; but Munden has none that you can properly pin down, and call *his*. When you think he has exhausted his battery of looks, in unaccountable warfare with your gravity, suddenly he sprouts out an entirely new set of features, like Hydra. He is not one, but legion. Not so much a comedian, as a company. If his name could be multiplied like his countenance, it might fill a play-bill. He, and he alone, literally *makes faces*: applied to any other person, the phrase is a mere figure, denoting certain modifications of the human countenance. Out of some invisible wardrobe he dips for faces, as his friend Suett used for wigs, and fetches them out as easily. We should not be surprised to see him some day put out the head of a river horse; or come forth a pewit, or lapwing, some feathered metamorphosis.

We have seen this gifted actor in Sir Christopher Curry—in Old Dornton—diffuse a glow of sentiment which has made the pulse of a crowded theatre beat like that of one man; when he has come in aid of the pulpit, doing good to the moral heart of a people. We have seen some faint approaches to this sort of excellence in other players. But in what has been truly denominated the "sublime of farce," Munden stands out as single and unaccompanied as Hogarth. Hogarth, strange to tell, had no followers. The school of Munden began, and must end, with himself.

Can any man *wonder*, like him? can any man *see ghosts*, like him? or *fight with his own shadow*—sessa—as he does in that strangely-neglected thing, the Cobler of Preston—where his alternations from the Cobler to the Magnifico, and from the Magnifico to the Cobler, keep the brain of the spectator in as wild a ferment, as if some Arabian Night were being acted before him, or as if Thalaba were no tale! Who like him can throw, or ever attempted to throw, a supernatural interest over the commonest daily-life objects? A table, or a joint stool, in his conception, rises into a dignity equivalent to Cassiopeia's chair. It is invested with constellatory importance. You could not speak of it with more deference, if it were mounted into the firmament. A beggar in the hands of Michael Angelo, says Fuseli, rose the Patriarch of Poverty. So the gusto of Munden antiquates and ennobles what it touches. His pots and his ladles are as grand and primal as the seething-pots and hooks seen in old prophetic vision. A tub of butter, contemplated by him, amounts to a Platonic idea. He understands a leg of mutton in its quiddity. He stands wondering, amid the commonplace materials of life, like primæval man, with the sun and stars about him.

Elia.

MODERN GALLANTRY.

In comparing modern with ancient manners, we are pleased to compliment ourselves upon the point of gallantry, as upon a thing altogether unknown to the old classic ages. This has been defined to consist in a certain obsequiousness, or deferential respect, paid to females, as females.

I shall believe that this principle actuates our conduct, when I can forget, that in the nineteenth century of the era, from which we date our civility, we are but just beginning to leave off the very frequent practice of whipping females in public, in common with the coarsest male offenders.

I shall believe it to be influential, when I can shut my eyes to the fact, that in England women are still occasionally—hanged.

I shall believe in it, when actresses are no longer subject to be hissed off a stage by gentlemen.

I shall believe in it, when Dorimant hands a fish-wife across the kennel; or assists the apple-woman to pick up her wandering fruit, which some unlucky dray has just dissipated.

I shall believe in it, when the Dorimants in humbler life, who would be thought in their way notable adepts in this refinement, shall act upon it in places where they are not known, or think themselves not observed—when I shall see the traveller for some rich tradesman part with his admired box coat, to spread it over the defenceless shoulders of the poor woman, who is passing to her parish on the roof of the same stage-coach with him, drenched in the rain—when I shall no longer see a woman standing up in the pit of a London theatre, till she is sick and faint with the exertion, with men about her, seated at their ease, and jeering at her distress; till one, that seems to have more manners or conscience than the rest, significantly declares "she should be welcome to his seat, if she were a little younger and handsomer." Place this dapper warehouseman, or that rider, in a circle of their own female acquaintance, and you shall confess you have not seen a politer-bred man in Lothbury.

Lastly, I shall begin to believe that there is some such principle, influencing our conduct, when more than one half of the drudgery and coarse servitude of the world shall cease to be performed by women.

Until that day comes, I shall never believe this boasted point to be any thing more than a conventional fiction; a pageant got up between the sexes, in a certain rank, and at a certain time of life, in which both find their account equally.

I shall be even disposed to rank it among the salutary fictions of life, when in polite circles I shall see the same attentions paid to age as to youth, to homely features as to handsome, to coarse complexions as to clear—to the woman, as she is a woman, not as she is a beauty, a fortune, or a title.

I shall believe it to be something more than a name, when a well-dressed gentleman in a well-dressed company can advert to the topic of *female old age* without exciting, and intending to excite a sneer:—when the phrases "antiquated virginity," and such a one has "overstaid her market," pronounced in good company, shall raise immediate offence in man, or woman, that shall hear them spoken.

Joseph Paice, of Bread-street-hill, merchant, and one of the Directors of the South Sea company—the same to whom Edwards, the Shakspeare commentator, has addressed a fine sonnet—was the only pattern of consistent gallantry I have met with. He took me under his shelter at an early age, and bestowed some pains upon me. I owe to his precepts and example whatever there is of the man of business (and that is not much) in my composition. It was not his fault that I did not profit more. Though bred a Presbyterian, and brought up a merchant, he was the finest gentleman of his time. He had not *one* system of attention to females in the drawing room, and *another* in the shop, or at the stall. I do not mean that he made no distinction. But he never lost sight of sex, or overlooked it in the casualties of a disadvantageous situation. I have seen him stand bare-headed—smile, if you please—to a poor servant girl, while she has been inquiring of him the way to some street—in such a posture of unforced civility, as neither to embarrass her in the acceptance, nor himself in the offer, of it. He was no dangler, in the common acceptation of the word, after women: but he reverenced and upheld, in every form in which it came before him, *womanhood.* I have seen him—nay, smile not—tenderly escorting a market-woman, whom he had encountered in a shower, exalting his umbrella over her poor basket of fruit, that it might receive no damage, with as much carefulness as if she had been a Countess. To the reverend form of Female Eld he would yield the wall (though it were to an ancient beggar-woman) with more ceremony than we can afford to show our grandams. He was the Preux Chevalier of Age; the Sir Calidore, or Sir Tristan, to those who have no Calidores or Tristans to defend them. The roses, that had long faded thence, still bloomed for him in those withered and yellow cheeks.

He was never married, but in his youth he paid his addresses to the beautiful Susan Winstanley — old Winstanley's daughter of Clapton—who dying in the early days of their courtship, confirmed in him the resolution of perpetual bachelorship. It was during their short courtship, he told me, that he had been one day treating his mistress with a profusion of civil speeches—the common gallantries—to which kind of thing she had hitherto manifested no repugnance—but in this instance with no effect. He could not obtain from her a decent acknowledgment in return. She rather seemed to resent his compliments. He could not set it down to caprice, for the lady had always shown herself above that littleness. When he ventured on the following day, finding her a little better humoured, to expostulate with her on her coldness of yesterday, she confessed, with her usual frankness, that she had no sort of dislike to his attentions; that she could even endure some high-flown compliments; that a young woman placed in her situation had a right to expect all sort of civil things said to her; that she hoped, she could digest a dose of adulation, short of insincerity, with as little injury to her humility as most young women: but that—a little before he had commenced his compliments—she had overheard him by accident, in rather rough language, rating a young woman, who had not brought home his cravats quite to the appointed time, and she thought to herself, "As I am Miss Susan Winstanley, and a young lady—a reputed beauty, and known to be a fortune,—I can have my choice of the finest speeches from the mouth of this very fine gentleman who is courting me—but if I had been poor Mary Such-a-one, (*naming the milliner*)—and had failed of bringing home the cravats to the appointed hour—though perhaps I had sat up half the night to forward them—what sort of compliments should I have received then?—And my woman's pride came to my assistance; and I thought, that if it were only to do *me* honour, a female, like myself, might have received handsomer usage: and I was determined not to accept any fine speeches, to the compromise of that sex, the belonging to which was after all my strongest claim and title to them."

I think the lady discovered both generosity, and a just way of thinking, in this rebuke which she gave her lover; and I have sometimes imagined, that the uncommon strain of courtesy, which through life regulated the actions and behaviour of my friend towards all of womankind indiscriminately, owed its happy origin to this seasonable lesson from the lips of his lamented mistress.

I wish the whole female world would entertain the same notion of these things, that Miss Winstanley showed. Then we should see something of the spirit of consistent gallantry; and no longer witness the anomaly of the same man—a pattern of true politeness to a wife—of cold contempt, or rudeness, to a sister—the idolater of his female mistress—the disparager and despiser of his no less female aunt, or unfortunate—still female—maiden cousin. Just so much respect as a woman derogates from her own sex, in whatever condition placed—her handmaid, or dependant—she deserves to have diminished from herself on that score; and probably will feel the diminution, when youth, and beauty, and advantages, not inseparable from sex, shall lose of their attraction. What a woman should demand of a man in courtship, or after it, is first—respect for her as she is a woman;—and next to that—to be respected by him above all other women. But let her stand upon her female character, as upon a foundation; and let the attentions, incident to individual preference, be so many pretty additaments, and ornaments—as many, and as fanciful, as you please—to that main structure. Let her first lesson be—with sweet Susan Winstanley—to *reverence her sex*.

ELIA.

THE GENTLE GIANTESS.

The widow Blacket, of Oxford, is the largest female I ever had the pleasure of beholding. There may be her parallel upon the earth, but surely I never saw it. I take her to be lineally descended from the maid's aunt of Brainford, who caused Master Ford such uneasiness. She hath Atlantean shoulders; and, as she stoopeth in her gait—with as few offences to answer for in her own particular as any of Eve's daughters—her back seems broad enough to bear the blame of all the peccadillos that have been committed since Adam. She girdeth her waist—or what she is pleased to esteem as such—nearly up to her shoulders, from beneath which, that huge dorsal expanse, in mountainous declivity, emergeth. Respect for her alone preventeth the idle boys, who follow her about in shoals, whenever she cometh abroad, from getting up and riding.—But her presence infallibly commands a reverence. She is indeed, as the Americans would express it, something awful. Her person is a burthen to herself, no less than to the ground which bears her. To her mighty bone, she hath a pinguitude withal, which makes the depth of winter to her the most desirable season. Her distress in the warmer solstice is pitiable. During the months of July and August, she usually renteth a cool cellar, where ices are kept, whereinto she descendeth when Sirius rageth. She dates from a hot Thursday—some twenty-five years ago. Her apartment in summer is pervious to the four winds. Two doors, in north and south direction, and two windows, fronting the rising and the setting sun, never closed, from every cardinal point, catch the contributory breezes. She loves to enjoy what she calls a quadruple draught. That must be a shrewd zephyr, that can escape her. I owe a painful face-ach, which oppresses me at this moment, to a cold caught, sitting by her, one day in last July, at this receipt of coolness. Her fan in ordinary resembleth a banner spread, which she keepeth continually on the alert to detect the least breeze. She possesseth an active and gadding mind, totally incommensurate with her person. No one delighteth more than herself in country exercises and pastimes. I have passed many an agreeable holiday with her in her favourite park at Woodstock. She performs her part in these delightful ambulatory excursions by the aid of a portable garden chair. She setteth out with you at a fair foot gallop, which she keepeth up till you are both well breathed, and then she reposeth for a few seconds. Then she is up again, for a hundred paces or so, and again resteth—her movement, on these sprightly occasions, being something between walking and flying. Her great weight seemeth to propel her forward, ostrich-fashion. In this kind of relieved marching I have traversed with her many scores of acres on those well-wooded and well-watered domains. Her delight at Oxford is in the public walks and gardens, where, when the weather is not too oppressive, she passeth much of her valuable time. There is a bench at Maudlin, or rather, situated between the frontiers of that and ******'s college——some litigation latterly, about repairs, has vested the property of it finally in ******'s—where at the hour of noon she is ordinarily to be found sitting—so she calls it by courtesy—but in fact, pressing and breaking of it down with her enormous settlement; as both those Foundations, who, however, are good-natured enough to wink at it, have found, I believe, to their cost. Here she taketh the fresh air, principally at vacation times, when the walks are freest from interruption of the younger fry of students. Here she passeth her idle hours, not idly, but generally accompanied with a book—blest if she can but intercept some resident Fellow (as usually there are some of that brood left behind at these periods); or stray Master of Arts (to most of whom she is better known than their dinner bell); with whom she may confer upon any curious topic of literature. I have seen these shy gownsmen, who truly set but a very slight value upon female conversation, cast a hawk's eye upon her from the length of Maudlin grove, and warily glide off into another walk—true monks as they are, and ungently neglecting the delicacies of her polished converse, for their own perverse and uncommunicating solitariness! Within doors her principal diversion is music, vocal and instrumental, in both which she is no mean professor. Her voice is wonderfully fine; but till I got used to it, I confess it staggered me. It is for all the world like that of a piping bulfinch, while from her size and stature you would expect notes to drown the deep organ. The shake, which most fine singers reserve for the close or cadence, by some unaccountable flexibility, or tremulousness of pipe, she carrieth quite through the composition; so that her time, to a common air or ballad, keeps double motion, like the earth—running the primary circuit of the tune, and still revolving upon its own axis. The effect, as I said before, when you are used to it, is as agreeable as it is altogether new and surprising. The spacious apartment of her outward frame lodgeth a soul in all respects disproportionate. Of more than mortal make, she evinceth withal a trembling sensibility, a yielding infirmity of purpose, a quick susceptibility to reproach, and all the train of diffident and blushing virtues, which for their habitation usually seek out a feeble frame, an attenuated and meagre constitution. With more than man's bulk, her humours and occupations are eminently feminine. She sighs—being six foot high. She languisheth—being two feet wide. She worketh slender sprigs upon the delicate muslin—her fingers being capable of moulding a Colossus. She sippeth her wine out of her glass daintily—her capacity being that of a tun of Heidelburg. She goeth mincingly with those feet of hers—whose solidity need not fear the black ox's pressure. Softest, and largest of thy sex, adieu! by what parting attribute may I salute thee—last and best of the Titanesses—Ogress, fed with milk instead of blood—not least, or least handsome, among Oxford's stately structures—Oxford, who, in its deadest time of vacation, can never properly be said to be empty, having thee to fill it.

ELIA.

THE

London Magazine.

JANUARY, 1823.

REJOICINGS UPON THE NEW YEAR'S COMING OF AGE.

THE *Old Year* being dead, and the *New Year* coming of age, which he does, by Calendar Law, as soon as the breath is out of the old gentleman's body, nothing would serve the young spark but he must give a dinner upon the occasion, to which all the *Days* in the year were invited. The *Festivals*, whom he deputed as his Stewards, were mightily taken with the notion. They had been engaged time out of mind, they said, in providing mirth and good cheer for mortals below; and it was time they should have a taste of their own bounty. It was stiffly debated among them, whether the *Fasts* should be admitted. Some said, the appearance of such lean, starved guests, with their mortified faces, would pervert the ends of the meeting. But the objection was overruled by *Christmas Day*, who had a design upon *Ash Wednesday* (as you shall hear), and a mighty desire to see how the old Domine would behave himself in his cups. Only the *Vigils* were requested to come with their lanterns, to light the gentlefolks home at night.

All the *Days* came to their day. Covers were provided for three hundred and sixty-five guests at the principal table; with an occasional knife and fork at the side-board for the *Twenty-Ninth of February*.

I should have told you, that cards of invitation had been issued. The carriers were the *Hours*; twelve little, merry, whirligig foot-pages, as you should desire to see, that went all round, and found out the persons invited well enough, with the exception of *Easter Day*, *Shrove Tuesday*, and a few such *Moveables*, who had lately shifted their quarters.

Well, they all met at last, foul *Days*, fine *Days*, all sorts of *Days*, and a rare din they made of it. There was nothing but, Hail! fellow *Day*, well met—brother *Day*—sister *Day*,—only *Lady Day* kept a little on the aloof, and seemed somewhat scornful. Yet some said, *Twelfth Day* cut her out and out, for she came in a tiffany suit, white and gold, like a Queen on a frost-cake, all royal, glittering, and *Epiphanous*. The rest came, some in green, some in white—but old *Lent and his family* were not yet out of mourning. Rainy *Days* came in, dripping; and sunshiny *Days* helped them to change their stockings. *Wedding Day* was there in his marriage finery, a little the worse for wear; *Pay Day* came late, as he always does; and *Doomsday* sent word—he might be expected.

April Fool (as my young lord's jester) took upon himself to marshal the guests, and wild work he made with it. It would have posed old Erra Pater to have found out any given *Day* in the year, to erect a scheme upon—good *Days*, bad *Days*, were so shuffled together, to the confounding of all sober horoscopy.

He had stuck the *Twenty First of June* next to the *Twenty Second of December*, and the former looked like a Maypole siding a marrow-bone. *Ash Wednesday* got wedged in (as was concerted) betwixt *Christmas* and *Lord Mayor's Days*. Lord! how he laid about him! Nothing but barons of beef and turkeys would go down with him—to the great greasing and detriment of his new sackcloth bib and tucker. And still *Christmas Day* was at his elbow, plying him with the wassail-bowl, till he roared, and hiccup'd, and protested there was no faith in dried ling, but commended it to the devil for a sour, windy, acrimonious, censorious, hypo-crit-crit-critical mess, and no dish for a gentleman. Then he dipt his fist into the middle of the great custard that stood before his *left-hand neighbour*, and daubed his hungry beard all over with it, till you would have taken him for the *Last Day in December*, it so hung in icicles.

At another part of the table, *Shrove Tuesday* was helping the *Second of September* to some cock broth,—which courtesy the latter returned with the delicate thigh of a hen pheasant—so there was no love lost for that matter. The *Last of Lent* was spunging upon *Shrovetide's* pancakes; which *April Fool* perceiving, told him he did well, for pancakes were proper to a *good fry-day*.

In another part, a hubbub arose about the *Thirtieth of January*, who, it seems, being a sour puritanic character, that thought nobody's meat good or sanctified enough for him, had smuggled into the room a calves' head, which he had had cooked at home for that purpose, thinking to feast thereon incontinently; but as it lay in the dish, *March Manyweathers*, who is a very fine lady, and subject to the megrims, suddenly screamed out there was a "human head in the platter," and raved about Herodias' daughter to that degree, that the obnoxious viand was obliged to be removed; nor did she recover her stomach till she had gulped down a *Restorative*, confected of *Oak Apple*, which the merry *Twenty Ninth of May* always carries about with him for that purpose.

The King's health being called for after this, a notable dispute arose between the *Twelfth of August* (a zealous old Whig gentlewoman), and the *Twenty Third of April* (a new-fangled lady of the Tory stamp), as to which of them should have the honour to propose it. *August* grew hot upon the matter, affirming time out of mind the prescriptive right to have lain with her, till her rival had basely supplanted her; whom she represented as little better than a *kept* mistress, who went about in *fine clothes*, while she (the legitimate BIRTHDAY) had scarcely a rag, &c.

April Fool, being made mediator, confirmed the right in the strongest form of words to the appellant, but decided for peace' sake that the exercise of it should remain with the present possessor. At the same time, he slily rounded the first lady in the ear, that an action might lie against the Crown for *bi-geny*.

It beginning to grow a little duskish, *Candlemas* lustily bawled out for lights, which was opposed by all the *Days*, who protested against burning day-light. Then fair water was handed round in silver ewers, and the *same lady* was observed to take an unusual time in *washing* herself.

May Day, with that sweetness which is peculiar to her, in a neat speech proposing the health of the founder, crowned her goblet (and by her example the rest of the company) with garlands. This being done, the lordly *New Year* from the upper end of the table, in a cordial but somewhat lofty tone, returned thanks. He felt proud on an occasion of meeting so many of his worthy father's late tenants, promised to improve their farms, and at the same time to abate (if any thing was found unreasonable) in their rents.

At the mention of this, the four *Quarter Days* involuntarily looked at each other, and smiled; *April Fool* whistled to an old tune of "New Brooms;" and a surly old rebel at the farther end of the table (who was discovered to be no other than the *Fifth of November*), muttered out, distinctly enough to be heard by the whole company, words to this effect, that, "when the old one is gone, he is a fool that looks for a better." Which rudeness of his the guests resenting, unanimously voted his expulsion; and the male-content was thrust out neck and heels into the cellar, as the properest place for such a *boutefeu* and firebrand as he had shown himself.

Order being restored—the young lord (who, to say truth, had been a little ruffled, and put beside his oratory) in as few, and yet as obliging words as possible, assured them of entire welcome; and, with a graceful turn, singling out poor *Twenty Ninth of February*, that had sate all this while mum-chance at the side-board, begged to couple his health with that of the good company before him—which he drank accordingly; observing, that he had not seen his honest face any time these four years, with a number of endearing expressions besides. At the same time, removing the solitary *Day* from the forlorn seat which had been assigned him, he stationed him at his own board, somewhere between the *Greek Calends* and *Latter Lammas*.

Ash Wednesday, being now called upon for a song, with his eyes fast stuck in his head, and as well as the Canary he had swallowed would give him leave, struck up a Carol, which *Christmas Day* had taught him for the nonce; and was followed by the latter, who gave "Miserere" in fine style, hitting off the mumping tones and lengthened drawl of *Old Mortification* with infinite humour. *April Fool* swore they had exchanged conditions: but *Good Friday* was observed to look extremely grave; and *Sunday* held her fan before her face, that she might not be seen to smile.

Shrove-tide, Lord Mayor's Day, and *April Fool*, next joined in a glee—

Which is the properest day to drink?

in which all the *Days* chiming in, made a merry burden.

They next fell to quibbles and conundrums. The question being proposed, who had the greatest number of followers—the *Quarter Days* said, there could be no question as to that; for they had all the creditors in the world dogging their heels. But *April Fool* gave it in favour of the *Forty Days before Easter*; because the debtors in all cases out-numbered the creditors, and they kept *lent* all the year.

All this while, *Valentine's Day* kept courting pretty *May*, who sate next him, slipping amorous *billets-doux* under the table, till the *Dog Days* (who are naturally of a warm constitution,) began to be jealous, and to bark and rage exceedingly. *April Fool*, who likes a bit of sport above measure, and had some pretensions to the lady besides, as being but a cousin once removed,—clapped and halloo'd them on; and as fast as their indignation cooled, those mad wags, the *Ember Days*, were at it with their bellows, to blow it into a flame; and all was in a ferment: till old Madam *Septuagesima* (who boasts herself the *Mother of the Days*) wisely diverted the conversation with a tedious tale of the lovers which she could reckon when she was young; and of one Master *Rogation Day* in particular, who was for ever putting the *question* to her, but she kept him at a distance, as the chronicle would tell—by which I apprehend she meant the Almanack. Then she rambled on to the *Days that were gone*, the *good old Days*, and so to the *Days before the Flood*—which plainly showed her old head to be little better than crazed and doited.

Day being ended, the *Days* called for their cloaks and great coats, and took their leaves. *Lord Mayor's Day* went off in a Mist, as usual; *Shortest Day* in a deep black Fog, that wrapt the little gentleman all round like a hedge-hog. Two *Vigils*—so watchmen are called in heaven—saw *Christmas Day* safe home—they had been used to the business before. Another *Vigil*—a stout, sturdy patrole, called the *Eve of St. Christopher*—seeing *Ash Wednesday* in a condition little better than he should be, e'en whipt him over his shoulders, pick-a-back fashion, and *Old Mortification* went floating home, singing—

On the bat's back do I fly,

and a number of old snatches besides, between drunk and sober, but very few Aves or Penitentiaries (you may believe me) were among them. *Longest Day* set off westward in beautiful crimson and gold—the rest, some in one fashion, some in another; —but *Valentine* and pretty *May* took their departure together in one of the prettiest silvery twilights a Lover's Day would wish to set in.

Elia's Ghost.

A CHARACTER OF THE LATE ELIA,

BY A FRIEND.

This gentleman, who for some months past had been in a declining way, hath at length paid his final tribute to nature. He just lived long enough (it was what he wished) to see his papers collected into a volume. The pages of the London Magazine will henceforth know him no more.

Exactly at twelve last night his queer spirit departed, and the bells of Saint Bride's rang him out with the old year. The mournful vibrations were caught in the dining room of his friends T. and H.; and the company, assembled there to welcome in another First of January, checked their carousals in mid-mirth, and were silent. Janus wept. The gentle P———r, in a whisper, signified his intention of devoting an Elegy; and Allan C———, nobly forgetful of his countrymen's wrongs, vowed a Memoir to his *manes*, full and friendly as a Tale of Lyddalcross.

To say truth, it is time he were gone. The humour of the thing, if there was ever much in it, was pretty well exhausted; and a two years' and a half existence has been a tolerable duration for a phantom.

I am now at liberty to confess, that much which I have heard objected to my late friend's writings was well-founded. Crude they are, I grant you—a sort of unlicked, incondite things—villainously pranked in an affected array of antique modes and phrases. They had not been *his*, if they had been other than such; and better it is, that a writer should be natural in a self-pleasing quaintness, than to affect a naturalness (so called) that should be strange to him. Egotistical they have been pronounced by some who did not know, that what he tells us, as of himself, was often true only (historically) of another; as in his Fourth Essay (to save many instances)—where under the *first person* (his favourite figure) he shadows forth the forlorn estate of a country-boy placed at a London school, far from his friends and connections—in direct opposition to his own early history.—If it be egotism to imply and twine with his own identity the griefs and affections of another—making himself many, or reducing many unto himself—then is the skilful novelist, who all along brings in his hero, or heroine, speaking of themselves, the greatest egotist of all; who yet has never, therefore, been accused of that narrowness. And how shall the intenser dramatist escape being faulty, who doubtless, under cover of passion uttered by another, oftentimes gives blameless vent to his most inward feelings, and expresses his own story modestly?

My late friend was in many respects a singular character. Those who did not like him, hated him; and some, who once liked him, afterwards became his bitterest haters. The truth is, he gave himself too little concern what he uttered, and in whose presence. He observed neither time nor place, and would e'en out with what came uppermost. With the severe religionist he would pass for a free-thinker; while the other faction set him down for a bigot, or persuaded themselves that he belied his sentiments. Few understood him; and I am not certain that at all times he quite understood himself. He too much affected that dangerous figure—irony. He sowed doubtful speeches, and reaped plain, unequivocal hatred.—He would interrupt the gravest discussion with some light jest; and yet, perhaps, not quite irrelevant in ears that could understand it. Your long and much talkers hated him. The informal habit of his mind, joined to an inveterate impediment of speech, forbade him to be an orator; and he seemed determined that no one else should play that part when he was present. He was *petit* and ordinary in his person and appearance. I have seen him sometimes in what is called good company, but where he has been a stranger, sit silent, and be suspected for an odd fellow; till some unlucky occasion provoking it, he would stutter out some senseless pun (not altogether senseless perhaps, if rightly taken), which has stamped his character for the evening. It was hit or miss with him; but nine times out of ten, he contrived by this device to send away a whole company his enemies. His conceptions rose kindlier than his utterance, and his happiest *impromptus* had the appearance of effort. He has been accused of trying to be witty, when in truth he was but struggling to give his poor thoughts articulation. He chose his companions for some individuality of character which they manifested.—Hence, not many persons of science, and few professed *literati*, were of his councils. They were, for the most part, persons of an uncertain fortune; and, as to such people commonly nothing is more obnoxious than a gentleman of settled (though moderate) income, he passed with most of them for a great miser. To my knowledge this was a mistake. His *intimados*, to confess a truth, were in the world's eye a ragged regiment. He found them floating on the surface of society; and the colour, or something else, in the weed pleased him. The burrs stuck to him—but they were good and loving burrs for all that. He never greatly cared for the society of what are called good people. If any of these were scandalised (and offences were sure to arise), he could not help it. When he has been remonstrated with for not making more concessions to the feelings of good people, he would retort by asking, what one point did these good people ever concede to him? He was temperate in his meals and diversions, but always kept a little on this side of abstemiousness. Only in the use of the Indian weed he might be thought a little excessive. He took it, he would say, as a solvent of speech. Marry—as the friendly vapour ascended, how his prattle would curl up sometimes with it! the ligaments, which tongue-tied him, were loosened, and the stammerer proceeded a statist!

I do not know whether I ought to bemoan or rejoice that my old friend is departed. His jests were beginning to grow obsolete, and his stories to be found out. He felt the approaches of age; and while he pretended to cling to life, you saw how slender were the ties left to bind him. Discoursing with him latterly on this subject, he expressed himself with a pettishness, which I thought unworthy of him. In our walks about his suburban retreat (as he called it) at Shacklewell, some children belonging to a school of industry had met us, and bowed and curtseyed, as he thought, in an especial manner to *him*. "They take me for a visiting governor," he muttered earnestly. He had a horror, which he carried to a foible, of looking like any thing important and parochial. He thought that he approached nearer to that stamp daily. He had a general aversion from being treated like a grave or respectable character, and kept a wary eye upon the advances of age that should so entitle him. He herded always, while it was possible, with people younger than himself. He did not conform to the march of time, but was dragged along in the procession. His manners lagged behind his years. He was too much of the boy-man. The *toga virilis* never sate gracefully on his shoulders. The impressions of infancy had burnt into him, and he resented the impertinence of manhood. These were weaknesses; but such as they were, they are a key to explicate some of his writings.

He left little property behind him. Of course, the little that is left (chiefly in India bonds) devolves upon his cousin Bridget. A few critical dissertations were found in his escrutoire, which have been handed over to the Editor of this Magazine, in which it is to be hoped they will shortly appear, retaining his accustomed signature.

He has himself not obscurely hinted that his employment lay in a public office. The gentlemen in the Export department of the East India House will forgive me, if I acknowledge the readiness with which they assisted me in the retrieval of his few manuscripts. They pointed out in a most obliging manner the desk, at which he had been planted for forty years; showed me ponderous tomes of figures, in his own remarkably neat hand, which, more properly than his few printed tracts, might be called his "Works." They seemed affectionate to his memory, and universally commended his expertness in book-keeping. It seems he was the inventor of some ledger, which should combine the precision and certainty of the Italian double-entry (I think they called it) with the brevity and facility of some newer German system—but I am not able to appreciate the worth of the discovery. I have often heard him express a warm regard for his associates in office, and how fortunate he considered himself in having his lot thrown in amongst them. There is more sense, more discourse, more shrewdness, and even talent, among these clerks (he would say) than in twice the number of authors by profession that I have conversed with. He would brighten up sometimes upon the "old days of the India House," when he consorted with Woodroffe, and Wissett, and Peter Corbet (a descendant and worthy representative, bating the point of sanctity, of old facetious bishop Corbet), and Hoole who translated Tasso, and Bartlemy Brown whose father (God assoil him therefore) modernized Walton—and sly warm-hearted old Jack Cole (King Cole they called him in those days), and Campe, and Fombelle—and a world of choice spirits, more than I can remember to name, who associated in those days with Jack Burrell (the *bon vivant* of the South Sea House), and little Eyton (said to be a *fac simile* of Pope—he was a miniature of a gentleman) that was cashier under him, and Dan Voight of the Custom House that left the famous library.

Well, Elia is gone—for aught I know, to be reunited with them—and these poor traces of his pen are all we have to show for it. How little survives of the wordiest authors! Of all they said or did in their lifetime, a few glittering words only! His Essays found some favourers, as they appeared separately; they shuffled their way in the crowd well enough singly; how they will *read*, now they are brought together, is a question for the publishers, who have thus ventured to draw out into one piece his "weaved-up follies."

PHIL-ELIA.

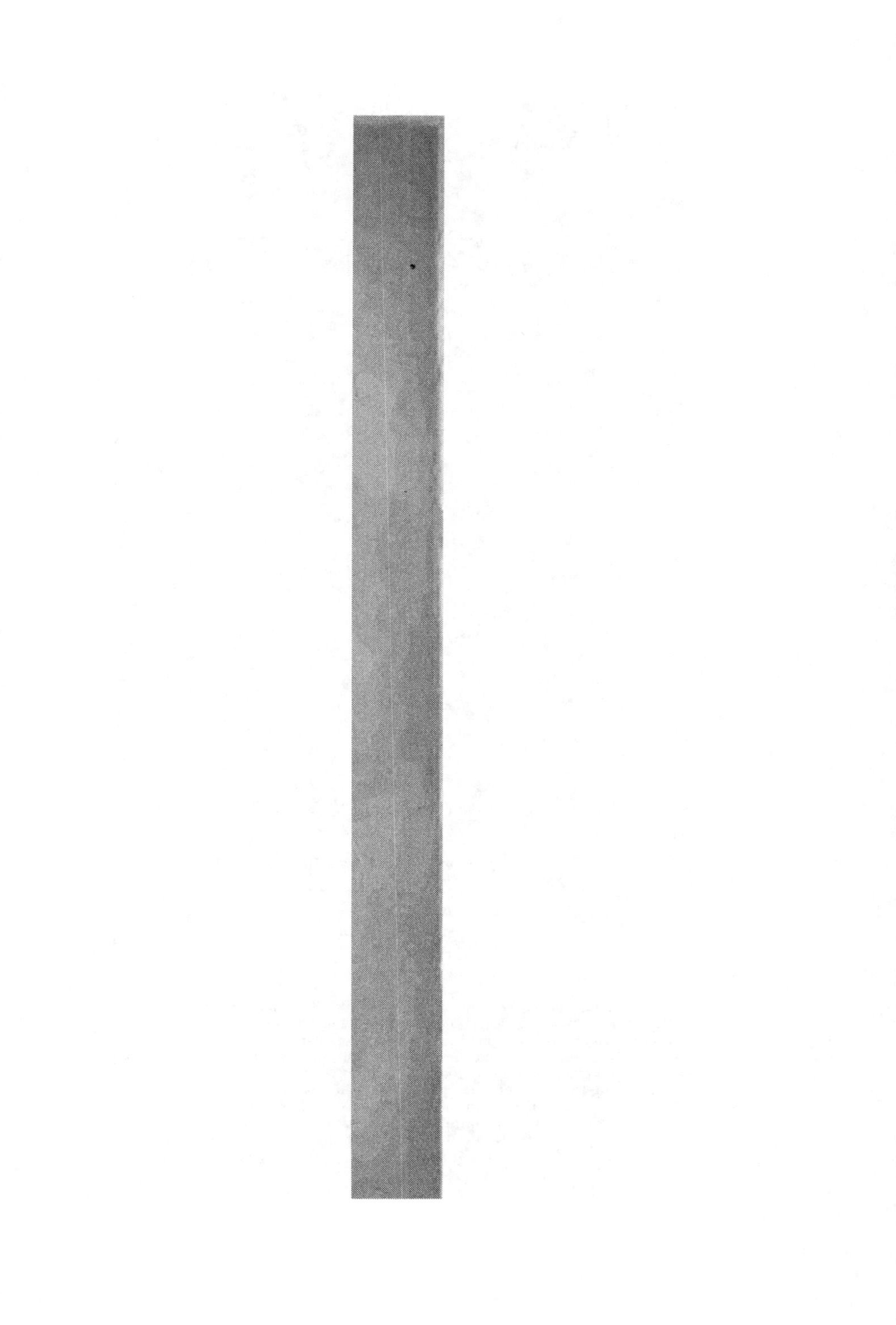

OLD CHINA.

I HAVE an almost feminine partiality for old china. When I go to see any great house, I inquire for the china closet, and next for the picture gallery. I cannot defend the order of preference, but by saying, that we have all some taste or other, of too ancient a date to admit of our remembering distinctly that it was an acquired one. I can call to mind the first play, and the first exhibition, that I was taken to; but I am not conscious of a time when china jars and saucers were introduced into my imagination.

I had no repugnance then—why should I now have?—to those little, lawless, azure-tinctured grotesques, that under the notion of men and women, float about, uncircumscribed by any element, in that world before perspective—a china tea-cup.

I like to see my old friends—whom distance cannot diminish—figuring up in the air (so they appear to our optics), yet on *terra firma* still—for so we must in courtesy interpret that speck of deeper blue, which the decorous artist, to prevent absurdity, has made to spring up beneath their sandals.

I love the men with women's faces, and the women, if possible, with still more womanish expressions.

Here is a young and courtly Mandarin, handing tea to a lady from a salver—two miles off. See how distance seems to set off respect! And here the same lady, or another—for likeness is identity on tea-cups—is stepping into a little fairy boat, moored on the hither side of this calm garden river, with a dainty mincing foot, which in a right angle of incidence (as angles go in our world) must infallibly land her in the midst of a flowery mead—a furlong off on the other side of the same strange stream!

Farther on—if far or near can be predicated of their world—see horses, trees, pagodas, dancing the hays.

Here—a cow and rabbit couchant, and co-extensive—so objects show, seen through the lucid atmosphere of fine Cathay!

I was pointing out to my cousin last evening, over our Hyson, (which we are old fashioned enough to drink unmixed still of an afternoon) some of these *speciosa miracula* upon a set of extraordinary old blue china (a recent purchase) which we were now for the first time using; and could not help remarking, how favourable circumstances had been to us of late years, that we could afford to please the eye sometimes with trifles of this sort—when a passing sentiment seemed to over-shade the brows of my companion. I am quick at detecting these summer clouds in Bridget.

"I wish the good old times would come again," she said, "when we were not quite so rich. I do not mean, that I want to be poor; but there was a middle state;"—so she was pleased to ramble on,—"in which I am sure we were a great deal happier. A purchase is but a purchase, now that you have money enough and to spare. Formerly it used to be a triumph. When we coveted a cheap luxury (and, O! how much ado I had to get you to consent to it in those times!) we were used to have a debate two or three days before, and to weigh the *for* and *against*, and think what we might spare out of, and what saving we could hit upon, that should be an equivalent. A thing was worth buying then, when we felt the money that we paid for it.

"Do you remember the brown suit, which you made to hang upon you, till all your friends cried shame upon you, it grew so thread-bare—and all because of that folio Beaumont and Fletcher, which you dragged home late at night, from Barker's in Covent-garden? Do you remember how we eyed it for weeks before we could make up our minds to the purchase, and had not come to a determination till it was near ten o'clock of the Saturday night, when you set off from Islington, fearing you should be too late—and when the old bookseller with some grumbling opened his shop, and by the twinkling taper (for he was setting bedwards) lighted out the relic from his dusty treasures—and when you lugged it home, wishing it were twice as cumbersome—and when you presented it to me—and when we were exploring the perfectness of it (*collating* you called it)—and while I was repairing some of the loose leaves with paste, which your impatience would not suffer to be left till day-break—was there no pleasure in being a poor man? or can those neat black clothes which you wear now, and are so careful to keep brushed, since we have become rich and finical, give you half the honest vanity, with which you flaunted it about in that over-worn suit—your old corbeau—for four or five weeks longer than you should have done, to pacify your conscience for the mighty sum of fifteen—or sixteen shillings was it?—a great affair we thought it then—which you had lavished on the old folio? Now you can afford to buy any book that pleases you, but I do not see that you ever bring me home any nice old purchases now.

"When you came home with twenty apologies for laying out a less number of shillings upon that print after Lionardo, which we christened the 'Lady Blanch;' when you looked at the purchase, and thought of the money—and thought of the money, and looked again at the picture—was there no pleasure in being a poor man? Now, you have nothing to do but to walk into Colnaghi's (as W—— calls it) and buy a wilderness of Lionardos. Yet do you?

"Then, do you remember our pleasant walks to Enfield, and Potter's Bar, and Waltham, when we had a holyday—holydays, and all other fun, are gone, now we are rich—and the little hand-basket in which I used to deposit our day's fare of savory cold lamb and salad—and how you would pry about at noon-tide for some decent house, where we might go in, and produce our store—only paying for the ale that you must call for—and speculate upon the looks of the landlady, and whether she was likely to allow us a table-cloth,—and wish for such another honest hostess, as Izaak Walton has described many a one on the pleasant banks of the Lea, when he went a fishing—and sometimes they would prove obliging enough, and sometimes they would look grudgingly upon us—but we had cheerful looks still for one another, and would eat our plain food savorily, scarcely grudging Piscator his Trout Hall? Now, when we go out a day's pleasuring, which is seldom moreover, we *ride* part of the way—and go into a fine inn, and order the best of dinners, never debating the expense—which, after all, never has half the relish of those chance country snaps, when we were at the mercy of uncertain usage, and a precarious welcome.

"You are too proud to see a play anywhere now but in the pit or boxes. Do you remember where it was we used to sit, when we saw the Battle of Hexham, and the Surrender of Calais, and Bannister and Mrs. Bland in the Children in the Wood—when we squeezed out our shillings a-piece to sit three or four times in a season in the one-shilling gallery—where you felt all the time that you ought not to have brought me—and more strongly I felt obligation to you for having brought me—and the pleasure was the better for a little shame—and when the curtain drew up, what cared we for our place in the house, or what mattered it where we were sitting, when our thoughts were with Rosalind in Arden, or with Viola at the Court of Illyria? You used to say, that the gallery was the best place of all for enjoying a play socially—that the relish of such exhibitions must be in proportion to the infrequency of going—that the company we met there, not being in general readers of plays, were obliged to attend the more, and did attend, to what was going on, on the stage—because a word lost would have been a chasm, which it was impossible for them to fill up. With such reflections we consoled our pride then—and I appeal to you, whether, as a woman, I met generally with less attention and accommodation, than I have done since in more expensive situations in the house? The getting in indeed, and the crowding up those inconvenient staircases, was bad enough,—but there was still a law of civility to women recognised to quite as great an extent as we have ever found it in the other passages—and how a little difficulty overcome heightened the snug seat, and the play, afterwards! Now we can only pay our money, and walk in. You cannot see, you say, in the galleries now. I am sure we saw, and heard too, well enough then—but sight, and all, I think, is gone with our poverty.

"There was pleasure in eating strawberries, before they became quite common—in the first dish of peas, while they were yet dear—to have them for a nice supper, a treat. What treat can we have now? If we were to treat ourselves now—that is, to have dainties a little above our means, it would be selfish and wicked. It is the very little more that we allow ourselves beyond what the actual poor can get at, that makes what I call a treat—when two people living together, as we have done, now and then indulge themselves in a cheap luxury, which both like; while each apologises, and is willing to take both halves of the blame to his single share. I see no harm in people making much of themselves in that sense of the word. It may give them a hint how to make much of others. But now—what I mean by the word—we never do make much of ourselves. None but the poor can do it. I do not mean the veriest poor of all, but persons as we were, just above poverty.

"I know what you were going to say, that it is mighty pleasant at the end of the year to make all meet—and much ado we used to have every Thirty-first Night of December to account for our exceedings—many a long face did you make over your puzzled accounts, and in contriving to make it out how we had spent so much—or that we had not spent so much—or that it was impossible we should spend so much next year—and still we found our slender capital decreasing—but then, betwixt ways, and projects, and compromises of one sort or another, and talk of curtailing this charge, and doing without that for the future—and the hope that youth brings, and laughing spirits (in which you were never poor till now), we pocketed up our loss, and in conclusion, with 'lusty brimmers' (as you used to quote it out of *hearty cheerful Mr. Cotton*, as you called him), we used to welcome in the 'coming guest.' Now, we have no reckoning at all at the end of an old year—no flattering promises about the new year doing better for us."

Bridget is so sparing of her speech on most occasions, that when she gets into a rhetorical vein, I am careful how I interrupt it. I could not help, however, smiling at the phantom of wealth which her dear imagination had conjured up out of a clear income of poor — hundred pounds a year. "It is true we were happier when we were poorer, but we were also younger, my cousin. I am afraid we must put up with the excess, for if we were to shake the superflux into the sea, we should not much mend ourselves. That we had much to struggle with, as we grew up together, we have reason to be most thankful. It strengthened, and knit our compact closer. We could never have been what we have been to each other, if we had always had the sufficiency which you now complain of. The resisting power—those natural dilations of the youthful spirit, which circumstances cannot straiten—with us are long since passed away. Competence to age is supplemental youth; a sorry supplement indeed, but I fear the best that is to be had. We must ride, where we formerly walked; live better, and lie softer—and shall be wise to do so—than we had means to do in those good old days you speak of. Yet could those days return—could you and I once more walk our thirty miles a-day—could Bannister and Mrs. Bland again be young, and you and I be young to see them—could the good old one shilling gallery days return—they are dreams, my cousin, now—but could you and I at this moment, instead of this quiet argument by our well-carpeted fire-side, sitting on this luxurious sofa—be once more struggling up those inconvenient stair-cases, pushed about, and squeezed, and elbowed by the poorest rabble of poor gallery scramblers—could I once more hear those anxious shrieks of yours—and the delicious *Thank God, we are safe*, which always followed when the top-most stair, conquered, let in the first light of the whole cheerful theatre down beneath us—I know not the fathom line that ever touched a descent so deep as I would be willing to bury more wealth than Crœsus had, or the great Jew R—— is supposed to have, to purchase it. And now do just look at that merry little Chinese waiter holding an umbrella, big enough for a bed-tester, over the head of that pretty insipid half-Madona-ish chit of a lady in that very blue summer house."

Elia.

THE

LONDON MAGAZINE.

MARCH, 1823.

THE LION'S HEAD.

Elia is *not* dead!—We thought as much—and even hinted our thought in the number for January. The following letter declaring Elia's existence is in his own handwriting, and was left by his own hand. We never saw a man so extremely alive, as he was, to the injury done him:

"Elia returns his thanks to the facetious Janus Weathercock, who, during his late unavoidable excursion to the Isles of Sark, Guernsey, and Jersey, took advantage of his absence to plot a sham account of his death; and to impose upon the town a posthumous Essay, signed by his Ghost—which, how like it is to any of the undoubted Essays of the author, may be seen by comparing it with his volume just published. One or two former papers, with his signature, which are not re-printed in the volume, he has reason to believe were pleasant forgeries by the same ingenious hand."

RITSON *versus* JOHN SCOTT THE QUAKER.

Critics I read on other men,
And Hypers upon them again.—*Prior.*

I HAVE in my possession Scott's "Critical Essays on some of the Poems of several English Poets,"—a handsome octavo, bought at the sale of Ritson's books; and enriched (or deformed, as some would think it) with MS. annotations in the handwriting of that redoubted Censor. I shall transcribe a few, which seem most characteristic of both the writers—Scott, feeble, but amiable—Ritson, coarse, caustic, clever; and, I am to suppose, not amiable. But they have proved some amusement to me; and, I hope, will produce some to the reader, this rainy season, which really damps a gentleman's wings for any original flight, and obliges him to ransack his shelves, and miscellaneous reading, to furnish an occasional or make-shift paper. If the sky clears up, and the sun dances this Easter (as they say he is wont to do), the town may be troubled with something more in his own way the ensuing month from its poor servant to command.

ELIA.

DYER'S RUINS OF ROME.

——— The pilgrim oft
At dead of night 'mid his oraison hears
Aghast the voice of time disparting towers,
Tumbling all precipitate down-dash'd,
Rattling around, loud thund'ring to the moon;
While murmurs sooth each awful interval
Of ever falling waters.

Scott.

There is a very bold transposition in this passage. A superficial reader, not attending to the sense of the epithet *ever*, might be ready to suppose that the *intervals* intended were those between the *falling of the waters*, instead of those between the *falling of the towers.*

Ritson.

A beauty, as in Thomson's Winter—

——— Cheerless towns, far distant, never blest,
Save when its annual course the caravan
Bends to the golden coast of rich Cathay,
With news of human kind.*

A superficial person—Mr. Scott, for instance, would be apt to connect the last clause in this period with the line foregoing—"bends to the coast of Cathay with news," &c. But has a reader nothing to do but to sit passive, while the connexion is to glide into his ears like oil?

DENHAM'S COOPER'S HILL.

The stream is so transparent, pure, and clear,
That, had the self-enamour'd youth gazed here,
So fatally deceived he had not been,
While he the bottom, not his face had seen.

Scott.

The last two lines have more music than Denham's can possibly boast.

Ritson.

May I have leave to conjecture, that in the very last line of all, the word "the" has erroneously crept in? I am persuaded that the poet wrote "his." To my mind, at least, this reading, in a surprising degree, heightens the idea of the extreme clearness and transparency of the stream, where a man might see *more than his face* (as it were) in it.

COLLINS'S ORIENTAL ECLOGUES.

Scott.

The second of these little pieces, called Hassan, or the Camel Driver, is of superior character. This poem contradicts history in one principal instance; the merchants of the east travel in numerous caravans, but Hassan is introduced travelling alone

---

* May I have leave to notice an instance of the same agreeable discontinuity in my friend Lloyd's admirable poem on Christmas?

——— Where the broad-bosom'd hills,
Swept with perpetual clouds, of Scotland rise,
Me fate compels to tarry.

in the desart. But this circumstance detracts little from our author's merit; adherence to historical fact is *seldom* required in poetry.

Ritson.

It is *always*, where the poet unnecessarily transports you to the ends of the world. If he must plague you with exotic scenery, you have a right to exact strict local imagery and costume. Why must I learn Arabic, to read nothing after all but Gay's Fables in another language?

Scott.

Abra is introduced in a grove, wreathing a flowery chaplet for her hair. Shakspeare himself could not have devised a more natural and pleasing incident, than that of the monarch's attention being attracted by her song:

Great Abbas chanced that fated morn to stray,
By love conducted from the chase away.
Among the vocal vales he heard her song—

Ritson.

Ch—t?

O stay thee, Agib, for my feet deny,
No longer friendly to my life, to fly—

Scott.

From the pen of Cowley such an observation as Secander's, that "his feet were no longer friendly to his life," might have been expected; but Collins rarely committed such violations of simplicity.

Ritson.

Pen of Cowley! impudent goose-quill, how darest thou guess what Cowley would have written?

GRAY'S CHURCH-YARD ELEGY.

Save where the beetle wheels—

Scott.

The beetle was introduced into poetry by Shakspeare * * *. Shakspeare has made the most of his description; indeed far too much, considering the occasion:

——to black Hecate's summons
The shard-born beetle with his drowsy hum
Hath rung night's yawning peal.

The imagination must be indeed fertile, which could produce this ill-placed exuberance of imagery. The poet, when composing this passage, must have had in his mind all the remote ideas of Hecate, a heathen Goddess, of a beetle, of night, of a peal of bells, and of that action of the muscles, commonly called a gape or yawn.

Ritson.

Numbscull! that would limit an infinite head by the square contents of thy own numbscull.

Scott.

The great merit of a poet is not, like Cowley, Donne, and Denham, to say what no man but himself has thought, but what every man besides himself has thought; but no man expressed, or, at least, expressed so well.

Ritson.

In other words, all *that* is poetry, which Mr. Scott has thought, as well as the poet; but *that* cannot be poetry, which was not obvious to Mr. Scott, as well as to Cowley, Donne, and Denham.

Scott.

Mr. Mason observes of the language in this part [the Epitaph], that it has a Doric delicacy. It has, indeed, what I should rather term a *happy rusticity*.

Ritson.

Come, see
Rural felicity.

GOLDSMITH'S DESERTED VILLAGE.

No busy steps the grass-grown footway tread,
But all the bloomy flush of life is fled—
All but yon widow'd solitary thing,
That feebly bends beside the plashy spring;
She, wretched matron, forced, in age, for bread,
To strip the brook with mantling cresses spread.

Scott.

Our author's language, in this place, is very defective in correctness. After mentioning the general privation of the "bloomy flush of life," the exceptionary "all but" includes, as a part of that "bloomy flush," an aged decrepid matron; that is to say, in plain prose, "the bloomy flush of life is all fled but one old woman."

Ritson.

Yet Milton could write:

Far from all resort of mirth,
Save the cricket on the hearth,
Or the bell-man's drowsy charm—

and I dare say he was right. O never let a quaker, or a woman, try their hand at being witty, any more than a Tom Brown affect to speak by the spirit!

Scott.

—Aaron Hill, who, although, in general, a bombastic writer, produced some pieces of merit, particularly the Caveat, an allegorical satire on Pope.

Ritson.

Say rather his verses on John Dennis, beginning "Adieu, unsocial excellence!" which are implicitly a finer satire on Pope than twenty Caveats. All that Pope could or did say against Dennis, is there condensed; and what he should have said, and did not, for him, is there too.*

THOMSON'S SEASONS.

Address to the Angler to spare the young fish.

If yet too young, and easily deceived,
A worthless prey scarce bends your pliant rod,
Him, piteous of his youth, and the short space
He has enjoy'd the vital light of heaven,
Soft disengage, and back into the stream
The speckled infant throw.——

Scott.

The praise bestowed on a preceding passage, cannot be justly given to this. There is in it an attempt at dignity above the occasion. Pathos seems to have been intended, but affectation only is produced.

Ritson.

It is not affectation, but it is the mock heroic of pathos, introduced purposely and wisely to attract the reader to a proposal, which from the unimportance of the subject—a poor little fish—might else have escaped his attention—as children learn, or may learn, humanity to animals from the mock romantic "Perambulations of a Mouse."

HAYMAKING.

——Infant hands
Trail the long rake; or, with the fragrant load
O'er-charged, amid the kind oppression roll.

Scott.

"Kind oppression" is a phrase of that sort, which one scarcely knows whether to blame or praise: it consists of two words, directly opposite in their signification; and yet, perhaps, no phrase whatever could have better conveyed the idea of an easy uninjurious weight—

Ritson.

—and yet he does not know whether to blame or praise it!

On the Death of Mr. Dennis.

* Adieu, unsocial excellence! at last
Thy foes are vanquish'd, and thy fears are past:
Want, the grim recompense of truth like thine,
Shall now no longer dim thy destined shrine.
The impatient envy, the disdainful air,
The front malignant, and the captious stare,
The furious petulance, the jealous start,
The mist of frailties that obscured thy heart—
Veil'd in thy grave shall unremember'd lie;
For these were parts of Dennis born to die.
But there's a nobler deity behind;
His reason dies not, and has friends to find:
Though here revenge and pride withheld his praise,
No wrongs shall reach him through his future days;
The rising ages shall redeem his name,
And nations read him into lasting fame.
In his defects untaught, his labour'd page
Shall the slow gratitude of Time engage.
Perhaps some story of his pitied woe,
Mix'd in faint shades, may with his memory go,
To touch fraternity with generous shame,
And backward cast an unavailing blame
On times too cold to taste his strength of art,
Yet warm contemners of too weak a heart.
Rest in thy dust, contented with thy lot,
Thy good remember'd, and thy bad forgot.

* * * * * * *

SHEEP-SHEARING.

——By many a dog
Compell'd——
* * * * *
The clamour much of men, and boys, and dogs—
* * * * *

Scott.

The mention of *dogs* twice was superfluous; it might have been easily avoided.——

Ritson.

Very true—by mentioning them only once.

Scott.

Nature is rich in a variety of minute but striking circumstances; some of which engage the attention of one observer, and some that of another.

Ritson.

This lover of truth never uttered a truer speech. Give me a lie with a spirit in it.

Air, earth, and ocean, smile immense.—

Scott.

The bombastic "immense smile of air," &c. better omitted.

Ritson.

Quite Miltonic—"enormous bliss" —and both, I presume, alike *caviare* to the Quaker.

He comes! he comes! in every breeze the power
Of philosophic melancholy comes!
His near approach, the sudden-starting tear,
The glowing cheek, the mild dejected air,
The soften'd feature, and the beating heart,
Pierced deep with many a virtuous pang, declare.

Scott.

This fine picture is greatly injured by a few words. The power should have been said to come "upon the breeze;" not "in every breeze;" an expression which indicates a multiplicity of approaches. If he came "in every breeze," he must have been always coming——

Ritson.

—and so he was.

——The branching Oronoque
Rolls a brown deluge, and the native drives
To dwell aloft on life-sufficing trees,
At once his dome, his robe, his food, and arms.
Swell'd by a thousand streams, impetuous hurl'd
From all the roaring Andes, huge descends
The mighty Orellana. *Scarce the muse*
Dares stretch her wing o'er this enormous mass
Of rushing water: *scarce she dares attempt*
The sea-like Plata; to whose dread expanse,
Continuous depth, and wond'rous length of course,
Our floods are rills. With unabated force
In silent dignity they sweep along,
And traverse realms unknown, and blooming wilds,
And fruitful desarts, worlds of solitude,
Where the sun smiles, and seasons teem, in vain,
Unseen and unenjoy'd. Forsaking these,
O'er peopled plains they fair-diffusive flow,
And many a nation feed, and circle safe
In their fair bosom many a happy isle,
The seat of blameless Pan, yet undisturb'd
By Christian crimes, and Europe's cruel sons.
Thus pouring on, they proudly seek the deep,
Whose vanquish'd tide, recoiling from the shock,
Yields to this liquid weight of half the globe,
And Ocean trembles for his green domain.

Scott.

Poets not unfrequently aim at aggrandising their subject, by avowing their inability to describe it. This is a puerile and inadequate expedient. Thomson has here, perhaps inadvertently, descended to this feeble art of exaggeration.

Ritson.

A magnificent passage in spite of Duns Scotus! The poet says not a word about his "inability to describe," nor seems to be thinking about his readers at all. He is confessing his own feelings, awe-struck with the contemplation of such o'erwhelming objects; in the same spirit with which he designates the den of the "green serpent" in another place—

—Which ev'n imagination fears to tread—

——A dazzling deluge reigns, and all
From pole to pole is undistinguish'd blaze—

Scott.

From pole to pole, strictly speaking, is improper. *The poet* meant, "from one part of the horizon to the other."

Ritson.

From *his* pole to *thy* pole was a more downward declension than "from the centre thrice," &c.

Ohe! jam satis.

POOR RELATIONS.

A Poor Relation is—the most irrelevant thing in nature,—a piece of impertinent correspondency,—an odious approximation,—a haunting conscience,—a preposterous shadow, lengthening in the noon-tide of your prosperity,—an unwelcome remembrancer,—a perpetually recurring mortification,—a drain on your purse,—a more intolerable dun upon your pride,—a drawback upon success,—a rebuke to your rising,—a stain in your blood,—a blot on your scutcheon,—a rent in your garment,—a death's head at your banquet,—Agathocles' pot,—a Mordecai in your gate,—a Lazarus at your door,—a lion in your path,—a frog in your chamber,—a fly in your ointment,—a mote in your eye,—a triumph to your enemy, an apology to your friends,—the one thing not needful,—the hail in harvest,—the ounce of sour in a pound of sweet,—the bore *par excellence*.

He is known by his knock. Your heart telleth you "That is Mr. —." A rap, between familiarity and respect; that demands, and, at the same time, seems to despair of, entertainment. He entereth smiling, and—embarrassed. He holdeth out his hand to you to shake, and—draweth it back again. He casually looketh in about dinner time—when the table is full. He offereth to go away, seeing you have company—but is induced to stay. He filleth a chair, and your visitor's two children are accommodated at a side table. He never cometh upon open days, when your wife says with some complacency, "My dear, perhaps Mr. —— will drop in to-day." He remembereth birth-days—and professeth he is fortunate to have stumbled upon one. He declareth against fish, the turbot being small—yet suffereth himself to be importuned into a slice against his first resolution. He sticketh by the port—yet will be prevailed upon to empty the remainder glass of claret,—if a stranger press it upon him. He is a puzzle to the servants, who are fearful of being too obsequious, or not civil enough, to him. The guests think "they have seen him before." Every one speculateth upon his condition; and the most part take him to be—a tide-waiter. He calleth you by your Christian name, to imply that his other is the same with your own. He is too familiar by half, yet you wish he had less diffidence. With half the familiarity, he might pass for a casual dependent; with more boldness, he would be in no danger of being taken for what he is. He is too humble for a friend, yet taketh on him more state than befits a client. He is a worse guest than a country tenant, inasmuch as he bringeth up no rent—yet 'tis odds, from his garb and demeanour, that your other guests take him for one. He is asked to make one at the whist table; refuseth on the score of poverty, and—resents being left out. When the company break up, he proffereth to go for a coach—and lets the servant go. He recollects your grandfather; and will thrust in some mean, and quite unimportant anecdote of—the family. He knew it when it was not quite so flourishing as "he is blest in seeing it now." He reviveth past situations, to institute what he calleth—favourable comparisons. With a reflecting sort of congratulation, he will inquire the price of your furniture; and insults you with a special commendation of your window-curtains. He is of opinion that the urn is the more elegant shape, but, after all, there was something more comfortable about the old tea-kettle—which you must remember. He dare say you must find a great convenience in having a carriage of your own, and appealeth to your lady if it is not so. Inquireth if you have had your arms done on vellum yet; and did not know till lately, that such-and-such had been the crest of the family. His memory is unseasonable; his compliments perverse; his talk a trouble; his stay pertinacious; and when he goeth away, you dismiss his chair into a corner, as precipitately as possible, and feel fairly rid of two nuisances.

There is a worse evil under the sun, and that is—a female Poor Relation. You may do something with the other; you may pass him off tolerably well; but your indigent she-Relative is hopeless. "He is an old humourist," you may say, "and affects to go threadbare. His circumstances are better than folks would take them to be. You are fond of having a Character at your table, and truly he is one." But in the indications of female poverty there can be no disguise. No woman dresses below herself from caprice. The truth must out without shuffling. "She is plainly related to the L——s; or what does she at their house?" She is, in all probability, your wife's cousin. Nine times out of ten, at least, this is the case. Her garb is something between a gentlewoman and a beggar, yet the former evidently predominates. She is most provokingly humble, and ostentatiously sensible to her inferiority. He may require to be repressed sometimes—*aliquando sufflaminandus erat*—but there is no raising her. You send her soup at dinner, and she begs to be helped—after the gentlemen. Mr. —— requests the honour of taking wine with her; she hesitates between Port and Madeira, and chooses the former—because he does. She calls the servant *Sir*; and insists on not troubling him to hold her plate. The housekeeper patronizes her. The children's governess takes upon her to correct her, when she has mistaken the piano for a harpsichord.

Richard Amlet, Esq. in the play, is a notable instance of the disadvantages, to which this chimerical notion of *affinity constituting a claim to acquaintance*, may subject the spirit of a gentleman. A little foolish blood is all that is betwixt him and a lady with a great estate. His stars are perpetually crossed by the malignant maternity of an old woman, who persists in calling him "her son Dick." But she has wherewithal in the end to recompense his indignities, and float him again upon the brilliant surface, under which it had been her seeming business and pleasure all along to sink him. All men, besides, are not of Dick's temperament. I knew an Amlet in real life, who, wanting Dick's buoyancy, sank indeed. Poor W—— was of my own standing at Christ's, a fine classic, and a youth of promise. If he had a blemish, it was too much pride; but its quality was inoffensive; it was not of that sort which hardens the heart, and serves to keep inferiors at a distance; it only sought to ward off derogation from itself. It was the principle of self-respect carried as far as it could go, without infringing upon that respect, which he would have every one else equally maintain for himself. He would have you to think alike with him on this topic. Many a quarrel have I had with him, when we were rather older boys, and our tallness made us more obnoxious to observation in the blue clothes, because I would not thrid the alleys and blind ways of the town with him, to elude notice, when we have been out together on a holiday in the streets of this sneering and prying metropolis. W—— went, sore with these notions, to Oxford, where the dignity and sweetness of a scholar's life, meeting with the alloy of a humble introduction, wrought in him a passionate devotion to the place, with a profound aversion from the society. The servitor's gown (worse than his school array) clung to him with Nessian venom. He thought himself ridiculous in a garb, under which Latimer must have walked erect; and in which Hooker, in his young days, possibly flaunted in a vein of no discommendable vanity. In the depth of college shades, or in his lonely chamber, the poor student slunk from observation. He found shelter among books, which insult not; and studies, that ask no questions of a youth's finances. He was lord of his library, and seldom cared for looking out beyond his domains. The healing influence of studious pursuits was upon him, to soothe and to abstract. He was almost a healthy man; when the waywardness of his fate broke out against him with a second and worse malignity. The father of W——— had hitherto exercised the humble profession of house painter at N——, near Oxford. A supposed interest with some of the heads of colleges had now induced him to take up his abode in that city, with the hope of being employed upon some public works which were talked of. From that moment I read in the countenance of the young man, the determination which at length tore him from academical pursuits for ever. To a person unacquainted with our Universities, the distance between the gownsmen and the townsmen, as they are called---the trading part of the latter especially---is carried to an excess that would appear harsh and incredible. The temperament of W——'s father was diametrically the reverse of his own. Old W—— was a little, busy, cringing tradesman, who, with his son upon his arm, would stand bowing and scraping, cap in hand, to any thing that wore the semblance of a gown---insensible to the winks, and opener remonstrances of the young man, to whose chamber-fellow, or equal in standing perhaps, he was thus obsequiously and gratuitously ducking. Such a state of things could not last. W—— must change the air of Oxford, or be suffocated. He chose the former; and let the sturdy moralist, who strains the point of the filial duties as high as they can bear, censure the dereliction; he cannot estimate the struggle. I stood with W——, the last afternoon I ever saw him, under the eaves of his paternal dwelling. It was in the fine lane leading from the High-street to the back of ***** college, where W—— kept his rooms. He seemed thoughtful, and more reconciled. I ventured to rally him---finding him in a better mood---upon a representation of the Artist Evangelist, which the old man, whose affairs were beginning to flourish, had caused to be set up in a splendid sort of frame over his really handsome shop, either as a token of prosperity, or badge of gratitude to his saint. W—— looked up at the Luke, and like Satan, "knew his mounted sign---and fled." A letter on his father's table the next morning announced, that he had accepted a commission in a regiment about to embark for Portugal. He was among the first who perished before the walls of St. Sebastian.

I do not know how, upon a subject which I began with treating half seriously, I should have fallen upon a recital so eminently painful; but this theme of poor relationship is replete with so much matter for tragic as well as comic associations, that it is difficult to keep the account distinct without blending. The earliest impressions which I received on this matter, are certainly not attended with any thing painful, or very humiliating, in the recalling. At my father's table (no very splendid one) was to be found, every Saturday, the mysterious figure of an aged gentleman, clothed in neat black, of a sad yet comely appearance. His deportment was of the essence of gravity; his words few or none; and I was not to make a noise in his presence. I had little inclination to have done so—for my cue was to admire in silence. A particular elbow chair was appropriated to him, which was in no case to be violated. A peculiar sort of sweet pudding, which appeared on no other occasion, distinguished the days of his coming. I used to think him a prodigiously rich man. All I could make out of him was, that he and my father had been schoolfellows a world ago at Lincoln, and that he came from the Mint. The Mint I knew to be a place where all the money was coined—and I thought he was the owner of all that money. Awful ideas of the Tower twined themselves about his presence. He seemed above human infirmities and passions. A sort of melancholy grandeur invested him. From some inexplicable doom I fancied him obliged to go about in an eternal suit of mourning. A captive—a stately being, let out of the Tower on Saturdays. Often have I wondered at the temerity of my father, who, in spite of an habitual general respect, which we all in common manifested towards him, would venture now and then to stand up against him in some argument, touching their youthful days. The houses of the ancient city of Lincoln are divided (as most of my readers know) between the dwellers on the hill, and in the valley. This marked distinction formed an obvious division between the boys who lived above (however brought together in a common school), and the boys whose paternal residence was on the plain; a sufficient cause of hostility in the code of these young Grotiuses. My father had been a leading Mountaineer; and would still maintain the general superiority, in skill and hardihood, of the *Above Boys* (his own faction), over the *Below Boys* (so were they called), of which party his contemporary had been a chieftain. Many and hot were the skirmishes on this topic—the only one upon which the old gentleman was ever brought out—and bad blood bred; even sometimes almost to the recommencement (so I expected) of actual hostilities. But my father, who scorned to insist upon advantages, generally contrived to turn the conversation upon some adroit by-commendation of the old Minster; in the general preference of which, before all other cathedrals in the island, the dweller on the hill, and the plain-born, could meet on a conciliating level, and lay down their less important differences. Once only I saw the old gentleman really ruffled, and I remember with anguish the thought that came over me: "Perhaps he will never come here again." He had been pressed to take another plate of the viand, which I have already mentioned as the indispensable concomitant of his visits. He had refused, with a resistance amounting to rigour—when my aunt, an old Lincolnian, but who had something of this, in common with my cousin Bridget, that she would sometimes press civility out of season—uttered the following memorable application—"Do take another slice, Mr. Billet, for you do not get pudding every day." The old gentleman said nothing at the time—but he took occasion in the course of the evening, when some argument had intervened between them, to utter with an emphasis which chilled the company, and which chills me now as I write it—"Woman, you are superannuated." John Billet did not survive long, after the digesting of this affront; but he survived long enough to assure me that peace was actually restored; and, if I remember aright, another pudding was discreetly substituted in the place of that which had occasioned the offence. He died at the Mint (Anno 1781) where he had long held, what he accounted, a comfortable independence; and with five pounds, fourteen shillings, and a penny, which were found in his escrutoire after his decease, left the world, blessing God that he had enough to bury him, and that he had never been obliged to any man for a sixpence. This was—a Poor Relation.

ELIA.

THE CHILD ANGEL:—A DREAM.

I CHANCED upon the prettiest, oddest, fantastical thing of a dream the other night, that you shall hear of. I had been reading the "Loves of the Angels," and went to bed with my head full of speculations, suggested by that extraordinary legend. It had given birth to innumerable conjectures; and, I remember, the last waking thought, which I gave expression to on my pillow, was a sort of wonder, "what could come of it."

I was suddenly transported, how or whither I could scarcely make out—but to some celestial region. It was not the real heavens neither—not the downright Bible heaven—but a kind of fairy-land heaven, about which a poor human fancy may have leave to sport and air itself, I will hope, without presumption.

Methought—what wild things dreams are!—I was present—at what would you imagine?—at an angel's gossiping.

Whence it came, or how it came, or who bid it come, or whether it came purely of its own head, neither you nor I know—but there lay, sure enough, wrapt in its little cloudy swaddling bands—a Child Angel.

Sun-threads—filmy beams—ran through the celestial napery of what seemed its princely cradle. All the winged orders hovered round, watching when the new-born should open its yet closed eyes: which, when it did, first one, and then the other—with a solicitude and apprehension, yet not such as, stained with fear, dims the expanding eye-lids of mortal infants—but as if to explore its path in those its unhereditary palaces—what an inextinguishable titter that time spared not celestial visages! Nor wanted there to my seeming—O the inexplicable simpleness of dreams!—bowls of that cheering nectar,

—which mortals *caudle* call below—

Nor were wanting faces of female ministrants,—stricken in years, as it might seem—so dextrous were those heavenly attendants to counterfeit kindly similitudes of earth, to greet with terrestrial child-rites the young Present, which earth had made to heaven.

Then were celestial harpings heard, not in full symphony as those by which the spheres are tutored; but, as loudest instruments on earth speak oftentimes, muffled; so to accommodate their sound the better to the weak ears of the imperfect-born. And, with the noise of those subdued soundings, the Angelet sprang forth, fluttering its rudiments of pinions—but forthwith flagged and was recovered into the arms of those full-winged angels. And a wonder it was to see how, as years went round in heaven—a year in dreams is as a day—continually its white shoulders put forth buds of wings, but, wanting the perfect angelic nutriment, anon was shorn of its aspiring, and fell fluttering—still caught by angel hands—for ever to put forth shoots, and to fall fluttering, because its birth was not of the unmixed vigour of heaven.

And a name was given to the Babe Angel, and it was to be called *Ge-Urania*, because its production was of earth and heaven.

And it could not taste of death, by reason of its adoption into immortal palaces; but it was to know weakness, and reliance, and the shadow of human imbecility; and it went with a lame gait; but in its goings it exceeded all mortal children in grace and swiftness. Then pity first sprang up in angelic bosoms; and yearnings (like the human) touched them at the sight of the immortal lame one.

And with pain did then first those Intuitive Essences, with pain and strife to their natures (not grief), put back their bright intelligences, and reduce their etherial minds, schooling them to degrees and slower processes, so to adapt their lessons to the gradual illumination (as must needs be) of the half-earth-born; and what intuitive notices they could not repel (by reason that their nature is to know all things at once), the half-heavenly novice, by the better part of its nature, aspired to receive into its understanding; so that Humility and Aspiration went on even-paced in the instruction of the glorious Amphibium.

But, by reason that Mature Humanity is too gross to breathe the air of that super-subtile region, its portion was, and is, to be a child for ever.

And because the human part of it might not press into the heart and inwards of the palace of its adoption, those full-natured angels tended it by turns in the purlieus of the palace, where were shady groves and rivulets, like this green earth from which it came: so Love, with Voluntary Humility, waited upon the entertainment of the new-adopted.

And myriads of years rolled round (in dreams Time is nothing), and still it kept, and is to keep, perpetual childhood, and is the Tutelar Genius of Childhood upon earth, and still goes lame and lovely.

By the banks of the river Pison is seen, lone-sitting by the grave of the terrestrial Mirzah, whom the angel Nadir loved, a Child; but not the same which I saw in heaven. A pensive hue overcasts its lineaments; nevertheless, a correspondency is between the child by the grave, and that celestial orphan, whom I saw above; and the dimness of the grief upon the heavenly, is as a shadow or emblem of that which stains the beauty of the terrestrial. And this correspondency is not to be understood but by dreams.

And in the archives of heaven I had grace to read, how that once the angel Nadir, being exiled from his place for mortal passion, upspringing on the wings of parental love (such power had parental love for a moment to suspend the else irrevocable law) appeared for a brief instant in his station; and, depositing a wondrous Birth, straightway disappeared, and the palaces knew him no more. And this charge was the self-same Babe, who goeth lame and lovely—but Mirzah sleepeth by the river Pison.

ELIA.

NUGÆ CRITICÆ:

BY THE AUTHOR OF ELIA.

No. I.

DEFENCE OF THE SONNETS OF SIR PHILIP SYDNEY.

SYDNEY's Sonnets—I speak of the best of them—are among the very best of their sort. They fall below the plain moral dignity, the sanctity, and high yet modest spirit of self-approval, of Milton, in his compositions of a similar structure. They are in truth what Milton, censuring the Arcadia, says of that work (to which they are a sort of after-tune or application), "vain and amatorious" enough, yet the things in their kind (as he confesses to be true of the romance) may be "full of worth and wit." They savour of the Courtier, it must be allowed, and not of the Commmonwealthsman. But Milton was a Courtier when he wrote the Masque at Ludlow Castle, and still more a Courtier when he composed the Arcades. When the national struggle was to begin, he becomingly cast these vanities behind him; and if the order of time had thrown Sir Philip upon the crisis which preceded the Revolution, there is no reason why he should not have acted the same part in that emergency, which has glorified the name of a later Sydney. He did not want for plainness or boldness of spirit. His letter on the French match may testify, he could speak his mind freely to Princes. The times did not call him to the scaffold.

The Sonnets which we oftenest call to mind of Milton were the compositions of his maturest years. Those of Sydney, which I am about to produce, were written in the very hey-day of his blood. They are stuck full of amorous fancies—far-fetched conceits, *befitting his occupation;* for True Love thinks no labour to send out Thoughts upon vast, and more than Indian voyages, to bring home rich pearls, outlandish wealth, gums, jewels, spicery, to sacrifice in self-depreciating similitudes, as shadows of true amiabilities in the Beloved. We must be Lovers—or at least the cooling touch of time, the *circum præcordia frigus,* must not have so damped our faculties, as to take away our recollection that we were once so—before we can duly appreciate the glorious vanities, and graceful hyperboles, of the passion. The images which lie before our feet (though by some accounted the only natural) are least natural for the high Sydnean love to express its fancies by. They may serve for the loves of Catullus or the dear Author of the Schoolmistress; for passions that creep and whine in Elegies and Pastoral Ballads. I am sure Milton never loved at this rate. I am afraid some of his addresses (*ad Leonoram* I mean) have rather erred on the farther side; and that the poet came not much short of a religious indecorum, when he could thus apostrophise a singing-girl:

Angelus unicuique suus (sic credite gentes)
Obtigit ætheriis ales ab ordinibus.
Quid mirum, Leonora, tibi si gloria major,
Nam tua præsentem vox sonat ipsa Deum?
Aut Deus, aut vacui certè mens tertia cœli
Per tua secretò guttura serpit agens;
Serpit agens, facilisque docet mortalia corda
Sensim immortali assuescere posse sono.
QUOD SI CUNCTA QUIDEM DEUS EST, PER CUNCTAQUE FUSUS,
IN TE UNÂ LOQUITUR, CÆTERA MUTUS HABET.

This is loving in a strange fashion; and it requires some candour of construction (besides the slight darkening of a dead language) to cast a veil over the ugly appearance of something very like blasphemy in the last two verses. I think the Lover would have been staggered, if he had gone about to express the same thought in English. I am sure, Sydney has no flights like this. His extravaganzas do not strike at the sky, though he takes leave to adopt the pale Dian into a fellowship with his mortal passions.

I.

With how sad steps, O Moon, thou climb'st the skies;
How silently; and with how wan a face!
What! may it be, that even in heavenly place
That busy Archer his sharp arrows tries?

Sure, if that long-with-love-acquainted eyes
Can judge of love, thou feel'st a lover's case;
I read it in thy looks; thy languisht grace
To me, that feel the like, thy state descries.
Then, even of fellowship, O Moon, tell me,
Is constant love deem'd there but want of wit?
Are beauties there as proud as here they be?
Do they above love to be loved, and yet
Those lovers scorn, whom that love doth possess?
Do they call *virtue* there—*ungratefulness*?

The last line of this poem is a little obscured by transposition. He means, Do they call ungratefulness there a virtue?

II.

Come, Sleep, O Sleep, the certain knot of peace,
The baiting place of wit, the balm of woe,
The poor man's wealth, the prisoner's release,
The indifferent judge between the high and low;
With shield of proof shield me from out the prease*
Of those fierce darts despair at me doth throw;
O make in me those civil wars to cease:
I will good tribute pay, if thou do so.
Take thou of me sweet pillows, sweetest bed;
A chamber deaf to noise, and blind to light;
A rosy garland, and a weary head.
And if these things, as being thine by right,
Move not thy heavy grace, thou shalt in me,
Livelier than elsewhere, STELLA's image see.

III.

The curious wits, seeing dull pensiveness
Bewray itself in my long-settled eyes—
Whence those same fumes of melancholy rise,
With idle pains, and missing aim, do guess.
Some, that know how my spring I did address,
Deem that my Muse some fruit of knowledge plies;
Others, because the Prince my service tries,
Think, that I think state-errors to redress:
But harder judges judge, ambition's rage,
Scourge of itself, still climbing slippery place,
Holds my young brain captiv'd in golden cage.
O fools, or over-wise! alas, the race
Of all my thoughts hath neither stop nor start,
But only STELLA's eyes, and STELLA's heart.

IV.

Because I oft in dark abstracted guise
Seem most alone in greatest company,
With dearth of words, or answers quite awry,
To them that would make speech of speech arise;
They deem, and of their doom the rumour flies,
That poison foul of bubbling *Pride* doth lie
So in my swelling breast, that only I
Fawn on myself, and others do despise:
Yet *Pride*, I think, doth not my Soul possess,
Which looks too oft in his unflattering glass:
But one worse fault—*Ambition*—I confess,
That makes me oft my best friends overpass,
Unseen, unheard—while Thought to highest place
Bends all his powers, even unto STELLA's grace.

V.

Having this day my horse, my hand, my lance
Guided so well, that I obtained the prize,
Both by the judgment of the English eyes,
And of some sent from that *sweet enemy*,—France;
Horsemen my skill in horsemanship advance;
Townfolks my strength; a daintier judge applies
His praise to sleight, which from good use doth rise;
Some lucky wits impute it but to chance;
Others, because of both sides I do take
My blood from them, who did excel in this,
Think Nature me a man of arms did make.
How far they shot awry! the true cause is,
STELLA look'd on, and from her heav'nly face
Sent forth the beams which made so fair my race.

VI.

In martial sports I had my cunning tried,
And yet to break more staves did me address,
While with the people's shouts (I must confess)
Youth, luck, and praise, even fill'd my veins with pride—
When Cupid, having me (his slave) descried
In Mars's livery, prancing in the press,
"What now, Sir Fool!" said he; "I would no less:
Look here, I say." I look'd, and STELLA spied,
Who, hard by, made a window send forth light.
My heart then quak'd, then dazzled were mine eyes;
One hand forgat to rule, th'other to fight;
Nor trumpet's sound I heard, nor friendly cries.
My foe came on, and beat the air for me,—
Till that her blush made me my shame to see.

* Press.

VII.

No more, my dear, no more these counsels try;
O give my passions leave to run their race;
Let Fortune lay on me her worst disgrace;
Let folk, o'er-charged with brain, against me cry.
Let clouds bedim my face, break in mine eye;
Let me no steps, but of lost labour, trace;
Let all the earth with scorn recount my case—
But do not will me from my love to fly.
I do not envy Aristotle's wit,
Nor do aspire to Cæsar's bleeding fame;
Nor aught do care, though some above me sit;
Nor hope, nor wish, another course to frame,
But that which once may win thy cruel heart,
Thou art my wit, and thou my virtue art.

VIII.

LOVE still a boy, and oft a wanton, is,
School'd only by his mother's tender eye;
What wonder then, if he his lesson miss,
When for so soft a rod dear play he try?
And yet my STAR, because a sugar'd kiss
In sport I suck'd, while she asleep did lie,
Doth lour, nay chide, nay threat, for only this.
Sweet, it was saucy LOVE, not humble I.
But no 'scuse serves; she makes her wrath appear
In beauty's throne—see now, who dares come near
Those scarlet judges, threat'ning bloody pain?
O heav'nly Fool, thy most-kiss-worthy face
Anger invests with such a lovely grace,
That anger's self I needs must kiss again.

IX.

I never drank of Aganippe well,
Nor ever did in shade of Tempe sit,
And Muses scorn with vulgar brains to dwell;
Poor lay-man I, for sacred rites unfit.
Some do I hear of Poets' fury tell,
But (God wot) wot not what they mean by it;
And this I swear by blackest brook of hell,
I am no pick-purse of another's wit.
How falls it then, that with so smooth an ease
My thoughts I speak, and what I speak doth flow
In verse, and that my verse best wits doth please?
Guess we the cause—what is it thus?—fye, no.
Or so?—much less. How then? sure thus it is,
My lips are sweet, inspired with STELLA's kiss.

X.

Of all the kings that ever here did reign,
Edward, named Fourth, as first in praise I name,
Not for his fair outside, nor well-lined brain—
Although less gifts imp feathers oft on Fame.
Nor that he could, young-wise, wise-valiant, frame
His sire's revenge, join'd with a kingdom's gain;
And, gain'd by Mars, could yet mad Mars so tame,
That Balance weigh'd what Sword did late obtain.
Nor that he made the Floure-de-luce so 'fraid,
Though strongly hedged of bloody Lion's paws,
That witty Lewis to him a tribute paid.
Nor this, nor that, nor any such small cause—
But only, for this worthy knight durst prove
To lose his crown rather than fail his love.

XI.

O happy Thames, that didst my STELLA bear,
I saw thyself, with many a smiling line
Upon thy cheerful face, Joy's livery wear,
While those fair planets on thy streams did shine;
The boat for joy could not to dance forbear;
While wanton winds, with beauty so divine
Ravish'd, stay'd not, till in her golden hair
They did themselves (O sweetest prison) twine.
And fain those Æol's youth there would their stay
Have made; but, forced by nature still to fly,
First did with puffing kiss those locks display.
She, so dishevel'd, blush'd; from window I
With sight thereof cried out, O fair disgrace,
Let honour's self to thee grant highest place!

XII.

Highway, since you my chief Parnassus be;
And that my Muse, to some ears not unsweet,
Tempers her words to trampling horses' feet,
More soft than to a chamber melody,—
Now, blessed You, bear onward blessed Me
To Her, where I my heart safe left shall meet,
My Muse and I must you of duty greet
With thanks and wishes, wishing thankfully.
Be you still fair, honour'd by public heed,
By no encroachment wrong'd, nor time forgot;
Nor blamed for blood, nor shamed for sinful deed.
And that you know, I envy you no lot
Of highest wish, I wish you so much bliss,
Hundreds of years you STELLA's feet may kiss.

Of the foregoing, the 1st, the 2d, and the last sonnet, are my favourites. But the general beauty of them all is, that they are so perfectly characteristical. The spirit of "learning and of chivalry,"—of which union, Spenser has entitled Sydney to have been the "president,"—shines through them. I confess I can see nothing of the "jejune" or "frigid" in them; much less of the "stiff" and "cumbrous"—which I have sometimes heard objected to the Arcadia. The verse runs off swiftly and gallantly. It might have been tuned to the trumpet; or tempered (as himself expresses it) to "trampling horses' feet." They abound in felicitous phrases—

O heav'nly Fool, thy most kiss-worthy face— *8th Sonnet.*

——— Sweet pillows, sweetest bed,
A chamber deaf to noise, and blind to light,
A rosy garland, and a weary head.
2d Sonnet.

——— That sweet enemy—France—
5th Sonnet.

But they are not rich in words only, in vague and unlocalised feelings—the failing too much of some poetry of the present day—they are full, material, and circumstantiated. Time and place appropriates every one of them. It is not a fever of passion wasting itself upon a thin diet of dainty words,* but a transcendent passion pervading and illuminating action, pursuits, studies, feats of arms, the opinions of contemporaries and his judgment of them. An historical thread runs through them, which almost affixes a date to them; marks the *when* and *where* they were written.

I have dwelt the longer upon what I conceive the merit of these poems, because I have been hurt by the wantonness (I wish I could treat it by a gentler name) with which a favourite critic of our day takes every occasion of insulting the memory of Sir Philip Sydney. But the decisions of the Author of Table Talk, &c. (most profound and subtle where they are, as for the most part, just) are more safely to be relied upon, on subjects and authors he has a partiality for, than on such as he has conceived an accidental prejudice against. Milton wrote Sonnets, and was a king-hater; and it was congenial perhaps to sacrifice a courtier to a patriot. But I was unwilling to lose a *fine idea* from my mind. The noble images, passions, sentiments, and poetical delicacies of character, scattered all over the Arcadia (spite of some stiffness and encumberment), justify to me the character which his contemporaries have left us of the writer. I cannot think with Mr. Hazlitt that Sir Philip Sydney was that *opprobrious thing*, which a foolish nobleman in his insolent hostility chose to term him. I call to mind the epitaph of Lord Brooke, to guide me to juster thoughts of him; and I repose upon the beautiful lines in the "Friend's

* A profusion of verbal dainties, with a disproportionate lack of matter and circumstance, is I think one reason of the coldness with which the public has received the poetry of a nobleman now living; which, upon the score of exquisite diction alone, is entitled to something better than neglect. I will venture to copy one of his Sonnets in this place, which for quiet sweetness, and unaffected morality, has scarcely its parallel in our language.

TO A BIRD THAT HAUNTED THE WATERS OF LACKEN IN THE WINTER.

By Lord Thurlow.

O melancholy Bird, a winter's day,
Thou standest by the margin of the pool,
And, taught by God, dost thy whole being school
To Patience, which all evil can allay.
God has appointed thee the Fish thy prey;
And given thyself a lesson to the Fool
Unthrifty, to submit to moral rule,
And his unthinking course by thee to weigh.
There need not schools, nor the Professor's chair,
Though these be good, true wisdom to impart.
He who has not enough, for these, to spare
Of time, or gold, may yet amend his heart,
And teach his soul, by brooks, and rivers fair:
Nature is always wise in every part.

Passion for his Astrophel," printed with the Elegies of Spenser and others.

You knew—who knew not Astrophel?
(That I should live to say I knew,
And have not in possession still!)—
Things known permit me to renew—
  Of him you know his merit such,
  I cannot say—you hear—too much.

Within these woods of Arcady
He chief delight and pleasure took;
And on the mountain Partheny,
Upon the chrystal liquid brook,
  The Muses met him every day,
  That taught him sing, to write, and say.

When he descended down the mount,
His personage seemed most divine;
A thousand graces one might count
Upon his lovely chearful eyne.
  To hear him speak, and sweetly smile,
  You were in Paradise the while.

A sweet attractive kind of grace;
A full assurance given by looks;
Continual comfort in a face,
The lineaments of Gospel books—
  I trow that count'nance cannot lye,
  Whose thoughts are legible in the eye.

* * * *

Above all others this is he,
Which erst approved in his song,
That love and honour might agree,
And that pure love will do no wrong.
  Sweet saints, it is no sin or blame
  To love a man of virtuous name.

Did never Love so sweetly breathe
In any mortal breast before:
Did never Muse inspire beneath
A Poet's brain with finer store:
  He wrote of Love with high conceit,
  And Beauty rear'd above her height.

Or let any one read the deeper sorrows (grief running into rage) in the Poem,—the last in the collection accompanying the above,—which from internal testimony I believe to be Lord Brooke's,—beginning with "Silence augmenteth grief,"—and then seriously ask himself, whether the subject of such absorbing and confounding regrets could have been *that thing* which Lord Oxford termed him. L.

THE OLD MARGATE HOY.

I am fond of passing my vacations (I believe I have said so before) at one or other of the Universities. Next to these my choice would fix me at some woody spot, such as the neighbourhood of Henley affords in abundance, upon the banks of my beloved Thames. But somehow or other my cousin contrives to wheedle me once in three or four seasons to a watering place. Old attachments cling to her in spite of experience. We have been dull at Worthing one summer, duller at Brighton another, dullest at Eastbourn a third, and are at this moment doing dreary penance at—Hastings!—and all because we were happy many years ago for a brief week at—Margate. That was our first sea-side experiment, and many circumstances combined to make it the most agreeable holyday of my life. We had neither of us seen the sea, and we had never been from home so long together in company.

Can I forget thee, thou old Margate Hoy, with thy weather-beaten, sun-burnt captain, and his rough accommodations—ill exchanged for the foppery and fresh-water niceness of the modern steam packet? To the winds and waves thou committedst thy goodly freightage, and didst ask no aid of magic fumes, and spells, and boiling cauldrons. With the gales of heaven thou wentest swimmingly; or, when it was their pleasure, stoodest still with sailor-like patience. Thy course was natural, not forced, as in a hot-bed; nor didst thou go poisoning the breath of ocean with sulphureous smoke—a great sea-chimæra, chimneying and furnacing the deep; or liker to that sea-god parching up Scamander.

Can I forget thy honest, yet slender crew, with their coy reluctant responses (yet to the suppression of any thing like contempt) to the raw questions, which we of the great city would be ever and anon putting to them, as to the uses of this or that strange naval implement. 'Specially can I forget thee, thou happy medium, thou shade of refuge between us and them, conciliating interpreter of their skill to our simplicity, comfortable ambassador between sea and land!—whose sailor-trowsers did not more convincingly assure thee to be an adopted denizen of the former, than thy white cap, and whiter apron over them, with thy neat-fingered practice in thy culinary vocation, bespoke thee to have been of inland nurture heretofore—a master cook of Eastcheap? How busily didst thou ply thy multifarious occupation, cook, mariner, attendant, chamberlain; here, there, like another Ariel, flaming at once about all parts of the deck, yet with kindlier ministrations—not to assist the tempest, but, as if touched with a kindred sense of our infirmities, to soothe the qualms which that untried motion might haply raise in our crude land-fancies. And when the o'er-washing billows drove us below deck (for it was far gone in October, and we had stiff and blowing weather) how did thy officious ministerings, still catering for our comfort, with cards, and cordials, and thy more cordial conversation, alleviate the closeness and the confinement of thy else (truth to say) not very savoury, nor very inviting, little cabin!

With these additaments to boot, we had on board a fellow-passenger, whose discourse in verity might have beguiled a longer voyage than we meditated, and have made mirth and wonder abound as far as from Thames to the Azores. He was a dark, Spanish-complexioned young man, remarkably handsome, with an officer-like assurance, and an insuppressible volubility of assertion. He was, in fact, the greatest liar I had met with then, or since. He was none of your hesitating half story-tellers (a most painful description of mortals) who go on sounding your belief, and only giving you as much as they see you can swallow at a time—the nibbling pickpockets of your patience—but one who committed downright, day-light depredations upon his neighbour's faith. He did not stand shivering upon the brink, but was a hearty thorough-paced liar, and plunged at once into the depths of your credulity. I partly believe, he made pretty sure of his company. Not many rich, not many wise, or learned, composed at that time the common stowage of a Margate packet. We were, I am afraid, a set of as unfledged Londoners (let our enemies give it a worse name) as Thames or Tooley-street at that time of day could have supplied. There might be an exception or two among us, but I scorn to make any invidious distinctions among such a jolly, companionable ship's company, as those were whom I sailed with. Something too must be conceded to the *Genius Loci*. Had the confident fellow told us half the legends on land, which he favoured us with on the other element, I flatter myself, the good sense of most of us would have revolted. But we were in a new world, with every thing unfamiliar about us, and the time and place disposed us to the reception of any prodigious marvel whatsoever. Time has obliterated from my memory much of his wild fablings; and the rest would appear but dull, as written, and to be read on shore. He had been Aid-de-camp (among other rare accidents and fortunes) to a Persian prince, and at one blow had stricken off the head of the King of Carimania on horseback. He, of course, married the Prince's daughter. I forget what unlucky turn in the politics of that court, combining with the loss of his consort, was the reason of his quitting Persia; but with the rapidity of a magician he transported himself, along with his hearers, back to England, where we still found him in the confidence of great ladies. There was some story of a Princess—Elizabeth, if I remember,—having entrusted to his care an extraordinary casket of jewels, upon some extraordinary occasion—but as I am not certain of the name or circumstance at this distance of time, I must leave it to the Royal daughters of England to settle the honour among themselves in private. I cannot call to mind half his pleasant wonders; but I perfectly remember, that in the course of his travels he had seen a phœnix; and he obligingly undeceived us of the vulgar error, that there is but one of that species at a time, assuring us that they were not uncommon in some parts of Upper Egypt. Hitherto he had found the most implicit listeners. His dreaming fancies had transported us beyond the "ignorant present." But when (still hardying more and more in his triumphs over our simplicity), he went on to affirm that he had actually sailed through the legs of the Colossus at Rhodes, it really became necessary to make a stand. And here I must do justice to the good sense and intrepidity of one of our party, a youth, that had hitherto been one of his most deferential auditors, who, from his recent reading, made bold to assure the gentleman, that there must be some mistake, as "the Colossus in question had been destroyed long since:" to whose opinion, delivered with all modesty, our hero was obliging enough to concede thus much, that "the figure was indeed a little damaged." This was the only opposition he met with, and it did not at all seem to stagger him, for he proceeded with his fables, which the same youth appeared to swallow with still more complacency than ever,—confirmed, as it were, by the extreme candour of that concession. With these prodigies he wheedled us on till we came in sight of the Reculvers, which one of our own company (having been the voyage before) immediately recognising, and pointing out to us, was considered by us as no ordinary seaman.

All this time sate upon the edge of the deck quite a different character. It was a lad, apparently very poor, very infirm, and very patient. His eye was ever on the sea, with a smile; and, if he caught now and then some snatches of these wild legends, it was by accident, and they seemed not to concern him. The waves to him whispered more pleasant stories. He was as one, being with us, but not of us. He heard the bell of dinner ring without stirring; and when some of us pulled out our private stores—our cold meat and our salads—he produced none, and seemed to want none. Only a solitary biscuit he had laid in; provision for the one or two days and nights, to which these vessels then were oftentimes obliged to prolong their voyage. Upon a nearer acquaintance with him, which he seemed neither to court nor decline, we learned that he was going to Margate, with the hope of being admitted into the Infirmary there for sea bathing. His disease was a scrofula, which appeared to have eaten all over him. He expressed great hopes of a cure; and when we asked him, whether he had any friends where he was going, he replied, "he *had* no friends."

These pleasant, and some mournful passages, with the first sight of the sea, co-operating with youth, and a sense of holydays, and out-of-door adventure, to me that had been pent up in populous cities for many months before,—have left upon my mind the fragrance as of summer days gone by, bequeathing nothing but their remembrance for cold and wintery hours to chew upon.

Will it be thought a digression (it may spare some unwelcome comparisons), if I endeavour to account for the *dissatisfaction* which I have heard so many persons confess to have felt (as I did myself feel in part on this occasion), *at the sight of the sea for the first time*? I think the reason usually given—referring to the incapacity of actual objects for satisfying our preconceptions of them —scarcely goes deep enough into the question. Let the same person see a lion, an elephant, a mountain, for the first time in his life, and he shall perhaps feel himself a little mortified. The things do not fill up that space, which the idea of them seemed to take up in his mind. But they have still a correspondency to his first notion, and in time grow up to it, so as to produce a very similar impression; enlarging themselves (if I may say so) upon familiarity. But the sea remains a disappointment.—Is it not, that in *the latter* we had expected to behold (absurdly, I grant, but, I am afraid, by the law of imagination unavoidably) not a definite object, as those wild beasts, or that mountain compassable by the eye, but *all the sea at once*, THE COMMENSURATE ANTAGONIST OF THE EARTH!—I do not say we tell ourselves so much, but the craving of the mind is to be satisfied with nothing less. I will suppose the case of a young person of fifteen (as I then was) knowing nothing of the sea, but from description. He comes to it for the first time—all that he has been reading of it all his life, and *that* the most enthusiastic part of life,—all he has gathered from narratives of wandering seaman; what he has gained from true voyages, and what he cherishes as credulously from romance and poetry; crowding their images, and exacting strange tributes from expectation.—He thinks of the great deep, and of those who go down unto it; of its thousand isles, and the vast continents it washes; of its receiving the mighty Plata, or Orellana, into its bosom, without disturbance, or sense of augmentation; of Biscay swells, and the mariner

For many a day, and many a dreadful night,
Incessant labouring round the stormy Cape;

of fatal rocks, and the "still-vexed Bermoothes;" of great whirlpools, and the water-spout; of sunken ships, and sumless treasures swallowed up in the unrestoring depths; of fishes, and quaint monsters, to which all that is terrible on earth—

Be but as buggs to frighten babes withal,
Compared with the creatures in the sea's
entral;

of naked savages, and Juan Fernandez; of pearls, and shells; of coral beds, and of enchanted isles; of mermaids' grots.—

I do not assert that in sober earnest he expects to be shown all these wonders at once, but he is under the tyranny of a mighty faculty, which haunts him with confused hints and shadows of all these; and when the actual object opens first upon him, seen (in tame weather too most likely) from our unromantic coasts—a speck, a slip of sea-water, as it shews to him—what can it prove but a very unsatisfying and even diminutive entertainment? Or if he has come to it from the mouth of a river, was it much more than the river widening? and, even out of sight of land, what had he but a flat watery horizon about him, nothing comparable to the vast o'er-curtaining sky, his familiar object, seen daily without dread or amazement?—Who, in similar circumstances, has not been tempted to exclaim with Charoba, in the poem of Gebir,

Is this the mighty ocean?—is this *all*?

I love town, or country; but this detestable Cinque Port is neither. I hate these scrubbed shoots, thrusting out their starved foliage from between the horrid fissures of dusty innutritious rocks; which the amateur calls "verdure to the edge of the sea." I require woods, and they show me stunted coppices. I cry out for the water-brooks, and pant for fresh streams, and inland murmurs. I cannot stand all day on the naked beech watching the capricious hues of the sea, shifting like the colours of a dying mullet. I am tired of looking out at the windows of this island-prison. I would fain retire into the interior of my cage. While I gaze upon the sea, I want to be on it, over it, across it. It binds me in with chains, as of iron. My thoughts are abroad. I should not so feel in Staffordshire. There is no home for me here. There is no sense of home at Hastings. It is a place of fugitive resort, an heterogeneous assemblage of sea-mews and stock-brokers, Amphitrites of the town, and misses that coquet with the Ocean. If it were what it was in its primitive shape, and what it ought to have remained, a fair honest fishing-town, and no more, it were something—with a few straggling fishermen's huts scattered about, artless as its cliffs, and with their materials filched from them, it were something. I could abide to dwell with Mescheck; to assort with fisher-swains, and smugglers. There are, or I dream there are, many of this latter occupation here. Their faces become the place. I like a smuggler. He is the only honest thief. He robs nothing but the revenue,—an abstraction I never greatly cared about. I could go out with them in their mackarel boats, or about their less ostensible business, with some satisfaction. I can even tolerate those poor victims to monotony, who from day to day pace along the beech, in endless progress and recurrence, to watch their illicit countrymen—townsfolk or brethren perchance—whistling to the sheathing and unsheathing of their cutlasses (their only solace), who under the mild name of preventive service, keep up a legitimated civil warfare, in the deplorable absence of a foreign one, to show their detestation of run hollands, and zeal for old England. But it is the visitants from town, that come here to *say* they have been here, with no more relish of the sea than a pond perch, or a dace might be supposed to have, that are my aversion. I feel like a foolish dace in these regions, and have as little toleration for myself here, as for them. What can they want here? if they had a true relish of the ocean, why have they brought all this land luggage with them? or why pitch their civilized tents in the desart? What mean these scanty book-rooms—marine libraries, as they entitle them—if the sea were, as they would have us believe, a book "to read strange matter in?" what are their foolish concert-rooms, if they come, as they would fain be thought to do, to listen to the music of the waves? All is false and hollow pretension. They come, because it is the fashion, and to spoil the nature of the place. They are mostly, as I have said, stock-brokers; but I have watched the better sort of them—now and then, an honest citizen (of the old stamp), in the simplicity of his heart, shall bring down his wife and daughters, to taste the sea breezes. I always know the date of their arrival. It is easy to see it in their countenance. A day or two they go wandering on the shingles, picking up cockle-shells, and thinking them great things; but, in a poor week, imagination slackens; they begin to discover that cockles produce no pearls, and then—O then!—if I could interpret for the pretty creatures (I know they have not the courage to confess it themselves) how gladly would they exchange their sea-side rambles for a Sunday walk on the green-sward of their accustomed Twickenham meadows!

I would ask of one of these sea-charmed emigrants, who think they truly love the sea, with its wild usages, what would their feelings be, if some of the unsophisticated aborigines of this place, encouraged by their courteous questionings here, should venture, on the faith of such assured sympathy between them, to return the visit, and come up to see—London. I must imagine them with their fishing-tackle on their back, as we carry our town necessaries. What a sensation would it cause in Lothbury? What vehement laughter would it not excite among

> The daughters of Cheapside, and wives of
> Lombard-street.

I am sure that no town-bred, or inland-born subjects, can feel their true and natural nourishment at these sea-places. Nature, where she does not mean us for mariners and vagabonds, bids us stay at home. The salt foam seems to nourish a spleen. I am not half so good-natured as by the milder waters of my natural river. I would exchange these sea-gulls for swans, and scud a swallow for ever about the banks of Thamesis.

ELIA.

LETTER OF ELIA TO ROBERT SOUTHEY, ESQUIRE.

Sir,—You have done me an unfriendly office, without perhaps much considering what you were doing. You have given an ill name to my poor Lucubrations. In a recent Paper on Infidelity, you usher in a conditional commendation of them with an exception; which, preceding the encomium, and taking up nearly the same space with it, must impress your readers with the notion, that the objectionable parts in them are at least equal in quantity to the pardonable. The censure is in fact the criticism; the praise—a concession merely. Exceptions usually follow, to qualify praise or blame. But there stands your reproof, in the very front of your notice, in ugly characters, like some bugbear, to frighten all good Christians from purchasing. Through you I am become an object of suspicion to preceptors of youth, and fathers of families. "*A book, which wants only a sounder religious feeling to be as delightful as it is original.*" With no further explanation, what must your readers conjecture, but that my little volume is some vehicle for heresy or infidelity? The quotation, which you honour me by subjoining, oddly enough, is of a character, which bespeaks a temperament in the writer the very reverse of *that* your reproof goes to insinuate. Had you been taxing me with superstition, the passage would have been pertinent to the censure. Was it worth your while to go so far out of your way to affront the feelings of an old friend, and commit yourself by an irrelevant quotation, for the pleasure of reflecting upon a poor child, an exile at Genoa?

I am at a loss what particular Essay you had in view (if my poor ramblings amount to that appellation) when you were in such a hurry to thrust in your objection, like bad news, foremost.—Perhaps the Paper on "Saying Graces" was the obnoxious feature. I have endeavoured there to rescue a voluntary duty—good in place, but never, as I remember, literally commanded—from the charge of an undecent formality. Rightly taken, Sir, that Paper was not against Graces, but Want of Grace; not against the ceremony, but the carelessness and slovenliness so often observed in the performance of it.

Or was it *that* on the "New Year"—in which I have described the feelings of the merely natural man, on a consideration of the amazing change, which is supposable to take place on our removal from this fleshly scene?—If men would honestly confess their misgivings (which few men will) there are times when the strongest Christians of us, I believe, have reeled under questionings of such staggering obscurity. I do not accuse you of this weakness. There are some who tremblingly reach out shaking hands to the guidance of Faith—Others who stoutly venture into the dark (their Human Confidence their leader, whom they mistake for Faith); and, investing themselves beforehand with Cherubic wings, as they fancy, find their new robes as familiar, and fitting to their supposed growth and stature in godliness, as the coat they left off yesterday—Some whose hope totters upon crutches—Others who stalk into futurity upon stilts.

The contemplation of a Spiritual

World,—which, without the addition of a misgiving conscience, is enough to shake some natures to their foundation—is smoothly got over by others, who shall float over the black billows, in their little boat of No-Distrust, as unconcernedly as over a summer sea. The difference is chiefly constitutional.

One man shall love his friends and his friends' faces; and, under the uncertainty of conversing with them again, in the same manner and familiar circumstances of sight, speech, &c. as upon earth—in a moment of no irreverent weakness—for a dream-while—no more—would be almost content, for a reward of a life of virtue (if he could ascribe such acceptance to his lame performances), to take up his portion with those he loved, and was made to love, in this good world, which he knows—which was created so lovely, beyond his deservings. Another, embracing a more exalted vision—so that he might receive indefinite additaments of power, knowledge, beauty, glory, &c.—is ready to forego the recognition of humbler individualities of earth, and the old familiar faces. The shapings of our heavens are the modifications of our constitution; and Mr. Feeble Mind, or Mr. Great Heart, is born in every one of us.

Some (and such have been accounted the safest divines) have shrunk from pronouncing upon the final state of any man; nor dare they pronounce the case of Judas to be desperate. Others (with stronger optics), as plainly as with the eye of flesh, shall behold a *given king* in bliss, and a *given chamberlain* in torment; even to the eternising of a cast of the eye in the latter, his own self-mocked and good humouredly-borne deformity on earth, but supposed to aggravate the uncouth and hideous expression of his pangs in the other place. That one man can presume so far, and that another would with shuddering disclaim such confidences, is, I believe, an effect of the nerves purely.

If in either of these Papers, or elsewhere, I have been betrayed into some levities—not affronting the sanctuary, but glancing perhaps at some of the out-skirts and extreme edges, the debateable land between the holy and the profane regions—(for the admixture of man's inventions, twisting themselves with the name of religion itself, has artfully made it difficult to touch even the alloy, without, in some men's estimation, soiling the fine gold)—if I have sported within the purlieus of serious matter—it was, I dare say, a humour—be not startled, Sir—which I have unwittingly derived from yourself. You have all your life been making a jest of the Devil. Not of the scriptural meaning of that dark essence—personal or allegorical; for the nature is no where plainly delivered. I acquit you of intentional irreverence. But indeed you have made wonderfully free with, and been mighty pleasant upon, the popular idea and attributes of him. A noble Lord, your brother Visionary, has scarcely taken greater liberties with the material keys, and merely Catholic notion of St. Peter.—You have flattered him in prose: you have chanted him in goodly odes. You have been his Jester; Volunteer Laureat, and self-elected Court Poet to Beëlzebub.

You have never ridiculed, I believe, what you thought to be religion, but you are always girding at what some pious, but perhaps mistaken folks, think to be so. For this reason I am sorry to hear, that you are engaged upon a life of George Fox. I know you will fall into the error of intermixing some comic stuff with your seriousness. The Quakers tremble at the subject in your hands. The Methodists are shy of you, upon account of *their* founder. But, above all, our Popish brethren are most in your debt. The errors of that church have proved a fruitful source to your scoffing vein. Their Legend has been a Golden one to you. And here, your friends, Sir, have noticed a noteable inconsistency. To the imposing rites, the solemn penances, devout austerities of that communion; the affecting though erring piety of their hermits; the silence and solitude of the Chartreux—their crossings, their holy waters—their Virgin, and their saints—to these, they say, you have been indebted for the best feelings, and the richest imagery, of your Epic poetry. You have drawn copious drafts upon Loretto. We thought at one time you were going post to Rome—but that in the facetious commentaries, which it is your custom to append so plentifully, and (some say) injudiciously, to your loftiest performances in this kind, you spurn the uplifted toe, which you but just now seemed to court; leave his holiness in the lurch; and show him a fair pair of Protestant heels under your Romish vestment. When we think you already at the wicket, suddenly a violent cross wind blows you transverse—

> ten thousand leagues awry.
> Then might we see
> Cowls, hoods, and habits, with their wearers, tost
> And flutter'd into rags; then reliques, beads,
> Indulgences, dispenses, pardons, bulls,
> The sport of winds.

You pick up pence by showing the hallowed bones, shrine, and crucifix; and you take money a second time by exposing the trick of them afterwards. You carry your verse to Castle Angelo for sale in a morning; and, swifter than a pedlar can transmute his pack, you are at Canterbury with your prose ware before night.

Sir, is it that I dislike you in this merry vein? The very reverse. No countenance becomes an intelligent jest better than your own. It is your grave aspect, when you look awful upon your poor friends, which I would deprecate.

In more than one place, if I mistake not, you have been pleased to compliment me at the expence of my companions. I cannot accept your compliment at such a price. The upbraiding a man's poverty naturally makes him look about him, to see whether he be so poor indeed as he is presumed to be. You have put me upon counting my riches. Really, Sir, I did not know I was so wealthy in the article of friendships. There is ——, and ——, whom you never heard of, but exemplary characters both, and excellent church-goers; and N., mine and my father's friend for nearly half a century; and the enthusiast for Wordsworth's poetry, T. N. T., a little tainted with Socinianism, it is to be feared, but constant in his attachments, and a capital critic; and ——, a sturdy old Athanasian, so that sets all to rights again; and W., the light, and warm-as-light hearted, Janus of the London; and the translator of Dante, still a curate, modest and amiable C.; and Allan C., the large-hearted Scot; and P——r, candid and affectionate as his own poetry; and A—p, Coleridge's friend; and G—n, his more than friend; and Coleridge himself, the same to me still, as in those old evenings, when we used to sit and speculate (do you remember them, Sir?) at our old Salutation tavern, upon Pantisocracy and golden days to come on earth; and W—th (why, Sir, I might drop my rent-roll here; such goodly farms and manors have I reckoned up already. In what possessions has not this last name alone estated me!—but I will go on)—and M., the noble-minded kinsman, by wedlock, of W——th; and H. C. R., unwearied in the offices of a friend; and Clarkson, almost above the narrowness of that relation, yet condescending not seldom heretofore from the labours of his world-embracing charity to bless my humble roof; and the gall-less and single-minded Dyer; and the high-minded associate of Cook, the veteran Colonel, with his lusty heart still sending cartels of defiance to old Time; and, not least, W. A. the last and steadiest left to me of that little knot of whist-players, that used to assemble weekly, for so many years, at the Queen's Gate (you remember them, Sir?) and called Admiral Burney friend.

I will come to the point at once. I believe you will not make many exceptions to my associates so far. But I have purposely omitted some intimacies, which I do not yet repent of having contracted, with two gentlemen, diametrically opposed to yourself in principles. You will understand me to allude to the authors of Rimini and of the Table Talk. And first, of the former.—

It is an error more particularly incident to persons of the correctest principles and habits, to seclude themselves from the rest of mankind, as from another species; and form into knots and clubs. The best people, herding thus exclusively, are in danger of contracting a narrowness. Heat and cold, dryness and moisture, in the natural world, do not fly asunder, to split the globe into sectarian parts and separations; but mingling, as they best may, correct the malignity of any single predominance. The analogy holds, I suppose, in the moral world. If all the good people were to ship themselves off to Terra Incognitas, what, in humanity's name, is to become of the refuse? If the persons, whom I have chiefly in view, have not pushed matters to this extremity yet, they carry them as far as they can go. Instead of mixing with the infidel and the free-thinker—in the room of opening a negociation, to try at least to find out at which gate the error entered—they huddle close together, in a weak fear of infection, like that pusillanimous underling in Spenser—

> This is the wandering wood, this Error's den;
> A monster vile, whom God and man does hate:
> Therefore, I reed, beware. Fly, fly, quoth then
> The fearful Dwarf.

and, if they be writers in orthodox journals—addressing themselves only to the irritable passions of the unbeliever—they proceed in a safe system of strengthening the strong hands, and confirming the valiant knees; of converting the already converted, and proselyting their own party. I am the more convinced of this from a passage in the very Treatise which occasioned this letter. It is where, having recommended to the doubter the writings of Michaelis and Lardner, you ride triumphant over the necks of all infidels, sceptics, and dissenters, from this time to the world's end, upon the wheels of two unanswerable deductions. I do not hold it meet to set down in a Miscellaneous Compilation like this, such religious words as you have thought fit to introduce into the pages of a petulant Literary Journal. I therefore beg leave to substitute *numerals*, and refer to the Quarterly Review (for July) for filling of them up. "Here," say you, "as in the history of 7, if these books are authentic, the events which they relate must be true; if they were written by 8, 9 is 10 and 11." Your first deduction, if it means honestly, rests upon two identical propositions; though I suspect an unfairness in one of the terms, which this would not be quite the proper place for explicating. At all events *you* have no cause to triumph; you have not been proving the premises, but refer for satisfaction therein to very long and laborious works, which may well employ the sceptic a twelvemonth or two to digest, before he can possibly be ripe for your conclusion. When he has satisfied himself about the premises, he will concede to you the inference, I dare say, most readily.—But your latter deduction, *viz.* that because 8 has written a book concerning 9, therefore 10 and 11 was certainly his meaning, is one of the most extraordinary conclusions *per saltum* that I have had the good fortune to meet with. As far as 10 is verbally asserted in the writings, all sects must agree with you; but you cannot be ignorant of the many various ways in which the doctrine of the ********* has been understood, from a low figurative expression (with the Unitarians) up to the most mysterious actuality; in which highest sense alone you and your church take it. And for 11, and that there is *no other possible conclusion*—to hazard this in the face of so many thousands of Arians and Socinians, &c., who have drawn so opposite a one, is such a piece of theological hardihood, as, I think, warrants me in concluding that, when you sit down to pen theology, you do not at all consider your opponents; but have in your eye, merely and exclusively, readers of the same way of thinking with yourself, and therefore have no occasion to trouble yourself with the quality of the logic, to which you treat them.

Neither can I think, if you had had the welfare of the poor child—over whose hopeless condition you whine so lamentably and (I must think) unseasonably—seriously at heart, that you could have taken the step of sticking him up *by name*—T. H. is as good as *naming* him—to perpetuate an outrage upon the parental feelings, as long as the Quarterly Review shall last.—Was it necessary to specify an individual case, and give to Christian compassion the appearance of personal attack? Is this the way to conciliate unbelievers, or not rather to widen the breach irreparably?

I own I could never think so considerably of myself as to decline the society of an agreeable or worthy man upon difference of opinion only. The impediments and the facilitations to a sound belief are various and inscrutable as the heart of man. Some believe upon weak principles. Others cannot feel the efficacy of the strongest. One of the most candid, most upright, and single-meaning men, I ever knew, was the late Thomas Holcroft. I believe he never said one thing and meant another, in his life; and, as near as I can guess, he never acted otherwise than with the most scrupulous attention to conscience. Ought we to wish the character false, for the sake of a hollow compliment to Christianity?

Accident introduced me to the acquaintance of Mr. L. H.—and the experience of his many friendly qualities confirmed a friendship between us. You, who have been misrepresented yourself, I should hope, have not lent an idle ear to the calumnies which have been spread abroad respecting this gentleman. I was admitted to his household for some years, and do most solemnly aver that I believe him to be in his domestic relations as correct as any man. He chose an ill-judged subject for a poem; the peccant humours of which have been visited on him tenfold by the artful use, which his adversaries have made, of an *equivocal term*. The subject itself was started by Dante, but better because brieflier treated of. But the crime of the Lovers, in the Italian and the English poet, with its aggravated enormity of circumstance, is not of a kind (as the critics of the latter well knew) with those conjunctions, for which Nature herself has provided no excuse, because no temptation. —It has nothing in common with the black horrors, sung by Ford and Massinger. The familiarising of it in tale or fable may be for that reason incidentally more contagious. In spite of Rimini, I must look upon its author as a man of taste, and a poet. He is better than so, he is one of the most cordial-minded men I ever knew, and matchless as a fire-side companion. I mean not to affront or wound your feelings when I say that, in his more genial moods, he has often reminded me of you. There is the same air of mild dogmatism—the same condescending to a boyish sportiveness—in both your conversations. His hand-writing is so much the same with your own, that I have opened more than one letter of his, hoping, nay, not doubting, but it was from you, and have been disappointed (he will bear with my saying so) at the discovery of my error. L. H. is unfortunate in holding some loose and not very definite speculations (for at times I think he hardly knows whither his premises would carry him) on marriage—the tenets, I conceive, of the Political Justice, carried a little further. For any thing I could discover in his practice, they have reference, like those, to some future possible condition of society, and not to the present times. But neither for these obliquities of thinking (upon which my own conclusions are as distant as the poles asunder)—nor for his political asperities and petulancies, which are wearing out with the heats and vanities of youth—did I select him for a friend; but for qualities which fitted him for that relation. I do not know whether I flatter myself with being the occasion, but certain it is, that, touched with some misgivings for sundry harsh things which he had written aforetime against our friend C.,—before he left this country he sought a reconciliation with that gentleman (himself being his own introducer), and found it.

L. H. is now in Italy; on his departure to which land with much regret I took my leave of him and of his little family—seven of them, Sir, with their mother—and as kind a set of little people (T. H. and all), as affectionate children, as ever blessed a parent. Had you seen them, Sir, I think you could not have looked upon them as so many little Jonases—but rather as pledges of the vessel's safety, that was to bear such a freight of love.

I wish you would read Mr. H.'s lines to that same T. H. "six years old, during a sickness:"—

> Sleep breaks at last from out thee,
> My little patient boy—

(they are to be found in the 47th page of "Foliage")—and ask yourself how far they are out of the spirit of Christianity. I have a letter from Italy, received but the other day, into which L. H. has put as much heart, and as many friendly yearnings after old associates, and native country, as, I think, paper can well hold. It would do you no hurt to give that the perusal also.

From the *other gentleman* I neither expect nor desire (as he is well assured) any such concessions as L. H. made to C. What hath soured him, and made him to suspect his friends of infidelity towards him, when there was no such matter, I know not. I stood well with him for fifteen years (the proudest of my life), and have ever spoke my full mind of him to some, to whom his panegyric must naturally be least tasteful. I never in thought swerved from him, I never betrayed him, I never slackened in my admiration of him, I was the same to him (neither better nor worse) though he could not see it, as in the days when he thought fit to trust me. At this instant, he may be preparing for me some compliment, above my deserts, as he has sprinkled many such among his admirable books, for which I rest his debtor; or, for any thing I know, or can guess to the contrary, he may be about to read a lecture on my weaknesses. He is welcome to them (as he was to my humble hearth), if they can divert a spleen, or ventilate a fit of sullenness. I wish he would not quarrel with the world at the rate he does; but the reconciliation must be effected by himself, and I despair of living to see that day. But, protesting against much that he has written, and some things which he chooses to do; judging him by his conversation which I enjoyed so long, and relished so deeply; or by his books, in those places where no clouding passion intervenes—I should belie my own conscience, if I said less, than that I think W. H. to be, in his natural and healthy state, one of the wisest and finest spirits breathing. So far from being ashamed of that intimacy, which was betwixt us, it is my boast that I was able for so many years to have preserved it entire; and I think I shall go to my grave without finding, or expecting to find, such another companion. But I forget my manners—you will pardon me, Sir—I return to the correspondence.—

Sir, you were *pleased* (you know where) to invite me to a compliance with the wholesome forms and doctrines of the Church of England. I take your advice with as much kindness, as it was meant. But I must think the invitation rather more kind than seasonable. I am a Dissenter. The last sect, with which you can remember me to have made common profession, were the Unitarians. You would think it not very pertinent, if (fearing that all was not well with you), I were gravely to invite you (for a remedy) to attend with me a course of Mr. Belsham's Lectures at Hackney. Perhaps I have scruples to some of your forms and doctrines. But if I come, am I secure of civil treatment?—The last time I was in any of your places of worship was on Easter Sunday last. I had the satisfaction of listening to a very sensible sermon of an argumentative turn, delivered with great propriety, by one of your bishops. The place was Westminster Abbey. As such religion, as I have, has always acted on me more by way of sentiment than argumentative process, I was not unwilling, after sermon ended, by no unbecoming transition, to pass over to some serious feelings, impossible to be disconnected from the sight of those old tombs, &c. But, by whose order I know not, I was debarred that privilege even for so short a space as a few minutes; and turned, like a dog or some profane person, out into the common street; with feelings, which I could not help, but not very genial to the day or the discourse. I do not know that I shall ever venture myself again into one of your Churches.

You had your education at Westminster; and doubtless among those dim aisles and cloisters, you must have gathered much of that devotional feeling in those young years, on which your purest mind feeds still—and may it feed! The antiquarian spirit, strong in you, and gracefully blending ever with the religious, may have been sown in you among those wrecks of splendid mortality. You owe it to the place of your education; you owe it to your learned fondness for the architecture of your ancestors; you owe it to the venerableness of your ecclesiastical establishment, which is daily lessened and called in question through these practices—to speak aloud your sense of them; never to desist raising your voice against them, till they be totally done away with and abolished; till the doors of Westminster Abbey be no longer closed against the decent, though low-in-purse, enthusiast, or blameless devotee, who must commit an injury against his family economy, if he would be indulged with a bare admission within its walls. You owe it to the decencies, which you wish to see maintained in its impressive services, that our Cathedral be no longer an object of inspection to the poor at those times only, in which they must rob from their attendance on the worship every minute which they can bestow upon the fabrick. In vain the public prints have taken up this subject, in vain such poor nameless writers as myself express their indignation. A word from you, Sir—a hint in your Journal—would be sufficient to fling open the doors of the Beautiful Temple again, as we can remember them when we were boys. At that time of life, what would the imaginative faculty (such as it is) in both of us, have suffered, if the entrance to so much reflection had been obstructed by the demand of so much silver!—If we had scraped it up to gain an occasional admission (as we certainly should have done) would the sight of those old tombs have been as impressive to us (while we had been weighing anxiously prudence against sentiment) as when the gates stood open, as those of the adjacent Park; when we could walk in at any time, as the mood brought us, for a shorter or longer time, as *that* lasted? Is the being shown over a place the same as silently for ourselves detecting the genius of it? In no part of our beloved Abbey now can a person find entrance (out of service time) under the sum of *two shillings*. The rich and the great will smile at the anticlimax, presumed to lie in these two short words. But you can tell them, Sir, how much quiet worth, how much capacity for enlarged feeling, how much taste and genius, may coexist, especially in youth, with a purse incompetent to this demand.—A respected friend of ours, during his late visit to the metropolis, presented himself for admission to Saint Paul's. At the same time a decently clothed man, with as decent a wife, and child, were bargaining for the same indulgence. The price was only two-pence each person. The poor but decent man hesitated, desirous to go in; but there were three of them, and he turned away reluctantly. Perhaps he wished to have seen the tomb of Nelson. Perhaps the Interior of the Cathedral was his object. But in the state of his finances, even sixpence might reasonably seem too much. Tell the Aristocracy of the country (no man can do it more impressively); instruct them of what value these insignificant pieces of money, these minims to their sight, may be to their humbler brethren. Shame these Sellers out of the Temple. Show the poor, that you can sometimes think of them in some other light than as mutineers and mal-contents. Conciliate them by such kind methods to their superiors, civil and ecclesiastical. Stop the mouths of the railers; and suffer your old friends, upon the old terms, again to honour and admire you. Stifle not the suggestions of your better nature with the stale evasion, that an indiscriminate admission would expose the Tombs to violation. Remember your boy-days. Did you ever see, or hear, of a mob in the Abbey, while it was free to all? Do the rabble come there, or trouble their heads about such speculations? It is all that you can do to drive them into your churches; they do not voluntarily offer themselves. They have, alas! no passion for antiquities; for tomb of king or prelate, sage or poet. If they had, they would be no longer the rabble.

For forty years that I have known the Fabrick, the only well-attested charge of violation adduced, has been—a ridiculous dismemberment committed upon the effigy of that amiable spy, Major André. And is it for this—the wanton mischief of some school-boy, fired perhaps with raw notions of Transatlantic Freedom—or the remote possibility of such a mischief occurring again, so easily to be prevented by stationing a constable within the walls, if the vergers are incompetent to the duty

—is it upon such wretched pretences, that the people of England are made to pay a new Peter's Pence, so long abrogated; or must content themselves with contemplating the ragged Exterior of their Cathedral? The mischief was done about the time that you were a scholar there. Do you know any thing about the unfortunate relic?—can you help us in this emergency to find the nose?—or can you give Chantry a notion (from memory) of its pristine life and vigour? I am willing for peace' sake to subscribe my guinea towards a restoration of the lamented feature.

I am, Sir,

Your humble servant,

ELIA.

GUY FAUX.

A VERY ingenious and subtle writer, whom there is good reason for suspecting to be an Ex-Jesuit, not unknown at Douay some five-and-twenty years since (he will not obtrude himself at M——th again in a hurry), about a twelvemonth back, set himself to prove the character of the Powder Plot conspirators to have been that of heroic self-devotedness and true Christian martyrdom. Under the mask of Protestant candour, he actually gained admission for his treatise into a London weekly paper, not particularly distinguished for its zeal towards either religion. But, admitting Catholic principles, his arguments are shrewd and incontrovertible. He says—

> Guy Faux was a fanatic, but he was no hypocrite. He ranks among *good haters.* He was cruel, bloody-minded, reckless of all considerations but those of an infuriated and bigoted faith; but he was a true son of the Catholic Church, a martyr and a confessor, for all that. He who can prevail upon himself to devote his life for a cause, however we may condemn his opinions or abhor his actions, vouches at least for the honesty of his principles and the disinterestedness of his motives. He may be guilty of the worst practices, but he is capable of the greatest. He is no longer a slave, but free. The contempt of death is the beginning of virtue. The hero of the Gunpowder-Plot was, if you will, a fool, a madman, an assassin; call him what names you please: still he was neither knave nor coward. He did not propose to blow up the Parliament and come off, scot-free, himself; he showed that he valued his own life no more than theirs in such a cause—where the integrity of the Catholic faith and the salvation of perhaps millions of souls was at stake. He did not call it a murder, but a sacrifice which he was about to achieve: he was armed with the Holy Spirit and with fire: he was the Church's chosen servant and her blessed martyr. He comforted himself as "the best of cut-throats." How many wretches are there that would have undertaken to do what he

intended for a sum of money, if they could have got off with impunity! How few are there who would have put themselves in Guy Faux's situation to save the universe! Yet in the latter case we affect to be thrown into greater consternation than at the most unredeemed acts of villainy, as if the absolute disinterestedness of the motive doubled the horror of the deed! The cowardice and selfishness of mankind are in fact shocked at the consequences to themselves (if such examples are held up for imitation), and they make a fearful outcry against the violation of every principle of morality, lest they too should be called on for any such tremendous sacrifices—lest they in their turn should have to go on the forlorn hope of extra-official duty. *Charity begins at home*, is a maxim that prevails as well in the courts of conscience as in those of prudence. We would be thought to shudder at the consequences of crime to others, while we tremble for them to ourselves. We talk of the dark and cowardly assassin; and this is well, when an individual shrinks from the face of an enemy, and purchases his own safety by striking a blow in the dark: but how the charge of cowardly can be applied to the public assassin, who, in the very act of destroying another, lays down his life as the pledge and forfeit of his sincerity and boldness, I am at a loss to devise. There may be barbarous prejudice, rooted hatred, unprincipled treachery, in such an act; but he who resolves to take all the danger and odium upon himself, can no more be branded with cowardice, than Regulus devoting himself for his country, or Codrus leaping into the fiery gulf. A wily Father Inquisitor, coolly and with plenary authority condemning hundreds of helpless, unoffending victims, to the flames or to the horrors of a living tomb, while he himself would not suffer a hair of his head to be hurt, is to me a character without any qualifying trait in it. Again; the Spanish conqueror and hero, the favourite of his monarch, who enticed thirty thousand poor Mexicans into a large open building, under promise of strict faith and cordial good-will, and then set fire to it, making sport of the cries and agonies of these deluded creatures, is an instance of uniting the most hardened cruelty with the most heartless selfishness. His plea was keeping no faith with heretics: this was Guy Faux's too; but I am sure at least that the latter kept faith with himself: he was in earnest in his professions. *His* was not gay, wanton, unfeeling depravity; he did not murder in sport; it was serious work that he had taken in hand. To see this arch-bigot, this heart-whole traitor, this pale miner in the infernal regions, skulking in his retreat with his cloak and dark lanthorn, moving cautiously about among his barrels of gunpowder loaded with death, but not yet ripe for destruction, regardless of the lives of others, and more than indifferent to his own, presents a picture of the strange infatuation of the human understanding, but not of the depravity of the human will, without an equal. There were thousands of pious Papists privy to and ready to applaud the deed when done:—there was no one but our old fifth-of-November friend, who still flutters in rags and straw on the occasion, that had the courage to attempt it. In him stern duty and unshaken faith prevailed over natural frailty.

It is impossible, upon Catholic principles, not to admit the force of this reasoning; we can only not help smiling (with the writer) at the simplicity of the gulled editor, swallowing the dregs of Loyola for the very quintessence of sublimated reason in England at the commencement of the nineteenth century. We will just, as a contrast, show what we Protestants (who are a party concerned) thought upon the same subject, at a period rather nearer to the heroic project in question.

The Gunpowder Treason was the subject which called forth the earliest specimen which is left us of the pulpit eloquence of Jeremy Taylor. When he preached the Sermon on that anniversary, which is printed at the end of the folio edition of his Sermons, he was a young man just commencing his ministry, under the auspices of Archbishop Laud. From the learning, and maturest oratory, which it manifests, one should rather have conjectured it to have proceeded from the same person after he was ripened by time into a Bishop and Father of the Church.—"And, really, these *Romano-barbari* could never pretend to any precedent for an act so barbarous as theirs. Adramelech, indeed, killed a king, but he spared the people; Haman would have killed the people, but spared the king; but that both king and people, princes and judges, branch and rush and root, should die at once (as if Caligula's wish were actuated, and all England upon one head), was never known till now, that all the malice of the world met in this as in a centre. The Sicilian even-song, the matins of St. Bartholomew, known for the pitiless and damned massacres, were but κάπνυ σκιᾶς ὄναρ, the dream of the shadow of smoke, if compared with this great fire. *In tam occupato sæculo fabulas vulgares nequitia non invenit.* This was a busy age; Herostratus must have invented a more sublimed malice than the burning of one temple, or not have been so much as spoke of since the discovery of the powder treason. But I must make more haste, I shall not else climb the sublimity of this impiety. Nero was sometimes the *populare odium*, was popularly hated, and deserved it too, for he slew his master, and his wife, and all his family, once or twice over,—opened his mother's womb,—fired the city, laughed at it, slandered the Christians for it; but yet all these were but *principia malorum*, the very first rudiments of evil. Add, then, to these, Herod's master-piece at Ramah, as it was deciphered by the tears and sad threnes of the matrons in an universal mourning for the loss of their pretty infants; yet this of Herod will prove but an infant wickedness, and that of Nero the evil but of one city. I would willingly have found out an example, but see I cannot; should I put into the scale the extract of all the old tyrants famous in antique stories,—

Bistonii stabulum regis, Busiridis aras,
Antiphatæ mensas, et Taurica regna
Thoantis;—

should I take for true story the highest cruelty as it was fancied by the most hieroglyphical Egyptian, this alone would weigh them down, as if the Alps were put in scale against the dust of a balance. For had this accursed treason prospered, we should have had the whole kingdom mourn for the inestimable loss of its chiefest glory, its life, its present joy, and all its very hopes for the future. For such was their destined malice, that they would not only have inflicted so cruel a blow, but have made it incurable, by cutting off our supplies of joy, the whole succession of the Line Royal. Not only the vine itself, but all the *gemmulæ*, and the tender olive branches, should either have been bent to their intentions, and made to grow crooked, or else been broken.

"And now, after such a sublimity of malice, I will not instance in the sacrilegious ruin of the neighbouring temples, which needs must have perished in the flame,—nor in the disturbing the ashes of our intombed kings, devouring their dead ruins like sepulchral dogs,—these are but minutes, in respect of the ruin prepared for the living temples:—

Stragem sed istam non tulit
Christus cadentum Principum
Impune, ne forsan sui
Patris periret fabrica.

Ergo quæ poterit lingua retexere
Laudes, Christe, tuas, qui domitum struis
Infidum populum cum Duce perfido!"

In such strains of eloquent indignation did Jeremy Taylor's young oratory inveigh against that stupendous attempt, which he truly says had no parallel in ancient or modern times. A century and a half of European crimes has elapsed since he made the assertion, and his position remains in its strength. He wrote near the time in which the nefarious project had like to have been completed. Men's minds still were shuddering from the recentness of the escape. It must have been within his memory, or have been sounded in his ears so young by his parents, that he would seem, in his maturer years, to have remembered it. No wonder then that he describes it in words that burn. But to us, to whom the tradition has come slowly down, and has had time to cool, the story of Guido Vaux sounds rather like a tale, a fable, and an invention, than true history. It supposes such gigantic audacity of daring, combined with such more than infantile stupidity in the motive,—such a combination of the fiend and the monkey,—that credulity is almost swallowed up in contemplating the singularity of the attempt. It has accordingly, in some degree, shared the fate of fiction. It is familiarized to us in a kind of serio-ludicrous way, like the story of *Guy of Warwick*, or *Valentine and Orson*. The way which we take to perpetuate the memory of this deliverance is well adapted to keep up this fabular notion. Boys go about the streets annually with a beggarly scarecrow dressed up, which is to be burnt, indeed, at night, with holy zeal; but, meantime, they beg a penny for *poor Guy*: this periodical petition, which we have heard from our infancy,—combined with the dress and appearance of the effigy, so well calculated to move compassion,—has the effect of quite removing from our fancy the horrid circumstances of the story which is thus commemorated; and in *poor Guy* vainly should we try to recognize any of the features of that tremendous madman in iniquity, Guido Vaux, with his horrid crew of accomplices, that sought to emulate earthquakes and bursting volcanoes in their more than mortal mischief.

Indeed, the whole ceremony of burning Guy Faux, or *the Pope*, as he is indifferently called, is a sort of *Treason Travestie*, and admirably adapted to lower our feelings upon this memorable subject. The printers of the little duodecimo *Prayer Book*, printed by T. Baskett,* in 1749, which has the effigy of his sacred Majesty George II. piously prefixed, have illustrated the service (a very fine one in itself) which is appointed for the Anniversary of this Day, with a print, which it is not very easy to describe, but the contents appear to be these:—The scene is a room, I conjecture, in the king's palace. Two persons,—one of whom I take to be James himself, from his wearing his hat while the other stands bareheaded,—are intently surveying a sort of speculum, or magic mirror, which stands upon a pedestal in the midst of the room, in which a little figure of Guy Faux with his dark lantern approaching the door of the Parliament House is made discernible by the light proceeding from a *great eye* which shines in from the topmost corner of the apartment, by which eye the pious artist no doubt meant to designate Providence. On the other side of the mirror, is a figure doing something, which puzzled me when a child, and continues to puzzle me now. The best I can make of it is, that it is a conspirator busy laying the train,—but then, why is he represented in the king's chamber?—Conjecture upon so fantastical a design is vain, and I only notice the print as being one of the earliest graphic representations which woke my childhood into wonder, and doubtless combined with the mummery before-mentioned, to take off the edge of that horror which the naked historical mention of Guido's conspiracy could not have failed of exciting.

Now that so many years are past since that abominable machination was happily frustrated, it will not, I hope, be considered a profane sporting with the subject, if we take no very serious survey of the consequences that would have flowed from this plot if it had had a successful issue. The first thing that strikes us, in a selfish point of view, is the material change which it must have produced in the course of the nobility. All the ancient peerage being extinguished, as it was intended, at one blow, the *Red-Book* must have been closed for ever, or a new race of peers must have been created to supply the deficiency; as the first part of this dilemma is a deal too shocking to think of, what a fund of mouth-watering reflections does this give rise to in the breast of us plebeians of A. D. 1823. Why you or I, reader, might have been Duke of ——— or Earl of ———: I particularize no titles, to avoid the least suspicion of intention to usurp the dignities of the two noblemen whom I have in my eye:—but a feeling more dignified than envy sometimes excites a sigh, when I think how the posterity of Guido's Legion of Honour (among whom you or I might have been) might have rolled down "dulcified," as Burke expresses it, "by an exposure to the influence of heaven in a long flow of generations, from the hard, acidulous, metallic tincture of the spring."† What new orders of merit, think you, this English Napoleon would have chosen? Knights of the Barrel, or Lords of the Tub, Grand Almoners of the Cellar, or Ministers of Explosion. We should have given the Train *couchant*, and the Fire *rampant* in our arms; we should have quartered the dozen white matches in our coats;—the Shallows would have been nothing to us.

* The same, I presume, upon whom the clergyman in the song of the *Vicar and Moses*, not without judgment, passes this memorable censure—

> Here, Moses, the King:—
> 'Tis a scandalous thing
> That this Baskett should print for the Crown.

† Letter to a Noble Lord.

Turning away from these mortifying reflections, let us contemplate its effects upon the *other house,* for they were all to have gone together,— King, Lords, Commons———

To assist our imagination, let us take leave to suppose,—and we do it in the harmless wantonness of fancy,—to suppose that the tremendous explosion had taken place in our days;—we better know what a House of Commons is in our days, and can better estimate our loss;—let us imagine, then, to ourselves, the United Members sitting in full conclave above—Faux just ready with his train and matches below; in his hand a "reed tipt with fire"—he applies the fatal engine———

To assist our notions still further, let us suppose some lucky dog of a reporter, who had escaped by miracle upon some plank of St. Stephen's benches, and came plump upon the roof of the adjacent Abbey, from whence descending, at some neighbouring coffee-house, first wiping his clothes and calling for a glass of lemonade, he sits down and reports what he had heard and seen (quorum pars magna fuit) for the *Morning Post* or the *Courier,*—we can scarcely imagine him describing the event in any other words but some such as these:—

"A *Motion* was put and carried, That this House do *adjourn:* That the Speaker do *quit the Chair.* The House ROSE amid clamours for Order."

In some such way the event might most technically have been conveyed to the public. But a poetical mind, not content with this dry method of narration, cannot help pursuing the effects of this tremendous blowing up, this adjournment in the air *sine die.* It sees the benches mount,—the Chair first, and then the benches, and first the Treasury Bench, hurried up in this nitrous explosion; the Members, as it were, pairing off; Whigs and Tories taking their friendly apotheosis together, (as they did their sandwiches below in Bellamy's room). Fancy, in her flight, keeps pace with the aspiring legislators, she sees the awful seat of order mounting till it becomes finally fixed a constellation, next to Cassiopeia's chair,—the wig of him that sat in it taking its place near Berenice's curls. St. Peter, at Heaven's wicket,—no, not St. Peter,—St. Stephen, with open arms, receives his own———

While Fancy beholds these celestial appropriations, Reason, no less pleased, discerns the mighty benefit which so complete a renovation must produce below. Let the most determined foe to corruption, the most thorough-paced redresser of abuses, try to conceive a more absolute purification of the House than this was calculated to produce;—why, Pride's Purge was nothing to it;—the whole borough-mongering system would have been got rid of, fairly *exploded;*—with it, the senseless distinctions of party must have disappeared; faction must have vanished; corruption have expired in air. From Hundred, Tything, and Wapentake, some new Alfred would have convened, in all its purity, the primitive Wittenagemot,—fixed upon a basis of property or population, permanent as the poles———

From this dream of universal restitution, Reason and Fancy with difficulty awake to view the real state of things. But, blessed be Heaven, St. Stephen's walls are yet standing, all her seats firmly secured; nay, some have doubted (since the Septennial Act) whether gunpowder itself, or any thing short of a *Committee above stairs,* would be able to shake any one member from his seat;—that great and final improvement to the Abbey, which is all that seems wanting,—the removing Westminster-hall and its appendages, and letting in the view of the Thames,—must not be expected in our days. Dismissing, therefore, all such speculations as mere tales of a tub, it is the duty of every honest Englishman to endeavour, by means less wholesale than Guido's, to ameliorate, without extinguishing, Parliaments; to hold the *lantern* to the dark places of corruption; to apply the *match* to the rotten parts of the system only; and to wrap himself up, not in the muffling mantle of conspiracy, but in the warm, honest *cloak* of integrity and patriotic intention.

ELIA.

NUGÆ CRITICÆ:

BY THE AUTHOR OF ELIA.

No. II.

ON A PASSAGE IN THE TEMPEST.

As long as I can remember the play of the Tempest, one passage in it has always set me upon wondering. It has puzzled me beyond measure. In vain I strove to find the meaning of it. I seemed doomed to cherish infinite hopeless curiosity.

It is where Prospero, relating the banishment of Sycorax from Argier, adds—

> —— For one thing that she did
> They would not take her life—

how have I pondered over this, when a boy! how have I longed for some authentic memoir of the witch to clear up the obscurity!—Was the story extant in the Chronicles of Algiers? Could I get at it by some fortunate introduction to the Algerine ambassador? Was a voyage thither practicable? The Spectator (I knew) went to Grand Cairo, only to measure a pyramid. Was not the object of my quest of at least as much importance?—The blue-eyed hag—could *she* have done any thing good or meritorious? might that Succubus relent? then might there be hope for the devil. I have often admired since, that none of the commentators have boggled at this passage—how they could swallow this camel—such a tantalising piece of obscurity, such an abortion of an anecdote.

At length I think I have lighted upon a clue, which may lead to show what was passing in the mind of Shakspeare, when he dropped this imperfect rumour. In the "accurate description of Africa, by John Ogilby (Folio) 1670," page 230, I find written, as follows. The marginal title to the narrative is—

Charles the Fifth besieges Algier.

In the last place, we will briefly give an account of the Emperour Charles the Fifth, when he besieg'd this city; and of the great loss he suffer'd therein.

This Prince in the year one thousand five hundred forty one, having embarqued upon the sea an army of twenty two thousand men aboard eighteen gallies, and an hundred tall ships, not counting the barques and shallops, and other small boats, in which he had engaged the principal of the Spanish and Italian nobility, with a good number of the knights of Maltha; he was to land on the coast of Barbary, at a cape call'd Matifou. From this place unto the city of Algier a flat shore or strand extends itself for about four leagues, the which is exceeding favourable to gallies. There he put ashore with his army, and in a few days caused a fortress to be built, which unto this day is call'd the Castle of the Emperor.

In the mean time the city of Algier took the alarm, having in it at that time but eight hundred Turks, and six thousand Moors, poor-spirited men, and unexercised in martial affairs; besides it was at that time fortifi'd onely with walls, and had no out-works: insomuch that by reason of its weakness, and the great forces of the Emperour, it could not in appearance escape taking. In fine, it was attaqued with such order, that the army came up to the very gates, where the Chevalier de Sauignac, a Frenchman by nation, made himself remarkable above all the rest, by the miracles of his valour. For having repulsed the Turks, who having made a sally at the gate call'd Babason, and there desiring to enter along with them, when he saw that they shut the gate upon him, he ran his ponyard into the same, and left it sticking deep therein. They next fell to battering the city by the force of cannon; which the assailants so weakened, that in that great extremity the defendants lost their courage, and resolved to surrender.

But as they were thus intending, there was a witch of the town, whom the history doth not name, which went to seek out Assam Aga, that commanded within, and pray'd him to make it good yet nine days longer, with assurance, that within that time he should infallibly see Algier delivered from that siege, and the whole army of the enemy dispersed, so that Christians should be as cheap as Birds. In a word, the thing did happen in the manner as foretold; for upon the twenty-first day of October in the same year, there fell a continual rain upon the land, and so furious a storm at sea, that one might have seen ships hoisted into the clouds, and in one instant again precipitated into the bottom of the water: insomuch that that same dreadful tempest was followed with the loss of fifteen gallies, and above an hundred other vessels; which was the cause why the Emperour, seeing his army wasted by the bad weather, pursued by a famine, occasioned by wrack of his ships, in which was the greatest part of his victuals and ammunition, he was constrain'd to raise the siege, and set sail for Sicily, whither he retreated with the miserable reliques of his fleet.

In the mean time that witch being acknowledged the deliverer of Algier, was richly remunerated, and the credit of her charms authorized. So that ever since witchcraft hath been very freely tolerated; of which the Chief of the town, and even those who are esteem'd to be of greatest sanctity among them, such as are the Marabou's, a religious order of their sect, do for the most part make profession of it, under a goodly pretext of certain revelations which they say they have had from their prophet Mahomet.

And hereupon those of Algier, to palliate the shame and the reproaches that are thrown upon them for making use of a witch in the danger of this siege, do say that the loss of the forces of Charles V, was caused by a prayer of one of their Marabou's, named Cidy Utica, which was at that time in great credit, not under the notion of a magitian, but for a person of a holy life. Afterwards in remembrance of their success, they have erected unto him a small mosque without the Babason gate, where he is buried, and in which they keep sundry lamps burning in honour of him: nay they sometimes repair thither to make their *sala*, for a testimony of greater veneration.

Can it be doubted for a moment, that the dramatist had come fresh from reading some *older narrative* of this deliverance of Algier by a witch, and transferred the merit of the deed to his Sycorax, exchanging only the "rich remuneration," which did not suit his purpose, to the simple pardon of her life? Ogilby wrote in 1670; but the authorities to which he refers for his Account of Barbary are—Johannes de Leo, or Africanus—Louis Marmol—Diego de Haedo—Johannes Gramaye—Bræves—Cel. Curio—and Diego de Torres—names totally unknown to me—and to which I beg leave to refer the curious reader for his fuller satisfaction.

L.

AMICUS REDIVIVUS.

> Where were ye, Nymphs, when the remorseless deep
> Closed o'er the head of your loved Lycidas?

I DO not know when I have experienced a stranger sensation, than on seeing my old friend G. D., who had been paying me a morning visit a few Sundays back, at my cottage, near Islington, upon taking leave, instead of turning down the right hand path by which he had entered—with staff in hand, and at noon day, deliberately march right forwards into the midst of the stream that runs by us, and totally disappear.

A spectacle like this at dusk would have been appalling enough; but, in the broad open daylight, to witness such an unreserved motion towards self-destruction in a valued friend, took from me all power of speculation.

How I found my feet, I know not. Consciousness was quite gone. Some spirit, not my own, whirled me to the spot. I remember nothing but the silvery apparition of a good white head emerging; nigh which a staff (the hand unseen that wielded it) pointed upwards, as feeling for the skies. In a moment (if time was in that time) he was on my shoulders, and I—freighted with a load more precious than his who bore Anchises.

And here I cannot but do justice to the officious zeal of sundry passers by, who, albeit arriving a little too late to participate in the honours of the rescue,* in philanthropic shoals came thronging to communicate their advice as to the recovery; prescribing variously the application, or non-application, of salt, &c. to the person of the patient. Life meantime was ebbing fast away, amidst the stifle of conflicting judgments,

* The topography of my cottage, and its relation to the river, will explain this; as I have been at some cost to have the whole engraved (in time, I hope, for our next number), as well for the satisfaction of the reader, as to commemorate so signal a deliverance.

when one, more sagacious than the rest, by a bright thought, proposed sending for the Doctor. Trite as the counsel was, and impossible, as one should think, to be missed on,—shall I confess?—in this emergency, it was to me as if an Angel had spoken. Great previous exertions—and mine had not been inconsiderable—are commonly followed by a debility of purpose. This was a moment of irresolution.

MONOCULUS—for so, in default of catching his true name, I choose to designate the medical gentleman who now appeared—is a grave middle-aged person, who, without having studied at the college, or truckled to the pedantry of a diploma, hath employed a great portion of his valuable time in experimental processes upon the bodies of unfortunate fellow-creatures, in whom the vital spark, to mere vulgar thinking, would seem extinct, and lost for ever. He omitteth no occasion of obtruding his services, from a case of common surfeit-suffocation to the ignobler obstructions, sometimes induced by a too wilful application of the plant *Cannabis* outwardly. But though he declineth not altogether these drier extinctions, his occupation tendeth for the most part to water-practice; for the convenience of which, he hath judiciously fixed his quarters near the grand repository of the stream mentioned, where, day and night, from his little watch-tower, at the Middleton's Head, he listeneth to detect the wrecks of drowned mortality—partly, as he saith, to be upon the spot—and partly, because the liquids which he useth to prescribe to himself and his patients, on these distressing occasions, are ordinarily more conveniently to be found at these common hostelries, than in the shops and phials of the apothecaries. His ear hath arrived to such finesse by practice, that it is reported, he can distinguish a plunge at a furlong and a half distance; and can tell, if it be casual or deliberate. He weareth a medal, suspended over a suit, originally of a sad brown, but which, by time, and frequency of nightly divings, has been dinged into a true professional sable. He passeth by the name of Doctor, and is remarkable for wanting his left eye. His remedy—after a sufficient application of warm blankets, friction, &c. is a simple tumbler, or more, of the purest Cogniac, with water, made as hot as the convalescent can bear it. Where he findeth, as in the case of my friend, a squeamish subject, he condescendeth to be the taster; and showeth, by his own example, the innocuous nature of the prescription. Nothing can be more kind or encouraging than this procedure. It addeth confidence to the patient, to see his medical adviser go hand in hand with himself in the remedy. When the doctor swalloweth his own draught, what peevish invalid can refuse to pledge him in the potion? In fine, MONOCULUS is a humane, sensible man, who, for a slender pittance, scarce enough to sustain life, is content to wear it out in the endeavour to save the lives of others—his pretensions so moderate, that with difficulty I could press a crown upon him, for the price of restoring the existence of such an invaluable creature to society as G. D.

It was pleasant to observe the effect of the subsiding alarm upon the nerves of the dear absentee. It seemed to have given a shake to memory, calling up notice after notice, of all the providential deliverances he had experienced in the course of his long and innocent life. Sitting up in my couch—my couch which, naked and void of furniture hitherto, for the salutary repose which it administered, shall be honoured with costly valance, at some price, and henceforth be a state-bed at Colebrook,—he discoursed of marvellous escapes—by carelessness of nurses—by pails of gelid, and kettles of the boiling element, in infancy—by orchard pranks, and snapping twigs, in schoolboy frolics—by descent of tiles at Trumpington, and heavier tomes at Pembroke—by studious watchings, inducing frightful vigilance—by want, and the fear of want, and all the sore throbbings of the learned head.—Anon, he would burst out into little fragments of chaunting—of songs long ago—ends of deliverance-hymns, not remembered before since childhood, but coming up now, when his heart was made tender as a child's—for the *tremor cordis*, in the retrospect of a recent deliverance, as in a case of impending danger, acting upon an innocent heart, will produce a self-tenderness, which we should do ill to christen cowardice; and Shakspeare, in the latter crisis, has made his good Sir Hugh to remember the sitting by Babylon, and to mutter of shallow rivers.

Waters of Sir Hugh Middleton,—what a spark you were like to have extinguished for ever! Your salubrious streams to this City, for now near two centuries, would hardly have atoned for what you were in a moment washing away. Mockery of a river—liquid artifice—wretched conduit! henceforth rank with canals, and sluggish aqueducts. Was it for this, that, smit in boyhood with the explorations of that Abyssinian traveller, I paced the vales of Amwell to explore your tributary springs, to trace your salutary waters through green Hertfordshire, and cultured Enfield parks?—Ye have no swans—no naiads—no river God—or did the benevolent hoary aspect of my friend tempt ye to suck him in, that ye also might have the tutelary genius of your waters?

Had he been drowned in Cam, there would have been some consonancy in it; but what willows had ye to wave and rustle over his moist sepulture?—or, having no *name*, besides that unmeaning assumption of *eternal novity*, did ye think to get one by the noble prize, and henceforth to be termed the STREAM DYERIAN?

And could such spacious virtue find a grave
Beneath the imposthumed bubble of a wave?

I protest, George, you shall not venture out again—no, not by daylight—without a sufficient pair of spectacles—in your musing moods especially. Your absence of mind we have borne, till your presence of body came to be called in question by it. You shall not go wandering into Euripus with Aristotle, if we can help it. Fie, man, to turn dipper at your years, after your many tracts in favour of sprinkling only!

I have nothing but water in my head o' nights since this frightful accident. Sometimes I am with Clarence in his dream. At others, I behold Christian beginning to sink, and crying out to his good brother Hopeful (that is me), "I sink in deep waters; the billows go over my head, all the waves go over me. Selah." Then I have before me Palinurus, just letting go the steerage. I cry out too late to save. Next follow—a mournful procession—*suicidal faces*, saved against their wills from drowning; dolefully trailing a length of reluctant gratefulness, with ropy weeds pendant from locks of watchet hue—constrained Lazari—Pluto's half-subjects—stolen fees from the grave—bilking Charon of his fare. At their head Arion——or is it G. D.?—in his singing garments marcheth singly, with harp in hand, and votive garland, which Machaon (or Doctor Hawes) snatcheth straight, intending to suspend it to the stern God of Sea. Then follow dismal streams of Lethe, in which the half-drenched on earth are constrained to drown downright, by wharfs where Ophelia twice acts her muddy death.—

And, doubtless, there is some notice in that invisible world, when one of us approacheth (as my friend did so lately) to their inexorable precincts. When a soul knocks once, twice, at death's door, the sensation aroused within the palace must be considerable; and the grim Feature, by modern science so often dispossessed of his prey, must have learned by this time to pity Tantalus.

A pulse assuredly was felt along the line of the Elysian shades, when the near arrival of G. D. was announced by no equivocal indications. From their seats of Asphodel arose the gentler and the graver ghosts—poet, or historian—of Grecian or of Roman lore—to crown with unfading chaplets the half-finished love-labours of their unwearied scholiast. Him Markland expected—him Tyrwhitt hoped to encounter—him the sweet lyrist of Peter House, whom he had barely seen upon earth,* with newest airs prepared to greet——; and, patron of the gentle Christ's-boy,—who should have been his patron through life—the mild Askew, with longing aspirations, leaned foremost from his venerable Æsculapian chair, to welcome into that happy company the matured virtues of the man, whose tender scions in the boy he himself upon earth had so prophetically fed and watered.

ELIA.

* GRAIUM *tantùm vidit.*

LONDON MAGAZINE.

DECEMBER, 1823.

The following admirable letter seems to refer to the observations on Kant, contained in the Opium Eater's Letters. Perhaps that acute logician may be able to discover its meaning: or if not, he may think it worth preserving as an illustration of Shakspeare's profound knowledge of character displayed in Ancient Pistol.

Can Neptune sleep?—Is Willich dead?—Him who wielded the trident of Albion! Is it thus you trample on the ashes of my friend? All the dreadful energies of thought—all the sophistry of fiction and the triumphs of the human intellect are waving o'er his peaceful grave. "He understood not Kant." Peace then to the harmless invincible. I have long been thinking of presenting the world with a Metaphysical Dictionary—of elucidating Locke's romance.—I await with impatience Kant in English. Give me that! Your letter has awakened me to a sense of your merits. Beware of squabbles; I know the literary infirmities of man. Scott rammed his nose against mortals—he grasped at death for fame to chaunt the victory.

THINE.

How is the Opium Eater?

THE

London Magazine.

SEPTEMBER, 1824.

BLAKESMOOR IN H——SHIRE.

I do not know a pleasure more affecting than to range at will over the deserted apartments of some fine old family mansion. The traces of extinct grandeur admit of a better passion than envy; and contemplations on the great and good, whom we fancy in succession to have been its inhabitants, weave for us illusions, incompatible with the bustle of modern occupancy, and vanities of foolish present aristocracy. The same difference of feeling, I think, attends us between entering an empty and a crowded church. In the latter it is chance but some present human frailty—an act of inattention on the part of some of the auditory—or a trait of affectation, or worse, vain-glory, on that of the preacher—puts us by our best thoughts, disharmonising the place and the occasion. But wouldst thou know the beauty of holiness?—go alone on some week-day, borrowing the keys of good Master Sexton, traverse the cool aisles of some country church—think of the piety that has kneeled there—the congregations, old and young, that have found consolation there—the meek pastor—the docile parishioner—with no disturbing emotions, no cross conflicting comparisons—drink in the tranquillity of the place, till thou thyself become as fixed and motionless as the marble effigies that kneel and weep around thee.

Journeying northward lately, I could not resist going some few miles out of my road, to look upon the remains of an old great house with which I had been impressed in this way in infancy. I was apprized that the owner of it had lately pulled it down; still I had a vague notion that it could not all have perished, that so much solidity with magnificence could not have been crushed all at once into the mere dust and rubbish which I found it.

The work of ruin had proceeded with a swift hand indeed, and the demolition of a few weeks had reduced it to—an antiquity.

I was astonished at the indistinction of every thing. Where had stood the great gates? What bounded the court-yard? Whereabout did the out-houses commence? a few bricks only lay as representatives of that which was so stately and so spacious.

Death does not shrink up his human victim at this rate. The burnt ashes of a man weigh more in their proportion.

Had I seen these brick-and-mortar knaves at their process of destruction, at the plucking of every pannel I should have felt the varlets at my heart. I should have cried out to them to spare a plank at least out of the cheerful store-room, in whose hot window-seat I used to sit, and read Cowley, with the grass-plat before, and the hum and flappings of that one solitary wasp that ever haunted it, about me—it is in mine ears now, as oft as summer returns—or a pannel of the yellow room.

Why, every plank and pannel of that house for me had magic in it. The tapestried bed-rooms—tapestry so much better than painting—not adorning merely, but peopling the wainscots—at which childhood ever and anon would steal a look, shifting its coverlid (replaced as quickly) to exercise its tender courage in a momentary eye-encounter with those stern bright visages, staring reciprocally—all Ovid on the walls, in colours vivider than his descriptions. Actæon in mid sprout, with the unappeasable prudery of Diana; and the still more provoking, and almost culinary coolness of Dan Phœbus, eel-fashion, deliberately divesting of Marsyas.

Then, that haunted room—in which old Mrs. Battle died—whereinto I have crept, but always in the day-time, with a passion of fear; and a sneaking curiosity, terror-tainted, to hold communication with the past.—*How shall they build it up again?*

It was an old deserted place, yet not so long deserted but that traces of the splendour of past inmates were everywhere apparent. Its furniture was still standing—even to the tarnished gilt leather battledores, and crumbling feathers of shuttlecocks, in the nursery, which told that children had once played there. But I was a lonely child, and had the range at will of every apartment, knew every nook and corner, wondered and worshipped everywhere.

The solitude of childhood is not so much the mother of thought, as it is the feeder of love, and silence, and admiration. So strange a passion for the place possessed me in those years, that, though there lay—I shame to say how few roods distant from the mansion—half hid by trees, what I judged some romantic lake—such was the spell which bound me to the house, and such my carefulness not to pass its strict and proper precincts, that the idle waters lay unexplored for me; and not till late in life, curiosity prevailing over elder devotion, I found, to my astonishment, a pretty brawling brook had been the Lacus Incognitus of my infancy. Variegated views, extensive prospects—and those at no great distance from the house--I was told of such--what were they to me, being out the boundaries of my Eden?—So far from a wish to roam, I would have drawn, methought, still closer the fences of my chosen prison; and have been hemmed in by a yet securer cincture of those excluding garden walls. I could have exclaimed with that garden-loving poet—

Bind me, ye woodbines, in your twines;
Curl me about, ye gadding vines;
And oh so close your circles lace,
That I may never leave this place:
But, lest your fetters prove too weak,
Ere I your silken bondage break,
Do you, O brambles, chain me too,
And, courteous briars, nail me through.*

I was here as in a lonely temple. Snug firesides—the low-built roof—parlours ten feet by ten—frugal boards, and all the homeliness of home—these were the condition of my birth—the wholesome soil which I was planted in. Yet, without impeachment to their tenderest lessons, I am not sorry to have had glances of something beyond; and to have taken if but a peep, in childhood, at the contrasting accidents of a great fortune.

To have the feeling of gentility, it is not necessary to have been born gentle. The pride of ancestry may be had on cheaper terms than to be obliged to an importunate race of ancestors; and the coat-less antiquary, in his unemblazoned cell, revolving the long line of a Mowbray's or De Clifford's pedigree—at those sounding names may warm himself into as gay a vanity as those who do inherit them. The claims of birth are ideal merely: and what herald shall go about to strip me of an idea? Is it trenchant to their swords? can it be hacked off as a spur can? or torn away like a tarnished garter?

* Marvell, on Appleton House, to the Lord Fairfax.

What, else, were the families of the great to us? what pleasure should we take in their tedious genealogies, or their capitulatory brass monuments? What to us the uninterrupted current of their bloods, if our own did not answer within us to a cognate and correspondent elevation?

Or wherefore, else, O tattered and diminished 'Scutcheon—that hung upon the time-worn walls of thy princely stairs, BLAKESMOOR!—have I in childhood so oft stood poring upon thy mystic characters—thy emblematic supporters, with their prophetic "Resurgam"—till, every dreg of peasantry purging off, I received into myself Very Gentility?—Thou wert first in my morning eyes; and, of nights, hast detained my steps from bedward, till it was but a step from gazing at thee to dreaming on thee.

This is the only true gentry by adoption; the veritable change of blood, and not, as empirics have fabled, by transfusion.

Who it was by dying that had earned the splendid trophy, I know not, I inquired not; but its fading rags, and colours cobweb-stained, told, that its subject was of two centuries back.

And what if my ancestor at that date was some Damœtas—feeding flocks, not his own, upon the hills of Lincoln—did I in less earnest vindicate to myself the family trappings of this once proud Ægon?—repaying by a backward triumph the insults he might possibly have heaped in his life-time upon my poor pastoral progenitor.

If it were presumption so to speculate, the present owners of the mansion had least reason to complain. They had long forsaken the old house of their fathers for a newer trifle; and I was left to appropriate to myself what images I could pick up, to raise my fancy, or to soothe my vanity.

I was the true descendant of those old W——s; and not the present family of that name, who had fled the old waste places.

Mine was that gallery of good old family portraits, which as I have traversed, giving them in fancy my own family name, one—and then another—would seem to smile, reaching forward from the canvas, to recognise the new relationship; while the rest looked grave, as it seemed, at the vacancy in their dwelling, and thoughts of fled posterity.

That Beauty with the cool blue pastoral drapery, and a lamb—that hung next the great bay window—with the bright yellow H——shire hair, and eye of watchet hue—so like my Alice!—I am persuaded, she was a true Elia—Mildred Elia, I take it.

From her, and from my passion for her—for I first learned love from a picture—Bridget took the hint of those pretty whimsical lines, which thou mayst see, if haply thou hast never seen them, Reader, in the margin.* But my Mildred grew not old, like the imaginary Helen.

Mine too, BLAKESMOOR, was thy noble Marble Hall, with its mosaic pavements, and its Twelve Cæsars—stately busts in marble—ranged round: of whose countenances, young

---

* "High-born Helen, round your dwelling,
  These twenty years I've paced in vain:
Haughty beauty, thy lover's duty
  Hath been to glory in his pain.

High-born Helen, proudly telling
  Stories of thy cold disdain;
I starve, I die, now you comply,
  And I no longer can complain.

These twenty years I've lived on tears,
  Dwelling for ever on a frown;
On sighs I've fed, your scorn my bread;
  I perish now you kind are grown.

Can I, who loved my beloved
  But for the scorn 'was in her eye,'
Can I be moved for my beloved,
  When she returns me sigh for sigh?

reader of faces as I was, the frowning beauty of Nero, I remember, had most of my wonder, but the mild Galba had my love. There they stood in the coldness of death, yet freshness of immortality.

Mine too thy lofty Justice Hall, with its one chair of authority, high-backed, and wickered, once the terror of luckless poacher, or self-forgetful maiden——so common since, that bats have roosted in it.

Mine too—whose else?—thy costly fruit garden, with its sun-baked southern wall; the ampler pleasure-garden, rising backwards from the house, in triple terraces, with flower-pots now of palest lead, save that a speck here and there, saved from the elements, bespake their pristine state to have been gilt and glittering; the verdant quarters backwarder still; and, stretching still beyond, in old formality, thy firry wilderness, the haunt of squirrel, and the day-long murmuring woodpigeon—with that antique image in the centre, God or Goddess I wist not; but child of Athens or old Rome paid never a sincerer worship to Pan or to Sylvanus in their native groves, than I to that fragmental mystery.

Was it for this, that I kissed my childish hands too fervently in your idol worship, walks and windings of BLAKESMOOR! for this, or what sin of mine, has the plough passed over your pleasant places? I sometimes think that as men, when they die, do not die all, so of their extinguished habitations there may be a hope—a germ to be revivified.

ELIA.

ORIGINAL LETTER OF JAMES THOMSON.

THE following very interesting letter has been recovered from oblivion, or at least from neglect, by our friend Elia, and the public will no doubt thank him for the deed. It is without date or superscription in the manuscript, which (as our contributor declares) was in so "fragmentitious" a state as to perplex his transcribing faculties in the extreme. The poet's love of nature is quite evident from one part of it; and the "poetical posture of his affairs" from another. Whether regarded as elucidating the former or the latter, it is a document not a little calculated to excite the attention of the curious as well as the critical. We could ourselves write an essay-full of conjectures from the grounds it affords both with respect to the author's poems and his pride. But we must take another opportunity, or leave it to his next biographer.

DEAR SIR,

I would chide you for the slackness of your correspondence; but having blamed you wrongeously* last time,I shall say nothing till I hear from you, which I hope will be soon.

There's a little business I would communicate to you before I come to the more entertaining part of our correspondence.

I'm going (hard task) to complain, and beg your assistance. When I came up here I brought very little money along with me; expecting some more upon the selling of Widehope, which was to have been sold that day my mother was buried. Now it is unsold yet, but will be disposed of as soon as it can be conveniently done; though indeed it is perplexed with some difficulties. I was a long time living here at my own charges, and you know how expensive that is: this, together with the furnishing of myself with clothes, linen, one thing and another, to fit me for any business of this nature here, necessarily obliged me to contract some debts. Being a stranger, it is a wonder how I got any credit; but I cannot expect it will be long sustained, unless I immediately clear it. Even now, I believe it is at a crisis—my friends have no money to send me, till the land is sold; and my creditors will not wait till then. You know what the consequence would be. Now the assistance I would beg of you, and which I know, if in your power, you will not refuse me, is a letter of credit on some merchant, banker, or such like person in London, for the matter of twelve pounds; till I get money upon the selling of the land, which I am at last certain of, if you could either give it me yourself, or procure it: though you owe it not to my merit, yet you owe it to your own nature, which I know so well as to say no more upon the subject: only allow me to add, that when I first fell upon such a project, (the only thing I have for it in my present circumstances,) knowing the selfish inhumane temper of the generality of the world, you were the first person that offered to my thoughts, as one to whom I had the confidence to make such an address.

Now I imagine you are seized with a fine romantic kind of melancholy on the fading of the year—now I figure you wandering, philosophical and pensive, amidst brown withered groves; whiles the leaves rustle under your feet, the sun gives a farewell parting gleam, and the birds—

Stir the faint note, and but attempt to sing.

Then again, when the heavens wear a more gloomy aspect, the winds whistle and the waters spout, I see you in the well-known cleugh, beneath the solemn arch of tall, thick, embowering trees, listening to the amusing lull of the many steep, moss-grown cascades; while deep, divine contemplation, the genius of the place, prompts each swelling, awful thought.

* *Sic in MS.*

ancestral thumbs; dear, cracked spinnet of dearer Louisa! Without mention of mine, be dumb, thou thin accompanier of her thinner warble! A veil be spread over the dear delighted face of well-deluded father, who now haply listening to cherubic notes, scarce feels sincerer pleasure than when she awakened thy time-shaken chords responsive to the twitterings of that slender image of a voice.

We were not without our literary talk either. It did not extend far, but, as far as it went, it was good. It was bottomed well; had good grounds to go upon. In *the cottage* was a room, which tradition authenticated to have been the same in which Glover, in his occasional retirements, had penned the greater part of his Leonidas. This circumstance was nightly quoted, though none of the present inmates, that I could discover, appeared ever to have met with the poem in question. But that was no matter. Glover had written there, and the anecdote was pressed into the account of the family importance. It diffused a learned air through the apartment, the little side casement of which (the poet's study window), opening upon a superb view as far as to the pretty spire of Harrow, over domains and patrimonial acres, not a rood nor square yard whereof our host could call his own, yet gave occasion to an immoderate expansion of—vanity shall I call it?—in his bosom, as he showed them in a glowing summer evening. It was all his, he took it all in, and communicated rich portions of it to his guests. It was a part of his largess, his hospitality; it was going over his grounds; he was lord for the time of showing them, and you the implicit lookers-up to his magnificence.

He was a juggler, who threw mists before your eyes—you had no time to detect his fallacies. He would say "hand me the *silver* sugar-tongs;" and, before you could discover it was a single spoon, and that *plated*, he would disturb and captivate your imagination by a misnomer of "the urn" for a tea kettle; or by calling a homely bench a sofa. Rich men direct you to their furniture, poor ones divert you from it; he neither did one nor the other, but by simply assuming that every thing was handsome about him, you were positively at a demur what you did, or did not see, at *the cottage*. With nothing to live on, he seemed to live upon every thing. He had a stock of wealth in his mind; not that which is properly termed *Content*, for in truth he was not to be *contained* at all, but overflowed all bounds by the force of a magnificent self-delusion.

Enthusiasm is catching; and even his wife, a sober native of North Britain, who generally saw things more as they were, was not proof against the continual collision of his credulity. Her daughters were rational and discreet young women; in the main, perhaps, not insensible to their true circumstances. I have seen them assume a thoughtful air at times. But such was the preponderating opulence of his fancy, that I am persuaded, not for any half hour together, did they ever look their own prospects fairly in the face. There was no resisting the vortex of his temperament. His riotous imagination conjured up handsome settlements before their eyes, which kept them up in the eye of the world too, and seem at last to have realized themselves; for they both have married since, I am told, more than respectably.

It is long since, and my memory waxes dim on some subjects, or I should wish to convey some notion of the manner in which the pleasant creature described the circumstances of his own wedding-day. I faintly remember something of a chaise and four, in which he made his entry into Glasgow on that morning to fetch the bride home, or carry her thither, I forget which. It so completely made out the stanza of the old ballad—

> When we came down through Glasgow town,
> We were a comely sight to see;
> My love was clad in black velvet,
> And I myself in cramasie.

I suppose it was the only occasion, upon which his own actual splendour at all corresponded with the world's notions on that subject. In homely cart, or travelling caravan, by whatever humble vehicle they chanced to be transported in less prosperous days, the ride through Glasgow came back upon his fancy, not as a humiliating contrast, but as a fair occasion for reverting to that one day's state. It seemed an "equipage etern" from which no power of fate or fortune, once mounted, had power thereafter to dislodge him.

There is some merit in putting a handsome face upon indigent circumstances. To bully and swagger away the sense of them before strangers, may not be always discommendable. Tibbs, and Bobadil, even when detected, have more of our admiration than contempt. But for a man to put the cheat upon himself; to play the Bobadil at home; and, steeped in poverty up to the lips, to fancy himself all the while chin-deep in riches, is a strain of constitutional philosophy, and a mastery over fortune, which was reserved for my old friend Captain Jackson.

ELIA.

BIOGRAPHICAL MEMOIR OF MR. LISTON.

The subject of our Memoir is lineally descended from Johan De L'Estonne (see Doomesday Book, where he is so written) who came in with the Conqueror, and had lands awarded him at Lupton Magna, in Kent. His particular merits or services, Fabian, whose authority I chiefly follow, has forgotten, or perhaps thought it immaterial, to specify. Fuller thinks that he was standard-bearer to Hugo De Agmondesham, a powerful Norman Baron, who was slain by the hand of Harold himself at the fatal battle of Hastings. Be this as it may, we find a family of that name flourishing some centuries later in that county. John Delliston, Knight, was high sheriff for Kent, according to Fabian, *quinto Henrici Sexti;* and we trace the lineal branch flourishing downwards—the orthography varying, according to the unsettled usage of the times, from Delleston to Leston, or Liston, between which it seems to have alternated, till, in the latter end of the reign of James I, it finally settled into the determinate and pleasing dissyllabic arrangement which it still retains. Aminadab Liston, the eldest male representative of the family of that day, was of the strictest order of Puritans. Mr. Foss, of Pall Mall, has obligingly communicated to me an undoubted tract of his, which bears the initials only, A. L. and is entitled " the Grinning Glass: or Actor's Mirrour, wherein the vituperative Visnomy of vicious Players for the Scene is as virtuously reflected back upon their mimetic Monstrosities as it has viciously (hitherto) vitiated with its vile Vanities her Votarists." A strange title, but bearing the impress of those absurdities with which the title pages of that pamphlet-spawning age abounded. The work bears date 1617. It preceded the Histriomastix by fifteen years; and as it went before it in time, so it comes not far short of it in virulence. It is amusing to find an ancestor of Liston's thus bespattering the players at the commencement of the seventeenth century. " Thinketh He (the actor), with his costive countenances, to wry a sorrowing soul out of her anguish, or by defacing the divine denotement of destinate dignity (daignely described in the face humane and no other) to reinstamp the Paradice-plotted similitude with a novel and naughty approximation (not in the first intention) to those abhorred and ugly God-forbidden correspondences, with flouting Apes' jeering gibberings, and Babion babbling-like, to hoot out of countenance all modest measure, as if our sins were not sufficing to stoop our backs without He wresting and crooking his members to mistimed mirth (rather malice) in deformed fashion, leering when he should learn, prating for praying, goggling his eyes (better upturned for grace), whereas in Paradice (if we can go thus high for His profession) that devilish Serpent appeareth his undoubted Predecessor, first induing a mask like some roguish roistering Roscius

(I spit at them all) to beguile with Stage shows the gaping Woman, whose Sex hath still chiefly upheld these Mysteries, and are voiced to be the chief Stage-haunters, where, as I am told, the custom is commonly to mumble (between acts) apples, not ambiguously derived from that pernicious Pippin (worse in effect than the Apples of Discord) whereas sometimes the hissing sounds of displeasure, as I hear, do lively reintonate that snake-taking-leave, and diabolical goings off, in Paradice."

The puritanic effervescence of the early Presbyterians appears to have abated with time, and the opinions of the more immediate ancestors of our subject to have subsided at length into a strain of moderate Calvinism. Still a tincture of the old leaven was to be expected among the posterity of A. L.

Our hero was an only son of Habakuk Liston, settled as an Anabaptist minister upon the patrimonial soil of his ancestors. A regular certificate appears, thus entered in the church book at Lupton Magna "*Johannes, filius Habakuk et Rebeccæ Liston, Dissentientium, natus quinto Decembri* 1780, *baptizatus, sexto Februarii sequentis; Sponsoribus J. et W. Woollaston, unâ cum Maria Merryweather.*" The singularity of an Anabaptist minister conforming to the child rites of the church, would have tempted me to doubt the authenticity of this entry, had I not been obliged with the actual sight of it, by the favour of Mr. Minns, the intelligent and worthy parish clerk of Lupton. Possibly, some expectation in point of worldly advantages from some of the sponsors, might have induced this unseemly deviation, as it must have appeared, from the practice and principles of that generally rigid sect. The term *Dissentientium* was possibly intended by the orthodox clergyman as a slur upon the supposed inconsistency. What, or of what nature, the expectations we have hinted at, may have been, we have now no means of ascertaining. Of the Wollastons no trace is now discoverable in the village. The name of Merryweather occurs over the front of a grocer's shop at the western extremity of Lupton

Of the infant Liston we find no events recorded before his fourth year, in which a severe attack of the measles bid fair to have robbed the rising generation of a fund of innocent entertainment. He had it of the confluent kind, as it is called, and the child's life was for a week or two despaired of His recovery he always attributes (under Heaven) to the humane interference of one Doctor Wilhelm Richter, a German empiric, who, in this extremity, prescribed a copious diet of *Saur Kraut,* which the child was observed to reach at with avidity, when other food repelled him; and from this change of diet his restoration was rapid and complete We have often heard him name the circumstance with gratitude, and it is not altogether surprising, that a relish for this kind of aliment, so abhorrent and harsh to common English palates, has accompanied him through life. When any of Mr. Liston's intimates invite him to supper, he never fails of finding, nearest to his knife and fork, a dish of *Saur Kraut.*

At the age of nine we find our subject under the tuition of the Rev. Mr. Goodenough (his father's health not permitting him probably to instruct him himself), by whom he was inducted into a competent portion of Latin and Greek, with some mathematics, till the death of Mr. Goodenough, in his own seventieth, and Master Liston's eleventh year, put a stop for the present to his classical progress.

We have heard our hero with emotions, which do his heart honour, describe the awful circumstances attending the decease of this worthy old gentleman. It seems they had been walking out together, master and pupil, in a fine sunset, to the distance of three quarters of a mile west of Lupton, when a sudden curiosity took Mr Goodenough to look down upon a chasm, where a shaft had been lately sunk in a mining speculation (then projecting, but abandoned soon after, as not answering the promised success, by Sir Ralph Shepperton, Knight, and member for the county). The old clergyman leaning over, either with incaution, or sudden giddiness (probably a mixture of both), suddenly lost his footing, and, to use Mr. Liston's phrase, disappeared; and was doubtless broken into a thousand pieces. The sound of his head, &c dashing successively upon the projecting masses of the chasm, had such an effect upon the child, that a serious sickness ensued, and even for many years after his recovery he was not once seen so much as to smile.

The joint death of both his parents, which happened not many months after this disastrous accident, and were probably (one or both of them) accelerated by it, threw our youth upon the protection of his maternal great aunt, Mrs. Sittingbourn. Of this aunt we have never heard him speak but with expressions amounting almost to reverence. To the influence of her early counsels and manners, he has always attributed the firmness with which, in maturer years, thrown upon a way of life, commonly not the best adapted to gravity and self-retirement, he has been able to maintain a serious character, untinctured with the levities incident to his profession. Ann Sittingbourn (we have seen her portrait by Hudson) was stately, stiff, tall, with a cast of features strikingly resembling the subject of this memoir. Her estate in Kent was spacious and well-wooded; the house, one of those venerable old mansions which are so impressive in childhood, and so hardly forgotten in succeeding years. In the venerable solitudes of Charnwood, among thick shades of the oak and beech (this last his favourite tree), the young Liston cultivated those contemplative habits which have never entirely deserted him in after years. Here he was commonly in the summer months to be met with, with a book in his hand—not a play-book—meditating Boyle's Reflections was at one time the darling volume, which in its turn was superseded by Young's Night Thoughts, which has continued its hold upon him through life. He carries it always about him; and it is no uncommon thing for him to be seen, in the refreshing intervals of his occupation, leaning against a side scene, in a sort of Herbert of Cherbury posture, turning over a pocket edition of his favourite author.

But the solitudes of Charnwood were not destined always to obscure the path of our young hero. The premature death of Mrs. Sittingbourn, at the age of 70, occasioned by incautious burning of a pot of charcoal in her sleeping chamber, left him in his 19th year nearly without resources. That the stage at all should have presented itself as an eligible scope for his talents, and, in particular, that he should have chosen a line so foreign to what appears to have been his turn of mind, may require some explanation.

At Charnwood then we behold him thoughtful, grave, ascetic. From his cradle averse to flesh meats, and strong drink; abstemious even beyond the genius of the place; and almost in spite of the remonstrances of his great aunt, who, though strict, was not rigid; water was his habitual drink, and his food little beyond the mast, and beech nuts, of his favourite groves. It is a medical fact, that this kind of diet, however favourable to the contemplative powers of the primitive hermits, &c., is but ill adapted to the less robust minds and bodies of a later generation. Hypochondria almost constantly ensues. It was so in the case of the young Liston. He was subject to sights, and had visions. Those arid beech nuts, distilled by a complexion naturally adust, mounted into an occiput, already prepared to kindle by long seclusion, and the fervour of strict Calvinistic notions. In the glooms of Charnwood he was assailed by illusions, similar in kind to those which are related of the famous Anthony of Padua. Wild antic faces would ever and anon protrude themselves upon his *sensorium*. Whether he shut his eyes, or kept them open, the same illusions operated. The darker and more profound were his cogitations, the droller and more whimsical became the apparitions. They buzzed about him thick as flies, flapping at him, flouting him, hooting in his ear, yet with such comic appendages, that what at first was his bane, became at length his solace; and he desired no better society than that of his merry phantasmata. We shall presently find in what way this remarkable phenomenon influenced his future destiny.

On the death of Mrs. Sittingbourn, we find him received into the family of Mr. Willoughby, an eminent Turkey merchant, resident in Birchin-lane, London. We lose a little while here the chain of his history; by what inducements this gentleman was determined to make him an inmate of his house. Probably he had had some personal kindness for Mrs. Sittingbourn formerly; but however it was, the young man was here treated more like a son than a clerk, though he was nominally but the latter. Different avocations, the change of scene, with that alternation of business and recreation, which in its greatest perfection is to be had only in London, appear to have weaned him in a short time from the hypochondriacal affections which had beset him at Charnwood.

In the three years which followed his removal to Birchin-lane, we find him making more than one voyage to the Levant, as chief factor for Mr. Willoughby, at the Porte. We could easily fill our biography with the pleasant passages which we have heard him relate as having happened to him at Constantinople, such as his having been taken up on suspicion of a design of penetrating the seraglio, &c.; but with the deepest convincement of this gentleman's own veracity, we think that some of the stories are of that whimsical, and others of that romantic nature, which, however diverting, would be out of place in a narrative of this kind, which aims not only at strict truth, but at avoiding the very appearance of the contrary.

We will now bring him over the seas again, and suppose him in the counting-house in Birchin-lane, his protector satisfied with the returns of his factorage, and all going on so smoothly that we may expect to find Mr. Liston at last an opulent merchant upon 'Change, as it is called. But see the turns of destiny! Upon a summer's excursion into Norfolk, in the year 1801, the accidental sight of pretty Sally Parker, as she was called (then in the Norwich company), diverted his inclinations at once from commerce; and he became, in the language of common-place biography, stage-struck. Happy for the lovers of mirth was it, that our hero took this turn; he might else have been to this hour that unentertaining character, a plodding London merchant.

We accordingly find him shortly after making his *debut*, as it is called, upon the Norwich boards, in the season of that year, being then in the 22d year of his age. Having a natural bent to tragedy, he chose the part of Pyrrhus in the Distressed Mother, to Sally Parker's Hermione. We find him afterwards as Barnwell, Altamont, Chamont, &c.; but, as if nature had destined him to the sock, an unavoidable infirmity absolutely discapacitated him for tragedy. His person at this latter period, of which I have been speaking, was graceful, and even commanding; his countenance set to gravity; he had the power of arresting the attention of an audience at first sight almost beyond any other tragic actor. But he could not hold it. To understand this obstacle we must go back a few years to those appalling reveries at Charnwood. Those illusions, which had vanished before the dissipation of a less recluse life, and more free society, now in his solitary tragic studies, and amid the intense calls upon feeling incident to tragic acting, came back upon him with tenfold vividness. In the midst of some most pathetic passage, the parting of Jaffier with his dying friend, for instance, he would suddenly be surprised with a fit of violent horse laughter. While the spectators were all sobbing before him with emotion, suddenly one of those grotesque faces would peep out upon him, and he could not resist the impulse. A timely excuse once or twice served his purpose, but no audiences could be expected to bear repeatedly this violation of the continuity of feeling. He describes them (the illusions) as so many demons haunting him, and paralysing every effect. Even now, I am told, he cannot recite the famous soliloquy in Hamlet, even in private, without immoderate bursts of laughter. However, what he had not force of reason sufficient to overcome, he had good sense enough to turn into emolument, and determined to make a commodity of his distemper. He prudently exchanged the buskin for the sock, and the illusions instantly ceased; or, if they occurred for a short season, by their very co-operation added a zest to his comic vein; some of his most catching faces being (as he expresses it) little more than transcripts and copies of those extraordinary phantasmata.

We have now drawn out our hero's existence to the period when he was about to meet for the first time the sympathies of a London audience. The particulars of his success since have been too much before our eyes to render a circumstantial detail of them expedient. I shall only mention that Mr. Willoughby, his resentments having had time to subside, is at present one of the fastest friends of his old renegado factor; and that Mr. Liston's hopes of Miss Parker vanishing along with his unsuccessful suit to Melpomene, in the autumn of 1811 he married his present lady, by whom he has been blest with one son, Philip; and two daughters, Ann, and Augustina.

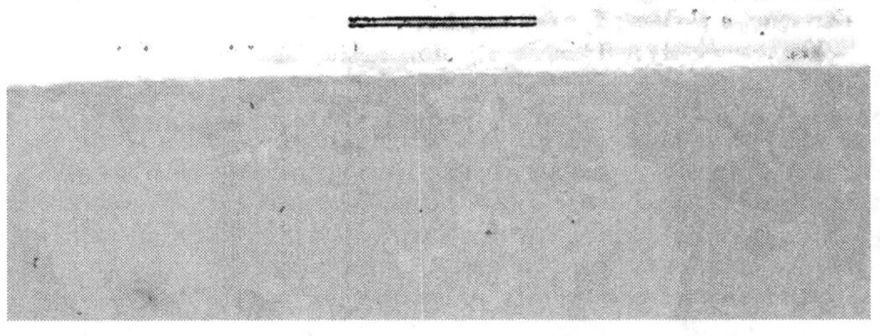

A VISION OF HORNS.

My thoughts had been engaged last evening in solving the problem, why in all times and places the *horn* has been agreed upon as the symbol, or honourable badge, of married men. Moses' horn, the horn of Ammon, of Amalthea, and a cornucopia of legends besides, came to my recollection, but afforded no satisfactory solution, or rather involved the question in deeper obscurity. Tired with the fruitless chase of inexplicant analogies, I fell asleep, and dreamed in this fashion.

Methought certain scales or films fell from my eyes, which had hitherto hindered these little tokens from being visible. I was somewhere in the Cornhill (as it might be termed) of some Utopia. Busy citizens jostled each other, as they may do in our streets, with care (the care of making a penny) written upon their foreheads; and *something else*, which is rather imagined, than distinctly imaged, upon the brows of my own friends and fellow-townsmen.

In my first surprise I supposed myself gotten into some forest—Arden, to be sure, or Sherwood; but the dresses and deportment, all civic, forbade me to continue in that delusion. Then a scriptural thought crossed me (especially as there were nearly as many Jews and Christians among them), whether it might not be the children of Israel going up to besiege Jericho. I was undeceived of both errors by the sight of many faces which were familiar to me. I found myself strangely (as it will happen in dreams) at one and the same time in an unknown country, with known companions. I met old friends, not with new faces, but with their old faces oddly adorned in front, with each man a certain corneous excrescence. Dick Mitis, the little cheesemonger in St. * * * *'s Passage, was the first that saluted me, with his hat off—you know Dick's way to a customer—and, I not being aware of him, he thrust a strange beam into my left eye, which pained and grieved me exceedingly; but, instead of apology, he only grinned and fleered in my face, as much as to say "it is the custom of the country," and passed on.

I had scarce time to send a civil message to his lady, whom I have always admired as a pattern of a wife,—and do indeed take Dick and her to be a model of conjugal agreement and harmony,—when I felt an ugly smart in my neck, as if something had gored it behind, and turning round, it was my old friend and neighbour, Dulcet, the confectioner, who, meaning to be pleasant, had thrust his protuberance right into my nape, and seemed proud of his power of offending.

Now I was assailed right and left, till in my own defence I was obliged to walk sideling and wary, and look about me, as you guard your eyes in London streets; for the horns thickened, and came at me like the ends of umbrellas poking in one's face.

I soon found that these towns-folk were the civillest best-mannered people in the world, and that if they had offended at all, it was entirely owing to their blindness. They do not know what dangerous weapons they protrude in front, and will stick their best friends in the eye with provoking complacency. Yet the best of it is, they can see the beams on their neighbours' foreheads, if they are as small as motes, but their own beams they can in no wise discern.

There was little Mitis, that I told you I just encountered—he has simply (I speak of him at home in his own shop) the smoothest forehead in his own conceit—he will stand you a quarter of an hour together contemplating the serenity of it in the glass, before he begins to shave himself in a morning—yet you saw what a desperate gash he gave me.

Desiring to be better informed of the ways of this extraordinary people, I applied myself to a fellow of some assurance, who (it appeared) acted as a sort of interpreter to strangers—he was dressed in a military uniform, and strongly resembled Colonel ———, of the guards,—and "pray, Sir," said I, "have all the inhabitants of your city these troublesome excrescences? I beg pardon, I see you have none. You perhaps are single." "Truly, Sir," he replied with a smile, "for the most part we have, but not all alike. There are some, like Dick, that sport but one tumescence. Their ladies have been tolerably faithful—have confined themselves to a single aberration or so—these we call Unicorns. Dick, you must know, is my Unicorn. [He spoke this with an air of invincible assurance.] Then we have Bicorns, Tricorns, and so on up to Millecorns. [Here methought I crossed and blessed myself in my dream.] Some again we have—there goes one—you see how happy the rogue looks—how he walks smiling, and perking up his face, as if he thought himself the only man. He is not married yet, but on Monday next he leads to the altar the accomplished widow Dacres, relict of our late sheriff."

"I see, Sir," said I, "and observe that he is happily free from the national *goitre* (let me call it), which distinguishes most of your countrymen."

"Look a little more narrowly," said my conductor.

I put on my spectacles, and observing the man a little more diligently, above his forehead I could mark a thousand little twinkling shadows dancing the horn-pipe, little hornlets, and rudiments of horn, of a soft and pappy consistence (for I handled some of them), but which, like coral out of water, my guide informed me would infallibly stiffen and grow rigid within a week or two from the expiration of his bachelorhood.

Then I saw some horns strangely growing out behind, and my interpreter explained these to be married men, whose wives had conducted themselves with infinite propriety since the period of their marriage, but were thought to have antedated their good men's titles, by certain liberties they had indulged themselves in, prior to the ceremony. This kind of gentry wore their horns backwards, as has been said, in the fashion of the old pig-tails; and as there was nothing obtrusive or ostentatious in them, nobody took any notice of it.

Some had pretty little budding antlers, like the first essays of a young faun. These, he told me, had wives, whose affairs were in a hopeful way, but not quite brought to a conclusion.

Others had nothing to show, only by certain red angry marks and swellings in their foreheads, which itched the more they kept rubbing and chafing them, it was to be hoped that something was brewing.

I took notice that every one jeered at the rest, only none took notice of the sea-captains, yet these were as well provided with their tokens as the best among them. This kind of people, it seems, taking their wives upon so contingent tenures, their lot was considered as nothing but natural,—so they wore their marks without impeachment, as they might carry their cockades, and nobody respected them a whit the less for it.

I observed, that the more sprouts grew out of a man's head, the less weight they seemed to carry with them; whereas, a single token would now and then appear to give the wearer some uneasiness. This shows that use is a great thing.

Some had their adornings gilt, which needs no explanation; while others, like musicians, went sounding theirs before them—a sort of music which I thought might very well have been spared.

It was pleasant to see some of the citizens encounter between themselves; how they smiled in their sleeves at the shock they received from their neighbour, and none seemed conscious of the shock which their neighbour experienced in return.

Some had great corneous stumps, seemingly torn off and bleeding. These, the interpreter warned me, were husbands who had retaliated upon their wives, and the badge was in equity divided between them.

While I stood discerning of these things, a slight tweak on my cheek unawares, which brought tears into my eyes, introduced to me my friend Placid, between whose lady and a certain male cousin, some idle flirtations I remember to have heard talked of; but that was all. He saw he had somehow hurt me, and asked my pardon with that round unconscious face of his, and looked so tristful and contrite for his no-offence, that I was ashamed for the man's penitence. Yet I protest it was but a scratch. It was the least little hornet of a horn that could be framed. "Shame on the man," I secretly exclaimed, "who could thrust so much as the value of a hair into a brow so unsuspecting and inoffensive. What then must they have to answer for, who plant great, monstrous, timber-like, projecting antlers upon the heads of those whom they call their friends, when a puncture of this atomical tenuity made my eyes to water at this rate All the pincers at Surgeons' Hall cannot pull out for Placid that little hair."

I was curious to know what became of these frontal excrescences, when the husbands died; and my guide informed me that the chemists in their country made a considerable profit by them, extracting from them certain subtle essences —and then I remembered, that nothing was so efficacious in my own for restoring swooning matrons, and wives troubled with the vapours, as a strong sniff or two at the composition, appropriately called hartshorn—far beyond *sal volatile.*

Then also I began to understand, why a man, who is the jest of the company, is said to be the butt—as much as to say, such a one butteth with the horn.

I inquired if by no operation these wens were ever extracted; and was told, that there was indeed an order of dentists, whom they call canonists in their language, who undertook to restore the forehead to its pristine smoothness; but that ordinarily it was not done without much cost and trouble; and when they succeeded in plucking out the offending part, it left a painful void, which could not be filled up; and that many patients who had submitted to the excision, were eager to marry again, to supply with a good second antler the baldness and deformed gap left by the extraction of the former, as men losing their natural hair substitute for it a less becoming periwig.

Some horns I observed beautifully taper, smooth, and (as it were) flowering. These I understand were the portions brought by handsome women to their spouses; and I pitied the rough, homely, unsightly deformities on the brows of others, who had been deceived by plain and ordinary partners. Yet the latter I observed to be by far the most common—the solution of which I leave to the natural philosopher.

One tribute of married men I particularly admired at, who, instead of horns, wore, engrafted on their forehead, a sort of horn-book. "This," quoth my guide, "is the greatest mystery in our country, and well worth an explanation. You must know that all infidelity is not of the senses. We have as well intellectual, as material, wittols. These, whom you see decorated with the Order of the Book—are triflers, who encourage about their wives' presence the society of your men of genius (their good friends, as they call them)—literary disputants, who ten to one out-talk the poor husband, and commit upon the understanding of the woman a violence and estrangement in the end, little less painful than the coarser sort of alienation. Whip me these knaves—[my conductor here expressed himself with a becoming warmth]—whip me them, I say, who with no excuse from the passions, in cold blood seduce the minds, rather than the persons, of their friends' wives; who, for the tickling pleasure of hearing themselves prate, dehonestate the intellects of married women, dishonouring the husband in what should be his most sensible part. If I must be—[here he used a plain word] let it be by some honest sinner like myself, and not by one of these gad-flies, these debauchers of the understanding, these flattery-buzzers." He was going on in this manner, and I was getting insensibly pleased with my friend's manner (I had been a little shy of him at first), when the dream suddenly left me, vanishing—as Virgil speaks—through the gate of Horn.

ELIA.

UNITARIAN PROTESTS:

IN A LETTER TO A FRIEND OF THAT PERSUASION NEWLY MARRIED.

Dear M——, Though none of your acquaintance can with greater sincerity congratulate you upon this happy conjuncture than myself, one of the oldest of them, it was with pain I found you, after the ceremony, depositing in the vestry-room what is called a Protest. I thought you superior to this little sophistry. What, after submitting to the service of the Church of England—after consenting to receive a boon from her, in the person of your amiable consort—was it consistent with sense, or common good manners, to turn round upon her, and flatly taunt her with false worship? This language is a little of the strongest in your books and from your pulpits, though there it may well enough be excused from religious zeal and the native warmth of nonconformity. But at the altar—the Church of England altar—adopting her forms and complying with her requisitions to the letter—to be consistent, together with the practice, I fear, you must drop the language of dissent. You are no longer sturdy Non Cons; you are there Occasional Conformists. You submit to accept the privileges communicated by a form of words, exceptionable, and perhaps justly, in your view; but, so submitting, you have no right to quarrel with the ritual which you have just condescended to owe an obligation to. They do not force you into their churches. You come voluntarily, knowing the terms. You marry in the name of the Trinity. There is no evading this by pretending that you take the formula with your own interpretation, (and so long as you can do this, where is the necessity of Protesting?): for the meaning of a vow is to be settled by the sense of the imposer, not by any forced construction of the taker: else might all vows, and oaths too, be eluded with impunity. You marry then essentially as Trinitarians; and the altar no sooner satisfied than, hey presto, with the celerity of a juggler, you shift habits, and proceed pure Unitarians again in the vestry. You cheat the Church out of a wife, and go home smiling in your sleeves that you have so cunningly despoiled the Egyptians. In plain English, the Church has married you in the name of so and so, assuming that you took the words in her sense, but you outwitted her; you assented to them in your sense only, and took from her what, upon a right understanding, she would have declined giving you.

This is the fair construction to be put upon all Unitarian marriages as at present contracted; and so long as you Unitarians could salve your consciences with the equivoque, I do not see why the Established Church should have troubled herself at all about the matter. But the Protesters necessarily see further. They have some glimmerings of the deception; they apprehend a flaw somewhere; they would fain be honest, and yet they must marry notwithstanding; for honesty's sake, they are fain to dehonestate themselves a little. Let me try the very words of your own Protest, to see what confessions we can pick out of them.

"As Unitarians therefore we (you and your newly espoused bride) most solemnly protest against the service (which yourselves have just demanded) because we are thereby called upon, not only tacitly to acquiesce, but to profess a belief in a doctrine which is a dogma, as we believe, totally unfounded." But do you profess that belief during the ceremony; or are you only called upon for the profession but do not make it? If the latter, then you fall in with the rest of your more consistent brethren, who waive the Protest; if the former, then, I fear, your Protest cannot save you.

Hard and grievous it is, that in any case an institution so broad and general as the union of man and wife should be so cramped and straitened by the hands of an imposing hierarchy, that to plight troth to a lovely woman a man must be necessitated to compromise his truth and faith to Heaven; but so it must be, so long as you chuse to marry by the forms of the Church over which that hierarchy presides.

Therefore, say you, we Protest. O poor and much fallen word Protest! It was not so that the first heroic reformers protested. They departed out of Babylon once for good and all; they came not back for an occasional contact with her altars; a dallying, and then a protesting against dalliance; they stood not shuffling in the porch, with a Popish foot within, and its lame Lutheran fellow without, halting betwixt. These were the true Protestants. You are—Protesters.

Besides the inconsistency of this proceeding, I must think it a piece of impertinence—unseasonable at least, and out of place, to obtrude these papers upon the officiating clergyman—to offer to a public functionary an instrument which by the tenor of his function he is not obliged to accept, but, rather, he is called upon to reject. Is it done in his clerical capacity? he has no power of redressing the grievance. It is to take the benefit of his ministry and then insult him. If in his capacity of fellow Christian only, what are your scruples to him, so long as you yourselves are able to get over them, and do get over them by the very fact of coming to require his services? The thing you call a Protest might with just as good a reason be presented to the churchwarden for the time being, to the parish clerk, or the pew opener.

The Parliament alone can redress your grievance, if any. Yet I see not how with any grace your people can petition for relief, so long as, by the very fact of your coming to Church to be married, they do *boná fide* and strictly relieve themselves. The Upper House, in particular, is not unused to these same things called Protests, among themselves. But how would this honorable body stare to find a noble Lord conceding a measure, and in the next breath, by a solemn Protest disowning it. A Protest there is a reason given for non-compliance, not a subterfuge for an equivocal occasional compliance. It was reasonable in the primitive Christians to avert from their persons, by whatever lawful means, the compulsory eating of meats which had been offered unto idols. I dare say the Roman Prefects and Exarchats had plenty of petitioning in their days. But what would a Festus, or Agrippa, have replied to a petition to that effect, presented to him by some evasive Laodicean, with the very meat between his teeth, which he had been chewing voluntarily rather than abide the penalty? Relief for tender consciences means nothing, where the conscience has previously relieved itself; that is, has complied with the injunctions which it seeks preposterously to be rid of. Relief for conscience there is properly none, but what by better information makes an act appear innocent and lawful, with which the previous conscience was not satisfied to comply. All else is but relief from penalties, from scandal incurred by a complying practice, where the conscience itself is not fully satisfied.

But, say you, we have hard measure, the Quakers are indulged with the liberty denied to us. They have, and dearly have they earned it. You have come in (as a sect at least) in the cool of the evening; at the eleventh hour. The Quaker character was hardened in the fires of persecution in the seventeenth century; not quite to the stake and faggot, but little short of that, they grew up and thrived against noisome prisons, cruel beatings, whippings, stockings. They have since endured a century or two of scoffs, contempts; they have been a bye-word, and a nay-word; they have stood unmoved: and the consequence of long conscientious resistance on one part is invariably, in the end, remission on the other The legislature, that denied you the tolerance, which I do not know that at that time you even asked, gave them the liberty which, without granting, they would have assumed. No penalties could have driven them into the Churches. This is the consequence of entire measures. Had the early Quakers consented to take oaths, leaving a Protest with the clerk of the court against them in the same breath with which they had taken them, do you in your conscience think that they would have been indulged at this day in their exclusive privilege of Affirming? Let your people go on for a century or so, marrying in your own fashion, and I will warrant them before the end of it the legislature will be willing to concede to them more than they at present demand.

Either the institution of marriage depends not for its validity upon hypocritical compliances with the ritual of an alien Church; and then I do not see why you cannot marry among yourselves, as the Quakers, without their indulgence, would have been doing to this day; or it does depend upon such ritual compliance, and then in your Protests you offend against a divine ordinance. I have read in the Essex-street Liturgy a form for the celebration of marriage. Why is this become a dead letter? O! it has never been legalised; that is to say, in the law's eye it is no marriage. But do you take upon you to say, in the view of the gospel it would be none? Would your own people at least look upon a couple so paired, to be none? But the case of dowries, alimonies, inheritances, &c. which depend for their validity upon the ceremonial of the Church by law established—are these nothing? That our children are not legally *Filii Nullius*—is this nothing? I answer, nothing; to the preservation of a good conscience, nothing; to a consistent christianity, less than nothing. Sad worldly thorns they are indeed, and stumbling blocks, well worthy to be set out of the way by a legislature calling itself Christian; but not likely to be removed in a hurry by any shrewd legislators, who perceive that the petitioning complainants have not so much as bruised a shin in the resistance; but, prudently declining the briars and the prickles, nestle quietly down in the smooth two-sided velvet of a Protesting Occasional Conformity.—I am, dear sir,

With much respect, yours, &c.

ELIA.

TO THE EDITOR OF THE LONDON MAGAZINE.

Dear Sir,—I send you a bantering Epistle to an Old Gentleman whose Education is supposed to have been Neglected. Of course, it was *suggested* by some Letters of your admirable Opium-Eater; the discontinuance of which has caused so much regret to myself in common with most of your readers. You will do me injustice by supposing, that in the remotest degree it was my intention to ridicule those Papers. The fact is, the most serious things may give rise to an innocent burlesque; and the more serious they are, the fitter they become for that purpose. It is not to be supposed, that Charles Cotton did not entertain a very high regard for Virgil, notwithstanding he travestied that Poet. Yourself can testify the deep respect I have always held for the profound learning and penetrating genius of our friend. Nothing upon earth would give me greater pleasure than to find that he has not lost sight of his entertaining and instructive purpose.

I am, dear Sir, yours and *his* sincerely,

Elia.

LETTER TO AN OLD GENTLEMAN

WHOSE EDUCATION HAS BEEN NEGLECTED.

My Dear Sir,—The question which you have done me the honour to propose to me, through the medium of our common friend Mr. Grierson, I shall endeavour to answer with as much exactness as a limited observation and experience can warrant.

You ask—or rather, Mr. Grierson in his own interesting language asks for you—"Whether a person at the age of sixty-three, with no more proficiency than a tolerable knowledge of most of the characters of the English alphabet at first sight amounts to, by dint of persevering application, and good masters,—a docile and ingenuous disposition on the part of the pupil always pre-supposed—may hope to arrive, within a presumable number of years, at that degree of attainments, which shall entitle the possessor to the character, which you are on so many accounts justly desirous of acquiring, of a *learned man*."

This is fairly and candidly stated—only I could wish that on one point you had been a little more explicit. In the mean time, I will take it for granted, that by a "knowledge of the alphabetic characters," you confine your meaning to the single powers only, as you are silent on the subject of the diphthongs, and harder combinations.

Why truly, Sir, when I consider the vast circle of sciences—it is not here worth while to trouble you with the distinction between learning and science—which a man must be understood to have made the tour of in these days, before the world will be willing to concede to him the title which you aspire to, I am almost disposed to reply to your inquiry by a direct answer in the negative.

However, where all cannot be compassed, a great deal that is truly valuable may be accomplished. I am unwilling to throw out any remarks that should have a tendency to damp a hopeful genius; but I must not in fairness conceal from you, that you have much to do. The consciousness of difficulty is sometimes a spur to exertion. Rome—or rather, my dear Sir, to borrow an illustration from a place, as yet more familiar to you—Rumford—Rumford—was not built in a day.

Your mind as yet, give me leave to tell you, is in the state of a sheet of white paper. We must not blot or blur it over too hastily. Or, to use an opposite simile, it is like a piece of parchment all be-scrawled and be-scribbled over with characters of no sense or import, which we must carefully erase and remove, before we can make way for the authentic characters or impresses, which are to be substituted in their stead by the corrective hand of science.

Your mind, my dear Sir, again resembles that same parchment, which we will suppose a little hardened by time and disuse. We may apply the characters, but are we sure that the ink will sink?

You are in the condition of a traveller, that has all his journey to begin. And again, you are worse off than the traveller which I have supposed—for you have already lost your way.

You have much to learn, which you have never been taught, and more, I fear, to unlearn, which you have been taught erroneously. You have hitherto, I dare say, imagined, that the sun moves round the earth. When you shall have mastered the true solar system, you will have quite a different theory upon that point, I assure you. I mention but this instance. Your own experience, as knowledge advances, will furnish you with many parallels.

I can scarcely approve of the intention, which Mr. Grierson informs me you had contemplated, of entering yourself at a common seminary, and working your way up from the lower to the higher forms with the children. I see more to admire in the modesty, than in the expediency, of such a resolution. I own I cannot reconcile myself to the spectacle of a gentleman at your time of life seated, as must be your case at first, below a Tyro of four or five—for at that early age the rudiments of education usually commence in this country. I doubt whether more might not be lost in the point of fitness, than would be gained in the advantages which you propose to yourself by this scheme.

You say, you stand in need of emulation; that this incitement is no where to be had but at a public school, that you should be more sensible of your progress by comparing it with the daily progress of those around you. But have you considered the nature of emulation; and how it is sustained at those tender years, which you would have to come in competition with? I am afraid you are dreaming of academic prizes and distinctions. Alas! in the university, for which you are preparing, the highest medal would be a silver penny, and you must graduate in nuts and oranges.

I know that Peter, the great Czar—or Emperor—of Muscovy, submitted himself to the discipline of a dock-yard at Deptford, that he might learn, and convey to his countrymen, the noble art of ship-building. You are old enough to remember him, or at least the talk about him. I call to mind also other great princes, who, to instruct themselves in the theory and practice of war, and set an example of subordination to their subjects, have condescended to enrol themselves as private soldiers, and, passing through the successive ranks of corporal, quarter-master, and the rest, have served their way up to the station, at which most princes are willing enough to set out—of General and Commander-in-Chief over their own forces. But—besides that there is oftentimes great sham and pretence in their show of mock humility—the competition which they stooped to was with their co-evals, however inferior to them in birth. Between ages so very disparate, as those which you contemplate, I fear there can no salutary emulation subsist.

Again, in the other alternative, could you submit to the ordinary reproofs and discipline of a day-school? Could you bear to be corrected for your faults? Or how would it look to see you put to stand, as must be the case sometimes, in a corner?

I am afraid the idea of a public school in your circumstances must be given up.

But is it impossible, my dear Sir, to find some person of your own age—if of the other sex, the more agreeable perhaps—whose information, like your own, has rather lagged behind their years, who should be willing to set out from the same point with yourself, to undergo the same tasks—thus at once inciting and sweetening each other's labours in a sort of friendly rivalry. Such a one, I think, it would not be difficult to find in some of the western parts of this island—about Dartmoor for instance

Or what if, from your own estate—that estate which, unexpectedly acquired so late in life, has inspired into you this generous thirst after knowledge, you were to select some elderly peasant, that might best be spared from the land; to come and begin his education with you, that you might till, as it were, your minds together—one, whose heavier progress might invite, without a fear of discouraging, your emulation? We might then see—starting from an equal post—the difference of the clownish and the gentle blood.

A private education then, or such a one as I have been describing, being determined on, we must in the next place look out for a preceptor: —for it will be some time before either of you, left to yourselves, will be able to assist the other to any great purpose in his studies.

And now, my dear Sir, if in describing such a tutor as I have imagined for you, I use a style a little above the familiar one in which I have hitherto chosen to address you, the nature of the subject must be my apology. *Difficile est de scientiis inscienter loqui*, which is as much as to say that "in treating of scientific matters it is difficult to avoid the use of scientific terms" But I shall endeavour to be as plain as possible. I am not going to present you with the *ideal* of a pedagogue, as it may exist in my fancy, or has possibly been realized in the persons of Buchanan and Busby. Something less than perfection will serve our turn. The scheme which I propose in this first or introductory letter has reference to the first four or five years of your education only; and in enumerating the qualifications of him that should undertake the direction of your studies, I shall rather point out the *minimum*, or *least*, that I shall require of him, than trouble you in the search of attainments neither common nor necessary to our immediate purpose.

He should be a man of deep and extensive knowledge. So much at least is indispensable. Something older than yourself, I could wish him, because years add reverence.

To his age and great learning, he should be blest with a temper and a patience, willing to accommodate itself to the imperfections of the slowest and meanest capacities. Such a one in former days Mr. Hartlib appears to have been, and such in our days I take Mr. Grierson to be; but our friend, you know, unhappily has other engagements I do not demand a consummate grammarian; but he must be a thorough master of vernacular orthography, with an insight into the accentualities and punctualities of modern Saxon, or English. He must be competently instructed (or how shall he instruct you?) in the tetralogy, or four first rules, upon which not only arithmetic, but geometry, and the pure mathematics themselves, are grounded. I do not require that he should have measured the globe with Cook, or Ortelius, but it is desirable that he should have a general knowledge (I do not mean a very nice or pedantic one) of the great division of the earth into four parts, so as to teach you readily to name the quarters. He must have a genius capable in some degree of soaring to the upper element, to deduce from thence the not much dissimilar computation of the cardinal points, or hinges, upon which those invisible phenomena, which naturalists agree to term *winds*, do perpetually shift and turn. He must instruct you, in imitation of the old Orphic fragments (the mention of which has possibly escaped you), in numeric and harmonious responses, to deliver the number of solar revolutions, within which each of the twelve periods, into which the *Annus Vulgaris*, or common year, is divided, doth usually complete and terminate itself. The intercalaries, and other subtle problems, he will do well to omit, till riper years, and course of study, shall have rendered you more capable thereof He must be capable of embracing all history, so as from the countless myriads of individual men, who have peopled this globe of earth—*for it is a globe*—by comparison of their respective births, lives, deaths, fortunes, conduct, prowess, &c. to pronounce, and teach you to pronounce, dogmatically and catechetically, who was the richest, who was the strongest, who was the wisest, who was the meekest man, that ever lived; to the facilitation of which solution, you will readily conceive, a smattering of biography would in no inconsiderable degree conduce. Leaving the dialects of men (in one of which I shall take leave to suppose you by this time at least superficially instituted), you will learn to ascend with him to the contemplation of that unarticulated language, which was before the written tongue; and, with the aid of the elder Phrygian or Æsopic key, to interpret the sounds by which the animal tribes communicate their minds—evolving moral instruction with delight from the dialogue of cocks, dogs, and foxes Or marrying theology with verse, from whose mixture a beautiful and healthy offspring may be expected, in your own native accents (but purified) you will keep time together to the profound harpings of the more modern or Wattsian hymnics.

Thus far I have ventured to conduct you to a "hill-side, whence you may discern the right path of a virtuous and noble education; laborious indeed at the first ascent, but else so smooth, so green, so full of goodly prospects and melodious sounds on every side, that the harp of Orpheus was not more charming."*

With my best respects to Mr. Grierson, when you see him,

I remain, dear Sir, your obedient servant,

April 1, 1823. ELIA.

* Milton's Tractate on Education, addressed to Mr Hartlib.

AUTOBIOGRAPHY OF MR. MUNDEN:

IN A LETTER TO THE EDITOR.

HARK'EE, Mr. Editor. A word in your ear. They tell me you are going to put me in print—in print, Sir. To publish my life. What is my life to you, Sir? What is it to you whether I ever lived at all? My life is a very good life, Sir. I am insured at the Pelican, Sir. I am threescore years and six—six; mark me, Sir: but I can play Polonius, which, I believe, few of your corre—correspondents can do, Sir. I suspect tricks, Sir: I smell a rat; I do, I do. You would cog the die upon us; you would, you would, Sir. But I will forestall you, Sir. You would be deriving me from William the Conqueror, with a murrain to you. It is no such thing, Sir. The town shall know better, Sir. They begin to smoke your flams, Sir. Mr. Liston may be born where he pleases, Sir: but I will not be born at Lup— Lupton Magna, for any body's pleasure, Sir. My son and I have looked over the great map of Kent together, and we can find no such place as you would palm upon us, Sir; palm upon us, I say. Neither Magna nor Parva, as my son says, and he knows Latin, Sir; Latin. If you write my life true, Sir, you must set down, that I, Joseph Munden, comedian, came into the world upon Allhallows' day, Anno Domini 1759—1759; no sooner nor later, Sir: and I saw the first light—the first light, remember, Sir, at Stoke Pogis—Stoke Pogis, comitatu Bucks, and not at Lup— Lup Magna, which I believe to be no better than moonshine—moonshine; do you mark me, Sir? I wonder you can put such flim flams upon us, Sir; I do, I do. It does not become you, Sir; I say it—I say it. And my father was an honest tradesman, Sir: he dealt in malt and hops, Sir, and was a Corporation man, Sir, and of the Church of England, Sir, and no Presbyterian; nor Ana— Anabaptist, Sir, however you may be disposed to make honest people believe to the contrary, Sir. Your bams are found out, Sir. The town will be your stale puts no longer, Sir; and you must not send us jolly fellows, Sir—we that are comedians, Sir,—you must not send us into groves and Charn— Charnwoods, a moping, Sir. Neither Charns, nor charnel houses, Sir. It is not our constitutions, Sir. I tell it you—I tell it you. I was a droll dog from my cradle. I came into the world tittering, and the midwife tittered, and the gossips spilt their caudle with tittering. And when I was brought to the font, the parson could not christen me for tittering. So I was never more than half baptized. And when I was little Joey, I made 'em all titter;—there was not a melancholy face to be seen in Pogis. Pure nature, Sir. I was born a comedian. Old Screwup, the undertaker, could tell you, Sir, if he were living. Why, I was obliged to be locked up every time there was to be a funeral at Pogis. I was—I was, Sir. I used to *grimace* at the mutes, as he called it, and put 'em out with my mops and my mows, till they could'nt stand at a door for me. And when I was locked up, with nothing but a cat in my company, I followed my bent with trying to make her laugh, and sometimes she would, and sometimes she would not. And my schoolmaster could make nothing of me: I had only to thrust my tongue in my cheek—in my cheek, Sir, and the rod dropped from his fingers: and so my education was limited, Sir. And I grew up a young fellow, and it was thought convenient to enter me upon some course of life that should make me serious; but it would'nt do, Sir. And I was articled to a drysalter. My father gave forty pounds premium with me, Sir. I can show the indent—dent—dentures, Sir. But I was born to be a comedian, Sir: so I ran away, and listed with the players, Sir; and I topt my parts at Amersham and Gerrard's Cross, and played my own father to his face, in his own town of Pogis, in the part of Gripe, when I was not full seventeen years of age, and he did not know me again, but he knew me afterwards; and then he laughed, and I laughed, and, what is better, the drysalter laughed, and gave me up my articles for the joke's sake: so that I came into court afterwards with clean hands—with clean hands—do you see, Sir?

[Here the manuscript becomes illegible for two or three sheets onwards, which we presume to be occasioned by the absence of Mr. Munden, jun. who clearly transcribed it for the press thus far. The rest (with the exception of the concluding paragraph, which seemingly is resumed in the first hand writing) appears to contain a confused account of some law-suit, in which the elder Munden was engaged; with a circumstantial history of the proceedings on a case of Breach of Promise of Marriage, made to or by (we cannot pick out which) Jemima Munden, spinster, probably the comedian's cousin, for it does not appear he had any sister; with a few dates, rather better preserved, of this great actor's engagements—as "Cheltenham (spelt Cheltnam) 1776;" "Bath, 1779;" "London, 1789;" together with stage anecdotes of Messrs. Edwin, Wilson, Lee Lewis, &c. over which we have strained our eyes to no purpose, in the hope of presenting something amusing to the public. Towards the end the manuscript brightens up a little, as we have said, and concludes in the following manner.]

——— stood before them for six and thirty years, [we suspect that Mr. Munden is here speaking of his final leave-taking of the stage] and to be dismissed at last. But I was heart-whole, heart-whole to the last, Sir. What though a few drops did course themselves down the old veteran's cheeks; who could help it, Sir? I was a giant that night, Sir; and could have played fifty parts, each as arduous as Dozy. My faculties were never better, Sir. But I was to be laid upon the shelf. It did not suit the public to laugh with their old servant any longer, Sir. [Here some moisture has blotted a sentence or two.] But I can play Polonius still, Sir; I can, I can.

Your servant, Sir,

JOSEPH MUNDEN.

EXCERPTIONS

FROM AN IDLER'S SCRAP-BOOK.

Times have consumed his works, saving some few *excerptions*
Raleigh.

GRAY'S LATIN ODE

ON THE MONASTERY OF THE GRANDE CHARTREUSE.

In a new Translation.

O TU severi *religio* loci. Some people have sadly puzzled themselves about this term *religio* "It must be the vow of the order," say these good folks: "aye, and there we have the *severity* of their rules." So that Gray, whose Christianity does not seem to have sat particularly *tight* about him, (unless we suppose that in his letters to Walpole, he thought it gave him more of the air of a *bel esprit* and an *esprit fort* to affect scepticism,) is smitten, according to these "word-catchers who live on syllables," with the love of a monastic life; and intends in good hearty earnest to shave his head, sew up his mouth, or only open it for the purpose of braying canticles and masticating parsneps, which, like Diocletian's cabbages, were to have been planted with his own fingers. Of this right apostolical resolution, I believe Gray never dreamed· no—not even in a make-believe trance of Parnassian inspiration. What would Dr Keate say to a lad who should render this first line, "*O thou! the religion of this place of austerities?*" But, "is not the monastery there?" Beyond the possibility of contradiction. "Like Scotland," it "stands where it did." But as regards Gray's poem, its standing where it did was a mere accidental circumstance: he has not a thought—no, not even a glancing association—connected with its grey walls, or the Latin graces before and after *pulse*, droned out by the cowled faquirs within them. It is the aspect of nature, in the surrounding vastness of her most rugged and most gloomy solitudes, that awakens the enthusiasm of Gray. Take the sketch of the scenery from the first pocket volume which chance may throw in your way. "On one hand is the rock with woods of pine-trees hanging over-head, and on the other a prodigious precipice, almost perpendicular, at the bottom of which rolls a deep torrent." Here we have the *religio* and here the *severi*, I suspect, notwithstanding that Gray is unauthorized in his use of the term *religio*. He certainly means a sort of *genius loci:* a power invisible and inaccessible, like Lucan's unknown demon of the Druidical forest of Marseilles· or rather its spirit; the influence by which it makes its presence felt But *religio* is employed to describe the impression of awe and reverence produced in the mind by some object of its solemn contemplation Gray, therefore, substitutes an active for the passive significance of the word, and transfers the religious awe from the mind to the object. making the effect to be the cause. But though it is easy to perceive his meaning, it is not so easy to convey it with the requisite fulness, and conciseness, and precision. Some translators have rendered *religio* by *genius*. They agree with me, therefore, in their general notion. but their expression of it is too definite in one sense, and too undefined in another. It is too definite, because it clothes an obscure abstraction with a gross and palpable form · we use, indeed, the words *genius* and *spirit* for the essence or energy of things; but where they are apostrophized they become personifications. It is too undefined, because it fails to communicate the impression of sacred horror excited by the original. There is no absolute prosopopœia: it is a *nescio quid* which the poet invocates; but it is a something which compels the instantaneous and involuntary sympathy and homage of the religious instincts. That there is a great difficulty in embodying this idea, must be evident from the fact, that Gray could only effect it by violating the philosophy of grammar. All the versions which have met my eye are too much in the nature of paraphrases They slur the diction of Gray, and sophisticate his sentiment. I think the Latin Ode of Gray should be done in the same number of lines, and in the metre which he himself loved when he versified in English. *Tentanda via*

Dread somewhat! hallowing to thyself this spot
  Of wildness, how to name thee? (for I deem
Less than a godhead presence haunteth not
  This antique forest and this native stream:

And we behold more near the visible God
  Midst these shagg'd cliffs, these rude hill-solitudes,
These rocks, which foot of man hath never trod,
  This dash of waters and this night of woods,

Than if beneath a citron arch he shone
  Fashion'd in molten gold by Phidias' hand—)
Hail!—if invoked aright, look gracious on!
  Here let my wearied youth glide calm to land.

Or should hard Fate's rebuff, e'en while I yearn
  For these endear'd retreats, this holy reign
Of silence, with the reflux swell return
  Me to the tossing midmost waves again;

Sire! (shall I call thee?) be the boon allow'd
  To share thy freedom in my drooping age;
Then steal me from the cares that vex the crowd,
  And safe receive me from their restless rage.

[About the year 18—, one R——d, a respectable London merchant (since dead), stood in the pillory for some alledged fraud upon the Revenue. Among his papers were found the following "Reflections," which we have obtained by favour of our friend Elia, who knew him well, and had heard him describe the train of his feelings upon that trying occasion almost in the words of the MS. Elia speaks of him as a man (with the exception of the peccadillo aforesaid) of singular integrity in all his private dealings, possessing great suavity of manner, with a certain turn for humour. As our object is to present human nature under every possible circumstance, we do not think that we shall sully our pages by inserting it.—*Editor.*]

REFLECTIONS IN THE PILLORY.

Scene, opposite the Royal Exchange.
Time, Twelve to One, Noon.

Ketch, my good fellow, you have a neat hand. Prithee, adjust this new collar to my neck gingerly. I am not used to these wooden cravats There, softly, softly. That seems the exact point between ornament and strangulation. A thought looser on this side. Now it will do. And have a care in turning me, that I present my aspect due vertically. I now face the orient. In a quarter of an hour I shift southward—do you mind?—and so on till I face the east again, travelling with the sun. No half points, I beseech you; N. N. by W. or any such elaborate niceties. They become the shipman's card, but not this mystery. Now leave me a little to my own reflections.

Bless us, what a company is assembled in honour of me! How grand I stand here! I never felt so sensibly before the effect of solitude in a crowd. I muse in solemn silence upon that vast miscellaneous rabble in the pit there. From my private box I contemplate with mingled pity and wonder the gaping curiosity of those underlings. There are my Whitechapel supporters. Rosemary Lane has emptied herself of the very flower of her citizens to grace my show. Duke's place sits desolate. What is there in my face, that strangers should come so far from the east to gaze upon it? [*Here an egg narrowly misses him*]. That offering was well meant, but not so cleanly executed By the tricklings, it should not be either myrrh or frankincence. Spare your presents, my friends; I am no-ways mercenary. I desire no missive tokens of your approbation. I am past those valentines. Bestow these coffins of untimely chickens upon mouths that water for them. Comfort your addle spouses with them at home, and stop the mouths of your brawling brats with such Olla Podridas, they have need of them [*A brick is let fly*] Disease not, I pray you, nor dismantle your rent and ragged tenements, to furnish me with architectural decorations, which I can excuse. This fragment might have stopped a flaw against snow comes. [*A coal flies.*] Cinders are dear, gentlemen This hubbling might have helped the pot boil, when your dirty cuttings from the shambles at three ha'-pence a pound shall stand at a cold simmer. Now, south about, Ketch. I would enjoy australian popularity.

What my friends from over the water! Old benchers—flies of a day—ephemeral Romans—welcome! Doth the sight of me draw souls from limbo? can it dispeople purgatory—ha!

What am I, or what was my father's house, that I should thus be set up a spectacle to gentlemen and others? Why are all faces, like Persians at the sun-rise, bent singly on mine alone? It was wont to be esteemed an ordinary visnomy, a quotidian merely. Doubtless, these assembled myriads discern some traits of nobleness, gentility, breeding, which hitherto have escaped the common observation—some intimations, as it were, of wisdom, valour, piety, and so forth. My sight dazzles; and, if I am not deceived by the too familiar pressure of this strange neckcloth that envelopes it, my countenance gives out lambent glories. For some painter now to take me in the lucky point of expression!—the posture so convenient—the head never shifting, but standing quiescent in a sort of natural frame But these artizans require a westerly aspect. Ketch, turn me.

Something of St. James's air in these my new friends How my prospects shift, and brighten! Now if Sir Thomas Lawrence be any where in that group, his fortune is made for ever I think I see some one taking out a crayon. I will compose my whole face to a smile, which yet shall not so predominate, but that gravity and gaiety shall contend as it were—you understand me? I will work up my thoughts to some mild rapture—a gentle enthusiasm us—which the artist may transfer in a manner warm to the canvass. I will inwardly apostrophize my tabernacle.

Delectable mansion, hail! House, not made of every wood! Lodging, that pays no rent; airy and commodious; which, owing no window tax, art yet all casement, out of which men have such pleasure in peering and overlooking, that they will sometimes stand an hour together to enjoy thy prospects! Cell, recluse from the vulgar! Quiet retirement from the great Babel, yet affording sufficient glimpses into it! Pulpit, that instructs without note or sermon-book, into which the preacher is inducted without tenth or first fruit! Throne, unshared and single, that disdainest a Brentford competitor! Honour without co-rival! Or hearest thou rather, magnificent theatre in which the spectator comes to see and to be seen? From thy giddy heights I look down upon the common herd, who stand with eyes upturned as if a winged messenger hovered over them; and mouths open, as if they expected manna. I feel, I feel, the true Episcopal yearnings. Behold in me, my flock, your true overseer! What though I cannot lay hands, because my own are laid, yet I can mutter benedictions. True *otium cum dignitate!* Proud Pisgah eminence! Pinnacle sublime! O Pillory, 'tis thee I sing! Thou younger brother to the gallows, without his rough and Esau palms; that with ineffable contempt surveyest beneath thee the grovelling stocks, which claims presumptuously to be of thy great race. Let that low wood know, that thou art far higher born! Let that domicile for groundling rogues and base earth-kissing varlets envy thy preferment, not seldom fated to be the wanton baiting-house, the temporary retreat, of poet and of patriot. Shades of Bastwick and of Prynne hover over thee—Defoe is there, and more greatly daring Shebbeare—from their (little more elevated) stations they look down with recognitions. Ketch, turn me.

I now veer to the north. Open your widest gates, thou proud Exchange of London, that I may look in as proudly! Gresham's wonder, hail! I stand upon a level with all your kings. They, and I, from equal heights, with equal superciliousness, o'er-look the plodding, money-hunting tribe below; who, busied in their sordid speculations, scarce elevate their eyes to notice your ancient, or my recent, grandeur. The second Charles smiles on me from three pedestals?* He closed the Exchequer; I cheated the Excise. Equal our darings, equal be our lot.

Are those the quarters? 'tis their fatal chime. That the ever-winged hours would but stand still! but I must descend, descend from this dream of greatness. Stay, stay, a little while, importunate hour hand. A moment or two, and I shall walk on foot with the undistinguished many. The clock speaks one. I return to common life. Ketch, let me out.

---

* A statue of Charles II. by the elder Cibber, adorns the front of the Exchange. He stands also on high, in the train of his crowned ancestors, in his proper order, *within* that building. But the merchants of London, in a superfœtation of loyalty, have, within a few years, caused to be erected another effigy of him on the ground in the centre of the interior. We do not hear that a fourth is in contemplation.—*Editor.*

THE LAST PEACH.

I AM the miserablest man living. Give me counsel, dear Editor. I was bred up in the strictest principles of honesty, and have past my life in punctual adherence to them. Integrity might be said to be ingrained in our family. Yet I live in constant fear of one day coming to the gallows.

Till the latter end of last autumn I never experienced these feelings of self-mistrust which ever since have embittered my existence. From the apprehension of that unfortunate man whose story began to make so great an impression upon the public about that time, I date my horrors. I never can get it out of my head that I shall some time or other commit a forgery, or do some equally vile thing. To make matters worse I am in a banking-house. I sit surrounded with a cluster of bank-notes. These were formerly no more to me than meat to a butcher's dog. They are now as toads and aspics. I feel all day like one situated amidst gins and pit-falls. Sovereigns, which I once took such pleasure in counting out, and scraping up with my little thin tin shovel (at which I was the most expert in the banking-house), now scald my hands When I go to sign my name I set down that of another person, or write my own in a counterfeit character I am beset with temptations without motive. I want no more wealth than I possess A more contented being than myself, as to money matters, exists not. What should I fear?

When a child I was once let loose, by favour of a Nobleman's gardener, into his Lordship's magnificent fruit garden, with free leave to pull the currants and the gooseberries, only I was interdicted from touching the wall fruit. Indeed, at that season (it was the end of Autumn) there was little left. Only on the South wall (can I forget the hot feel of the brick-work?) lingered the one last peach. Now peaches are a fruit which I always had, and still have, an almost utter aversion to. There is something to my palate singularly harsh and repulsive in the flavour of them. I know not by what demon of contradiction inspired, but I was haunted with an irresistible desire to pluck it. Tear myself as often as I would from the spot, I found myself still recurring to it, till, maddening with desire (desire I cannot call it), with wilfulness rather—without appetite—against appetite, I may call it—in evil hour I reached out my hand, and plucked it. Some few rain drops just then fell; the sky (from a bright day) became overcast; and I was a type of our first parents, after the eating of that fatal fruit I felt myself naked and ashamed, stripped of my virtue, spiritless The downy fruit, whose sight rather than savour had tempted me, dropt from my hand, never to be tasted. All the commentators in the world cannot persuade me but that the Hebrew word in the second chapter of Genesis, translated apple, should be rendered peach. Only this way can I reconcile that mysterious story.

Just such a child at thirty am I among the cash and valuables, longing to pluck, without an idea of enjoyment further. I cannot reason myself out of these fears: I dare not laugh at them. I was tenderly and lovingly brought up. What then? Who that in life's entrance had seen the babe F——, from the lap stretching out his little fond mouth to catch the maternal kiss, could have predicted, or as much as imagined, that life's very different exit? The sight of my own fingers torments me, they seem so admirably constructed for —— pilfering. Then that jugular vein, which I have in common ——; in an emphatic sense may I say with David, I am "fearfully made." All my mirth is poisoned by these unhappy suggestions. If, to dissipate reflection, I hum a tune, it changes to the "Lamentations of a Sinner." My very dreams are tainted I awake with a shocking feeling of my hand in some pocket.

Advise with me, dear Editor, on this painful heart-malady. Tell me, do you feel any thing allied to it in yourself? do you never feel an itching, as it were—a *dactylomania*—or am I alone? You have my honest confession. My next may appear from Bow-street.

SUSPENSURUS.

BARBARA S——

On the noon of the 14th of November, 1743 or 4, I forget which it was, just as the clock had struck one, Barbara S——, with her accustomed punctuality, ascended the long rambling staircase, with awkward interposed landing-places, which led to the office, or rather a sort of box with a desk in it, whereat sat the then Treasurer of (what few of our readers may remember) the Old Bath Theatre. All over the island it was the custom, and remains so I believe to this day, for the players to receive their weekly stipend on the Saturday. It was not much that Barbara had to claim.

This little maid had but just entered her eleventh year, but her important station at the theatre, as it seemed to her, with the benefits which she felt to accrue from her pious application of her small earnings, had given an air of womanhood to her steps and to her behaviour. You would have taken her to have been at least five years older

Till latterly she had merely been employed in choruses, or where children were wanted to fill up the scene. But the manager, observing a diligence and adroitness in her above her age, had for some few months past entrusted to her the performance of whole parts. You may guess the self consequence of the promoted Barbara. She had already drawn tears in young Arthur; had rallied Richard with infantine petulance in the Duke of York, and in her turn had rebuked that petulance when she was Prince of Wales. She would have done the elder child in Morton's pathetic after-piece to the life, but as yet the "Children in the Wood" was not.

Long after this little girl was grown an aged woman, I have seen some of these small parts, each making two or three pages at most, copied out in the rudest hand of the then prompter, who doubtless transcribed a little more carefully and fairly for the grown-up tragedy ladies of the establishment But such as they were, blotted and scrawled, as for a child's use, she kept them all; and in the zenith of her after reputation it was a delightful sight to behold them bound up in costliest Morocco, each single—each small part making a *book*—with fine clasps, gilt-splashed, &c. She had conscientiously kept them as they had been delivered to her; not a blot had been effaced or tampered with. They were precious to her for their affecting remembrancings. They were her principia, her rudiments; the elementary atoms, the little steps by which she pressed forwards to perfection. "What," she would say, "could Indian rubber, or a pumice stone, have done for these darlings?"

I am in no hurry to begin my story—indeed I have little or none to tell—so I will just mention an observation of hers connected with that interesting time.

Not long before she died I had been discoursing with her on the quantity of real present emotion which a great tragic performer experiences during acting I ventured to think, that though in the first instance such players must have possessed the feelings which they so powerfully called up in others, yet by frequent repetition those feelings must become deadened in great measure, and the performer trust to the memory of past emotion, rather than express a present one. She indignantly repelled the notion, that with a truly great tragedian the operation, by which such effects were produced upon an audience, could ever degrade itself into what was purely mechanical With much delicacy, avoiding to instance in her *self*-experience, she told me, that so long ago as when she used to play the part of the Little Son to Mrs. Porter's Isabella, (I think it was) when that impressive actress has been bending over her in some heart-rending colloquy, she has felt real hot tears come trickling from her, which (to use her powerful expression) have perfectly scalded her back.

I am not quite so sure that it was Mrs. Porter; but it was some great actress of that day The name is indifferent; but the fact of the scalding tears I most distinctly remember.

I was always fond of the society of the players, and am not sure that an impediment in my speech (which certainly kept me out of the pulpit) even more than certain personal disqualifications, which are often got over in that profession, did not prevent me at one time of life from adopting it. I have had the honour (I must ever call it) once to have been admitted to the tea-table of Miss Kelly. I have played at serious whist with Mr. Liston. I have chatted with ever good-humoured Mrs Charles Kemble. I have conversed as friend to friend with her accomplished husband I have been indulged with a classical conference with Macready; and with a sight of the Player-picture gallery at Mr. Matthews's, when the kind owner, to remunerate me for my love of the old actors (whom he loves so much) went over it with me, supplying to his capital collection, what alone the artist could not give them—voice; and their living motions Old tones, half-faded, of Dodd, and Parsons, and Baddeley, have lived again for me at his bidding Only Edwin he could not restore to me. I have supped with ——, but I am growing a coxcomb.

As I was about to say—at the desk of the then treasurer of the old Bath theatre—not Diamond's — presented herself the little Barbara S——

The parents of Barbara had been in reputable circumstances. The father had practised, I believe, as an apothecary in the town. But his practice from causes which I feel my own infirmity too sensibly that way to arraign—or perhaps from that pure infelicity which accompanies some people in their walk through life, and which it is impossible to lay at the door of imprudence—was now reduced to nothing. They were in fact in the very teeth of starvation, when the manager, who knew and respected them in better days, took the little Barbara into his company.

• At the period I commenced with, her slender earnings were the sole support of the family, including two younger sisters. I must throw a veil over some mortifying circumstances. Enough to say, that her Saturday's pittance was the only chance of a Sunday's (generally their only) meal of meat.

One thing I will only mention, that in some child's part, where in her theatrical character she was to sup off a roast fowl (O joy to Barbara!) some comic actor, who was for the night caterer for this stage dainty—in the misguided humour of his part, threw over the dish such a quantity of salt (O grief and pain of heart to Barbara!) that when he crammed a portion of it into her mouth, she was obliged sputteringly to reject it; and what with shame of her ill-acted part, and pain of real appetite at missing such a dainty, her little heart sobbed almost to breaking, till a flood of tears, which the well-fed spectators were totally unable to comprehend, mercifully relieved her.

This was the little starved, meritorious maid, who stood before old Ravenscroft, the treasurer, for her Saturday's payment.

Ravenscroft was a man, I have heard many old theatrical people besides herself say, of all men least calculated for a treasurer. He had no head for accounts, paid away at random, kept scarce any books, and summing up at the week's end, if he found himself a pound or so deficient, blest himself that it was no worse.

Now Barbara's weekly stipend was a bare half guinea.—By mistake he popped into her hand a—whole one.

Barbara tripped away

She was entirely unconscious at first of the mistake: God knows that Ravenscroft would never have discovered it.

But when she had got down to the first of those uncouth landing-places, she became sensible of an unusual weight of metal pressing her little hand.

Now mark the dilemma.

She was by nature a good child. From her parents and those about her she had imbibed no contrary influence. But then they had taught her nothing. Poor men's smoky cabins are not always porticoes of moral philosophy. This little maid had no instinct to evil, but then she might be said to have no fixed principle She had heard honesty commended, but never dreamed of its application to herself. She thought of it as something which concerned grown-up people—men and women She had never known temptation, or thought of preparing resistance against it

Her first impulse was to go back to the old treasurer, and explain to him his blunder. He was already so confused with age, besides a natural want of punctuality, that she would have had some difficulty in making him understand it. She saw *that* in an instant. And then it was such a bit of money! and then the image of a larger allowance of butcher's meat on their table next day came across her, till her little eyes glistened, and her mouth moistened. But then Mr. Ravenscroft had always been so good-natured, had stood her friend behind the scenes, and even recommended her promotion to some of her little parts. But again the old man was reputed to be worth a world of money. He was supposed to have fifty pounds a year clear of the theatre. And then came staring upon her the figures of her little stockingless and shoeless sisters. And when she looked at her own neat white cotton stockings, which her situation at the theatre had made it indispensable for her mother to provide for her, with hard straining and pinching from the family stock, and thought how glad she should be to cover their poor feet with the same—and how then they could accompany her to rehearsals, which they had hitherto been precluded from doing, by reason of their unfashionable attire,—in these thoughts she reached the second landing-place—the second, I mean from the top—for there was still another left to traverse.

Now virtue support Barbara!

And that never-failing friend did step in—for at that moment a strength not her own, I have heard her say, was revealed to her—a reason above reasoning—and without her own agency, as it seemed (for she never felt her feet to move) she found herself transported back to the individual desk she had just quitted, and her hand in the old hand of Ravenscroft, who in silence took back the refunded treasure, and who had been sitting (good man) insensible to the lapse of minutes, which to her were anxious ages; and from that moment a deep peace fell upon her heart, and she knew the quality of honesty.

A year or two's unrepining application to her profession brightened up the feet, and the prospects, of her little sisters, set the whole family upon their legs again, and released her from the difficulty of discussing moral dogmas upon a landing-place.

I have heard her say, that it was a surprise, not much short of mortification to her, to see the coolness with which the old man pocketed the difference, which had cost her such mortal throes

This anecdote of herself I had in the year 1800, from the mouth of the late Mrs. Crawford* then sixty-seven years of age (she died soon after), and to her struggles upon this childish occasion I have sometimes ventured to think her indebted for that power of rending the heart in the representation of conflicting emotions, for which in after years she was considered as little inferior (if at all so in the part of Lady Randolph) even to Mrs Siddons. ELIA.

---

* The maiden name of this lady was Street, which she changed, by successive marriages, for those of Dancer, Barry, and Crawford She was Mrs Crawford, and a third time a widow, when I knew her

THE THREE GRAVES;

Written during the time, now happily almost forgotten, of the Spy System.

CLOSE by the ever-burning brimstone beds,
Where Bedloe, Oates, and Judas, hide their heads,
I saw great Satan like a Sexton stand,
With his intolerable spade in hand,
Digging three graves. Of coffin shape they were,
For those who, coffinless, must enter there
With unblest rites. The shrouds were of that cloth,
Which Clotho weaveth in her blackest wrath:
The dismal tinct oppress'd the eye, that dwelt
Upon it long, like darkness to be felt.
The pillows to these baleful beds were toads,
Large, living, livid, melancholy loads,
Whose softness shock'd. Worms of all monstrous size
Crawl'd round; and one, upcoil'd, which never dies.
A doleful bell, inculcating despair,
Was always ringing in the heavy air.
And all about the detestable pit
Strange headless ghosts, and quarter'd forms, did flit;
Rivers of blood, from dripping traitors spilt,
By treachery stung from poverty to guilt.
I ask'd the Fiend, for whom those rites were meant?
"These graves," quoth he, "when life's brief oil is spent,
When the dark night comes, and they're sinking bedwards,
I mean for C——, O——, and E——."

QUATRAINS

TO THE EDITOR OF THE EVERY DAY-BOOK.

I LIKE you, and your book, ingenuous Hone!
  In whose capacious, all-embracing leaves
The very marrow of tradition's shown;
  And all that history—much that fiction—weaves.

By every sort of taste your work is graced.
  Vast stores of modern anecdote we find,
With good old story quaintly interlaced—
  The theme as various as the reader's mind.

Rome's lie-fraught legends you so truly paint—
  Yet kindly—that the half-turn'd Catholic
Scarcely forbears to smile at his own saint,
  And cannot curse the candid Heretic.

Rags, relics, witches, ghosts, fiends, crowd your page;
  Our fathers' mummeries we well-pleased behold;
And, proudly conscious of a purer age,
  Forgive some fopperies in the times of old.

Verse-honouring Phœbus, Father of bright *Days*,
  Must needs bestow on you both good and many,
Who, building trophies to his children's praise,
  Run their rich Zodiac through, not missing any.

Dan Phœbus loves your book—trust me, friend Hone—
  The title only errs, he bids me say:
For while such art—wit—reading—there are shown,
  He swears, 'tis not a work of *every day*.

C. LAMB.

THE SUPERANNUATED MAN.

—— *Sera tamen respexit*
Libertas.

If peradventure, Reader, it has been thy lot to waste the golden years of thy life—thy shining youth—in the irksome confinement of an office; to have thy prison days prolonged through middle age down to decrepitude and silver hairs, without hope of release or respite; to have lived to forget that there are such things as holidays, or to remember them but as the prerogatives of childhood; then, and then only, will you be able to appreciate my deliverance.

It is now six and thirty years since I took my seat at the desk in Mincing-lane. Melancholy was the transition at fourteen from the abundant play-time, and frequently-intervening vacations of school days, to the eight, nine, and sometimes ten hours' a-day attendance at a counting-house. But time partially reconciles us to any thing. I gradually became content—doggedly contented, as wild animals in cages.

It is true I had my Sundays to myself; but Sundays, admirable as the institution of them is for purposes of worship, are for that very reason the very worst adapted for days of unbending and recreation.*

* Our ancestors, the noble old Puritans of Cromwell's day, could distinguish between a day of religious rest and a day of recreation; and while they exacted a rigorous abstinence from all amusements (even to the walking out of nursery maids with their little charges in the fields) upon the Sabbath; in the lieu of the superstitious observance of the Saints days, which they abrogated, they humanely gave to the apprentices, and poorer sort of people, every alternate Thursday for a day of entire sport and recreation. A strain of piety and policy to be commended above the profane mockery of the Stuarts and their Book of Sports.

In particular, there is a gloom for me attendant upon a city Sunday, a weight in the air I miss the cheerful cries of London, the music, and the ballad singers—the buzz and stirring murmur of the streets. Those eternal bells depress me. The closed shops repel me. Prints, pictures, all the glittering and endless succession of knacks and gewgaws, and ostentatiously displayed wares of tradesmen, which make a week-day saunter through the less busy parts of the metropolis so delightful—are shut out. No book-stalls deliciously to idle over—No busy faces to recreate the idle man who contemplates them ever passing by—the very face of business a charm by contrast to his temporary relaxation from it. Nothing to be seen but unhappy countenances—or half-happy at best—of emancipated prentices and little tradesfolks, with here and there a servant maid that has got leave to go out, who, slaving all the week, with the habit has lost almost the capacity of enjoying a free hour; and livelily expressing the hollowness of a day's pleasuring. The very strollers in the fields on that day look any thing but comfortable.

But besides Sundays I had a day at Easter, and a day at Christmas, with a full week in the summer to go and air myself in my native fields of Hertfordshire. This last was a great indulgence; and the prospect of its recurrence, I believe, alone kept me up through the year, and made my durance tolerable. But when the week came round, did the glittering phantom of the distance keep touch with me? or rather was it not a series of seven uneasy days, spent in restless pursuit of pleasure, and a wearisome anxiety to find out how to make the most of them? Where was the quiet, where the promised rest? Before I had a taste of it, it was vanished. I was at the desk again, counting upon the fifty-one tedious weeks that must intervene before such another snatch would come. Still the prospect of its coming threw something of an illumination upon the darker side of my captivity. Without it, as I have said, I could scarcely have sustained my thraldom.

Independently of the rigours of attendance, I have ever been haunted with a sense (perhaps a mere caprice) of incapacity for business. This, during my latter years, had increased to such a degree, that it was visible in all the lines of my countenance. My health and my good spirits flagged. I had perpetually a dread of some crisis, to which I should be found unequal. Besides my day-light servitude, I served over again all night in my sleep, and would awake with terrors of imaginary false entries, errors in my accounts, and the like. I was fifty years of age, and no prospect of emancipation presented itself. I had grown to my desk, as it were; and the wood had entered into my soul.

My fellows in the office would sometimes rally me upon the trouble legible in my countenance, but I did not know that it had raised the suspicions of any of my employers, when, on the 5th of last month, a day ever to be remembered by me, L——, the junior partner in the firm, calling me on one side, directly taxed me with my bad looks, and frankly inquired the cause of them. So taxed, I honestly made confession of my infirmity, and added that I was afraid I should eventually be obliged to resign his service. He spoke some words of course to hearten me, and there the matter rested. A whole week I remained labouring under the impression that I had acted imprudently in my disclosure; that I had foolishly given a handle against myself, and had been anticipating my own dismissal. A week passed in this manner, the most anxious one, I verily believe, in my whole life, when on the evening of the 12th of April, just as I was about quitting my desk to go home (it might be about eight o'clock) I received an awful summons to attend the presence of the whole assembled firm in the formidable back parlour. I thought, now my time is surely come, I have done for myself, I am going to be told that they have no longer occasion for me. L——, I could see, smiled at the terror I was in, which was a little relief to me,—when to my utter astonishment B——, the eldest partner, began a formal harangue to me on the length of my services, my very meritorious conduct during the whole of the time (the deuce, thought I, how did he find out that? I protest I never had the confidence to think as much). He went on to descant upon the expediency of retiring at a certain time of life (how my heart panted!) and asking me a few questions as to the amount of my own property, of which I have a little, ended with a proposal, to which his three partners nodded a grave assent, that I should accept from the house, which I had served so well, a pension for life to the amount of two-thirds of my accustomed salary—a magnificent offer! I do not know what I answered between surprise and gratitude, but it was understood that I accepted their proposal, and I was told that I was free from that hour to leave their service. I stammered out a bow, and at just ten minutes after eight I went home—for ever. This noble benefit—gratitude forbids me to conceal their names—I owe to the kindness of the most munificent firm in the world—the house of Boldero, Merryweather, Bosanquet, and Lacy.

Esto Perpetua!

For the first day or two I felt stunned, overwhelmed. I could only apprehend my felicity; I was too confused to taste it sincerely. I wandered about, thinking I was happy, and knowing that I was not. I was in the condition of a prisoner in the old Bastile, suddenly let loose after a forty years' confinement. I could scarce trust myself with myself. It was like passing out of Time into Eternity—for it is a sort of Eternity for a man to have his Time all to himself. It seemed to me that I had more Time on my hands than I could ever manage. From a poor man, poor in Time, I was suddenly lifted up into a vast revenue; I could see no end of my possessions; I wanted some steward, or judicious bailiff, to manage my estates in Time for me. And here let me caution persons grown old in active business, not lightly, nor without weighing their own resources, to forego their customary employment all at once, for there may be danger in it. I feel it by myself, but I know that my resources are sufficient; and now that those first giddy raptures have subsided, I have a quiet home-feeling of the blessedness of my condition I am in no hurry. Having all holidays, I am as though I had none. If Time hung heavy upon me, I could walk it away; but I do *not* walk all day long, as I used to do in those old transient holidays, thirty miles a day, to make the most of them. If Time were troublesome, I could read it away, but I do *not* read in that violent measure, with which, having no Time my own but candle-light Time, I used to weary out my head and eye-sight in by-gone winters. I walk, read or scribble (as now) just when the fit seizes me. I no longer hunt after pleasure, I let it come to me. I am like the man

> ——— That's born, and has his years come to him,
> In some green desart.

"Years," you will say! "what is this superannuated simpleton calculating upon? He has already told us, he is past fifty."

I have indeed lived nominally fifty years, but deduct out of them the hours which I have lived to other people, and not to myself, and you will find me still a young fellow. For *that* is the only true Time, which a man can properly call his own, that which he has all to himself; the rest, though in some sense he may be said to live it, is other people's time, not his. The remnant of my poor days, long or short, is at least multiplied for me three-fold. My ten next years, if I stretch so far, will be as long as any preceding thirty. 'Tis a fair rule-of-three sum.

Among the strange fantasies which beset me at the commencement of my freedom, and of which all traces are not yet gone, one was, that a vast tract of time had intervened since I quitted the Counting House. I could not conceive of it as an affair of yesterday. The partners, and the clerks, with whom I had so many years and for so many hours in each day of the year been closely associated—being suddenly removed from them—they seemed as dead to me. There is a fine passage, which may serve to illustrate this fancy, in a Tragedy by Sir Robert Howard, speaking of a friend's death:

> ——— 'Twas but just now he went away;
> I have not since had time to shed a tear;
> And yet the distance does the same appear
> As if he had been a thousand years from me.
> Time takes no measure in Eternity.

To dissipate this awkward feeling, I have been fain to go among them once or twice since, to visit my old desk-fellows—my co-brethren of the quill—that I had left below in the state militant. Not all the kindness with which they received me could quite restore to me that pleasant familiarity, which I had heretofore enjoyed among them. We cracked some of our old jokes, but methought they went off but faintly. My old desk, the peg where I hung my hat, were appropriated to another. I knew it must be, but I could not take it kindly. D——l take me, if I did not feel some remorse—beast, if I had not,—at quitting my old compeers, the faithful partners of my toils for six and thirty years, that smoothed for me with their jokes and their conundrums the ruggedness of my professional road. Had it been so rugged then after all? or was I a coward simply? Well, it is too late to repent; and I also know, that these suggestions are a common fallacy of the mind on such occasions. But my heart smote me. I had violently broken the bands betwixt us. It was at least not courteous. I shall be some time before I get quite reconciled to the separation. Farewell, old cronies, yet not for long, for again and again I will come among ye, if I shall have your leave. Farewell Ch——, dry, sarcastic, and friendly! Do———, mild, slow to move, and gentlemanly! Pl———, officious to do, and to volunteer, good services!—and thou, thou dreary pile, fit mansion for a Gresham or a Whittington of old, stately House of Merchants; with thy labyrinthine passages, and light-excluding, pent-up offices, where candles for one half the year supplied the place of the sun's light; unhealthy contributor to my weal, stern fosterer of my living, farewell! In thee remain, and not in the obscure collection of some wandering bookseller, my "works!" There let them rest, as I do from my labours, piled on thy massy shelves, more MSS. in folio than ever Aquinas left, and full as useful! My mantle I bequeath among ye.

THE SUPERANNUATED MAN.—No. II.

A Clerk I was in London gay.—O'KEEFE.

A FORTNIGHT has passed since the date of my first communication. At that period I was approaching to tranquillity, but had not reached it. I boasted of a calm indeed, but it was comparative only. Something of the first flutter was left; an unsettling sense of novelty; the dazzle to weak eyes of unaccustomed light. I missed my old chains, forsooth, as if they had been some necessary part of my apparel. I was a poor Carthusian, from strict cellular discipline suddenly by some revolution returned upon the world. I am now as if I had never been other than my own master. It is natural to me to go where I please, to do what I please. I find myself at eleven o'clock in the day in Bond-street, and it seems to me that I have been sauntering there at that very hour for years past. I digress into Soho, to explore a book-stall. Methinks I have been thirty years a collector. There is nothing strange nor new in it. I find myself before a fine picture in a morning. Was it ever otherwise? What is become of Fish-street Hill? Where is Fenchurch-street? Stones of old Mincing-lane which I have worn with my daily pilgrimage for six and thirty years, to the footsteps of what toil-worn clerk are your everlasting flints now vocal? I indent the gayer flags of Pall Mall. It is Change time, and I am strangely among the Elgin marbles. It was no hyperbole when I ventured to compare the change in my condition to a passing into another world. Time stands still in a manner to me. I have lost all distinction of season. I do not know the day of the week, or of the month. Each day used to be individually felt by me in its reference to the foreign post days; in its distance from, or propinquity to, the next Sunday. I had my Wednesday feelings, my Saturday nights' sensations. The genius of each day was upon me distinctly during the whole of it, affecting my appetite, spirits, &c. The phantom of the next day, with the dreary five to follow, sate as a load upon my poor Sabbath recreations. What charm has washed that Ethiop white? What is gone of Black Monday? All days are the same. Sunday itself—that unfortunate failure of a holyday as it too often proved, what with my sense of its fugitiveness, and over-care to get the greatest quantity of pleasure out of it—is melted down into a week day. I can spare to go to church now, without grudging the huge cantle, which it used to seem to cut out of the holyday. I have Time for every thing. I can visit a sick friend. I can interrupt the man of much occupation when he is busiest. I can insult over him with an invitation to take a day's pleasure with me to Windsor this fine May-morning. It is Lucretian pleasure to behold the poor drudges, whom I have left behind in the world, carking and caring; like horses in a mill, drudging on in the same eternal round—and what is it all for? I recite those verses of Cowley, which so mightily agree with my constitution.

Business! the frivolous pretence
Of human lusts to shake off innocence:
Business! the grave impertinence.
Business! the thing which I of all things hate:
Business! the contradiction of my fate.

Or I repeat my own lines, written in my Clerk state:

Who first invented work—and bound the free
And holyday-rejoicing spirit down
To the ever-haunting importunity
Of business, in the green fields, and the town—
To plough, loom, anvil, spade—and oh! most sad,
To this dry drudgery of the desk's dead wood?
Who but the Being unblest, alien from good,
Sabbathless Satan! he who his unglad
Task ever plies 'mid rotatory burnings,
That round and round incalculably reel—
For wrath divine hath made him like a wheel—
In that red realm from whence are no returnings;
Where toiling, and turmoiling, ever and aye
He, and his thoughts, keep pensive worky-day!

O this divine Leisure!—Reader, if thou art furnished with the Old Series of the London, turn incontinently to the third volume (page 367), and you will see my present condition there touched in a "Wish" by a daintier pen than I can pretend to.' I subscribe to that Sonnet *toto corde*. A man can never have too much Time to himself, nor too little to do. Had I a little son, I would christen him NOTHING-TO-DO; he should do nothing. Man, I verily believe, is out of his element as long as he is operative. I am altogether for the life contemplative. Will no kindly earthquake come and swallow up those accursed cotton mills? Take me that lumber of a desk there, and bowl it down

As low as to the fiends.

I am no longer J——s D——n, Clerk to the Firm of, &c. I am Retired Leisure. I am to be met with in trim gardens. I am already come to be known by my vacant face and careless gesture, perambulating at no fixed pace, nor with any settled purpose. I walk about; not to and from. They tell me, a certain *cum dignitate* air, that has been buried so long with my other good parts, has begun to shoot forth in my person. I grow into gentility perceptibly. When I take up a newspaper, it is to read the state of the opera. *Opus operatum est.* I have done all that I came into this world to do. I have worked task work, and have the rest of the day to myself. J, D.

Beaufort-terrace, Regent-street;
Late of Ironmonger's-court, Fenchurch-street.

THE WEDDING.

I DO not know when I have been better pleased than at being invited last week to be present at the wedding of a friend's daughter. I like to make one at these ceremonies, which to us old people give back our youth in a manner, and restore our gayest season, in the remembrance of our own success, or the regrets, scarcely less tender, of our own youthful disappointments, in this point of a settlement. On these occasions I am sure to be in good humour for a week or two after, and enjoy a reflected honey-moon Being without a family, I am flattered with these temporary adoptions into a friend's family, I feel a sort of cousinhood, or uncleship, for the season; I am inducted into degrees of affinity, and, in the participated socialities of the little community, I lay down for a brief while my solitary bachelorship. I carry this humour so far, that I take it unkindly to be left out, even when a funeral is going on in the house of a dear friend. But to my subject.——

The union itself had been long settled, but its celebration had been hitherto deferred, to an almost unreasonable state of suspense in the lovers, by some invincible prejudices which the bride's father had unhappily contracted upon the subject of the too early marriages of females. He has been lecturing any time these five years—for to that length the courtship has been protracted—upon the propriety of putting off the solemnity, till the lady should have completed her five and twentieth year. We all began to be afraid that a suit, which as yet had abated of none of its ardours, might at last be lingered on, till passion had time to cool, and love go out in the experiment. But a little wheedling on the part of his wife, who was by no means a party to these overstrained notions, joined to some serious expostulations on that of his friends, who, from the growing infirmities of the old gentleman, could not promise ourselves many years' enjoyment of his company, and were anxious to bring matters to a conclusion during his life time, at length prevailed, and on Monday last the daughter of my old friend, Admiral ———, having attained the *womanly* age of nineteen, was conducted to the church by her pleasant cousin J——, who told some few years older.

Before the youthful part of my female readers express their indignation at the abominable loss of time occasioned to the lovers by the preposterous notions of my old friend, they will do well to consider the reluctance which a fond parent naturally feels at parting with his child. To this unwillingness, I believe, in most cases may be traced the difference of opinion on this point between child and parent, whatever pretences of interest or prudence may be held out to cover it. The hard-heartedness of fathers is a fine theme for romance-writers, a sure and moving topic, but is there not something untender, to say no more of it, in the hurry which a beloved child is sometimes in to tear herself from the parental stock, and commit herself to strange graftings? The case is heightened where the lady, as in the present instance, happens to be an only child. I do not understand these matters experimentally, but I can make a shrewd guess at the wounded pride of a parent upon these occasions. It is no new observation, I believe, that a lover in most cases has no rival so much to be feared as the father. Certainly there is a jealousy in *unparallel subjects*, which is little less heart-rending than the passion which we more strictly christen by that name Mothers' scruples are more easily got over; for this reason, I suppose, that the protection transferred to a husband is less a derogation and a loss to their authority than to the paternal Mothers, besides, have a trembling foresight, which paints the inconveniences (impossible to be conceived in the same degree by the other parent) of a life of forlorn celibacy, which the refusal of a tolerable match may entail upon their child Mothers' instinct is a surer guide here, than the cold reasonings of a father on such a topic To this instinct may be imputed, and by it alone may be excused, the unbeseeming artifices, by which some wives push on the matrimonial projects of their daughters, which the husband, however approving, shall entertain with comparative indifference A little shamelessness on this head is pardonable With this explanation, forwardness becomes a grace, and maternal importunity receives the name of a virtue. But the parson stays, while I preposterously assume his office, I am preaching, while the bride is on the threshold

Nor let any of my female readers suppose that the sage reflections which have just escaped me have the obliquest tendency of application to the young lady, who, it will be seen, is about to venture upon a change in her condition, at a *mature and competent age*, and not without the fullest approbation of both parents. I only deprecate *very hasty marriages*

It had been fixed that the ceremony should be gone through at an early hour, to give time for a little *dejeune* afterwards, to which a select party of friends had been invited. We were in church a little before the clock struck eight.

Nothing could be more judicious or graceful than the dress of the bride-maids—the three charming Miss Foresters—on this morning To give the bride an opportunity of shining singly, they had come habited all in green. I am ill at describing female apparel; but, while *she* stood at the altar in vestments white and candid as her thoughts, a sacrificial whiteness, *they* assisted in robes, such as might have become Diana's nymphs—Foresters indeed—as such who had not yet come to the resolution of putting off cold virginity. These young maids, not being so blest as to have a mother living, I am told, keep single for their father's sake, and live all together so happy with their remaining parent, that the hearts of their lovers are even broken with the prospect (so inauspicious to their hopes) of such uninterrupted and provoking home-comfort. Gallant girls! each a victim worthy of Iphigenia!

I do not know what business I have to be present in solemn places. I cannot divest me of an unseasonable disposition to levity upon the most awful occasions. I was never cut out for a public functionary. Ceremony and I have long shaken hands; but I could not resist the importunities of the young lady's father, whose gout unhappily confined him at home, to act as parent on this occasion, and *give away the bride*. Something ludicrous occurred to me at this most serious of all moments—a sense of my unfitness to have the disposal, even in imagination, of the sweet young creature beside me. I fear I was betrayed to some lightness, for the awful eye of the parson—and the rector's eye of Saint Mildred's in the Poultry is no trifle of a rebuke—was upon me in an instant, souring my incipient jest to the tristful severities of a funeral.

This was the only misbehaviour which I can plead to upon this solemn occasion, unless what was objected to me after the ceremony by one of the handsome Miss Turners, be accounted a solecism. She was pleased to say that she had never seen a gentleman before me give away a bride in black. Now black has been my ordinary apparel so long—indeed I take it to be the proper costume of an author—the stage sanctions it—that to have appeared in some lighter colours—a pea-green coat, for instance, like the bridegroom's—would have raised more mirth at my expense, than the anomaly had created censure. But I could perceive that the bride's mother, and some elderly ladies present (God bless them!), would have been well content, if I had come in any other colour than that. But I got over the omen by a lucky apologue, which I remembered out of Pilpay, or some Indian author, of all the birds being invited to the linnets' wedding, at which, when all the rest came in their gayest feathers, the raven alone apologised for his cloak, because "he had no other." This tolerably reconciled the elders. But with the young people all was merriment, and shakings of hands, and congratulations, and kissing away the bride's tears, and kissings from her in return, till a young lady, who assumed some experience in these matters, having worn the nuptial bands some four or five weeks longer than her friend, rescued her, archly observing, with half an eye upon the bridegroom, that at this rate she would have "none left."

My friend the Admiral was in fine wig and buckle on this occasion—a striking contrast to his usual neglect of personal appearance. He did not once shove up his borrowed locks (his custom ever at his morning studies) to betray the few grey stragglers of his own beneath them. He wore an aspect of thoughtful satisfaction. I trembled for the hour, which at length approached, when after a protracted *breakfast* of three hours—if stores of cold fowls, tongues, hams, botargoes, dried fruits, wines, cordials, &c. can deserve so meagre an appellation—the coach was announced, which was come to carry off the bride and bridegroom for a season, as custom has sensibly ordained, into the country; upon which design, wishing them a felicitous journey, let us return to the assembled guests

> As when a well-graced actor leaves the stage,
> The eyes of men
> Are idly bent on him that enters next.

So idly did we bend our eyes upon one another, when the chief performers in the morning's pageant had vanished. None told his tale None sipt her glass. The poor Admiral made an effort—it was not much. I had anticipated so far. Even the infinity of full satisfaction, that had betrayed itself through the prim looks and quiet deportment of his lady, began to wane into something of misgiving. No one knew whether to take their leaves or stay. We seemed assembled upon a silly occasion. In this crisis, betwixt tarrying and departure, I must do justice to a foolish talent of mine, which had otherwise like to have brought me into disgrace in the fore-part of the day, I mean, a power, in any emergency, of thinking and giving vent to all manner of strange nonsense. In this awkward dilemma I found it sovereign. I rattled off some of my most excellent absurdities. All were willing to be relieved, at any expense of reason, from the pressure of the intolerable vacuum which had succeeded to the morning bustle. By this means I was fortunate in keeping together the better part of the company to a late hour; and a rubber of whist (the Admiral's favourite game) with some rare strokes of chance as well as skill, which came opportunely on his side—lengthened out till midnight—dismissed the old gentleman at last to his bed with comparatively easy spirits

---

I have been at my old friend's various times since. I do not know a visiting place where every guest is so perfectly at his ease, no where, where harmony is so strangely the result of confusion. Every body is at cross purposes, yet the effect is so much better than uniformity. Contradictory orders, servants pulling one way; master and mistress driving some other, yet both diverse; visitors huddled up in corners; chairs unsymmetrised; candles disposed by chance; meals at odd hours, tea and supper at once, or the latter preceding the former; the host and the guest conferring, yet each upon a different topic, each understanding himself, and neither trying to understand or hear the other; draughts and politics, chess and political economy, cards and conversation on nautical matters, going on at once, without the hope, or indeed the wish, of distinguishing them, make it altogether the most perfect *concordia discors* you shall meet with. Yet somehow the old house is not quite what it should be. The Admiral still enjoys his pipe, but he has no Miss Emily to fill it for him. The instrument stands where it stood, but she is gone, whose delicate touch could sometimes for a short minute appease the warring elements. He has learnt, as Marvel expresses it, to "make his destiny his choice" He bears bravely up, but he does not come out with his flashes of wild wit so thick as formerly. His sea songs seldomer escape him. His wife, too, looks as if she wanted some younger body to scold and set to rights. We all miss a junior presence. It is wonderful how one young maiden freshens up, and keeps green, the paternal roof. Old and young seem to have an interest in her, so long as she is not absolutely disposed of. The youthfulness of the house is flown. Emily is married. ELIA.

THE CONVALESCENT.

A PRETTY severe fit of indisposition which, under the name of a nervous fever, has made a prisoner of me for some weeks past, and is but slowly leaving me, has reduced me to an incapacity of reflecting upon any topic foreign to itself. Expect no healthy conclusions from me this month, reader; I can offer you only sick men's dreams.

And truly the whole state of sickness is such: for what else is it but a magnificent dream for a man to lie a-bed, and draw day-light curtains about him; and, shutting out the sun, to induce a total oblivion of all the works which are going on under it? To become insensible to all the operations of life, except the beatings of one feeble pulse?

If there be a regal solitude, it is a sick bed. How the patient lords it there! what caprices he acts without controul! how king-like he sways his pillow—tumbling, and tossing, and shifting, and raising, and lowering, and thumping, and flatting, and moulding it, to the ever-varying requisitions of his throbbing temples.

He changes *sides* oftener than a politician. Now he lies full length,

---

* In this instance no other object was attained by depriving the musical public of their amusement on the Tuesday, for after all the new Opera was not produced on the following Saturday.

then half-length, obliquely, transversely, head and feet quite across the bed; and none accuses him of tergiversation. Within the four curtains he is absolute. They are his Mare Clausum.

How sickness enlarges the dimensions of a man's self to himself! he is his own exclusive object. Supreme selfishness is inculcated upon him as his only duty. 'Tis the Two Tables of the Law to him. He has nothing to think of but how to get well. What passes out of doors, or within them, so he hear not the jarring of them, affects him not.

A little while ago he was greatly concerned in the event of a law-suit, which was to be the making or the marring of his dearest friend. He was to be seen trudging about upon this man's errand to fifty quarters of the town at once, jogging this witness, refreshing that solicitor. The cause was to come on yesterday. He is absolutely as indifferent to the decision, as if it were a question to be tried at Pekin. Peradventure from some whispering, going on about the house, not intended for his hearing, he picks up enough to make him understand, that things went cross-grained in the Court yesterday, and his friend is ruined. But the word "friend," and the word "ruin," disturb him no more than so much jargon He is not to think of any thing but how to get better.

What a world of foreign cares are merged in that absorbing consideration!

He has put on the strong armour of sickness, he is wrapt in the callous hide of suffering; he keeps his sympathy, like some curious vintage under trusty lock and key, for his own use only.

He lies pitying himself, honing and moaning to himself; he yearneth over himself; his bowels are even melted within him, to think what he suffers; he is not ashamed to weep over himself

He is for ever plotting how to do some good to himself; studying little stratagems, and artificial alleviations

He makes the most of himself, dividing himself, by an allowable fiction, into as many distinct individuals, as he hath sore and sorrowing members. Sometimes he meditates—as of a thing apart from him—upon his poor aching head, and that dull pain which, dozing or waking, lay in it all the past night like a log, or palpable substance of pain, not to be removed without opening the very scull, as it seemed, to take it thence. Or he pities his long, clammy, attenuated fingers. He compassionates himself all over, and his bed is a very discipline of humanity, and tender heart

He is his own sympathiser, and instinctively feels that none can so well perform that office for him. He cares for few spectators to his tragedy. Only that punctual face of the old nurse pleases him, that announces his broths, and his cordials. He likes it because it is so unmoved, and because he can pour forth his feverish ejaculations before it as unreservedly as to his bed-post.

To the world's business he is dead. He understands not what the callings and occupations of mortals are: only he has a glimmering conceit of some such thing, when the doctor makes his daily call: and even in the lines of that busy face he reads no multiplicity of patients, but solely conceives of himself as *the sick man*. To what other uneasy couch the good man is hastening, when he slips out of his chamber, folding up his thin douceur so carefully for fear of rustling—is no speculation which he can at present entertain. He thinks only of the regular return of the same phenomenon at the same hour to-morrow.

Household rumours touch him not. Some faint murmur, indicative of life going on within the house, soothes him, while he knows not distinctly what it is. He is not to know any thing, not to think of any thing. Servants gliding up or down the distant staircase, treading as upon velvet, gently keep his ear awake, so long as he troubles not himself further than with some feeble guess at their errands. Exacter knowledge would be a burthen to him: he can just endure the pressure of conjecture. He opens his eye faintly at the dull stroke of the muffled knocker, and closes it again without asking "who was it?" He is flattered by a general notion that inquiries are making after him, but he cares not to know the name of the inquirer. In the general stillness, and awful hush of the house, he lies in state, and feels his sovereignty.

To be sick is to enjoy monarchal prerogatives. Compare the silent tread, and quiet ministry, almost by the eye only, with which he is served—with the careless demeanour, the unceremonious goings in and out (slapping of doors, or leaving of them open) of the very same attendants, when he is getting a little better—and you will confess, that from the bed of sickness (throne let me rather call it) to the elbow chair of convalescence, is a fall from dignity, amounting to a deposition.

How convalescence shrinks a man back to his pristine stature! where is now the space, which he occupied so lately, in his own, in the family's eye? The scene of his regalities, his sick room, which was his presence chamber, where he lay and acted his despotic fancies—how is it reduced to a common bed-room! The trimness of the very bed has something petty and unmeaning about it. It is *made* every day. How unlike to that wavy, many-furrowed, oceanic surface, which it presented so short a time since, when to *make* it was a service not to be thought of at oftener than three or four day revolutions, when the patient was with pain and grief to be lifted for a little while out of it, to submit to the encroachments of unwelcome neatness, and decencies which his shaken frame deprecated, then to be lifted into it again, for another three or four days' respite, to flounder it out of shape again, while every fresh furrow was a historical record of some shifting posture, some uneasy turning, some seeking for a little ease; and the shrunken skin scarce told a truer story than the crumpled coverlid.

Hushed are those mysterious sighs—those groans—so much more awful, while we knew not from what caverns of vast hidden suffering they proceeded. The Lernean pangs are quenched. The riddle of sickness is solved, and Philoctetes is become an ordinary personage.

Perhaps some relic of the sick man's dream of greatness survives in the still lingering visitations of the medical attendant. But how is he too changed with every thing else! Can this be he—this man of news—of chat—of anecdote—of every thing but physic—can this be he, who so lately came between the patient and his cruel enemy, as on some solemn embassy from Nature, erecting herself into a high mediating party?—Pshaw! 'tis some old woman.

Farewell with him all that made sickness pompous—the spell that hushed the household—the desart-like stillness, felt throughout its inmost chambers—the mute attendance—the inquiry by looks—the still softer delicacies of self-attention—the sole and single eye of distemper alonely fixed upon itself—world-thoughts excluded—the man a world unto himself—his own theatre—

What a speck is he dwindled into!

In this flat swamp of convalescence, left by the ebb of sickness, yet far enough from the terra firma of established health, your note, dear Editor, reached me, requesting—an article. In Articulo Mortis, thought I; but it is something hard—and the quibble, wretched as it was, relieved me. The summons, unseasonable as it appeared, seemed to link me on again to the petty businesses of life, which I had lost sight of; a gentle call to activity, however trivial, a wholesome weaning from that preposterous dream of self-absorption—the puffy state of sickness—in which I confess to have lain so long, insensible to the magazines, and monarchies, of the world alike, to its laws, and to its literature. The hypochondriac flatus is subsiding, the acres, which in imagination I had spread over—for the sick man swells in the sole contemplation of his single sufferings, till he becomes a Tityus to himself—are wasting to a span, and for the giant of self-importance, which I was so lately, you have me once again in my natural pretensions—the lean and meagre figure of your insignificant monthly contributor, ELIA.

IMPERFECT DRAMATIC ILLUSION.

A play is said to be well or ill acted in proportion to the scenical illusion produced. Whether such illusion can in any case be perfect, is not the question. The nearest approach to it, we are told, is, when the actor appears wholly unconscious of the presence of spectators. In tragedy—in all which is to affect the feelings—this undivided attention to his stage business, seems indispensable. Yet it is, in fact, dispensed with every day by our cleverest tragedians; and, while these references to an audience, in the shape of rant or sentiment, are not too frequent or palpable, a sufficient quantity of illusion for the purposes of dramatic interest may be said to be produced in spite of them. But, tragedy apart, it may be inquired whether in certain characters in comedy, especially those which are a little extravagant, or which involve some notion repugnant to the moral sense, it is not a proof of the highest skill in the comedian when, without absolutely appealing to an audience, he keeps up a tacit understanding with them; and makes them, unconsciously to themselves, a party in the scene. The utmost nicety is required in the mode of doing this; but we speak only of the great artists in the profession.

The most mortifying infirmity in human nature, to feel in ourselves, or to contemplate in another is, perhaps, cowardice. To see a coward *done to the life* upon a stage would produce any thing but mirth. Yet we most of us rememember Jack Bannister's cowards. Could any thing be more agreeable, more pleasant? We loved the rogues. How was this effected but by the exquisite art of the actor in a perpetual sub-insinuation to us the spectators, even in the extremity of the shaking fit, that he was not half such a coward as we took him for?—We saw all the common symptoms of the malady upon him; the quivering lip, the cowering knees, the teeth chattering; and could have sworn "that man was frightened." But we forgot all the while—or kept it almost a secret to ourselves—that he never once lost his self-possession; that he let out by a thousand droll looks and gestures—meant at *us*, and not at all supposed to be visible to his fellows in the scene, that his confidence in his own resources had never once deserted him. Was this a genuine picture of a coward? or not rather a likeness, which the clever artist contrived to palm upon us instead of an original; while we secretly connived at the delusion for the purpose of greater pleasure, than a more genuine counterfeiting of the imbecility, helplessness, and utter self-desertion, which we know to be concomitants of cowardice in real life, could have given us?

Why are misers so hateful in the world, and so endurable on the stage, but because the skilful actor by a sort of sub-reference, rather than direct appeal to us, disarms the character of a great deal of its odiousness, by seeming to engage *our* compassion for the insecure tenure by which he holds his money bags and parchments? By this subtle vent half of the hatefulness of the character—the self-closeness with which in real life it coils itself up from the sympathies of men—evaporates. The miser becomes sympathetic; *i. e.* is no genuine miser. Here again a diverting likeness is substituted for a very disagreeable reality.

Spleen, irritability—the pitiable infirmities of old men, which produce only pain to behold in the realities, counterfeited upon a stage, divert not altogether for the comic appendages to them, but in part from an inner conviction that they are *being acted* before us; that a likeness only is going on, and not the thing itself. They please by being done under the life, or beside it; not *to the life.* When Gatty acts an old man, is he angry indeed? or only a pleasant counterfeit, just enough of a likeness to recognise, without pressing upon us the uneasy sense of reality?

Comedians, paradoxical as it may seem, may be too natural. It was the case with a late actor. Nothing could be more earnest or true than the manner of Mr. Emery; this told excellently in his Tyke, and characters of a tragic cast. But when he carried the same rigid exclusiveness of attention to the stage business, and wilful blindness and oblivion of every thing before the curtain into his comedy, it produced a harsh and dissonant effect. He was out of keeping with the rest of the *Personæ Dramatis.* There was as little link between him and them as betwixt himself and the audience. He was a third estate, dry, repulsive, and unsocial to all. Individually considered, his execution was masterly. But comedy is not this unbending thing; for this reason, that the same degree of credibility is not required of it as to serious scenes. The degrees of credibility demanded to the two things may be illustrated by the different sort of truth which we expect when a man tells us a mournful or a merry story. If we suspect the former of falsehood in any one tittle, we reject it altogether. Our tears refuse to flow at a suspected imposition. But the teller of a mirthful tale has latitude allowed him. We are content with less than absolute truth. 'Tis the same with dramatic illusion. We confess we love in comedy to see an audience naturalized behind the scenes, taken in into the interest of the drama, welcomed as by-standers however. There is something ungracious in a comic actor holding himself aloof from all participation or concern with those who are come to be diverted by him. Macbeth must see the dagger, and no ear but his own be told of it; but an old fool in farce may think he *sees something*, and by conscious words and looks express it, as plainly as he can speak, to pit, box, and gallery. When an impertinent in tragedy, an Osric for instance, breaks in upon the serious passions of the scene, we approve of the contempt with which he is treated. But when the pleasant impertinent of comedy, in a piece purely meant to give delight, and raise mirth out of whimsical perplexities, worries the studious man with taking up his leisure, or making his house his home, the same sort of contempt expressed (however *natural*) would destroy the balance of delight in the spectators. To make the intrusion comic, the actor who plays the annoyed man must a little desert nature; he must, in short, be thinking of the audience, and express only so much dissatisfaction and peevishness as is consistent with the pleasure of comedy. In other words, his perplexity must seem half put on. If he repel the intruder with the sober set face of a man in earnest, and more especially if he deliver his expostulations in a tone, which in the world must necessarily provoke a duel: his real-life manner will destroy the whimsical and purely dramatic existence of the other character (which, to render it comic demands an antagonist comicality on the part of the character opposed to it), and convert what was meant for mirth, rather than belief, into a downright piece of impertinence indeed, which would raise no diversion in us, but rather stir pain, to see inflicted in earnest upon any worthy person. A very judicious actor (in most of his parts) seems to have fallen into an error of this sort in his playing with Mr. Wrench in the farce of Free and Easy.

Many instances would be tedious; these may suffice to show that comic acting at least does not always demand from the performer that strict abstraction from all reference to an audience, which is exacted of it; but that in some cases a sort of compromise may take place, and all the purposes of dramatic delight be attained by a judicious understanding, not too openly announced, between the ladies and gentlemen—on both sides of the curtain.

ELIA.

THE SORROWS OF ** ***.

I AM the most unfortunate of an unfortunate race. The most wretched of the wretched who have no rest for the soles of their feet.—Mistake me not—I am no Jew,—would I were but the meanest amongst the Hebrews!—but my unhappy despised generation labours under a sterner, though a similar, curse. We are a proverb and a bye-word—a mark for derision and scorn, even to the vilest of those scattered Israelites. We are sold into tenfold bondage and persecution. We are delivered over to slavery and to poverty—we are visited with numberless stripes.——No, tender-hearted Man of Bramber! we are not what thy sparkling eyes would seem to anticipate,—we are, alas! no negroes,—it were a merciful fate to us to be but Blackamoors. *They* have their snatches of rest and of joy even—their tabors, and pipes, and cymbals—*we* have neither song nor dance—misery alone is our portion—pain is in all our joints—and on our bosoms, and all about us, sits everlasting *shagreen.*—Dost thou not, by this time, guess at my tribe—

Dost thou not suspect my *ears?*

I am indeed, as thou discernest, an inferior horse—a Jerusalem colt; but why should I blush to "write myself down an ass?" My ancestors at least were free, and inhabited the desert!—My forefathers were noble,—though it must rob our patriarchs of some of their immortal bliss, if they can look down from their lower Indian heaven on their abject posterity!

* * * * * *

Fate,—I know not whether kindly or unkindly,—has cast my lot upon the coast. I have heard, there are some of my race who draw in sand-carts, or carry panniers, and are oppressed by those Coptic vagabonds, the Gypsies,—but I can conceive no oppressions greater than mine.—I can dream of no fardels more intolerable than those I bear; but think, rather with envy, of the passiveness of a pair of panniers, compared to the living burdens which gall and fret me by their continual efforts. A sand-bag might be afflictive, from its weight—but it could not kick with it, like a young lady. I should fear no stripes—from a basket of apples.—A load of green peas could not tear my tongue by tugging at my eternal bridle. All these are circumstances of my hourly afflictions,—when I am toiling along the beach—the most abject, and starved, and wretched of our sea-roamers—with one, or perhaps three, of my master's cruel customers, sitting upon my painful back. It may chance, for this ride, that I have been ravished from a hasty breakfast—full of hunger and wind—having at six o'clock suckled a pair of young ladies, in declines,—my own unweaned shaggy foal remaining all the time unnourished (think of that, mothers!) in his sorry stable. It is generally for some child or children that I am saddled thus early—for urchins fresh from the brine, full of spirits and mischief,—would to Providence it might please Mrs. D—— the Dipper, to suffocate the shrieking imps in their noisy immersion! The sands are allowed to be excellent for a gallop—but for the sake of the clatter, these infant demons prefer the shingles—and on this horrible footing I am raced up and down, till I can barely lift a leg. A brawny Scotch nursery wench, therefore, with sinews made all the more vigorous by the shrewd bracing sea air, lays lustily on my haunches with a toy whip—no toy however in her pitiless "red right hand:" and when she is tired of the exercise, I am made over to the next comer. This is probably the Master Buckle—and what hath my young cock, but a pair of artificial spurs—or huge corking-pins stuck at his abominable heels.—No

—gentle knight comes *pricking* o'er the plain.—

I am now treated, of course, like a cockchafer—and endeavour to rid myself of my tormentor; but the bruteling, to his infernal praise, is an excellent rider. At last the contrivance is espied, and my jockey drawn off by his considerate parent—not as the excellent Mr. Thomas Day would advise, with a Christian lecture on his cruelty—but with an admonition on the danger to his neck. His mother too kisses him in a frenzy of tenderness at his escape—and I am discharged with a character of spitefulness, and obstinacy, and all that is brutal in nature.

A young literary lady—blinded with tears, that make her stumble over the shingles—here approaches, book in hand, and mounts me,—with the charitable design, as I hope, of preserving me from a more unkindly rider. And, indeed, when I halt from fatigue, she only strikes me over the crupper, with a volume of Duke Christian of Lunenburg—(a Christian tale to be used so!)—till her concern for the binding of the novel compels her to desist. I am then parted with as incorrigibly lazy, and am mounted in turn by all the stoutest women in Margate, it being their fancy, as they declare, to ride leisurely.

Are *these* things to be borne?

Conceive me, simply, tottering under the bulk of Miss Wiggins, (who some aver is "all soul," but to me she is all body,) or Miss Huggins—the Prize Giantesses of England; either of them sitting like a personified lumbago on my loins!—Am I a Hindoo tortoise—an Atlas? Sometimes, Heaven forgive me, I think I *am* an ass to put up with such miseries—dreaming under the impossibility of throwing off my fardels—of ridding myself of myself—or in moments of less impatience, wishing myself to have been created at least an elephant, to bear these young women in their "towers," as they call them, about the coast.

Did they never read the fable of "Ass's Skin," under which covering a princess was once hidden by the malice of fairy Fate? If they have, it might inspire them with a tender shrinking and misgiving, lest, under our hapless shape, they should peradventure be oppressing and crushing some once dear relative or bosom-friend, some youthful intimate or school-fellow, bound to them, perhaps, by a mutual vow of eternal affection. Some of us, moreover, have titles which might deter a modest mind from degrading us. Who would think of riding, much less of flagellating the beautiful Duchess—or only a namesake of the beautiful Duchess of Devonshire? Who would think of wounding through our sides, the tender nature of the Lady Jane Grey? Who would care to goad Lord Wellington, or Nelson, or Duncan?—and yet these illustrious titles are all worn,—by my melancholy brethren. There is scarcely a distinguished family in the peerage—but hath an ass of their name.

Let my oppressors think of this and mount modestly, and let them use me—*a female*—tenderly, for the credit of their own feminine nature. Am I not capable, like them, of pain and fatigue—of hunger and thirst? Have I, forsooth, no rheumatic aches—no cholics and windy spasms, or stitches in the side—no vertigoes—no asthma—no feebleness or hystericks—no colds on the lungs? It would be but reasonable to presume I had all these, for my stable is bleak and damp—my water brackish and my food scanty—for my master is a Caledonian, and starves me.—I am almost one of those Scotch asses that "live upon a *brae!*"

* * * * * * *

Will you mention these things, honourable and humane Sir, † in your place in Parliament?

Friends of humanity!—Eschewers of West Indian sugar!—Patrons of black drudges,—pity also the brown and grizzle-grey! Suffer no sand—that hath been dragged by the afflicted donkey. Consume not the pannier-potatoe—that hath helped to overburthen the miserable ass! Do not ride on us, or drive us—or mingle with those who do. Die conscientiously of declines—and spare the consumption of our family milk. Think of our babes, and of our backs. Remember our manifold sufferings, and our meek resignation—our life-long martyrdom, and our mild martyr-like endurance. Think of the "languid patience" in our physiognomy!

I have heard of a certain French Metropolitan, who declared that the most afflicted and patient of animals was "de Jōb-horse:"—but surely he ought to have applied to *our* race the attributes and the name of the man of Uz!

A FEW WORDS ON "CHRISTMAS."

Close the shutters, and draw the curtains together, and pile fresh wood upon the hearth! Let us have, for once, an innocent *auto da fé*. Let the hoarded corks be brought forth, and branches of crackling laurel. Place the wine and fruit and the hot chesnuts upon the table.—And now, good folks and children, bring your chairs round to the blazing fire. Put some of those rosy apples upon your plates. We'll drink one glass of bright sherry "to our absent friends and readers," and then let us talk a little about Christmas.

And what is Christmas?

Why, it is the happiest time of the year. It is the season of mirth and cold weather. It is the time when Christmas-boxes and jokes are given; when mistletoe, and red-berried laurel, and soups, and sliding, and school-boys, prevail; when the country is illuminated by fires and bright faces; and the town is radiant with laughing children. Oranges, as rich as the fruit of the Hesperides, shine out in huge golden heaps. Cakes, frosted over (as if to rival the glittering snow) come forth by thousands from their summer (caves) ovens: and on every stall at every corner of every street are the roasted apples, like incense fuming on Pagan altars.

And *this* night is Christmas Eve. Formerly it was a serious and holy vigil. Our forefathers observed it strictly till a certain hour, and then requited their own forbearance with cups of ale and Christmas candles, with placing the *yule clog* on the fire, and roaring themselves thirsty till morning. Time has altered this. We are neither so good as our forefathers were—nor so bad. We go to bed sober; but we have forgotten their old devotions. Our conduct looks like a sort of compromise; so that we are not worse than our ancestors, we are satisfied not to be better: but let that pass.—What we now call Christmas Eve—(there is something very delightful in old terms: they had always their birth in reason or sentiment) was formerly *Mædrenack*, or *The Night of Mothers!* How beautifully does this recal to one's heart that holy tale—that wonderful nativity, which the eastern shepherds went by night to gaze at and adore—

(It was the winter wild,
When the heaven-born child
All meanly wrapp'd in the rude manger lay;)

a prodigy, which, had it been invention only, would have contained much that was immaculate and sublime; but, twined as it is with man's hopes and fears, is invested with a grand and overwhelming interest.

But to-night is Christmas Eve, and so we will be merry. Instead of toast and ale, we will content ourselves with our sherry and chesnuts; and we must put up with coffee or fragrant tea, instead of having the old *Wassail-bowl* which formed part of the inspiration of our elder poets. We were once admitted to the mysteries of that fine invention, and we respect it accordingly. Does any one wish to know its merits? Let him try what he can produce, on our hint, and be grateful to us for ever. The "Wassail-bowl" is, indeed, a great composition. It is not carved by Benvenuto Cellini (the outside *may*,—but it is not material), nor shaped by Michael Angelo from the marble quarries of Carrara; but it is a liquor fit for the lips of the Indian Bacchus, and worthy to celebrate his return from conquest. It is made—for, after all, we must descend to particulars—it is made of wine, with *some* water (but *parce, precor, precor!*) with spices of various sorts, and roasted apples, which float in triumph upon its top. The proportions of each are not important—in fact, they should be adapted to the taste of the drinkers. The only caution that seems necessary is to "spare the water." If the compositor should live in the neighbourhood of Aldgate, this hint may be deemed advisable; though we mean no affront to either him or the pump.

One mark and sign of Christmas is the *music;* rude enough, indeed, but generally gay, and speaking eloquently of the season. Music, at festival times, is common to most countries. In Spain, the serenader twangs his guitar: in Italy, the musician allures rich notes from his Cremona: in Scotland, the bagpipe drones out its miserable noise: in Germany, there is the horn, and the pipe in Arcady. We too, in our turn, have our Christmas "*Waits*," who witch us at early morning, before cock-crow, with strains and welcomings which belong to night. They wake us so gently that the music seems to have commenced in our dreams, and we listen to it till we sleep again. Besides this, we have our songs, from the young and the old, jocose and fit for the time. What old gentleman of sixty has not his stock—his one, or two, or three frolicksome verses. He sings them for the young folks, and is secure of their applause and his own private satisfaction. His wife, indeed, perhaps says "*Really*, my dear Mr. Williams, you should *now* give over these, &c." but he is more resolute from opposition, and gambols through his "Flowery meads of May," or "Beneath a shady bower," while the children hang on his thin, trembling, untuneable notes in delighted and delightful amaze.

Many years ago (some forty-one,—or two,—or three) when we were at home "for the Christmas holidays," we occasionally heard these things. What a budget of songs we had! None of them were good for much; but they were sung by joyful spirits, amidst fun and laughter, loud and in defiance of tune, and we were enchanted. There was "Bright Chanticleer proclaims the dawn,"—and "'Twas in the good ship Rover,"—and, "Buy my matches,"—(oh! what an accompaniment there was with the flat hand and the elbow)—"The lobster claw,"—and others. We should be sorry to strip them, like "majesty" in the riddle, of their merit first and last (our recollection) and reduce them to "a jest." Yet they were indeed a jest, and a very pleasant one.—Of all the songs, however, which become a time of feasting, there is none comparable to one written by Beaumont and Fletcher. It is racy, and rich, and sparkling. It has the strength and regal taste of Burgundy, and the etherial spirit of Champaigne. Does the reader wish to see it? Here it is: the words seem floating in wine.

God Lyæus—ever young,
Ever honour'd, ever sung;
Stain'd with blood of lusty grapes,
In a thousand lusty shapes,
Dance upon the mazer's brim,
In the crimson liquor swim;
From thy plenteous hand divine
Let a river run with wine!

What a rioter was he that wrote this!—His drink was not water from Hippocrene. His fountain flowed with wine. His goddess was a girl with purple lips; and his dreams were rich, like the autumn; but prodigal, wild, and Bacchanalian!

—Leaving now our *eve* of Christmas, its jokes, and songs, and warm hearths, we will indulge ourselves in a few words upon Christmas Day. It is like a day of victory. Every house and church is as green as spring. The laurel, that never dies,—the holly, with its armed leaves and scarlet berries,—the mistletoe, under which one sweet ceremonial is (we hope still) performed, are seen. Every brave shrub that has life and verdure seems to come forward to shame the reproaches of men, and to show them that the earth is never dead, never parsimonious. Then, what gay dresses are intermixed,—art rivalling nature!—Woe to the rabbits and the hares, and the nut-cracking squirrels, the foxes, and all children of the woods, for furriers shall spoil them of their coats, to keep woman (the wonder of creation) warm! And woe to those damsels (fair anachronisms) who will not fence out the sharp winter; for rheumatisms and agues shall be theirs, and catarrhs shall be their portion in spring.—But, look! what thing is this, awful and coloured like the rainbow,—blue, and red, and glistening yellow? Its vest is sky tinctured! The edges of its garments are like the sun! Is it

——A faery vision
Of some gay creature of the element,
That in the colours of the rainbow lives,
And plays i' the plighted clouds?—

No:—it is the Beadle of St. ——'s! How Christmas and consolatory he looks! How redolent of good cheer is he! He is a cornu-copia,—an abundance! What pudding-sleeves!—what a collar, red and a like beef-steak, is his! He is a walking refreshment! He looks like a *whole* parish,—full, important,—but untaxed. The children of charity gaze at him with a modest smile. The straggling boys look on him with confidence. They do not pocket their marbles. They do not fly from the familiar gutter. This is a red-letter day; and the cane is reserved for tomorrow.

London is not *too* populous at Christmas. But what there *is* of population looks more alive than at other times. Quick walking and heaps of invitations keep the blood warm. Every one seems hurrying to a dinner. The breath curls upwards like smoke through the frosty air; the eyes glisten; the teeth are shown; the muscles of the face are rigid, and the colour of the cheek has a fixed look, like a stain. Hunger is no longer an enemy. We feed him, like the ravenous tiger, till he pants and sleeps, or is quiet. Every body eats at Christmas. The rich feast as usual; but the tradesman leaves his moderate fare for dainties. The apprentice abjures his chop, and plunges at once into the luxuries of joints and puddings. The schoolboy is no longer at school. He dreams no more of the coming lesson or the lifted rod; but mountains of jelly rise beside him, and blancmange, with its treacherous foundations, threatens to overwhelm his fancy; roods of mince pies spread out their chequered riches before him; and figures (only real on the 6th of January) pass by him, one by one, like ghosts before the vision of the king of Scotland. Even the servant has his "once a year" bottle of port; and the beggar his "alderman in chains."

Oh! merry piping time of Christmas! Never let us permit thee to degenerate into distant courtesies and formal salutations. But let us shake our friends and familiars by the hand, as our fathers and their fathers did. Let them all come around us, and let us count how many the year has added to our circle. Let us enjoy the present, and laugh at the past. Let us tell old stories and invent new ones—innocent always, and ingenious if we can. Let us not meet to abuse the world, but to make it better by our individual example. Let us be patriots, but not men of party. Let us look *of the time*,—cheerful and generous, and endeavour to make others as generous and cheerful as ourselves.

Our next contributor calls his paper "Scraps of Criticism." We think that we know "the fine Roman hand,"—but let that pass. It is enough, perhaps, (for our readers) that the remarks are good. Whether we translate them from the Syriac or Chaldee, or transcribe them from vellum or papyrus, is a question which we cannot now explain. The two first "Scraps" refer to Gray's Poems, and take novel (and, what is better, just) exceptions to two passages which they contain.—Johnson has been abused more, perhaps, for undervaluing the merits of Gray, than for any of his offences against literature. For our own parts, we think that he has been abused unjustly. Were *we* to cast a stone at him, it would be for his life of Milton. But Gray has, of all poets in the English language, the least right to complain. His reputation is enormously too great for the foundation upon which it rests. No doubt that he had learning, and a pleasant way of communicating his thoughts. But his language is, beyond even that of his contemporaries, artificial; and his poems are not remarkable either for original thought or even felicity of expression. His "Elegy" is clearly the first of his compositions: there is a tender vein of melancholy running through it; and the reflections, generally speaking, if not very profound, are graceful and pleasing.—The "Scrap" upon the word "*villain*" is a very material one; inasmuch as it seems to be the *key*, or leading word, to the character of Richard, as it is seen on the stage. With regard to "Howell's Letters,"—certainly our friend Howell has taken an odd *pro* and *con* view of the same subject. Perhaps he had one eye for the good, and one for the bad—and saw with them alternately. Thus "to wink at a person's faults" is to shut the bad eye.

SCRAPS OF CRITICISM.

Perhaps in this neglected spot is laid
Some heart once pregnant with celestial fire;
Hands that the rod of empire might have sway'd,
Or waked to ecstacy the living lyre.

Gray's Elegy.

There has always appeared to me a vicious mixture of the figurative with the real in this admired passage. The first two lines may barely pass, as not bad. But the *hands* laid in the earth, must mean the identical five-finger'd organs of the body; and how does this consist with their occupation of *swaying rods*, unless their owner had been a schoolmaster; or *waking lyres*, unless he were literally a harper by profession? Hands that "might have held the plough," would have some sense, for that work is strictly manual; the others only emblematically or pictorially so. Kings now-a-days sway no rods, *alias* sceptres, except on their coronation day; and poets do not necessarily strum upon the harp or fiddle, as poets. When we think upon dead cold fingers, we may remember the honest squeeze of friendship which they returned heretofore; we cannot but with violence connect their living idea, as opposed to death, with uses to which they must become metaphorical (i. e. less real than dead things themselves) before we can so with any propriety apply them.

He saw, but, blasted with excess of light,
Closed his eyes in endless night.

Gray's Bard.

Nothing was ever more violently distorted, than this material fact of Milton's blindness having been occasioned by his intemperate studies, and late hours, during his prosecution of the defence against Salmasius—applied to the dazzling effects of too much mental vision. His corporal sight was blasted with corporal occupation; his inward sight was not impaired, but rather strengthened, by his task. If his course of studies had turned his brain, there would have been some fitness in the expression.

And since I cannot, I will prove a *villain*,
And hate the idle pleasures of these days.

Soliloquy in Richard III.

The performers, whom I have seen in this part, seem to mistake the import of the word which I have marked with italics. Richard does not mean, that because he is by shape and temper unfitted for a *courtier*, he is therefore determined to prove, in our sense of the word, a *wicked man*.

The word in Shakspeare's time had not passed entirely into the modern sense; it was in its passage certainly, and indifferently used as such; the beauty of a world of words in that age was in their being less definite than they are now, fixed, and petrified. *Villain* is here undoubtedly used for a *churl*, or *clown*, opposed to a *courtier*; and the incipient deterioration of the meaning gave the use of it in this place great spirit and beauty. A *wicked man* does not necessarily hate *courtly pleasures*; a *clown* is naturally opposed to them. The mistake of this meaning has, I think, led the players into that hard literal conception with which they deliver this passage, quite foreign, in my understanding, to the bold gay-faced irony of the soliloquy. Richard, upon the stage, looks round, as if he were literally apprehensive of some dog snapping at him; and announces his determination of procuring a looking-glass, and employing a tailor, as if he were prepared to put both in practice before he should get home— I apprehend "a world of figures here."

Howell's Letters. "The treaty of the match 'twixt our Prince [afterwards Charles I.] and the Lady Infanta, is now strongly a foot: she is a very comely lady, *rather of a Flemish complexion than Spanish, fair haired*, and carrieth a most pure mixture of red and white in her face. She is full and *big-lipp'd; which is held a beauty rather than a blemish, or rather excess in the Austrian family, it being a thing incident to most of that race*; she goes now upon 16, and is of a tallness agreeable to those years." This letter bears date, 5th Jan. 1622. Turn we now to a letter dated 16th May, 1626. The wind was now changed about, the Spanish match broken off, and Charles had become the husband of Henrietta. "I thank you for your late letter, and the several good tidings sent me from Wales. In requital I can send you gallant news, for we have now a most noble new Queen of England, who in true beauty is beyond the long-woo'd Infanta; for she was of a *fading flaxen hair, big-lipp'd*, and somewhat heavy-eyed; but this daughter of France, this youngest branch of Bourbon (being but in her cradle when the great Henry her father was put out of the world) is of a more *lovely and lasting complexion*, a dark brown; she hath eyes that sparkle like stars; and for her physiognomy, she may be said to be a mirror of perfection." He hath a rich account, in another letter, of Prince Charles courting this same Infanta. "There are Comedians once a week come to the Palace [at Madrid] where, under a great canopy, the Queen and the Infanta sit in the middle, our Prince and Don Carlos on the Queen's right hand, the king and the little Cardinal on the Infanta's left hand. I have seen the Prince have his eyes immovably fixed upon the Infanta half an hour together in a thoughtful speculative posture, *which sure would needs be tedious, unless affection did sweeten it.*" Again, of the Prince's final departure from that court. "The king and his two brothers accompanied his Highness to the Escurial, some twenty miles off, and would have brought him to the sea-side, but that the Queen is big, and hath not many days to go. When the King and He parted, there past wonderful great endearments and embraces *in divers postures* between them a long time; and in that place there is a pillar to be erected as a monument to posterity." This scene of royal congées assuredly gave rise to the popular, or reformed sign (as Ben Jonson calls it), of *The Salutation*. In the days of Popery, this sign had a more solemn import.

Happy beyond that man of Ross,
Whom mere content could ne'er engross,
Art *thou*,—with hope,—health,—"learned leisure,"
Friends—books—thy thoughts—an endless pleasure!
—Yet—yet—(for when was pleasure made
Sunshine all without a shade?)
Thou, perhaps, as now thou rovest
Through the busy scenes thou lovest
With an idler's careless look,
Turning some moth-pierced book,
Feel'st a sharp and sudden woe
For visions vanished long ago!—
And then thou think'st how time has fled
Over thy unsilver'd head,
Snatching many a fellow mind
Away, and leaving—what——behind?—
Nought, alas! save joy and pain
Mingled ever, like a strain
Of music where the discords vie
With the truer harmony.
So, perhaps, with thee the vein
Is sullied ever,—so the chain
Of habits and affections old,
Like a weight of solid gold,
Presseth on thy gentle breast,
Till sorrow rob thee of thy rest.

—Ay: So it is. Ev'n *I* (whose lot
The fairy Love so long forgot)
Seated beside this Sherris wine,
And near to books and shapes divine,
Which poets and the painters past
Have wrought in lines that aye shall last—
Ev'n I, with Shakspeare's self beside me,
And One, whose tender talk can guide me
Through fears, and pains, and troublous themes,—
Whose smile doth fall upon my dreams
Like sunshine on a stormy sea,—
Want *something*,—when I think of *thee*!

May 25, 1825. C.

www.ingramcontent.com/pod-product-compliance
Lightning Source LLC
LaVergne TN
LVHW012113170826
845678LV00001BA/23

* 9 7 8 0 3 4 4 9 9 0 4 4 1 *